At the Falls

Published for The Valentine,

the Museum of the Life & History

of Richmond, by The University of

North Carolina Press, Chapel Hill

& London

At the Falls

Richmond, Virginia, and Its People

Marie Tyler-McGraw

Illustrations:

p. i, photo by Pyramid Studios; pp. ii–iii, *View of Richmond from Hollywood Cemetery* (1854), by William MacLeod; p. xiii, *Richmond from the Hill above the Waterworks* (1834), engraving by W. J. Bennett, all from the Valentine, Richmond, Virginia

The paper in this book meets the guidelines for permanence and durability of the Committee on Production Guidelines for Book Longevity of the Council on Library Resources.

Library of Congress Cataloging-in-Publication Data

Tyler-McGraw, Marie.

At the falls : Richmond, Virginia, and its people / by Marie Tyler-McGraw.

p. cm.

Includes bibliographical references and index.

ISBN 0-8078-2163-2 (cloth : alk. paper). — ISBN 0-8078-4476-4 (pbk. : alk. paper)

1. Richmond (Va.)—History. I. Title.

F234.R557T94 1994

975.5'451—dc20 94-5727

CIP

98 97 96 95 94 5 4 3 2 1

For

all the

people of

Richmond.

They made

the city and

they are its

story.

Contents

Foreword *by Frank Jewell,* ix

Acknowledgments, xi

Introduction, 1

CHAPTER ONE   Views of the Falls, 9

CHAPTER TWO   Settlement at the Falls, 32

CHAPTER THREE   Village, Town, and Capital, 54

CHAPTER FOUR   Rocky Road to Richmond, 77

CHAPTER FIVE   Richmond's Great Expectations, 103

CHAPTER SIX   Confederate Richmond, 132

CHAPTER SEVEN   Reconstruction Richmond, 159

CHAPTER EIGHT   Sorting Out the New South City, 184

CHAPTER NINE   The Prism of Progress, 218

CHAPTER TEN   The Up-to-Date City, 244

CHAPTER ELEVEN   Tollbooths and the Costs of Change, 276

CHAPTER TWELVE   The Suburban City, 298

Notes, 319

Bibliographic Essay, 335

Index, 347

Foreword

IN 1985 the Valentine set out to create a new history of Richmond, Virginia, one to be based upon the finest scholarship in urban and social history and written for the general reader. For the first time Richmond was to be studied within the context of national and international urban systems. The new history would include whole groups of its residents—African Americans, women, Jews, evangelical Christians, and working people—and entire eras previously considered marginal to Richmond's familiar history as a state capital, capital of the Confederacy, and mid-twentieth-century stronghold of massive resistance.

The Valentine Board of Trustees and the museum staff made the new history of Richmond the keystone of an ambitious exhibition agenda over the next nine years. Each exhibition articulated new architecture for Richmond history and was presented as a work in progress toward the new history. This unity of purpose gave the museum's work a coherence and accountability that enabled it to seek and receive the support necessary to embark on so lengthy and consuming a project.

During a residency program supported by the Virginia Foundation for the Humanities and Public Policy in Charlottesville, Virginia, Valentine staff members met Dr. Marie Tyler-McGraw, a student of the history and folklore of the Upper South and a published writer. While a Fellow at the National Museum of American History, she had also conducted extensive research on Richmond history. Soon thereafter Dr. Tyler-McGraw joined the museum staff full-time, with principal responsibility for writing this book. While drafting and presenting successive chapters of the book to her colleagues at the museum for review and comment, she also contributed her expertise to the development and critiques of interpretive projects at the Valentine.

One of the most exciting and rewarding products of the Valentine's research and interpretation since 1985 has been the explosion in the number of new visitors drawn by the nature of the exhibitions and by public programs that seek their viewpoints, knowledge, experiences, and opinions. These exhibitions have brought Richmond and the Valentine national and international acclaim in newspapers, magazines, professional journals, and television, both for their unflinching focus on topics once deemed too incendiary to discuss publicly or dismissed as insignificant. The Valentine today has become a significant crossroads and gathering point for the entire Richmond community. It is no longer in fact or fancy the bastion of a privileged elite.

From Resistance to Renaissance: Race Relations in Richmond, 1945–1985 broke the taboo on public analysis of this difficult aspect of the city's history. *Free to Profess* addressed the relationship between the Virginia Statute for Religious Freedom and the first century of Jewish life in Richmond. *Jackson Ward: A Century of Community* examined one of the two most important black communities in the South.

In Bondage and Freedom: Antebellum Black Life in Richmond, the first major study comparing the lives of free blacks and slaves in the Western hemisphere before the Civil War, looked at the power of cities to erode the system of slavery; the place of African Americans in a market economy; and their central and essential role in Richmond's development. *Jim Crow* examined the rise of racist thought and practice in the last decades of the nineteenth century, along with the intensification of anti-Semitism in the Commonwealth after the Civil War.

Women's history came to the fore in *Dressed for Work: Women in the Workforce, 1900–1989*, a commentary on the social history of various women's roles and their place in the working world. The enormous impact of a variety of Protestant Christians on Richmond since the city's beginnings was explored in *I Believe: Evangelicalism in Southern Urban Culture*. And most recently, *Shared Spaces, Separate Lives* looked at nineteenth-century race relations within the context of urban households composed of free masters and slave servants — a condition at once of utmost intimacy and absolute isolation. *Creating History* (1994) begins an effort to distinguish between the past and the discipline of history and to present a popular exegesis of the epistemology of history.

In all, the long road to *At the Falls* has been a tremendously gratifying intellectual and community odyssey for the Valentine, one that called forth the finest efforts of Valentine historians, curators, conservators, designers, educators, development officers, and the entire museum staff. With this new history, we celebrate all the people of Richmond past and present whose special contributions built and today sustain this rich, complex, and fascinating city.

In history there is never a last word, and Richmond's past, present, and future are destined to be reconsidered many times. Another Richmond decades hence will demand its own account. The Valentine proudly presents this version, for our time, in this place.

Frank Jewell
Director, The Valentine
Richmond, Virginia

Acknowledgments

Writing a book that spans four hundred years of history is much like watching the landscape from a high-speed train. No sooner does the view come into focus and the eye pick out some interesting object than the entire scene is past and the eye must refocus. For such a tour, knowledgeable guides are imperative. David Goldfield, Ed Ayers, and Chris Silver served as consultants to the Valentine and made valuable comments on many aspects of the city's history. Their repeated readings of portions of the manuscript saved me from many errors, and their own writings were, and remain, instructive examples of how to do the work of history. The vision of Frank Jewell, director of the Valentine, initiated this project as well as the many other projects that have turned the Valentine into a model city and regional history museum.

The staff at the Valentine contributed in major ways to early drafts of this manuscript. Curators Barbara Batson, Jane Webb Smith, Colleen Callahan, Greg Galer, and Judy Harris shared with me the results of their own research for the series of exhibitions that took place at the Valentine between 1985 and 1992 and investigated important aspects of Richmond's history. They often called my attention to just the piece of evidence I wished for—or else the piece that destroyed a grand theory. Special appreciation goes to Gregg Kimball, who for much of this time was an esteemed colleague as well as a productive curator. I am particularly indebted to Juliette Bowles, a research associate who compiled much data with wit and insight, and to the cheerful aid and friendship of Judith Sheldon, Judy Harris again, Karen Holt Luetjen, Monica Beach, Penny Carmody, and Laura Daly.

The Valentine chose the illustrations for chapter 12, and Gregg Kimball supplied the captions. At the University of North Carolina Press, David Perry and Christi Stanforth offered sound advice and kept the end in view.

It was my good fortune to be near several excellent institutional resources while researching this manuscript. In the same building with me was the Valentine Library, a treasury of Richmond information presided over first by Lacy Dick and then by Teresa Roane. Two blocks west were the libraries of the Medical College of Virginia and the Museum of the Confederacy. Two blocks to the south was the Virginia State Library, where the unfailingly cheerful staff served up one precious gem after another. The historians on the publications staff there, knowledgeable in every aspect of Virginia and Richmond history, offered me much sound advice and good direction. Sandy Treadway, John Kneebone, Kip Campbell, and Brent Tarter are models of the dedication and collegiality that should characterize the pursuit for understanding in history. They were supportive and critical in excellent balance. Just over a mile to the west, Virginia Commonwealth University offers the papers of important Richmond organizations and individuals, while the Virginia Historical Society (VHS), another mile or so away, has a massive collection of Virginia and Richmond documents. The staff at the VHS was another source of helpful information.

My debts to readers are many and I hope that I have not slighted any of the people who were kind enough to read all or part of this manuscript and instruct me. Readers who made important suggestions include Ben Campbell, Noralee Frankel, Virginia Kerns, Barbara Melosh, Edward Steel, Barbara Howe, John Moeser, Douglas Egerton, Randall Miller, Svend Holsoe, Dave Smith, Peter Wallenstein, Phyllis Palmer, Jim Horton and Lois Horton, Barbara Carson, Mike Plunkett, Pat Sullivan, and Mick Nicholl. Robert Saunders of Christopher Newport College graciously sent a series of Richmond-related articles he had written.

Thanks and gratitude are due to Richmonders James Latimer, Drew Carneal, and Ann Hobson Freeman for their insights, research, and approachability. These writers give "local history" a good name. Interviews with Francis Foster, Ben Campbell, Tazewell Carrington, Tom Inge, and Alice Jackson Stuart and conversations with many other Richmonders gave me a renewed sense of the power and malleability of history.

When I came to this project I brought with me research done while I was a fellow at both the Virginia Foundation for the Humanities and Public Policy and at the African American Communities Project at the Smithsonian Institution. That research grounded me in several aspects of antebellum black Virginia history. I am grateful to both for their support of earlier research.

My last and greatest debt is to my partner, friend, and spouse, Howard Wachtel. He read the manuscript as a member of that endangered species, the informed General Reader; but more important was his steady and thoughtful support. His affirmation kept me working through the most difficult of times. My daughters, Elizabeth and Sarah, allowed me to complain a lot.

To have produced an error-free manuscript of this length and diversity would have taken an act of divine intervention which I neither deserved nor received. But there are few pleasures in life equal to the academic *Schadenfreude* of finding someone else's errors. In this, if in nothing else, I will surely give pleasure. For all failures of citation and interpretation, I am responsible. Neither the readers for the University of North Carolina Press, nor the staff at the Valentine, nor the consultants and colleagues asked to read the manuscript are to be held accountable.

At the Falls

Introduction

THE city of Richmond sits on the divide between the Tidewater and Piedmont sections of Virginia, ever reminded of its position in the state by the falls of the James River—eight miles of rock outcroppings, small islands, and water-gnarled vegetation that flow within the city. Above the city, the James finds its sources in the streams and rivers of the Allegheny and Blue Ridge highlands, which meet in the southern end of the Valley of Virginia. The river, turning in its path, rushes to the fall line where Richmond was built. Below that line, it broadens and flows slowly past old plantations toward Chesapeake Bay, while the hint of salt in the air and water grows steadily stronger.

This history of the city is titled "At the Falls" because it was the James River's fall line that drew Native Americans, Europeans, and unwilling Africans to the area that became Richmond. A site of exchanges and encounters for centuries, the falls was a fixed point in the geography of trade and travel for Indian groups in eastern North America. All of the English adventurers saw the commercial possibilities at first viewing. Soon after English settlement, slave ships debarked at Bermuda Hundred below the falls on the James and later at Rocky Ridge or Manchester. For many enslaved Africans, the first real view of the world they were brought to as traded commodities was the James River and, across it, the village of Richmond above the falls.

The title refers also to time's unbroken flow and its ability, like that of rushing water, to wear away everything that may seem solid—human lives, buildings, and theories. Memory persists, but the life of a city is elusive. Its elements do not willingly separate themselves into discrete categories where they may be weighed and measured and compared among their own kind. These elements prefer to mix, to blend, or to move so rapidly that, like rushing water, as soon as they are isolated and examined in one source, they are found to have changed in another.

It is this very complex of human elements that makes a city, and Richmond is no exception. Much of the drama in the city's history is provided by the contrast and tension between some of its central elements: the city's enthusiastic capitalism and the slave system that underpinned it; its love of tradition and its desire for modernity; its patriotic nationalism and its intense regionalism; its polite but powerful hierarchies and its streetcar strikes and sit-ins; its double-entry bookkeepers and its duelists. The history of the city is revealed in the constant renegotiation of these elements as they converge, confront, or amalgamate. Often a convergence of elements moved Richmond down a particular historic path when a slight variation in that convergence might have produced a very different outcome. What might have happened if President Lincoln had given concessions to the unionists who convened in Richmond in April 1861? When did the mood of Richmond turn toward secession, and how much of that mood swing was subtly orchestrated? Such historical speculation is done here not for its own sake but for the purpose of understanding the power of contingency in every human choice.

The themes that together create the story of the city at the falls appear early and recur regularly. The river was central to transportation and communication for Native Americans and, later, for Europeans and Africans. The river and its uses form a constant theme, from the early descriptions of great shad and sturgeon by the English adventurers to the less wondrous problems of pollution and sewage treatment plants, with their political implications for the late-twentieth-century city. A closely related idea is the constant of the falls as a trading site and a manufacturing site. Water power from the falls broke stones and provided Indians with chips and shards that became arrowheads, while water powered the city's mills and factories, which produced flour, iron, and paper products. Indian canoes and Newport's sail-rigged vessel with multiple rowers launched the history of the impact that transportation technology would have on Richmond. The construction and placement of canals, turnpikes, railroads, streetcars, automobiles, roads and highways, airports, interstate highways, and regional hub airports each affected the city's development in turn.

A city is also its people. Different peoples with varied ambitions and visions encountered each other near the falls area; this encounter is the second major theme. Aspiring and speculative, commercial and occasionally utopian, the area's inhabitants spoke in many voices and sometimes failed to leave any words. There are gaps in the record. Perhaps most of the people who have ever lived in Richmond would not find their lives in a city history that focuses on city government, planning, and policy. The city's early black residents and white women were the subject of debates, public records, legal proceedings, trials, and newspaper columns, but seldom spoke for themselves. Where a personal voice is missing, like that of Gabriel in his 1800 slave conspiracy, we must let action and artifacts speak.

This history of Richmond attempts to lower some of the barriers between public and private life. The Virginia Company understood that without women and families there would be no accumulation of capital in Virginia. If Richmond women felt limited in their role as base for the pyramid of ambition, they were tireless and ingenious in extending their roles as household managers and mothers, as guardians and interpreters of civility and morality, as arbiters of taste and consumers of products, as fund-raisers and administrators for every sort of civic improvement, and as laborers and investors. They are as responsible for the placement of monuments and the location of department stores as they are for suburban landscapes in the West End, boarding patterns in Fulton, church construction in Jackson Ward, and the preservation of John Marshall's home in the old Shockoe Hill neighborhood. In the early twentieth century they emerged in a true flowering of reform associations that were deeply rooted in the lives and work of city women for the previous century or more. Not all of their work was nonwage labor. Black women always worked, and after 1865 they received at least some wages. Research has also begun to uncover the connection of many white women with money-making enterprises and wage labor.

The sweeping and panoramic physical landscape, central to Richmond's history, forms a third theme. The small villages of the Powhatans were spread widely between the fall lines of major rivers and the Chesapeake Bay, but rivers, paths, and a knowledge of the land connected them into a confederated unity. In the same manner, English settlement patterns near the falls of the James created a community of widespread stores, courthouses, churches, and meeting places arrayed in space and connected by common purpose, not propinquity. Now, in the late twentieth century, Richmond finds itself returned to a sprawling urban landscape of suburban counties with nodes of specialized functions, not unlike the colonial community.

The fourth theme, present at the beginning, is that of the intercontinental nature of trade at the falls. From the aspirations of the Jamestown expedition through the ventures of William Byrd I to the international banking and finance functions of the present-day downtown, Richmond has been part of an evolving and geographically wide-ranging commercial system long based on tobacco. Richmond grew as a city within a rural hinterland from which it drew tobacco, wheat, and other sustaining products, but that hinterland also acted as a political restraint. Like many southern cities, Richmond developed trade links outside the region. When it began to grow, after the Revolution, it was initially connected by trade with New York, Philadelphia, and then Baltimore, the new nation's largest cities. As a northern-style manufacturing city in a southern setting, Richmond yearned to rival the major cities that received its shipping and trade, but these cities were well established before Richmond extended its commercial and industrial ambitions beyond the James River.

Citizen boosters delighted in Richmond's growth. Limited by its position as a river port connected to the coastal trade, it long remained near the top of a second tier of growing, bustling American cities. Richmond was the second city of the South, after New Orleans—a port city with which it had less in common than with a commercial river town like Buffalo, New York. Its near neighbors, Petersburg and Norfolk, were not serious rivals after Richmond began its industrial growth. Richmond's particular drama was that its efforts to emulate northern cities were often brought up short by a reminder, like Gabriel's Conspiracy or Nat Turner's Rebellion, that Richmond was restrained as well as sustained by its countryside. Local ordinances spoke to the effort to define and control slavery in Richmond even as the city absorbed more and more hired slaves in its commerce and industry. The evolution of a proslavery ideology in the press, the pulpit, and the legislature ultimately prevailed over Richmond's important commercial ties to the North.

The tension between Richmond's position as an American city aspiring to national and international trade and its role as a southern city, in which much of the population was held in a system of slavery or segregated from full civic participation, provides another theme. The political and physical effort to control the black population was paralleled by a philosophical effort to justify these activities in a society based on liberty and individualism—ideals whose main explicators were Virginians. Looking alternately north and south, Richmond was plagued by an ambivalence that caused the city to develop a certain obsession with self-definition. The shifting boundaries and changing landscapes of the city over time reflected its search for identity and dominant values: its rural-urban interconnection, its place in a national context, its racial mix and class negotiations, its myths and creation of traditions were elements in that search.

An enhanced version of its history and destiny shaped the city and influenced the built landscape and the creation of traditions and public rituals. These were sometimes agreed upon, sometimes imposed, and often reprocessed or newly conceived to fit changing circumstances. This evolving and negotiated view of the city became the basis for policy at any moment in the city's history. The view began with English visions of the New World and the British imperial system, which imposed early sets of expectations and descriptions on the falls of the James. As the American reality failed to embody early British expectations, a new politics and society were elaborated by Virginia tobacco planters, who created a legal code for African slavery and then adopted theories of republican liberty for themselves. Baptist evangelicalism soon provided an alternative worldview for eighteenth-century converts who found little comfort in planter hierarchy. From its beginning to the present, the city drew its values from competing sets of verities. Among the first and still viable were those values that referenced either the cavalier or the conversion experience, as circumstances required.

Richmond was both a capital city and a national city. More than for most American cities, its history is a national history; parts of it are known to every schoolchild. The exploration of the James River by the English and their first encounters with the Powhatans produced powerful national historic symbols in the forms of Capt. John Smith, Pocahontas, and John Rolfe. Richmond was the site of Patrick Henry's stirring pre-Revolutionary speech and some of Lafayette's military activities. The slogan "On to Richmond" reflected the military strategy for much of the Civil War, and the defeated Confederacy centered its memorialization in the city. All these events, as well as Virginia's several constitutional debates, gave the city national historical resonance, as well as a cast of larger-than-life historical characters who must be placed in the city's drama.

Much remains to be discovered about the actual economic history of the city, because that history has been hidden under the city's role as capital of the Confederacy and the subsequent Lost Cause version of history. Richmond's industrial development was influenced by the labor practices of chattel slavery, by the plantation paternalism of the hinterlands, and by a commerce that began with the processing and sale of tobacco and wheat. Businesses continued to favor low-wage and labor-intensive enterprises. Richmond's enterprise and energy near the end of the nineteenth century enveloped and manipulated Lost Cause rhetoric in commerce as well as politics. Taxes remained low, government services minimal, political debate muted by low participation levels. Appeals to racial and regional bias cloaked dissent. This pattern constituted a commercial and industrial policy that proved durable, if not innovative.

Alternate perspectives existed. The shaping of an official version of the city's social and political history was, at all times, actively subverted by the presence and opinions of others who were not directly consulted. Foremost among those others were Richmond's African Virginians, who represented several dissenting perspectives and whose lives were a central part of what made the city. Although those persons and perspectives long lacked civil power and thus could not influence the law directly, their existence shaped much of the city's political agenda. Beneath the official structure of white domination were shifting alliances and antagonisms. In one instance, Richmond's middle-class black women and Progressive white women created tentative alliances based on shared concerns for women in factories, but these working relationships often could not survive the scrutiny that highly politicized issues like women's suffrage brought to them.

In many ways, Richmond's urban growth was like that of other cities, with its attention to city services such as water, streetcars, gas, and cemeteries. But the Civil War changed the mental and physical landscape of the city, adding a southern memorial aspect to most of the city's space. Southern cities were the testing ground for racial segregation ordinances, a process begun before the Civil War and completed at the turn of the twentieth century. The parallel development of Jim Crow laws and Confederate monuments in Richmond restructured the physical and social space of the city, influencing its institutions and annexations. The historical vision of the United Daughters of the Confederacy held firm in twentieth-century Richmond, and it was hardly remarkable that the ideology of "massive resistance" in the 1950s should find its origins and explication in Richmond. Nor was it surprising that this ideology was quickly found to be uncongenial with the southern urban industrial policy of moderate and pragmatic conservatism.

Despite popular wisdom, hindsight is not twenty-twenty. A city's past, rich in variety and layered over upon itself, offers infinite possibilities for interpretation. Historians try to choose aspects that promise to reveal the heart of the city and illustrate its look and feel as well as the lives of its inhabitants. Studies of American cities once followed the longtime national focus on great men and great events by chronicling a city's entrepreneurs, politicians, and moments of high drama. This approach was particularly tempting in a city that represented the political and military center of the Confederacy, and most Richmond histories have reflected and enhanced its role as Holy City of the Lost Cause. The research and writing of the most recent generation of history scholars have addressed other issues and concerns. The social history techniques and topics of the last thirty years have provided compelling scholarship on the colonial Chesapeake, on African Americans, on women's lives, and on the comparative growth and structure of cities. The results are very useful for an examination of Richmond.

A word must be said about the use of terms in this book. Wherever possible, the terms by which people identified or described themselves are used. I have avoided the use of familiar but inadequate terms like "tribe" to describe groups of American Indians. I have used "Native American" where it does not seem distracting or confusing. Because Richmond's history has been so centered around issues of race, it is impossible not to use the term, although its meaning is socially constructed and reconstructed over generations. Wherever possible, I have avoided talking about "races" and have instead used the highly unsatisfactory and inaccurate dichotomies "black" and "white." Because our history has made much of these differences, it is impossible not to use some form of physical description, which is often provided only to give social, political, or economic contextual clues to an event or a policy and not because the shade of skin color has other meaning. That it should be this difficult to accurately describe individuals or that these labels are even necessary is an indication of both the local and national obsession with race as an ultimate definition and the extent to which the significance of an event hinges on the "race" of the participants.

Another equally weighted and confusing term is that of "class." Class is now often viewed through a variety of prisms, including neighborhood, occupation, religion, voluntary associations, and consumption patterns. The effort to determine which groups provided the dominant sets of values and how this dominance was maintained or undermined constitutes a promising approach to understanding class in Richmond. The city was the space in which the contest for influence, power, or inclusion took place. One way to view this contest is to follow the spatial development of Richmond as an emerging middle class rose above the grimy labor and tawdry commerce of Main Street, Rocketts, and the Basin to build their homes on the heights of Shockoe Hill and then spread east and west to suburban villas. In the meantime, industry grew along the James River's banks, neighborhoods grew to accommodate factory labor, and in the late nineteenth century, city neighborhoods divided by race. New functions for old city spaces or further refinement of old functions were spatial reflections of changes in the social order and culture.

A spirit of enterprise ran through the city from William Byrd I forward and pervaded all ranks and stations. Entrepreneurialism, individualism, evangelical religion, and racial control were important contexts from which class was derived, but all categories, if employed only as polarities, obscure the avenues and arenas of the middle ground where most residents lived their lives and where they crossed ambiguous boundaries daily.

Concepts of class and race and gender roles are constantly reformulated, and their evolution can be traced in such issues as "leadership recruitment"; the advent of the "race man [or] woman," whose "race work" was often a form of black community-building wedded to middle-class standards; and the social mobility of entrepreneurs. These roles are elusive elements, like the rushing water of the river, not the iron cages of immutable category. Historians attempt to recreate a world's *mentalité* by allowing its inhabitants, rather than later chroniclers, to attach significance to events. In the history of Richmond, that means different versions of and changing perspectives on the past. A history that encompasses almost four hundred years permits only hints and flashes of domestic interiors, of the sweetly pungent odor of tobacco and licorice, of difficult pregnancies, of baseball games on unbuilt lots, of dance cards and the best fishing spots, all of which evoke personal perspectives on a shared past.

The American city is often described as a mosaic, each stone complete but embedded in a larger and interconnected pattern that the historian must back away to see. A more useful image for Richmond and other American cities may be the kaleidoscope. Again, the stones or shards make a pattern, but it is not cemented in place. Each small turn of the cylinder moves them into a new pattern. The movement of even one fragment changes the whole pattern. Held to the light, the kaleidoscope may be instructive for understanding both Richmond's history and its future.

CHAPTER ONE

Views of the Falls

At the falls of the river the water rushed downstream in swirls, arches, and sprays, and hit with a steady roar against stone piles, jutting rock, and small green islands. The sound absorbed bird cries, the creak of branches, and human voices in the way that morning mist obscured the river's granite outcroppings. The people called Powhatan, who were a part of this place, chose to live a short distance downriver on a plateau above the banks of the falls. From this vantage point they could both hear and see who came toward their village.

In May of 1607, from a muddy new encampment farther down the river toward the sea, Capt. Christopher Newport, a one-armed veteran of English wars in the West Indies, led twenty-three men, including Capt. John Smith, upriver toward the falls. The rest of the assorted Englishmen engaged in this New World venture stayed behind to build defenses and plant corn. The men rowing upstream were watched, moment to moment, by the Powhatans in whose midst they had planted themselves; local chiefs greeted them each time they landed, and once the queen of the Appamatuck met them on the river bank. The Powhatans saw rivers as the center of their territory, not as the edges or boundaries. To travel upriver on what the English called the "King's river" or "James" was to travel through the very center of the Powhatan world.

The first encounter between the English and the Powhatans on the James River has had a central place in American history ever since members of Newport's party first put their experiences on paper. The town that grew up at the falls of the James was deeply enmeshed in this origins story. The narrative of beginnings on the James has always carried powerful symbolic meaning and has been used to explain and reexplain subsequent history in Richmond, in Virginia, and in the nation. A regional mythology overlay and obscured both the lives of Native Americans along the eastern Virginia rivers and the diverse motives and visions of the English adventurers. Richmond's early history was also national history.

By 1607, the English had already named a wide sweep of the North American continent "Virginia" for Elizabeth I, the Virgin Queen whose reign inspired, though it did not finance, the exploration of North America by Englishmen. The first permanent settlement and the river it was on were named for her dour nephew and successor, James I, who was king when Jamestown was founded in 1607. The England of the early seventeenth century faced a larger world of commerce with rising confidence and energy, envisioning American colonies as commercial enterprises as well as military outposts from which to search for precious metals.

As Newport's party left the Chesapeake Bay, the land was flat and the stream wide, with water clear to the gravel and sand bottom. The banks were dense with pines and oaks, sweet gum and yellow poplar except where rock outcroppings, shaped by the water, prevented growth or where fires had burned away underbrush. There the spring sun dappled the ground between the pines and hardwoods. Winter's ice storms had bent or broken great trees, and their branches reached up from the ground in stages of decomposition.

West of the settlement, the land rose slightly, and ash, cedar, cypress, and hickory appeared. From their shallop, Newport's men could see evidence of the spring freshets in the leaves and debris caught in the lower branches of young trees, and a dry mud still caked the riverbank's spring green. Despite the common-sense proposals that drew investors to the joint-stock company financing the Virginia expedition, some lingering hope remained that they might repeat the Spanish experience and find inland cities piled high with gold and silver. The gentlemen adventurers and soldiers believed that they had not come this distance merely to grub in the spring mud and slap at insects in Jamestown. Newport's party traveled upstream carrying the burden of European history and mythology, while those left behind to plant may have felt denied their opportunity for fame.

There were just over one hundred men in the group of adventurers sponsored by English merchants and led by world-seasoned professional soldiers. Its members included the younger sons of West Country gentry—men who hoped to gain a fortune, since they could inherit little—and villagers who came to London for work and, finding none, indentured themselves to Virginia. It was a period of perceived overpopulation in England, when many respectable English families were driven, by lack of work and land, out of the local areas to which they were intensely attached. The English indenture system was an old and honorable pattern of rising in the world through apprenticeship and journeyman status; a few journeymen could ultimately become masters of a craft. But after 1607 young men and women discovered what thousands more would learn—that indenture in Virginia often meant leaving behind the support of English law and finding, instead, illness and death. The lads and maids who emigrated to Virginia were suddenly thrust into a commercial world where the prizes of land and wealth excited ambition and broke down traditional obligations between master and indenture.[1]

THE Powhatan Indians, an Algonquian-speaking people, had lived in Virginia and near the falls of the James River for 1,400 years. In the early seventeenth century, they were clustered along major rivers east of the fall line, while the area to the west was claimed by Souian speakers. The Powhatan village at the falls was inhabited by one of the six Pamunkey groups that had been dominated since about 1580 by a man named Wahunsonacock, called Powhatan by the English. For a generation he extended his empire eastward along the rivers that moved toward the Chesapeake Bay; eventually he became the paramount chief, or *mamanatowic*, over 14,000 Algonquians in a loose confederation known as Tsenacommacah. The settlements along the James were at the center of his chiefdom, and the river was a cord that tied the villages together. Groups nearer Carolina and the Potomac were less completely under his control.

At the falls the local chief, or *werowance*, was his son Parahunt, who could raise fifty warriors. Just to the west of the Powhatan village were their enemies, the Monacans. Far north and west of the Monacans were the Iroquois, and near the coast south of the James were the Nottoway and Meherrin. The Iroquois had long made seasonal raids into the south and, after defeating the Hurons and the Eries, were turning their attention to the Powhatans and other southern peoples.

This unwelcome attention from the Iroquois was not the the first invasion in the living memory of the Powhatans. In recent decades, the Spanish had attempted a York River settlement, and subsequent battles between them and the Indians had killed significant numbers of both groups. The Spanish were driven out, but they left European diseases behind, and many Indian villages had been decimated. Just before the time of the Jamestown settlement, Powhatan had destroyed several villages that resisted his authority. For all these reasons, Powhatan may have hoped to make allies of the English and work them into his imperial design, just as they schemed to work him into theirs.

A tall, broad-shouldered man in his sixties with long gray hair, Powhatan cultivated a dark mien and a majestic demeanor. The English had no difficulty in identifying him as a mon-

Groups of Indians
aligned with Powhatan
were based along the
rivers of Tidewater
Virginia and used the
fall line extensively for
fishing and tool-making.
The Powhatan groups
knew of Europeans from
contacts that took place
even before the founding
of Jamestown, and Indian
populations had already
been affected by the
introduction of European
diseases. Map adapted
from Pocahontas's
People: The Powhatan
Indians of Virginia
through Four Centuries,
by Helen C. Rountree.
Copyright 1989 by the
University of Oklahoma
Press.

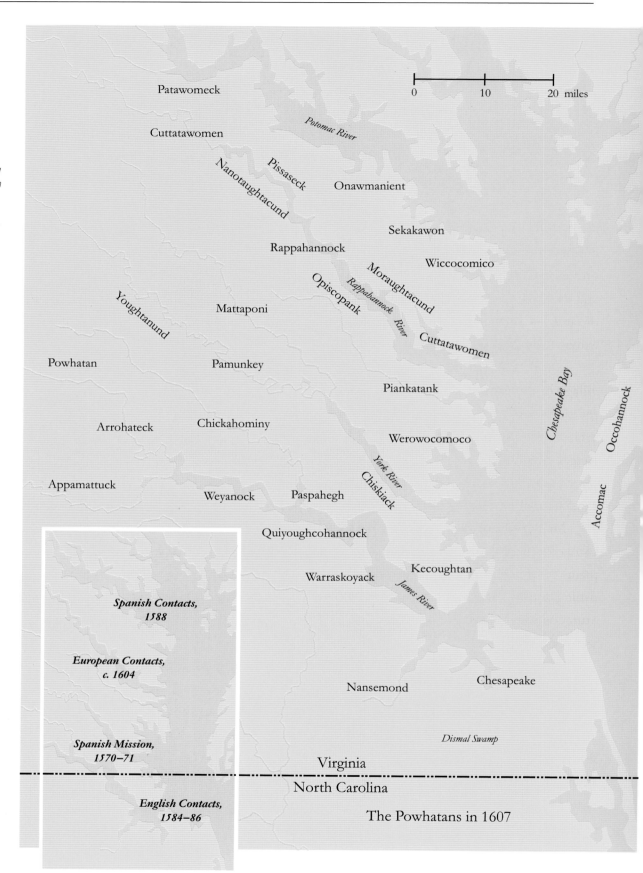

Spanish Contacts,
1588

European Contacts,
c. 1604

Spanish Mission,
1570–71

English Contacts,
1584–86

Patawomeck

Cuttatawomen

Potomac River

Pissaseck

Nanotaughtacund

Onawmanient

Sekakawon

Rappahannock

Wiccocomico

Moraughtacund

Opiscopank

Rappahannock River

Cuttatawomen

Youghtanund

Mattaponi

Powhatan

Pamunkey

Piankatank

Arrohateck

Chickahominy

Werowocomoco

York River

Chiskiack

Appamattuck

Weyanock

Paspahegh

Quiyoughcohannock

Kecoughtan

Warraskoyack

James River

Chesapeake Bay

Occohannock

Accomac

Nansemond

Chesapeake

Dismal Swamp

Virginia

North Carolina

The Powhatans in 1607

arch or ruler. He achieved his dominance through craft, intimidation, and war, but ruled by custom and tradition, and much of his power rested on personal dignity and prestige. Tributes exacted from each Tsenacommacah group represented a symbolic gesture of obedience and were also a means of storing valuable commodities like corn for ritual feasts and periods of famine. Copper and pearl-like shell interiors for ornament and display traveled widely in an extensive trade network that was centered near the falls.

A well-worn path ran downriver from the Powhatan village at the falls to the Arrohattec village of the Pamunkey. Another trail, marked by three notches on the trees, ran west along the north bank, to the mountains. These trails were trade routes and hunting paths in an area of exchange and seasonal expeditions that stretched from the Great Lakes to the southern Appalachian mountains. Since coastal Indians and others often came to the falls of major rivers in search of stone for tools and weapons or to cast their nets for spawning fish, these areas became natural centers for exchange.

Many, perhaps most, Virginia Indians lived along rivers, which were used to transport information, goods, and people and to supply food. The falls marked the place where the coastal plain met the Piedmont; here the river, no longer subject to the tides, was an excellent site for fishing and trade. Fish from the Chesapeake Bay might come as far as the rapids to spawn. Sturgeon weighing over one hundred pounds and shad described by the English as a yard long were caught in nets by the hundreds daily each spring.

The Indians along Virginia rivers lived in villages of ten to one hundred houses that the women made by sticking saplings in the ground and bending them together at the top. This frame, covered with bark, hides, or mats, had a smoke hole in the top and an entrance opening at ground level. Beds were platforms raised from the earth floor with forked sticks. Around the houses were fields in which Indian women grew vegetables and grains, especially corn, which was planted at varied times from early spring with beans, squashes, melons, and sunflowers; the corn stalk provided support for the vines of the other plants, and each crop in turn provided shade or nutrients for the others. Women used a field for five to twenty years, then left it for thirty to forty years to let the soil restore itself. Whether the cluster of houses slowly shifted to a new site or packed and moved completely was the decision of the women, who created and maintained the village and the family. Their centrality was acknowledged in the practice of tracing descent from the mother.[2]

To this abundant natural world with its developed indigenous society, the Englishmen of the Virginia Company brought experiences from the recent attempt to subdue Catholic Ireland: after 1556, Irish land had been confiscated and allocated to English proprietors. This practice provided an English model for colonization and plantation, but Elizabethan explorers, who expected to use military rather than entrepreneurial skills to achieve wealth and fame, failed in the late sixteenth century to make a permanent base on the North American mainland. While English policy wanted to use North American colonies as trading posts and military bases that would protect them from their European rivals and provide a place from which to search for metals or exotic plants, English merchants, less interested in rivaling the conquistadores of Spain, began to plan for long-term commercial possibilities in the New World. Native Americans were at least as much of a hindrance to commercial and imperial "regional planning" as the Irish had been.

Mercantile plans were accompanied by a new popular English literature of travel and exploration, including the promotional writings of Richard Hakluyt the younger, preeminent promoter of the possibilities of the New World. He emphasized the practical reasons for Virginia colonization, which had little to do with cities of gold and silver. Hakluyt predicted a favorable balance of trade for England from Virginia because "the subjectes of this realm for many years shall chaunge many cheape commodities of these parts for things of highe value not there esteemed" and predicted a decline among the many without work because "the wandring beggars that grow up idly and hurtful and burdensome to this realm, may there be unladen, better bred up and may people waste countries."[3]

The Virginia Company of London was created in 1606 by a charter from King James to Richard Hakluyt and "divers others" who still hoped for profit in precious metals but noted the value of plants for dyes and medicines, a passage to the Pacific Ocean, or a trade in iron, furs, potash, pitch, and tar. This enterprise was a joint-stock company composed of both gentry and merchant investors. While it received a charter from the king and was briefly under royal oversight, it was a private venture. Typical of its day, it had but a short amount of time in

Their rype corne.

Their greene corne.

Corne newly sprong.

Their sitting at meate.

The place of solemne prayer.

The howse wherin the Tombe of their Herounds standeth.

SECOTON·

This Indian village on the North Carolina coast looks much like the descriptions of Powhatan villages along the James a generation later. There is a gridlike orderliness to the parts of this village that may reflect a European interpretive overlay, but the design of the houses and the presence of several plantings of corn reflect the everyday culture of the Powhatans. **Village of Secota** (1585), watercolor by John White. Reprinted from America 1585: The Complete Drawings of John White, by Paul Hulton. Copyright 1984 by The University of North Carolina Press

which to make a profit from the stockholders' money before the shares and assets were sold to satisfy debts. Financial urgency pervaded all the activities of the Virginia Company's representatives and drove them to find, if not gold, at least a quickly profitable trade. Understanding that confidence bred further investment, they made enthusiastic claims in their dispatches to England: "This river which we have discovered is one of the famousest rivers that ever was found by any Christian."[4]

Newport, in his journey up the river to the falls, was offered food and drink by the Pamunkeys and was told that he would come to "an overfall of water." Three miles before the falls, the Englishmen reached the village presided over by Parahunt, which consisted of some twelve dwelling houses. It was located on a high hill, and the plain between the houses and the river had recently been planted in a series of small fields where corn, beans, tobacco, pumpkins, gourds, hemp, and flax grew. The English group was well received by Parahunt and participated in an evening of feasting understood by both groups as preliminary to an alliance. Parahunt and his warriors, dressed in handsome buckskin mantles and layers of pearl, copper, and shell necklaces, offered venison and corn cakes to the English, who pressed "hot drinks" of alcohol on their hosts. Traveling upstream to the falls of the river the next day, Newport's party, given more to commercial speculation than contemplation of nature, reasoned that the river might accommodate "100 water milnes for any uses."[5]

Parahunt persuaded Newport not to proceed any farther up the river, telling him that the territory above the falls was inhabited by the hostile Monacans. Newport contented himself with erecting a cross inscribed with King James's name and the year; he added his own name below it. Newport told an Indian guide, who reported it to Parahunt, that the two arms signified Powhatan and Newport and that the fastening in the middle represented their league of friendship.

The friendship proffered by both the Powhatans and the English was as artful and scheming as the answer Newport gave to his guide at the falls, and relations between the English and Powhatans became tense and then warlike. Further explorations made the Powhatans suspicious of English claims to be mere visitors and allies. After a trip to England, Newport returned the next year to march above the falls and meet with the Monacans. The governors

John Smith's map of Virginia illustrates that the Indians' presence on the landscape was pervasive and that the English explorers were thus obliged to negotiate with them. Both the English and the Powhatans understood the need to inspire awe in armed strangers, and this buckskin mantle, with its intricate shell embroidery, was mutually recognized as a symbol of power and majesty. Detail from Virginia map printed in volume 1 of The True Travels, Adventures, and Observations of Captaine John Smith . . . from the London Edition of 1629 (reprint, Richmond: Franklin Press, 1819), from the Valentine, Richmond, Virginia; Powhatan's mantle courtesy of Ashmolean Museum, Oxford University

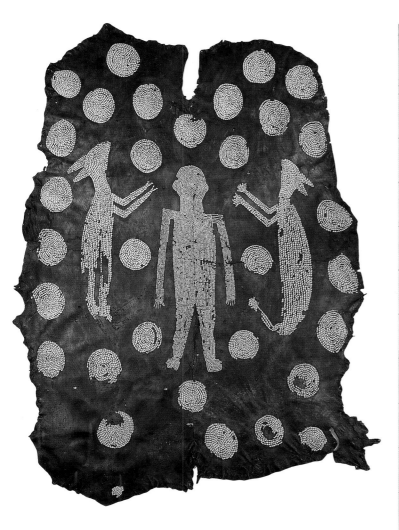

sent out by the Virginia Company had been instructed to plant settlements to the fall line of the James River, which was strategically important for control of the coastal basin and the protection of Jamestown.

Capt. Francis West made such an effort at the James River falls in 1609, but his soldiers stole food from the Powhatan village, whose warriors then attacked the English encampment near the river. The efforts of Capt. John Smith to placate the Indians did not reduce suspicion and hostility between the English adventurers, and the expedition was abandoned. Three years later, Sir Thomas Dale strove mightily to construct a garrison called Henrico near the site of the Arrohattec village below the falls. The steady English incursion into the heart of the Powhatan territory accelerated deteriorating relations and led to the first Anglo-Powhatan War, which lasted from 1609 to 1614 and in which the Powhatans ultimately suffered serious defeat.[6]

Dale's village of Henrico was notable for several reasons. It was here that colonist John Rolfe experimented with varieties of tobacco and where Pocahontas, a daughter of Powhatan and long a visitor to the English settlements, was kidnapped and held hostage as a part of the war between the English and Powhatans. The Jamestown settlers were originally instructed to make allies of the Indians, and some efforts to make treaties and to incorporate the two societies had continued despite hostilities. The most dramatic of these efforts was the marriage of Pocahontas to John Rolfe. Having been converted to Christianity while a hostage, she took the English name Rebecca. After her marriage to Rolfe, she bore a son, traveled to England, was presented at the court, and died as she was about to return to Virginia. The legend of this Indian princess, whose marriage brought a temporary cessation to Anglo-Powhatan wars, became the favorite English symbol of bonding with Virginia, and descent from Pocahontas served as a special claim upon the Virginia land.[7]

Promotional literature and the Virginia Company assumed that climate could be inferred from latitude alone and that Virginia could grow silkworms, tea, or wine grapes as readily as China, Greece, Italy, and Spain. Instead, tobacco became Virginia's profitable commodity after John Rolfe's experimental tobacco plants—milder than older strains—were sent to England in 1614. The subsequent rise in price stimulated a growth in production that made some planters wealthy by the early 1620s. Although the price for tobacco then declined, new arrivals and old

While the English marveled at the designs dyed on the skins of Indian women and observed Indian agricultural patterns and techniques, the true marvel may have *been the rapidity with which European artifacts and standards entered the lives of Native Americans, either casually or prescriptively. The young Pocahontas, described* *as wanton and athletic, became the sedate and anglicized Lady Rebecca of the portrait, and in a late-sixteenth-century drawing by John White, the Indian child carries* *an English doll.* **Pocahontas** *(1616), artist unknown, courtesy of the National Portrait Gallery, Smithsonian Institution;* **Indian Mother and Child** *reprinted from* America 1585: The Complete Drawings of John White, *by Paul Hulton. Copyright 1984 by The University of North Carolina Press*

Despite the early mis-givings of Charles I, the author of this treatise against tobacco, colonists were quick to adopt tobacco as a cash crop. The adaptation of a strain of tobacco suited to the Virginia soil earned the precarious colony a place in the mercantile world and provided the region with its characteristic plantation system, accompanied by indentured or slave labor. From the Valentine, Richmond, Virginia

DIEV · ET · MON · DROIT

By the King.

¶ A Proclamation concerning Tobacco.

Hereas in the Reigne of Our moſt deare and Royall Father, King I A M E S of bleſſed memozy, ſince Our acceſſe to the Crowne, ſeuerall Pzoclamations haue been made and publiſhed concerning Tobacco, Yet notwithſtanding all the care and pzouidence which hath hitherto been vſed, We finde the vnlimited deſire of gaine, and the inozdinate appetite of taking Tobacco, hath ſo farre pzeuailed, that Tobacco hath been continued to bee planted in great quanti=ties, in ſeuerall parts of this Our Realme, and a vaſt pzopoztion of vnſeruiceable Tobacco made and bzought from Our Colonies of Virginia , Summer Ilands, and other Our Fozreigne Plantations, beſides an incredible quantity of Braſill and Spaniſh Tobacco impozted hither, and ſecretly con=ueyed on Land. And it is now come to paſſe, That thoſe Our Fozreigne Plantations,that might become vſefull to this Kingdome, lingering onely vpon Tobacco, are in apparant danger to be vtterly ruined,vnleſſe Wee ſpeedily pzouide foz their ſubſiſtence;The bodies and manners of Our people are alſo in danger to bee cozrupted, and the wealth of this King=dome exhauſted by ſo vſeleſſe a Weede as Tobacco is, which beeing repzeſented vnto Us by the humble Petition of Our louing Subiects the Planters and Aduenturers in Virginia, and alſo by the like humble Petition of the Retailers and Sellers of Tobacco in and about Our Cities of London and Weſtminſter,Wee haue thought it wozthy of Our Pzincely care,as a mat=ter not only fit foz Our pzofit, ſ the pzofit of Our people, but much concerning Us in Our ho=nour and gouernment ſo to regulate the ſame , and compell due obedience thereto, that Our Fozreigne Plantations and Colonies may bee ſuppozted and encouraged, and they made vſe=full to this Kingdome, by applying themſelues to moze ſolide commodities, that the healths of Our Subiects may be pzeſerued the wealth of this Kingdome enlarged,and the manners of Our people ſo ozdered and gouerned, that the wozld may not iuſtly taxe Us, that theſe are at once endangered only by the licentious vſe of Tobacco. And therfoze hauing ſeriouſly adui=ſed hereof,Wee,by the aduice of Our Pziuie Councell,haue now reſolued vpon, and publiſhed theſe Our Coũmands following concerning Tobacco, which Our Royall will and pleaſure is, ſhall be in all things obſerued vpon paine of Our higheſt diſpleaſure,and of ſuch paines,pe=nalties and puniſhments, as by Our Court of Exchequer, and Court of Starre Chamber, and by any other Courts and miniſters of Juſtice, oz by Our Pzerogatiue Royall can be in=ſucted vpon the offendozs.

settlers alike continued to hope for another boom and continued to plant more tobacco and extend their acreage. As tobacco fields spread and planters sought more land from the crown, the Powhatan groups were pushed farther from their traditional land.

The Virginia Company still hoped to bring the Indians into an English world of industry and trade after the first Anglo-Powhatan war. Another fort, to replace the one fallen away at Henrico, was established nearby at Tuckahoe, and the eight miles of land between the falls and that fort was devoted to the support of a college for English and Indian youth. English sermons and broadsides implored donations for this college, which would convert and educate the Indians. A percentage of the profits from an iron works set up in 1619 six miles below the falls was to be used for Indian education.

For a dozen years the joint-stock company sent settlers, supplies, and directives from London to Jamestown and depleted its financial resources in a vain effort to make the colony profitable. The death rate remained high, and the company found it difficult to enforce its directives from the other side of the Atlantic. A major reorganization of the company in 1618 included a new land system designed to lure colonists and to enrich those already in Virginia. Settlers received one hundred acres of land and were granted fifty acres more for each person they brought into the colony. The company was to be paid a rent of one shilling per fifty acres. English law supplanted martial law in the 1618 reforms, and the colonists were given an assembly with decision-making powers. The company authorized the creation of autonomous little colonies called "particular plantations" within Virginia and for the first time gave control of the land to individual settlers or investors. Each particular plantation had its own organizers and backers in England; each was responsible for recruiting and transporting settlers. These little colonies, or "hundreds," soon evolved toward control by individual families and became the model for the Tidewater plantation system, in which a few entrepreneurial families were able to engross most of the best land.

The shift to the family as the economic and political base unit was purposeful. Women had arrived in Jamestown after 1607 in small numbers with each ship, but after its reorganization in 1618, the Virginia Company sponsored over one hundred women emigrants and made an effort to verify their virtuous conduct and domestic skills. The company hoped "to tye and roote the Planter's myndes to Virginia by the bonds of wives and children" and, in this hope, sent "young, handsome, and honestlie educated Maides." It was the misfortune of the maids to arrive just a few months before the major Indian attack of March 1622 and to then face the starving winter of 1622–23.[8]

The ambitious combination of enterprises near the falls, including the college, iron works, and corporate reorganization, was destroyed in the second Anglo-Powhatan War. The Indians' attack in 1622 demonstrated their conclusion that the white encroachment had no limits. Led by Opechancanough, brother of the deceased Powhatan, the Indians destroyed these ventures as well as any expectation of their peaceful submission to the English. Those settlers outside stockaded forts were killed, and those inside were called briefly back to Jamestown.

In desperate financial straits by 1622, the Virginia Company was quite ready to abandon notions of coexistence with the Indians and to advise the colonists to destroy them as a people. This the colonists were not powerful enough to do, but they could and did burn Indian villages, destroy corn fields, cut fishing lines, break treaties, and harass the Indians into drawing away from the areas of English settlement. The Indians had changed their tactics as well: rather than engaging the enemy in open fields, they now relied on surprise and ambush. The result was reciprocal forms of terror that went on for almost two generations as tobacco planters moved upriver along the James, York, Rappahannock, and Potomac.[9]

The Virginia Company finally failed in 1624 and was placed under the supervision of the crown, which divided its James River settlements into four incorporations. In 1634 the expanded area of settlement was organized into eight shires or counties in an attempt to place English political order on the Tidewater. One of those counties was Henrico, a large and sparsely settled area. Although each of these new counties was to be administered from a town, in essence no towns existed. There were "stores" set up as legal tobacco market centers, but no commercial towns resulted, and Jamestown remained an unhealthy and disorganized village. Settlers moved up the James and other rivers and out along lesser rivers and creeks looking for land which they could purchase from a grant or on which they could stake out headrights. The settlement of upriver lands was particularly haphazard, but a sense of sprawling rural neighborhood did develop in Henrico and other upriver counties, where settlers knew of each others' presence and activities though they gathered infrequently.[10]

The aged Opechancanough led a second war against the English in 1644, and his bowmen killed about five hundred outlying colonists, but the settlers captured Opechancanough and forced the Powhatans to a treaty. The Treaty of 1646 was made with a conveniently pliable chief of unknown affiliation whom the English called "emperor" and whom they invested with the power to cede all the mainland of eastern Virginia to the English and to declare all Indians of Virginia to be subject to the government at Jamestown. Many Powhatan groups were forced to move from land along the major rivers, and forts were constructed at the falls of each river. Fort Charles, constructed at the falls of the James, marked the beginning of continuous settlement there and functioned as a trading center for Powhatans and planters as well as a military outpost.

Under this treaty, on pain of death no Indians could enter the peninsula between the York and James rivers without wearing a striped coat, which signaled that they were messengers. English imperial policy in the mid-1640s created a pale of settlement and the beginnings of a reservation policy in Virginia, while the Jamestown government concerned itself with aligning the old Powhatan confederacy with the English and making them ever more dependent.[11]

In the first half-century of English occupation, the Indian population of the bay and rivers declined rapidly. Wars and skirmishes with the English and attacks from the northern or Iroquois tribes had an effect, but European illnesses were particularly devastating. Even affiliation with the English could cost the Indians dearly, as was evident when a combined force of English militiamen and Pamunkey warriors fought "foreign" Indians, probably Iroquois or Cherokee, near the falls of the James in 1656 and were badly defeated. Many Pamunkeys were slain in a battle that gave the name "Bloody Run" to the little stream running through the woods where they fought. The colonial council had to sue for peace and fixed wider boundaries on the north and south sides of the river; Indians could not enter this region. The Pamunkeys suffered the greatest battle losses, yet the new law restricted them most.

If the upriver English planters feared the movements of both Powhatans under treaty and

Indentured servants emigrated from England's major ports in the 1600s, drawing heavily on the immediate areas around cities like London, Liverpool, and Bristol. As the emigration of white servants waned in the late 1600s, the Chesapeake colonies turned toward Africa for labor, although the trade of the Royal African Company was still focused primarily on the West Indies. The African slave trade was carried out primarily on the east coast of Africa, where slaves were brought after capture. Map adapted from Philip D. Curtin, The Atlantic Slave Trade: A Census (Madison: University of Wisconsin Press, 1969), and from James Horn, "Servant Emigration to the Chesapeake in the Seventeenth Century," in The Chesapeake in the Seventeenth Century: Essays on Anglo-American Society, ed. Thad Tate and David Ammerman (Chapel Hill: University of North Carolina Press for the Institute of Early American History and Culture, 1979), by permission of the publishers.

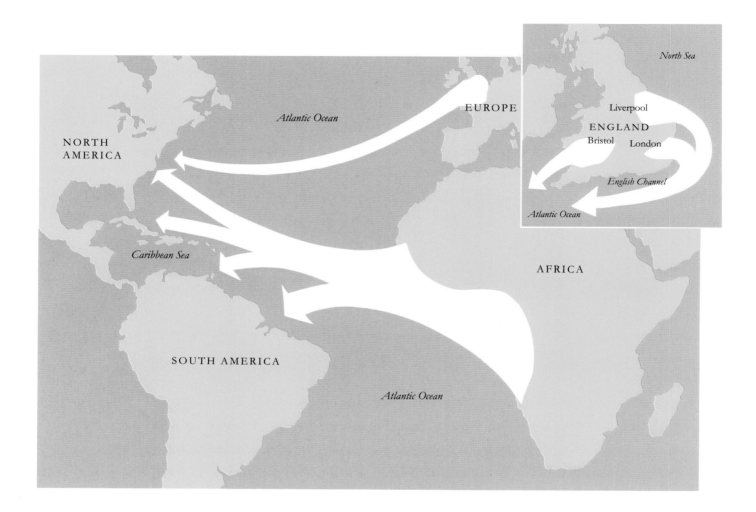

traveling parties of other Indians, they looked with equal anxiety to the rivers, where European imperial rivalries might manifest themselves in the form of hostile warships. While the threat to English settlements from the Spanish had diminished, trade wars with the Dutch in the 1660s and 1670s twice brought Dutch warships up the James River to burn tobacco. Caught up in the commercial conflicts of distant nation-states and wary of unseen presences in a stand of trees at the edge of a cornfield, Henrico planters felt unprotected and wanted more from their government. Tensions continued to mount, because the area had drawn a most combustible mixture of warring elements. In Henrico, English colonial policy met Powhatans, English gentlefolk and villagers, and transported Africans.[12]

In the 1650s the English government began passing a series of Navigation Acts designed to bring colonial outposts under parliamentary control, create trading monopolies, and impose a national imperial policy. English wars with the Netherlands in the same period broke the Dutch hold on trade in tobacco, furs, and slaves. An English slave trade with Africa became an important and profitable part of the commerce that grew up under the Navigation Acts. The English-based Royal African Company, formed late in the seventeenth century, acquired much of the Dutch slave trade from West Africa.

Africans purchased with British goods were transported in British ships to the West Indies, especially Jamaica; some were carried on to Virginia and others came after some time of seasoning in the West Indies, but their numbers, especially on the frontier, remained very small. By the 1670s, some few Africans worked alongside indentured servants on the plantations near the falls. Their status, while still uncertain, was moving slowly, statute by statute, toward a form of permanent bondage.

On the Henrico frontier in the 1670s, trade in furs and slaves was as important as trade in tobacco. Planters were often merchants and took advantage of the fact that traditional Indian trading paths crisscrossed the area. As fur-bearing animals became scarce in Europe, the trade of skins and hides shifted to North America. The market for American beaver pelts was now insatiable in Europe, and the beaver trade moved westward rapidly; those Indian groups who adopted it developed a dependency on European goods.[13]

In the falls area there was much to be gained in trade and much to be lost. Nathaniel Bacon, a privileged and impetuous young man who had created problems for himself and his family in England, arrived in Virginia in the spring of 1674 and bought land on the James, including a cleared plantation with dwelling and outbuildings at Curles Neck and undeveloped acreage near the falls. There he met William Byrd, son of a London goldsmith, whose shrewd appraisal of his own opportunities was an object lesson in entrepreneurship.

The Byrd family, so prominent in Richmond's history, began in Virginia with Thomas Stegge, who came to the colony in the 1630s and began trading on the James River in the 1640s. After the first Thomas Stegge was lost at sea in 1651, his son, also named Thomas Stegge, added to his inherited lands another 1,800 acres at the falls of the James. This parcel made up the Falls Plantation on the south side of the river. In 1660, Stegge purchased eight hundred more acres on the north side and, in the next year, went to live in a small stone house with a center chimney on the Falls Plantation, south of the river. This second Thomas Stegge died in 1671 and left the bulk of his estate, including the Falls Plantation, to his young nephew, William Byrd, who already lived in the colony.

Byrd was working to expand the land holdings left him by his uncle when he met Nathaniel Bacon, his new neighbor. Bacon had acquired Curles Plantation and intended both to farm that land and to build a trading house at the falls. Byrd and Bacon planned a partnership in anticipation of a lucrative trade with the Indians. Both were cousins by marriage of Frances Culpepper, wife of Governor William Berkeley. Ambitious men like William Byrd and Nathaniel Bacon took wives from well-connected families in the realistic expectation that such kinship would smooth their way in the world. A typical wife, whose status was assessed primarily by her husband's fortune, would share her husband's goals of advancement through politics, planting, and military service. Bacon was indeed shown preferment by Berkeley and appointed to the Governor's Council, although he attended few meetings.[14]

The pervasive presence of the Indians west of the falls prevented land-hungry Englishmen without kin or wealth from spreading out and claiming land. Surrounding these frontier settlers were Powhatan treaty lands and, beyond them, the land of Indian groups who had never agreed to a treaty. While land was abundant, it was not available. The Jamestown government, which protected treaty lands, also favored a small elite of planters in granting land. It was common for the monarch to reward favors or to repay debts through land grants in Virginia, and courtiers or wealthy merchants were the usual beneficiaries. Kinship or commercial relations with the Governor's Council also provided opportunity for land grants or public office. When planters with large holdings, like Nathaniel Bacon and William Byrd, appeared to agree with the unhappy English landless on the issues of Indian land and Governor Berkeley's alleged trade monopolies, it distracted attention from the preferment Byrd and Bacon received and created an artificial and temporary unity among the landless and the privileged on the frontier.

Early in 1676, a cycle of Indian raids and retaliation that had begun along the Potomac the previous year reached the James River falls. Bacon's overseer there, as well as three of William Byrd's men, were killed. Planters, their African and English servants, and land-hungry frontiersmen gathered to move against the Indians. Bacon, Byrd, and other planters took them rum at their encampment, and the unauthorized militia cheered Bacon into assuming command. They moved in April to attack the Indians and, although Governor Berkeley withheld permission, began campaigns against the Pamunkeys and Occaneechees, local tribes who were not connected to the Indian raids. As contemporary chroniclers of Bacon's Rebellion noted about the activities of those who attacked the Indians, "it matters not whether they be Friends or Foes Soe they be Indians." [15]

In the first part of the sprawling and episodic battles of Bacon's Rebellion, friendly Indians were taken unaware and murdered, their cache of furs and skins taken as booty. Although Governor Berkeley denounced Bacon and declared him a rebel, Bacon remained popular and was elected to the assembly in June. At Jamestown for the General Assembly meeting, Bacon obtained a pardon from Governor Berkeley but then left the governmental seat and returned with an army of followers and intimidated the assembly into giving him command of the Indian campaign.

While Bacon and his army looked for Indians near the falls of the James, Berkeley yet again declared Bacon a rebel. With apparent popular approval, Bacon attacked the weak and fragmented Powhatan Confederacy and then laid siege to Jamestown, forcing Berkeley out

The colonial policies of Gov. William Berkeley in Jamestown often seemed at odds with the interests of frontier planters and landless families at the edge of settlement, in such counties as Henrico. In Bacon's Rebellion, the unsuccessful attempt to overthrow Berkeley's government, planters armed their slaves and indentured servants to supplement the militia; each group may have hoped to gain either freedom or land by resisting the king's representative. **Governor William Berkeley,** artist and date unknown, courtesy of the Virginia State Library and Archives, Richmond

and burning the capital. Soon after, Bacon became ill and died and the revolt collapsed. Governor Berkeley, aware that the frontier area had many landless and unhappy young men with weapons, began to move toward accommodating men on the frontier at the expense of the Indians and the treaties that had been made with them.

In these campaigns, Bacon, Byrd and other gentlemen armed their indentured servants and their African slaves. Promises of shares in the booty of war and perhaps promises of freedom from indenture and slavery merged with genuine fear of Indian ambushes to impel servants to join the militia's campaigns. Certain wives of Henrico planters seemed particularly persuaded by Nathaniel Bacon's cause. Perhaps a resentment of the high Jamestown ladies and a fear that they might be hindered in their own family ambitions sent them out to rally support and to make speeches denouncing Governor Berkeley. At the rebellion's end, one woman, Sarah Grendon, did not receive the general pardon, and another, Lydia Chiesman, begged Governor Berkeley to hold her responsible for her husband's disloyalties. Another, Sarah Drummond, sailed to England to plead her husband's case and regain their property.[16]

While Byrd and Bacon were both recent immigrants from England, Byrd had planted himself firmly and pragmatically in the New World, while Bacon, with a young courtier's taste for vainglory, saw himself playing upon an English stage. The backdrop was Virginia, but his actions seemed directed toward an English audience and perhaps a triumphant return to England, where, if the outcome was favorable, his boldness would be applauded and feted. William Byrd initially sided with Bacon and the rebels, but when the rebellion assumed proportions beyond counter-raids on the Indians and possible acquisition of their land and furs, he prudently withdrew. His reward for this reversal was to be granted land that included Bacon's Quarter Branch. Both men got something they desired from Bacon's Rebellion. Byrd acquired land, and Bacon, in death, acquired the role of hero in the Restoration drama of the 1680s. There he was portrayed as a noble-souled giant among base money-grubbers of low birth.[17]

The turbulent events of 1676 reflected several realities of the Henrico County frontier. One of them was that most of the scattered English population in Henrico County did not want to distinguish between Indians living under the terms of treaties and Indians beyond the Jamestown government. They coveted the Indians' land and their stock of furs. A commission

appointed by the king concluded that the large landholders of the frontier were the main cul-
prits in attacking and robbing nearby Indians living under treaty. In this trespass the planters
were abetted by smallholders and ex–indentured servants who were willing to make common
cause with men they often resented in order to rid the area of Indians. During the seventeenth
century, English traders on the frontier were often as willing to enslave Indians as Africans,
and tax lists for this period in Henrico County show Indians held as slaves.[18]

Another reality of the Henrico frontier after Bacon was the scattered and subdued nature
of the Indian presence. Traces of the town of Powhatan below the falls appear in records after
the 1646 treaty that removed many Indian villages. A plat of Byrd family holdings in 1662
shows the Powhatan village still in existence on the north side of the James. These Powhatans
were still in Henrico County with ten bowmen, or adult males, according to a 1669 General
Assembly census. After that, the Pamunkeys long resident near the falls may have merged with
other Powhatan groups. The label "Powhite Indian cabins" appears on a 1701 plat of land on
Shockoe Creek.[19]

The English struggle for existence and dominance in the first half-century of the Virginia colonization project is legendary. Despite the vaunted New World abundance, the death
rate was extremely high. The Virginia Company sent over about 6,000 people between 1607
and 1624, but in 1624 there were only 1,200 people in Virginia. Thirty years later the population was about 20,000, and by 1662 about 40,000; in 1662 there was still no town worthy of
the name, although an "English nation" of sorts had been planted. Between 80 and 90 percent
of the total white arrivals in the Chesapeake came as servants. By 1670, Governor Berkeley
estimated a population of "above forty thousand persons, men, women, and children, and of
which there are two thousand black slaves, six thousand christian servants, for a short time."[20]

The successful planters of the first generation were mostly those ambitious men of lesser
status who made a large, crude reach for land and laborers to grow tobacco. Later, a few more
sons of the gentry and the family connections of merchants arrived with capital and bought
extensive estates, merging with the remnants or descendants of the first successful planters to
create a social and political elite. Virginia after seventy years was English, with a preponder-
ance of population from London and adjoining counties; Anglican in a pro forma manner;
hierarchical in that the colony was led by an emerging planter class that identified with the

country elite of late-seventeenth-century England. It was thinly populated and still predominantly male, with most of its people living on remote plantations or scattered along the riverbanks. It was also deeply affected by its experience of colonization and the long encounter with Native Americans. By the late seventeenth century, Virginia was securely part of an English empire, but the English colonials had reason to think of themselves as Virginians.[21]

CHAPTER TWO

Settlement at the Falls

One hundred years after Christopher Newport and his fellow adventurers ascended the James River and speculated on its commercial possibilities, the landscape at the falls gave little visual evidence that the region was part of an international trade system. Early-eighteenth-century maps in London's administrative councils, it is true, showed the region to be a part of the British Empire. The colonial assembly had parceled out the land and imposed a superficial political order upon it, incorporating the falls into the county of Henrico, with a courthouse at Varina. Yet property rights and political boundaries had modified the terrain only slightly in a century. Half-cleared fields dotted with stumps and the stark skeletons of girdled trees alternated with forests. Near the river were narrow wooden warehouses, and the small dwellings of planters and aspiring planters were scattered farther back. If one could measure wealth in acreage, as the English were generally willing to do, then a number of the dwellings were deceptively modest for the amount of land attached to them.[1]

The Indian village near the falls had dwindled to a few dwellings near the river, which housed the remnants of diverse Powhatan groups. The Monacans who lived above the falls had disappeared, and the site of their village was now a settlement called Manakintown, home to the French Protestants known as Huguenots. Some members of the Powhatans' empire lived nearby on clearly defined treaty land, and some Indians were held as slaves on frontier plantations. Forts built near the falls had fallen into ruin by the end of the 1600s, since the need to protect settlers from either Indians or hostile Europeans was gone.[2]

The Indian trails along the rise above the river were more distinctly worn from their new use in transporting hogsheads of tobacco to the warehouses from outlying plantations. Where the old trails were too narrow or steep, new paths had formed. The planter-merchants who lived near the falls of the James and on the Appomattox River dominated the Indian trade, sending packhorses far into the south and southwest to return with skins, furs, and Indian slaves. In the late seventeenth century, a fierce competition for the Indian trade existed between Abraham Wood, a prominent trader on the Appomattox River, and William Byrd I, who prevailed and became the most prominent Indian trader in Virginia.

The essential character of Richmond as a commercial center was established before it was a town. Its merchant culture was anticipated in the activities of its first families, who achieved their prominence through their willingness to seize whatever opportunities appeared before them. William Byrd I was a model of the aspiring planter, taking advantage of every opportunity to acquire land, trade with the Indians, buy and sell Indian and African slaves, produce and market tobacco, and compete for patronage offices in the colonial government.[3]

When Byrd's agents led pack horses west from the falls on Indian trails, they carried kettles, powder, guns, and beads to exchange for skins—especially deer, beaver, and raccoon. The relentless western movement of the fur trade changed the lives and habits of even those Indians outside English dominance and made them more dependent on European artifacts. Native Americans captured in intertribal wars were often purchased by Byrd's agents and brought back as slaves. Byrd also traded heavily in African slaves and in indentured servants. Late in the century, as the market for African slaves increased in Virginia, Byrd invested in a slave ship. He sold molasses, ginger, sugar, rum from Barbados, and English-manufactured items including shoes, brushes, files, horse collars, guns, hoes, and hats. To his great profit, his tobacco warehouse at the falls performed official government tobacco inspections and stored the tobacco of other planters. The first Byrd was a member of the House of Burgesses, Captain of the Henrico Militia, and member of the Council of State, from which offices he derived much of his preferment.

The community and the bonds that maintained it near the falls of the James in the late 1600s and early 1700s spread over a large expanse of countryside. Social and economic connections were regional and consisted of family, friends, and favors given and received. Farmhouses were linked by wagon roads and paths. The parish church, county courthouse, and tavern centered the region first at Varina and later at Richmond. Large landholders like Byrd were the social and political leaders; they served as justices of the peace, claimed the forward pews in church, and were chosen as delegates to the General Assembly. They also controlled the tobacco warehouses around which towns grew and supported the Warehouse Acts of 1713 and 1730, which established an inspection and grading system for tobacco. These acts gave their tobacco an advantage over that of small planters when merchants appeared in warehouse villages to offer credit and European goods.[4]

Although the fall line was still a frontier in the early eighteenth century, old tobacco

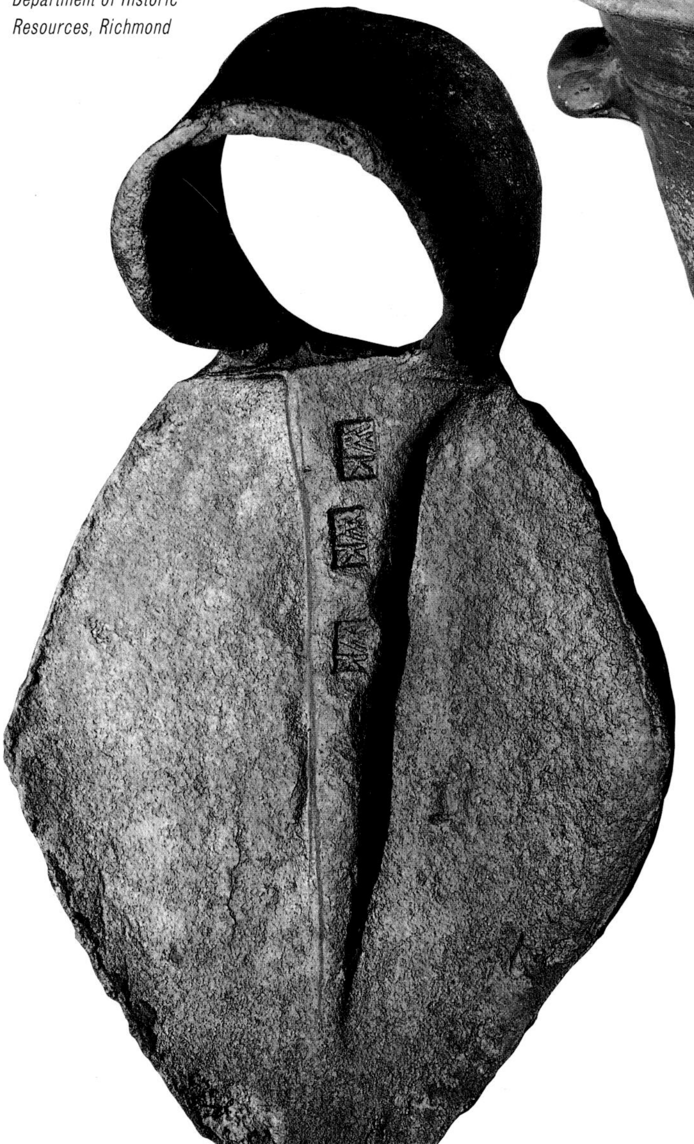

Household furnishings
were sparse and iron
implements scarce on
the Virginia frontier.
As population density
grew in the region near
the falls, ship's traders
and colonial agents for
English and Scottish
merchant firms found it
profitable to bring more
goods to the docks and
to keep stores of goods
available for customers.
Cooking pot and grub
hoe, photographed by
Katherine Wetzel, cour-
tesy of Archives, Virginia
Department of Historic
Resources, Richmond

fields and weathered frame dwellings gave the area a haphazard and worn appearance. Until the 1730s, English farmers followed the slash-and-burn techniques they had noted in Powhatan agriculture. Tobacco production up the James River to the falls depleted the sandy soil in a short time, and common practice was simply to move on to new land rather than actively restore the worn acreage. Old tobacco fields grew weeds or were used for grazing. In the mid-1700s, while tobacco was planted on new Piedmont soils, both Tidewater and Piedmont farmers moved to grain production in addition to tobacco. This gave rise to milling along Virginia rivers and, with the opening of European and West Indian grain markets, to a trade that rivaled the importance of the tobacco trade.[5]

While the physical landscape at the falls changed slowly for a century and more after Newport's journey, the area was fully part of the development of a Chesapeake society and economy. Most farms near the falls settlement were a few hundred acres in size, but some were several thousand acres. All these holdings were called "plantations," although it was the large ones that gave the word its particular American meaning. Planters of small or large acreage endeavored always to acquire more land for production to counter depleted soil or supplement low prices, and they usually responded to a drop in tobacco prices by planting more tobacco.[6]

Planters at the falls of the James built expecting to build again, preferring earthfast wooden houses not intended to last more than a generation. The early dwellings erected near the falls were most often one- or two-room split board buildings with end chimneys and a post-hole frame foundation set on or in the ground. Such buildings sagged, leaned, and even burned, but on the Virginia frontier they housed all levels of planters, as well as slaves and servants, and even served as churches. These buildings were used much longer in the Chesapeake than in the northern colonies, mainly because the massive capital investment involved in acquiring slaves and beginning a plantation meant that even large planters had to limit expenditures where they could. The cost of constructing a manor house or any sort of impressive dwelling was so great in the Chesapeake that even successful planters delayed until the early eighteenth century. As the Atlantic tobacco trade stabilized on the upper James and planters acquired both families and an increasing number of servants, larger structures were built with more outbuildings and separate housing for slaves.[7]

By the mid-1700s, a tobacco culture had matured in Tidewater Virginia, and its elements were recognizable throughout the trading world. This cartouche from the Frye-Jefferson map (1751) captures those elements: the well-dressed planter, his African slaves, his tobacco on the docks, and a possible transaction taking place. Courtesy of Colonial Williamsburg Foundation, Williamsburg, Virginia

High prices for tobacco in the early years of Virginia production were followed by a steady decline, somewhat balanced by lower production costs and the addition of acreage. In the second decade of the 1700s, the market started to expand when the French began importing Virginia tobacco and the Scottish tobacco factors began competing with English consignment firms. Despite the growing market for Chesapeake wheat and corn in Europe and the West Indies, tobacco remained the crop on which planters placed their hopes for rapid wealth.

A visitor to Richmond imagined that even the great bullfrogs in the river, "big as a man's foot," croaked "hogshead tobacco, knee deep, ancle deep, deeper and deeper."[8]

The economy of the Henrico frontier was closely related to the Atlantic economy; the rise and fall of tobacco prices on a world market caused planters to use credit extensively and to attempt to control their fixed costs. Land and labor were the keys to success and even to survival. The population remained predominantly youthful and male until the late 1600s, while opportunities for obtaining land and getting rich encouraged a driving materialism and individualism somewhat modified by the clear necessity of developing community structures. Before the eighteenth-century resurgence of tobacco prices and during the doldrums of the late 1600s, important changes took place in the population patterns and labor supply of the Chesapeake and the upper James.[9]

The number of white indentured servants in Virginia dropped as other colonies sought their labor and conditions improved in England. The short-lived attempts at English fortification of the falls in the early seventeenth century involved no women; but by the time the area began to support stores, warehouses, farms, and plantations in the 1660s, the shortage of women in the Virginia colony had begun to abate. The most profitable form of land use was a large land holding controlled and inhabited by one family unit, with as many indentured servants and slaves as possible. In this economic model, black and white women were central to the accumulation of wealth and property, but their role was essentially domestic and, high or low, they were isolated. Those women who lived in the river villages of Virginia—whether slave women or free—were at an advantage in their ability to connect with other women, with trade goods, and with the general circulation of information up and down the riverways.

Like their male counterparts, white indentured women worked very hard. Women were also vulnerable to sexual abuse by their masters; but if they survived indenture, they could make a good marriage and form part of an ambitious landowning family. Marriage after a seven-year indenture meant fewer children, and usually only half of those children survived, which again slowed down the rate of natural increase. Near the end of the seventeenth century, as the death rate declined and parents survived to raise families, planter families were able not only to secure their own position and power but to pass it on to their children.[10]

As white indenture declined in the late 1600s, many "new Africans" arrived on the James River to be sold at the dock at Bermuda Hundred, the dominant slave port, not far from the falls. Africans represented just over one person in every twenty in the colony in 1670; by 1700, more than one in four Virginians were African. By the 1730s, Virginia's slaves came directly from West Africa; almost two-fifths were from Biafra, while Angola and Senegambia also supplied significant numbers.

Virginia law moved to tighten control over Africans and white women. As early as the 1660s, neither English indenture law nor conversion to Christianity could lift the yoke of slavery from enslaved people or their children. Frontier conditions in the Chesapeake had provided weak legal protections for white women, especially indentured servants, but also provided fewer limits and restrictions on their activities. English law made women legally a part of their husbands, while Virginia statutes reduced Africans to property in order to control their labor. The systematic reduction of Africans to a labor commodity created a racial consciousness that made it less likely that white planter discontent over privilege and preferment in land acquisition would erupt in another rebellion.[11]

Although the legal fate of Africans was sealed after the slave code of 1705, many aspects of daily life and of relations between the races remained subject to local interpretation based on time and place. New Africans brought to Henrico plantations carried with them belief structures and practices that merged with English patterns. Superstitions and healing practices, food and cooking preferences, construction techniques, music styles, and the rhythms of agricultural labor were exchanged to create a "Virginian" pattern of daily life. Only slowly did these informal relations recede as the work patterns of masters, servants, slaves, and men and women diverged and they were less often employed in the same tasks. The hardest lot often fell to black women, who were sent to do field labor while some male slaves plowed and some were trained as carpenters or blacksmiths. Still, daily life meant frequent, casual, and unguarded exchanges among servants and laborers who were African, Indian, mulatto, or European.[12]

In August of 1681, on Malvern Hill, the Henrico County plantation of Thomas Cocke, a group described as "Negroes . . . , mulattoes, . . . and others in company with them" were weeding an orchard and drinking cider. They hailed passersby and asked them to stop and

Only about 20 percent of the Africans transported by the British slave trade between 1701 and 1810 went to North America. The appalling death rates in other colonies, such as the West Indies, fueled higher importation rates. The ending of the American slave trade in 1808 was largely due to the ability of the American slave population to grow through natural reproduction, not a decision by whites to turn away from slavery. Map adapted from Philip D. Curtin, The Atlantic Slave Trade: A Census (Madison: University of Wisconsin Press, 1969), by permission of the publisher

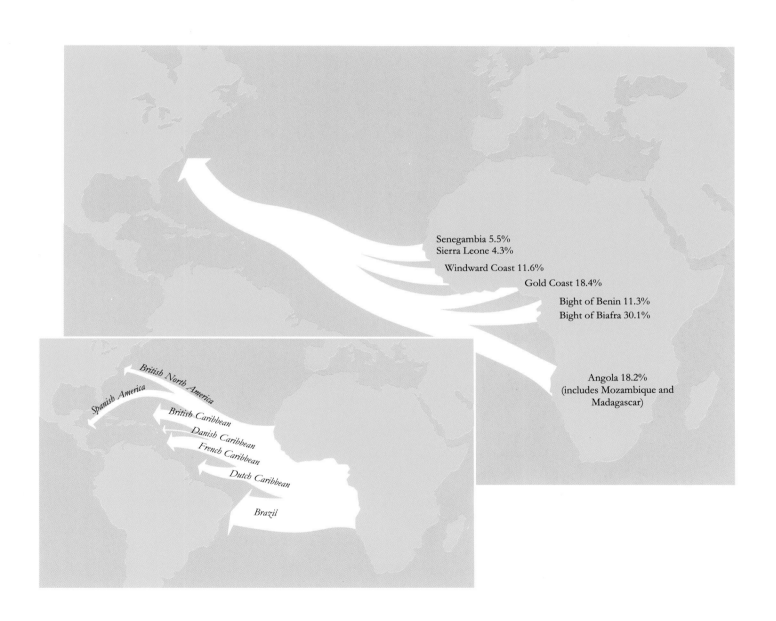

Senegambia 5.5%
Sierra Leone 4.3%

Windward Coast 11.6%

Gold Coast 18.4%

Bight of Benin 11.3%
Bight of Biafra 30.1%

Angola 18.2%
(includes Mozambique and Madagascar)

Spanish America
British North America
British Caribbean
Danish Caribbean
French Caribbean
Dutch Caribbean
Brazil

In the 1690s and after, the number of Africans on the upper James and in Virginia increased rapidly. More blacks were brought directly from Africa to the dock at Bermuda Hundred as tobacco cultivation expanded and white indenture declined. William Byrd I invested in a slave ship for this profitable trade. These new Africans had but recently experienced the fearful and often deadly passage to North America and were subjected to more legal restraints than earlier. A body of law that sanctioned slavery and codified its usages began to develop in the 1660s and was complete by 1705. **Slave Ship** (1700s), engraving by unknown artist, courtesy of Virginia Historical Society; slave leg irons from the Valentine, Richmond, Virginia

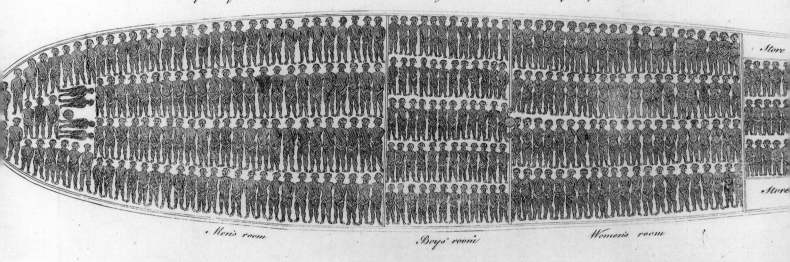

Plan of an African Ship's lower Deck, with Negroes, in the proportion of not quite one to a Ton.

Men's room   Boys' room   Women's room   Store   Store

share their refreshment. Many trips were made in the hot August sun to the outbuilding where the cider was stored. Faces grew flushed, and ribald comments were exchanged among the company, which included Katherine Watkins, wife of a nearby small landholder.[13]

There was no agreement about what happened late that afternoon, but several days later Mrs. Katherine Watkins walked the distance from her farm home to the houses of several of the county's justices of the peace to bring a complaint of rape against a young mulatto slave. Several witnesses supported her story, while others swore that she had enticed Mulatto Jack in the cider house. Although neither the wife nor the slave had any legal status and the court depositions preserve only the voices of white male witnesses, those voices place Mrs. Watkins and Jack in a scene of communal peasant labor and casual interactions at the same time that the courts began to proscribe such gatherings and to draw up special legislation for slaves who attacked white Virginians. Since no outcome is recorded for this case, it is sometimes concluded that Katherine Watkins's husband, Henry Watkins, refused to prosecute based on his Quaker beliefs, which prohibited sworn testimony.

These events took place in rural neighborhoods like Henrico and Chesterfield, which were anchored by county seats and parish churches but had no real towns or stores and few taverns. Still, people in the countryside knew which planters kept odd lots of merchandise for sale; they knew where the hard cider was stored and where men gathered to race their horses. When they were gathered together, at a militia muster or court day or outside a church, every sort of business was transacted informally, but agreements were binding. Kinship relations provided the basis for questions of guardianship and land title and created a web of meaning that obligated families across time and space.[14]

The falls settlement, in all its ramshackle sprawl, was connected with the Chesapeake, the British colonial empire, and the world. These connections can be traced on the maps of trade routes and on the designs of clay pipes found in excavations at Flowerdew Hundred on the James River below Richmond. Native Americans introduced Europeans and Africans to tobacco, and in both groups, men and women smoked with enthusiasm. Europeans developed a pipe mold, used extensively in the colonies, to make many uniform clay pipes. Careful research has determined that many of the pipes long thought to be patterned with Native

American designs were instead fashioned in European molds and decorated with West African designs by Africans living in close quarters with Europeans, before the advent of separate plantation quarters ended slaves' access to the molds. The pipes, with their origins in Native American culture, their forms fixed by European molds, and their West African designs, are eloquent testimony to the merger of three cultures on the Tidewater frontier.[15]

Few aspiring planters yet paused to note the fusion of traditions and practices that was creating a Virginia world. William Byrd I understood the single-minded attention to accumulation necessary to acquire wealth and power, but he also understood that accumulation would not be sufficient to make his family preeminent in Virginia or in England. He sent his two daughters, Ursula and Susan, and his son, William II, to England at tender ages for an education. He succeeded in raising the family from entrepreneurial wealth to intellectual eminence. William Byrd II became, as well as the founder of Richmond, the exemplar of the New World planter and the English gentleman of letters in America. Susan remained in England, while Ursula returned to marry Robert Beverly, the first historian of Virginia.[16]

William Byrd II, who returned to Virginia in 1704 upon his father's death, expanded his father's base of land and slave property using much the same techniques his father had used: steady aggrandizement of land and acquisition of state office. For forty years (1704–44), Byrd was active on both sides of the Atlantic in consolidating his colonial empire and establishing himself as a colonial gentleman. For the second twenty-year period, he worked closely with the two Mayo brothers, William and Joseph Mayo, who arrived at the falls around 1723 by way of Barbados.

Although the English government professed a commitment to establishing towns in Virginia, it suspended two acts passed by the Virginia Assembly in 1680 and 1705 to encourage town construction. The lack of towns was not disabling for either British trade or administration, and both English merchants and Virginia planter-politicians were comfortable enough with the system that emerged. When settlements began to grow, it was usually because they had a commercial function. The chief function of the little river villages of the eighteenth-century South was to store and ship local commodities and to sell a modest amount of im-

Son and heir of the ambitious William Byrd I, the second William Byrd received an English education and admission to the English Royal Society before returning to Virginia to become a member of the first real generation of Virginia colonial planter gentry. Byrd expanded his father's land and slave holdings and business enterprises, and he reluctantly agreed to give up his monopoly of trade at the falls. Pressed by the colonial assembly to set up a town at the site, Byrd may have named it Richmond to emphasize the site's similarity to the English town Richmond on the Thames and to promote the James River as another busy Thames, with its little ports as potential cities like those on the English river.

William Byrd II (c. 1704), attributed to Sir Godfrey Kneller, courtesy of the Virginia Historical Society, Richmond; **Richmond-on-Thames** (c. 1850), by J. Saddler after B. Foster, from the Valentine, Richmond, Virginia

ported goods. British ships and local crafts ascended the rivers and creeks to private plantation wharfs or public warehouses to which hogsheads of tobacco had been rolled.[17]

Scottish agents were often located near the warehouses on Virginia's rivers. After the 1707 Act of Union between Scotland and England, Glasgow merchants established stores run by their agents at most tobacco collection points on Virginia's rivers, and tobacco that was not already consigned directly to a British agent—usually that of the more middling planters— went to them. Trade and mercantile concerns acted as their own banks, accepting personal notes or money drafts for cash and extending credit for merchandise. A Scottish agent who ran a store near the falls in the early eighteenth century was advised that the mercantile reach of such a store extended approximately twelve or fourteen miles into the backcountry. The Warehouse Act of 1730, which provided for inspectors to grade tobacco at forty locations throughout the colony, made the James River falls one of those sites and pressured William Byrd II to lay out a town, disrupting his informal monopoly of tobacco warehousing.[18]

The second William Byrd, an inveterate journal keeper, recorded on 19 September 1733, his famous paragraph about the origins of Richmond: "When we got home we laid the foundations of two large Citys. One at Shacco's, to be called Richmond, and the other at the point of Appamattux River to be named Petersburgh. These Major Mayo offered to lay out into Lots without Fee or Reward. The Truth of it is, these two places being the uppermost landing of James and Appamattux Rivers, are naturally intended for Marts, where the Traffick of the Outer Inhabitants must center. Thus did we not build castles only, but also cities, in the air."[19]

There may have been as much irony as exuberance in this comment, since Byrd had been reluctant to place a town at the falls of the James. Most of the site's advantage as a fall line trade center had accrued to the Byrd family for some fifty years before the House of Burgesses pressured Byrd to lay out lots and offer them for sale. After lamenting that he would lose his monopoly on warehouses at the falls and vowing that he would not willingly sell an acre there, Byrd determined that town development was inevitable and had Mayo lay out the town, east of Shockoe Creek and north of the James River. In imposing a grid over the area's undulating ridges and valleys, Mayo used the pattern favored in colonial America but failed to incorporate either the example of nearby Williamsburg or the spectacular views offered from several heights in Richmond. The town plan was part of a commercial venture at the falls, and its authors were no less pragmatic than the practical Captain Newport of a century earlier.[20]

In April 1737 Major Mayo laid out thirty-four squares of four lots each. At the top of the grid were twelve large lots, varying in size from eight to seventeen acres, intended for suburban estates and given English names like "Hampstead." The smaller lots sold for seven pounds sterling in Virginia currency on the condition that within three years the purchaser build a house twenty-four by sixteen feet and fronting near the street.

As the settlement assumed a more regular appearance in the 1730s, the countryside was also changing. The rural setting, especially along the James River, added a dimension of grandeur to buildings that English visitors still saw as extremely modest for the homes of a rising gentry. Planters in the late 1600s had built small, constrained by high labor costs, but achieved a measure of privacy and social distance by moving servants, slaves, and much of the daily work to dependencies. Usually one or more of the outbuildings had but recently been the planter family's dwelling place and had now become a slave quarters. Storage and living functions were frequently combined. On Thomas Cocke's plantation, the outbuilding that held cider in a front room also held fish, stored in a back room that contained a bed. Inside the manor houses, the rising planters had more candles, more pewterware, more bedsteads and bed linen, more cooking equipment, and an occasional picture or looking glass; but they did not live a markedly different life from that of middling and poor classes.[21]

In the 1720s and 1730s, the Henrico County gentry began to build more imposing homes and to furnish them with goods distinctly superior to those available to lesser planters and the poor. The region began to display new Georgian manor houses of wood and brick, set back on a rise above the river. William Byrd I had moved his residence to Charles City County in 1690, and his son, William Byrd II, who had been content to live for almost a generation in a frame dwelling, put his mind and resources to building in the same county the imposing residence known as Westover. While William Mayo acquired land and seated himself in Goochland County, his younger brother, Joseph Mayo, purchased land below the falls and built Powhatan Seat, a two-story brick house, on a plateau overlooking the James River near the site of the Indian village.

At the request of William
Byrd II, Col. William Mayo
laid out the town at the
falls and measured
out thirty-two squares,
each one containing
four lots. Larger estates
surrounded this grid-
iron pattern. Richmond
received a limited town
charter in 1742, but
the town was not in-
corporated nor a town
government inaugurated
until 1782. 1737 map of
Richmond courtesy of the
Virginia State Library and
Archives, Richmond

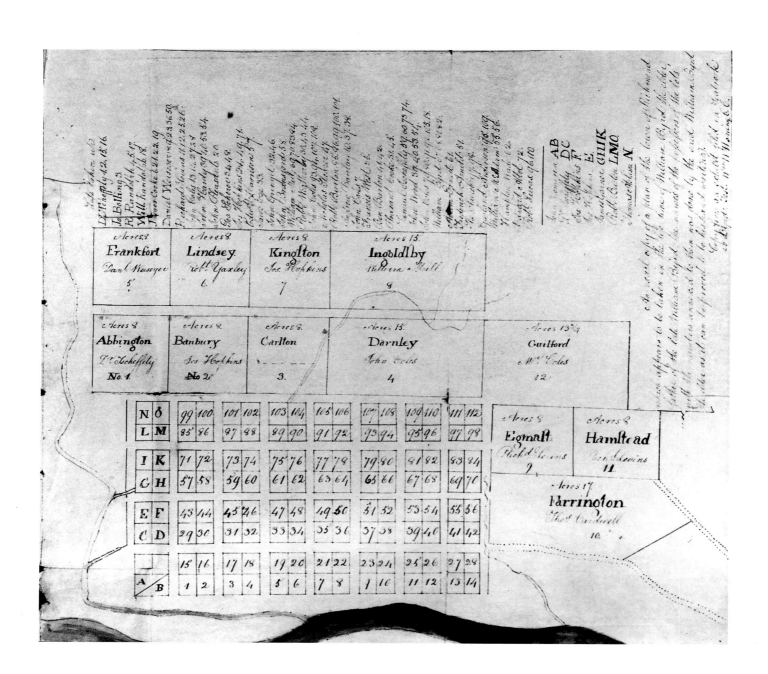

As the mid-1700s approached, prospering planters built large and imposing plantation houses such as Westover (left), the James River home of William Byrd II. These structures became the irrefutable evidence that a family was part of a recognizable colonial gentry. In the 1750s, William Byrd III built Belvidere (above), a less imposing residence but one that commanded a dramatic view of the falls of the James River. Placed on the western edge of Richmond, it seemed so rural that Byrd's first wife, Elizabeth Hill Carter Byrd, accurately feared she would "rusticate" there, far from all pleasing society. Westover photograph from the Valentine, Richmond, Virginia; **Belvidere, home of Bushrod Washington, Richmond, Virginia** (undated), watercolor by Benjamin Henry Latrobe, courtesy of the Maryland Historical Society, Baltimore

When "An Act for establishing the Town of Richmond" was passed by the General Assembly in May 1742, the village had a population of about 250, mostly settled along the river and the east side of Shockoe Creek. A stretch of open public land, required as a town common and donated by Byrd, ran along the river and the east bank of Shockoe Creek. Just west of the village grid was the "Public Warehouse at Shaccoe's," operated by Byrd under license from the General Assembly. In the same time period, licenses were granted for a ferry that crossed the James from Richmond to Rocky Ridge on the south bank and for three ordinaries to be kept in the homes of local residents who supplied simple food and drink to travelers, traders, and those waiting for the ferry. An Anglican chapel on an island in the James River was replaced in 1741 by an Anglican church placed on the hill above the village.

A road to Williamsburg followed the river east past Rocketts and the James River plantations in lower Henrico and Charles City counties. Another road climbed steeply from the tobacco warehouse at Shockoe Creek up the hill and westward irregularly to a dock at Westham, six miles upriver, where upcountry farm goods were unloaded. Once an Indian trail, then a path for fur traders, by the time of the town's incorporation this was a road along which hogsheads of tobacco bumped and rolled from Westham to Richmond.[22]

The householders who bought lots in Richmond reflected a diverse population. Like the Mayos, who came to Virginia via Barbados, and the redoubtable Captains Newport and Smith, many had experience in other parts of the British empire. Some, like the Huguenots, came to the area as refugees from European wars, and others, especially the Germans, were solicited to come. William Byrd II sent an agent and descriptive literature to Germany to encourage emigration, and the names of German families were featured prominently as early property holders. Jacob Ege, a silversmith from Württemberg, Germany, built a small one-and-a-half-story stone house, solidly constructed of river stone, with three dormer windows and chimneys at each end. Dr. Samuel Tschiffele, a German Swiss who served as the Virginia agent for the Helvetia Society, recruited German settlers in Pennsylvania and Germany for William Byrd II's land and new town. He also paid the little village the compliment of settling there himself. The doctor, a man of many hats, first advertised himself as a "Chimist and Practi-

Peter Jefferson, father of Thomas Jefferson, and Joshua Frye surveyed and mapped Virginia in the early 1750s. Their map was revised toward greater complexity several times before the American Revolution. This early version shows Richmond as a town for the first time; through the early eighteenth century Richmond was, as the map shows, a small trading center on the James River, set among well-established plantations and farms. Courtesy of Colonial Williamsburg Foundation, Williamsburg, Virginia

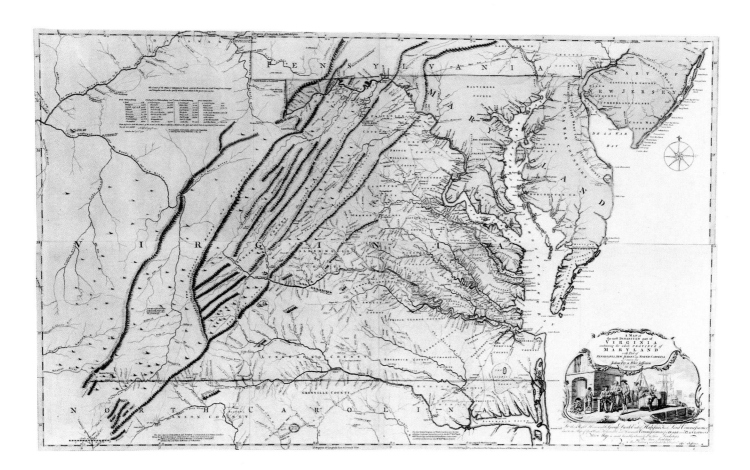

tioner of Physic" who would assay metals and ores in Richmond; a few years later he applied for a license to keep an ordinary at his home.[23]

In 1752 the General Assembly required that Richmond's streets be laid off and regularized; in the same year, the county seat was moved to Richmond, and a courthouse was constructed with a jail nearby. A decade later, the assembly mandated a pillory, stocks, and whipping post "neere the courthouse and ducking stoole" for all seventeen Virginia counties. The ducking stool, whose existence apparently preceded the other forms of public chastisement in Richmond, was the exclusive province of "brabbing women . . . [who] slander and scandalize their neighbors for which their poore husbands are often brought into chargeable and vexatious suits." Male boasting and slanderous gossip or insults often led to wrestling matches in which no holds were barred and participants might have an eye gouged out or an ear bitten off. For gentlemen, the duel emerged as a means of settling an offense against honor. The power of words to influence reputation was taken very seriously in Virginia, but women were more likely to be publicly shamed than men, who used private physical encounters to settle scores.[24]

The village of Richmond grew slowly for the rest of the colonial period, adding a few taverns (located in or next to the owner's home), warehouses, and stores. There were few overnight accommodations for women or families; they either stayed with relatives and close family friends or stayed home. The need for tobacco barrels gave work to coopers and blacksmiths, who also made cart wheels, plows, tubs, and kegs for butter and cider. Surpluses of grain, meat, butter, and cider from nearby farms were sold on market days. House lots often included gardens and outbuildings, corn cribs, pig sties, smokehouses, stables, and poultry coops. The master of a household, his wife and children, slaves, free blacks, and servants lived in close quarters in two- or three-room frame buildings.[25]

William Byrd II died in 1744, two years after Richmond was incorporated as a town. His widow continued at Westover, while his son and heir, William Byrd III, built a home called Belvidere just west of Richmond in the 1750s. A two-story frame house with a wide frontage and many windows, it drew much of its charm from its setting, which provided dramatic views of the James River and the falls. However charming, though, Belvidere was not as imposing as Westover, just as the third William Byrd was not as imposing as his grasping grandfather and many-talented father.

The first wife of William Byrd III, Elizabeth Hill Carter Byrd, complained of being left alone to rusticate in the country at Belvidere with only slaves, children, and the noise of the falls when he left, ostensibly for the French and Indian Wars and possibly for good. "I am afraid my youth and life will be buried in retirement and dissatisfaction," she wrote him in 1757. She died three years later, still alone, when she pulled a large press over upon herself. The marriage had been so publicly unhappy that there were rumours that she had committed suicide from the anxiety and distress of his desertion. Despite her own family's prominence, once she married, Elizabeth Byrd had no legal or social existence other than that given to her by her husband. Her property became his property, he had complete custody of any children, and she experienced a civil death. While the behavior of William Byrd III was an extreme example of neglect and abandonment, no married Virginia woman had the legal, financial, or social resources to defy her husband's wishes for her.[26]

When the improvident Byrd reached the end of his borrowing power, he devised a public land lottery to relieve his debt burden. In 1767, a notice appeared in the *Pennsylvania Gazette* that announced: "To be SOLD in Virginia by the subscriber . . . A valuable tract of land containing near 30,000 acres, lying upon both sides of James River, at the falls thereof, . . . including the landing at Westham, wherein warehouses are erected that receive the produce of the back country brought down the river in canoes to that place in order to be afterward shipped off from Shockoes." The lottery prizes included not just land but also the profits from tobacco inspections at Byrd's public warehouses, the ferry across the river, twenty-year leases on fisheries, a double forge, and a mill. In his advertisements Byrd evoked, for the first but far from the last time in Richmond's history, the chimera of navigation west on the James to the Blue Ridge Mountains, promising that obstructions would be cleared to within sixty or seventy miles of the Ohio River.[27]

Byrd was disappointed by the response to the lottery but held the drawing in November 1768 in Williamsburg. George Washington was among the winners of multiple parcels, having purchased, with Peyton Randolph and others, one hundred tickets for speculative purposes. Some less attentive winners failed to ever claim their prizes. In 1769, the year after the lottery, Richmond's population had increased to 574 from the 250 who lived at the falls when the area became a town in 1742. This growth prompted the first of the city's annexations, a half-mile-square section just west of the village on the land Byrd had divided for his lottery.

After the lottery, Byrd's fortunes continued to decline. He assigned his silver plate and plantation slaves to an English firm of creditors and spent his time gambling and gaming in Williamsburg. He sold Belvidere to Daniel Hylton, a Richmond merchant. He failed to join his fellow gentry in opposition to the crown, and they increasingly viewed him with distrust. Byrd committed suicide on New Year's Day in 1777.[28]

Byrd's suicide signaled the end of a century of dynastic expansion, consolidation, and power at the falls as well as the end of the colonial era. Just one hundred years before, his

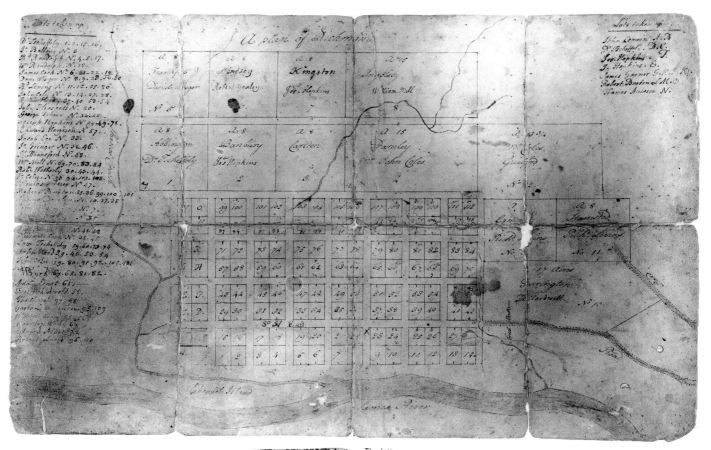

The lottery was a popular form of money-raising in Virginia when William Byrd III seized upon it as a solution to his indebtedness. The best-managed part of the entire scheme was the advertisement for the lottery, which ably described the advantages of the region at the falls of the James. The subsequent sale of lottery tickets, the hasty and premature drawing, and the number of lots that remained unclaimed all led to confusion in land titles for some decades afterward and did little to lessen Byrd's indebtedness. Map of lands claimed and lottery ticket courtesy of the Virginia State Library and Archives, Richmond

grandfather had emerged from Bacon's Rebellion rewarded for his support of the crown and colonial government against a rebellion. That same loyalty now made the financial problems of William Byrd III hopeless because only the legal preferment that the colonial gentry had created for themselves and had come to expect could save him. That system was now in shambles, as were his fortunes. It must have seemed to him that he had taken the same chances as his father had taken and his grandfather had wished to take—risked and borrowed money, traveled and played the role of Virginia gentleman. Yet it had not worked for him. Byrd could not, as most of his fellow planters did, transfer his allegiance from England to Virginia.

The once-powerful Byrd family now scattered, most of them far from the falls of the James. Richmond remained. While its wagon roads and footpaths led quickly out into the countryside, the grids imposed on each side of Shockoe Creek by the second and third William Byrds imposed an order and a sense of open access to the town. The village was still dominated by planter needs but lacked the imposing sense of private space that the plantation had. Richmond's pragmatic commercialism also lacked the elegance of Williamsburg, which had been planned as a political and cultural center, but Richmond had an energy that Williamsburg lacked.

Lying in the westward path of tobacco, slaves, and wheat, Richmond's small but diverse population claimed origins in West Africa, Northern Europe, the Caribbean, and east Virginia. As small as it was, at any one moment the village might contain great planters in town to visit their land and tobacco investments or the town's German artisans, mulatto craftsmen, English tavernkeepers, Scotch merchants, and "new Africans," all testing their ability to make their meanings known to the others. It was the anticipation of wealth from a system of trade across continents that, one way or another, brought all these people to the new town of Richmond.

CHAPTER THREE

Village, Town, and Capital

A few years before the American Revolution, an Englishman traveling in Virginia hired a boat and four black boatmen at a dollar a day to take him up the James River. After one night on board, the party landed at Shockoe and the Englishman noted in his travel diary, "There are three towns at this place. Richmond, the largest, is below the falls, and is separated only by a creek named Shokoes, from the town of Shokoes. On the south side of the river stands the town of Chesterfield, best known as Rocky Ridge." He added, "When a person arrives at Richmond his ears are continuously assailed with the prodigious noise and roaring of the falls, which almost stuns him and prevents him from sleeping at night."[1]

That roaring was greatest in the spring, when rain and melted snow at the river's source sent more water against the rocks. At the end of May 1771, when the fields and banks along the James River were already shading from the bright tones of spring into the darker greens of summer, the village of Richmond experienced a freshet, or spring flood, the likes of which had not been known in the region. Spring rains had soaked the soil, and water now ran in rivulets, streams, and creeks toward the James. Gathering quickly and moving rapidly, it roared down the river, taking the warehouses at Westham and their three hundred hogsheads of tobacco with it. Below the falls, Byrd's tobacco warehouse soon had water halfway up the lower tier of hogsheads, and the public warehouses at Shockoe were almost completely submerged. English goods unloaded at the docks were washed downstream. Hogsheads of tobacco could be seen bobbing, thirty and forty at a time, downriver from the warehouses.

After the rush of the flood, the high water remained. The crest was at least twenty feet higher than the one five years earlier. The lumber houses, where merchants stored their goods, and many dwellings were inundated. The *Virginia Gazette* quoted an "honest and well-known old negro named Joe" who declared that Indians told him their history contained no story of a more devastating flood. When the water receded, everything valuable had been swept from the low ground; even topsoil was carried away in flood-formed ravines. Carcasses of cattle were piled twelve to twenty feet high at snags in the current and were now emitting a stench that made the population fear "contagious disorder." The General Assembly met in Williamsburg in July to consider "the distressful situation of the sufferers" but provided relief only for planters who had lost tobacco in the warehouses.[2]

a

b

c

d

Tobacco from Virginia farms was transported to Richmond and then inspected and graded at a warehouse before being sold. Laws that required sorting and grading benefited the great planter, whose tobacco was likely to be of higher quality. This engraving shows tobacco being transported to market by double canoes, boat, wagon and four-horse team, and a hogshead rolled behind two horses. Courtesy of the Virginia State Library and Archives, Richmond

This natural disaster, which altered the landscape and damaged the man-made environment, was a prelude to a generation of change that swept away old forms and created new ones, nowhere more than in Richmond, which became the new capital of a new commonwealth within a new nation. Soon the town and the plantations along the James were caught up in another torrent—one of angry exchanges, retaliatory legislation, threats and counterthreats that forever altered the nature of politics and government in Virginia. The changes the American Revolution brought to Richmond and Virginia were ultimately more sweeping than any natural disaster, but they were just as difficult to predict when the colonials began to press for modification of the British mercantile system. In the last generation of the eighteenth century, the American Revolution made Richmond a city; republican and Enlightenment ideas of rationality and simplicity determined its most important architecture; evangelical Protestantism began its powerful career as the energetic engine of individual self-formation; and the town's black residents signaled that they were more than observers of these changes.

The structure of Virginia's quarrel with England was already in place when the General Assembly showed tender concern for the planter's tobacco but little interest in compensating other losses. By the time of the great freshet of 1771, most Virginia planters, especially those who dominated Virginia politics, were in debt to British firms in London, Liverpool, Glasgow, and Bristol, and to tobacco agents in trading towns like Richmond along Virginia's rivers. Richmond's prosperity was tied to the fortunes of the planters. There were good and bad years for tobacco crops, and markets varied with each shift in European political alliances. Tied to primary trade with England through the mercantile law that regulated the American colonies, planters along the James had neither the ships nor the legal authority to search out new markets. Caught without ready cash for the next crop year, planters borrowed money from each other and from the agent or firm that contracted for their tobacco.

In the mid-eighteenth century, Virginia tobacco planters incurred more debt to increase their purchases of luxury goods from England. The families of Virginia planters who subscribed to British periodicals such as *Country Magazine* began to define what were once luxuries as necessities and to emphasize their status through hospitality, consumption, and display. The large and handsome homes built during this period were furnished with silks and mahogany, porcelain and looking glasses.[3] Wealthy planters ordered expensive and specialized furniture and goods from England, while greater population density along the Chesapeake rivers meant merchants could also venture beyond essentials and stock a wider range of goods for the needs of middling planters and farmers within horseback- or cart-riding distance. The merchandise retrieved as muddy debris after the flood waters ebbed in 1771 included the fancy goods of British firms—goods intended to be bought on credit and carried from the Richmond dock to the domestic interiors of central Virginia.

Coming upriver from the Chesapeake Bay, merchant ships stopped at James River plantation docks to purchase tobacco and display their English goods to planter families. When the vessel reached the dock at Rocketts, just below the falls, the remaining merchandise was unloaded to make room for the tobacco weighed, graded, and stored in the Richmond warehouses. The merchandise stacked on the dock was piled haphazardly into storage buildings, and the merchants made little attempt to sort or display it. Nevertheless, the families of small planters and farmers, in town to sell tobacco or to grind wheat and corn, clustered about. They hefted iron skillets and fingered bits of lace and bolts of silk. Hammers and plows promised more efficient and productive farming, but bright-colored finery held the attraction of a direct link with England.

Planters, perennially short of cash, found ingenious ways to get pound notes, even though it meant they paid high rates for them. To sidestep colonial laws against high interest, planters concocted a ruse to draw bills of exchange on commercial companies in England or on individuals with whom they had no connection. Merchants in Virginia who bought these bills of exchange from planters knew they were fraudulent and knew that the planter would have to repay both the note's value and an additional 25 percent when the note was returned; but planters were willing to incur the penalty in order to have immediate use of the money. This devious method for acquiring cash provoked a grim humor from planters, who reportedly drew bills of exchange on such innocent parties as "the pump at Aldgate" and "the Bishop of London."[4]

The bonds of planter indebtedness in Virginia did not feel particularly constrictive until the tobacco market lost stability after 1750, when European wars disrupted Atlantic shipping and markets. Imperial wars between France and England interrupted Atlantic commerce, cost the British government dearly, and made British financial houses cautious in their lending policies. A depression followed the end of the Seven Years' War (known in the colonies as the French and Indian War), and not only did Virginia's planters, already deeply in debt from a series of poor crop years, find it difficult to borrow money, but their merchant creditors began dunning them for old debts. Planter debt was also based on the low prices at which they sold raw tobacco and the comparatively high prices for which they bought British goods. To expand their production, planters needed more slaves to work more tobacco acreage. In addition to luxury goods, merchants at the falls sold "new" Africans, disoriented and weakened by the long passage from West Africa. Manchester, just across the river from Richmond, was a major Virginia slave port and market through the late colonial period.[5]

In the same period, a challenge to the great planters' authority appeared in the form of middling planters in Hanover County, who defied Anglican authorities to meet in their own homes for religious worship. All tobacco was taxed to pay the Church of England ministry, but the great planters controlled the vestry and the hiring. Smaller planters were ready to listen to Baptists and New Side Presbyterians, who professed a religion in which an individual's worth was measured by his relationship with God, not with important planters.

A brief recovery in the late 1760s sent the great planters on a buying spree; when prices fell again in 1772, they were so overextended that many had to sell slaves or even their plantations to meet the demands of creditors. This crisis made some planters suspect that British merchants and the British government were out to ruin them, but even more felt that debt had compromised their independence. Planters who were called to account for debts felt that their honor had been challenged. Samuel Mordecai, chronicler of early Richmond, later echoed this assessment when he blamed the planter's plight on English and Scottish merchants; they united, he believed, to set low prices on the tobacco they purchased, because they had no social or family ties in Virginia. At the same time, Richmond's share of Virginia's export tobacco crop grew. In the years before the American Revolution, nearly one-sixth of the crop was sold in Richmond, primarily to agents for Scottish firms.[6]

The successful conclusion of the Seven Years' War saw Britain seeking new ways to raise money in order to pay for its military victory. The British understood that an overhaul of the imperial systems of taxation and administration was necessary but scarcely understood that increased efficiency in the Board of Trade or the Colonial Office would not be able to contain the colonial dynamic, which had an urgency of its own. Further, parliamentary efforts to raise revenue through new customs duties on imported goods were particularly vexing to Virginians, who imported so much. One of these duties, the Stamp Act, roused the assembly's Hanover delegate, Patrick Henry, to declare in 1765 that only a representative assembly had the right to tax colonists. Colonials increasingly viewed these imperial measures as unjustly burdensome, although ties to England, commercial and patriotic, remained strong. For more than a decade, England imposed, rescinded, and reimposed taxes. In response, Virginians considered closely where their interests lay.

Parliament's passage of the Coercive Acts of 1774 brought open colonial resistance, and planters in Virginia's counties organized Committees of Correspondence to connect themselves with emerging leaders in other colonies and to take charge of administrative duties and functions within Virginia as British officials departed. Merchants in Richmond and planters in the country around the village had already developed a network to petition the House of Burgesses or to monitor compliance with boycotts of British goods. While many town-dwelling American merchants and craftsmen remained loyal to England during these years, few Richmond citizens appeared unwilling to follow the county leadership into the rebellion.

"Loyal and Patriotick People" from Henrico County met at the courthouse in Richmond, soon after the Coercive Acts took effect, to affirm their resistance. A Virginia Convention met in Williamsburg in August 1774 and chose delegates to the First Continental Congress, which met in Philadelphia in September. That first extralegal meeting considered forms of resistance to British authority and resolved to meet again. The second Virginia Convention gathered in Richmond at the Henrico Parish Church, later St. John's Church, on 20 March 1775. The Anglican meetinghouse was the largest building in Richmond, but the press of 120 delegates so filled the pews and aisles that local spectators stood outside, listening through opened windows. This second meeting moved revolution out of the realm of abstract debate, as Patrick Henry's speech in favor of authorizing a Virginia militia reportedly ended with the fiery flourish, "I know not what course others may take, but as for me, give me liberty or give me death."[7]

Patrick Henry was a delegate to the second Virginia Convention meeting, held at St. John's Church in March 1775. Henry called for Virginia to strengthen its defenses and departed from conventional rhetoric to make a powerful and emotional speech in the manner of the evangelical Presbyterians near his home in Hanover, Virginia. **Patrick Henry** (1815), by Thomas Sully, courtesy of Colonial Williamsburg Foundation, Williamsburg, Virginia

A small parish church called St. John's Church, part of the colonial Anglican system, was built in Richmond in 1741. Such churches served as meetingplaces, although they were often without the services of an ordained Anglican priest. Many church functions were left to the vestry, who were members of local importance. **St. John's Church** (c. 1835), by John C. Bridgwood, from the Valentine, Richmond, Virginia

On the eve of the American Revolution there were some six hundred souls in Richmond. It was a youthful population and equally divided between white and black. The town itself had doubled in size in 1769 by moving west to absorb Shockoe Hill, which had been laid out as a part of William Byrd III's lottery. The General Assembly appointed trustees to handle town planning issues such as the location of wharves and the repair of streets. Town activity still centered in its older section—near the river along Main Street, where the Henrico courthouse and jail, the monthly market, and Bowler's and Cowley's taverns were located.

Richmond's oldest market area, at Seventeenth and Main streets, began as a motley collection of outdoor stalls and wagons near the town common. Late in the 1700s, the market was enclosed in a building, and a holding pen was constructed to display minor lawbreakers. This cage served a cautionary function for the public until it was demolished in 1827. Mutual Assurance Society policy, 1814, courtesy of the Virginia State Library and Archives, Richmond

Richmond suffered several British raids in the seven-year course of the American Revolution but was never the scene of protracted fighting or heavy engagements. The town's apparently secure position led the Williamsburg government to store documents there in 1777, and the war accelerated the development of coal and iron industries near Richmond. The state commissioned the building of a foundry, boring mill, and magazine known as the Westham Foundry, where coal from Chesterfield's Deep Run pits and iron ore carried downriver from the backcountry were converted to iron and cast into cannons.[8]

The usual military experience in Richmond was that of colonial armies passing through on their way to an engagement, but on 4 January 1781, General Benedict Arnold's flotilla of His Majesty's Ships left the lower James and turned toward Richmond. As Arnold's forces landed at Westover and advanced toward Richmond, Gov. Thomas Jefferson sent arms, military supplies, and public records to be stored at the Westham Foundry. Then Jefferson, his entourage, and many other citizens left the city. The British, unopposed, marched into Richmond, where Lt. Col. John Graves Simcoe of the Queen's Rangers continued up the Westham Road to the foundry and destroyed much of the plant's industrial capacity and some of the public records.

Simcoe's Rangers then marched back to Richmond, where they found the town almost deserted by the white population. They set fire to public buildings, the ropewalk along the river, warehouses, and workshops. When the British forces withdrew—a mere twenty-four hours after they arrived—looters scattered both county and state records. Although some shots may have been exchanged between local militiamen and the fringes of Arnold's army, the British army met no serious resistance in its brief campaign to Westham. Many slaves departed with the British. British General Clinton had promised freedom to slaves who would desert the American rebels, but there is evidence that Benedict Arnold and other British commanders considered slaves booty of war and sold many of those who believed that the British flag meant freedom.

This raid was a signal to Richmond that, after five years, the war had finally moved into Virginia. Gen. George Washington ordered a Continental Army detachment under the young Marquis de Lafayette to move against Arnold, who was now well settled in Portsmouth. After the necessary scrambling for supplies and money that accompanied all major expeditions in

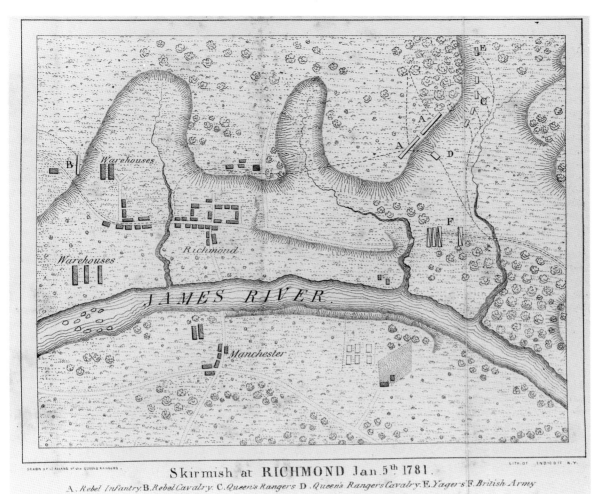

Skirmish at RICHMOND Jan 5th 1781.

A. *Rebel Infantry* B. *Rebel Cavalry* C. *Queen's Rangers* D. *Queen's Rangers Cavalry* E. *Yagers* F. *British Army*

Late in the Revolutionary War, British military forces turned their attention to Richmond in order to raid the town, disrupt its river commerce, and burn tobacco warehouses. This tactic was relatively successful for them on several occasions when they met little resistance from residents of the new state capital. **Skirmish at Richmond, Jan. 5th, 1781,** *published in* Simcoe's Military Journal *(New York: Bartlett and Welford, 1844), from the Valentine, Richmond, Virginia*

the American army, Lafayette marched his men to Richmond, arriving on 29 April. Governor Jefferson had ordered up the militias from surrounding counties, but they were extremely slow to muster, and Jefferson gloomily speculated on the effects of "this fatal tardiness."[9]

At first the British did exceedingly well in their late April campaign. They captured or disabled most of the ships in the James, plundered Manchester, and burned tobacco stored there. At the last minute, a show of strength by Lafayette's combined forces on the heights above Richmond forced the British commander to abandon his plan for a direct assault on the town.

A few weeks later, General Cornwallis arrived in Virginia from the south and united his army with the British forces already present. Again the British approached Richmond and its citizens fled. Cornwallis entered Richmond in mid-June, and his army systematically destroyed any items that might aid the war effort, especially tobacco. Then he marched off toward Yorktown.

While many slaves in Henrico and Chesterfield counties saw the arrival of the British as an opportunity to leave the region, some slaves and free blacks enlisted in the American cause.

James, a slave owned by William Armistead, was hired out in Richmond as a carpenter in the 1780s and lived apart from his master, sharing lodgings with another slave carpenter. During the Revolution he was recruited by General Lafayette to spy on the British troops and convey information to the American army. On the basis of his military work, he successfully petitioned for his freedom. **James Armistead Lafayette** *(1824), by John B. Martin, from the Valentine, Richmond, Virginia*

They reasoned that military service might provide an opening toward freedom and even citizenship, as it did in many societies. James Armistead, a slave carpenter hired out in Richmond and free from direct supervision, acted as a spy and courier for Lafayette; soldiers in Cornwallis's camp trusted him because he seemed to be simply a slave.[10]

Richmond's political experience during the Revolution was more important than its military experience because Virginia's capital moved there midway through the war. The move was only partly for reasons of wartime necessity. Piedmont planters, such as Thomas Jefferson, had long advocated moving the capital to a more central place in the state, more convenient for Piedmont and western planters as delegates or crop sellers. Williamsburg, a well-laid-out town of wide avenues, public squares, and imposing buildings, had remained a seasonal town, active only when the General Assembly met. Richmond's commercial life made it possible to keep taverns and printers and builders year-round.

In 1779 the General Assembly voted to move the capital of the new state from Williamsburg to Richmond, and in May 1780 the assembly met in Richmond for the first time, in a rented frame building. In June the assembly annexed land on which a new capitol would be built. The act that made Richmond the capital provided that six squares be set aside for public buildings. Thomas Jefferson, governor of Virginia in 1780 and deeply involved in the design for the new buildings in the new capital, at first anticipated a major building for each of the three branches of government.[11]

The movement of the capital west to Richmond from Williamsburg brought the apparatus of government upriver and gave the town at the falls not only a rapid infusion of new citizens but a new sense of solidity and permanence as well. No longer simply a site devised by nature and tobacco warehouses as a trade center, Richmond attracted a varied population of lawyers, clerks, printers, shoemakers, tailors, and artisans, who expanded commerce in the town while many drew their chief living from the state's government. These migrants up the

James were townspeople, accustomed to the amenities of Williamsburg, and they did not relish Richmond's raw and unbuilt appearance.

Among those moving to Richmond was the household of State Treasurer Jacquelin Ambler, including his wife, Rebecca; four young daughters; and Mary Lucas, a free mulatto hired by the Amblers, and her six-year-old son and infant daughter. The eldest daughter, Eliza Ambler, felt herself cut off from the society and ideas of Williamsburg, a condition as awful to contemplate as the appearance of British troops. Ambler's father had undertaken her education himself, not trusting the itinerant tutors of the day, who promised female education for "twenty-five pounds and a load of wood per year." She complained to a friend that "this famous Metropolis . . . will scarcely afford one comfort in life. With the exception of two or three families this little town is made up of Scotch factors, who inhabit small tenements scattered here and there from the river to the hill." [12]

Despite the uncertainties of war, land speculators and artisans in the building trades felt confident enough about the permanence of both the Revolutionary government and its legislative acts to turn their attention to Richmond. The town began a period of rapid growth, based primarily on its new governmental role but also on a steady expansion in regional trade in tobacco and wheat. The land and personal property tax lists in the 1780s showed a town of artisans and their apprentices, many of whom had only recently arrived in Richmond. Among them were free black and slave artisans. Richmond was notable for the number of skilled black workers clustered there; this number increased with the emancipations that followed the passage of a liberal Manumission Act in 1782. [13]

The invasion of the speculators seemed to have no limits, and in 1789 a group of outraged Richmond citizens addressed a complaint to the General Assembly, declaring that their "natural rights and privileges" had been invaded. The petitioners, they noted, had "been accustomed to uninterruptedly enjoy the advantages which nature liberally holds out to them in the large quantities of fish which she has bountifully stored our rivers. . . . [We] are likely to be disappointed of these advantages by reason of men called Speculators, who ransack earth, air, and water, for their private emolument, and under pretense of law divert a large part of the community of their natural rights and privileges. They have entered and actually surveyed the

Houses such as the Harvie-Wickham house were built after the Revolution by Richmond's new urban gentry of lawyers and government officials. With their outbuildings and gardens, they often recreated a plantation in town. Mutual Assurance Society policy, 1803, courtesy of the Virginia State Library and Archives, Richmond

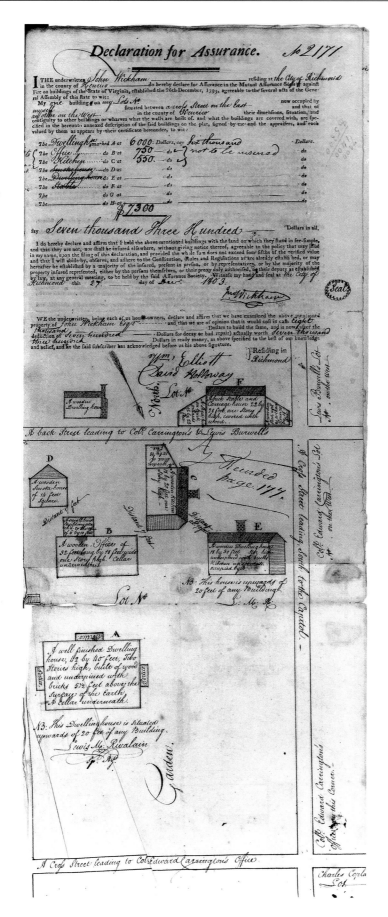

stream, the rocks, and the fishing stands in the falls of the James River, which always has been and ought to be considered as a Common for the good citizens at large."[14]

The fishermen's complaint showed that they could adapt the doctrine of natural rights to a call for protection of their customary rights. From the first resistance to British tax policy to the end of the eighteenth century, political ideas permeated the city and, combined with rapid growth, caused its society to be extremely fluid and almost volatile. Status was far from fixed. John Beckley, one of the town's first lawyers, had come to Virginia as an indentured servant. Dr. William Foushee, the first mayor, had studied medicine in Edinburgh and had an eye gouged in a Richmond tavern quarrel. James Armistead petitioned the legislature for his freedom on the basis of his information-gathering for General Lafayette during the Revolution. The free black population more than doubled in a decade.

The Manumission Act, which for the first time since 1711 permitted slaveholders to emancipate their slaves, was one manifestation of the brief congruence of evangelical religious principles and Enlightenment-based political principles in Revolutionary Virginia. In the wake of political upheaval, other changes arrived on the landscape and in the lives of residents. Richmond's transition from rural riverside trade town to political center created an expansive commercial and intellectual dynamic in which, for a few decades, almost anything seemed possible—even women preachers and an end to slavery.

Most Virginia slaveholders failed to note any contradiction between the Revolutionary rhetoric of liberty that they had freely employed and the state of permanent bondage in which the African American labor force found itself. Some planters and farmers who had felt discomfort with slavery joined with the Virginia Society of Friends, or Quakers, to pass the Manumission Act and then celebrated the passage of the act by freeing their slaves. Two of the most significant emancipations were those by Robert Carter and Robert Pleasants. Carter, who owned sixteen plantations in Virginia, freed five hundred slaves. Pleasants, a Henrico County planter and Quaker, freed seventy-eight slaves and deeded them land at Varina and Gravel Hill near Richmond; in 1784 the Quakers of Curles Neck Meeting began a school for the free blacks at Gravel Hill. These emancipations may have contributed directly to the growing number of free blacks in Richmond.[15]

Four generations of the Ege-Galt family, craftsmen and tavern-keepers, are represented here. German silversmith Jacob Ege's wife and their daughter Elizabeth stand on each side of Elizabeth Galt Williamson and her son Thomas. Such families were the town-dwelling providers of goods and services that made Richmond a trade center. **Portrait of Ege-Galt Family** *(date and artist unknown) courtesy of the Abby Aldrich Rockefeller Folk Art Center, Williamsburg, Virginia*

Among the Enlightenment ideas enacted into law was the Thomas Jefferson–sponsored Statute for Religious Freedom, proposed in 1779 and finally adopted in 1786. Its passage was preceded, in 1785, by the formation of the Protestant Episcopal Church in the old capitol building. This group acquired the Anglican St. John's Church but for many years met just as often in the new capitol, sharing the premises with Presbyterians. The personal and emotional religion of evangelical Protestantism was extremely attractive to many Virginians, both as an alternative to a gentry-defined sense of self-worth and for the sense of cohesiveness among its members. A great many conversions took place at the end of the American Revolution and for a dozen years afterward. Baptist evangelicalism attracted many black members to that church, and in Richmond, the Baptist Church organized in 1780 was almost equally divided between black and white.[16]

Baptists and Methodists far outnumbered other denominations in Richmond by the 1790s. Their faith in the teaching of the spirit gave women and slaves a voice in meetings and a place, for some decades, at the spiritual center of those churches. In the 1790s, the Baptist and Methodist general conferences attempted to end slavery among their members. This enterprise ran counter to the economic interests of the members and therefore failed, but the conversion of the slaves to evangelical Christianity made a powerful argument for their spiritual equality as "brothers" and "sisters." Among the Quakers, women were considered the spiritual equals of men. Those men and women with special gifts for speaking often traveled to bring religious messages to public meetings, and Richmond was visited by as many Quaker women as men.[17]

In 1790 Quakers organized the Virginia Abolition Society, which was centered in Richmond. Robert Pleasants was the society's president, and the officers were local Quakers and Methodists. Although the Abolition Society never acquired a large membership, it was, like the Statute for Religious Freedom, a sign of the times in Richmond. It marked an era of openness in thought, an era in which both religious and political ideals tended toward greater freedom.

Beth Shalome Hebrew Congregation was organized in 1789 by twenty-six heads of families. The Quakers established their first meeting inside the city in 1795 and constructed a brick meetinghouse in 1797. Roman Catholics established a mission in 1796, and the Methodists made Richmond a "station" in 1798. So much religious activity might seem to bespeak a pious city of dedicated religiosity, but most of the new congregations were composed of merchants, real estate speculators, and builders who were as vigorously in pursuit of business as they were of salvation. Thomas Scattergood, a Philadelphia Quaker who visited Richmond in 1793 to speak to a gathering of black residents, was aghast at the eager opportunism of Richmond and wrote, "O! The wickedness and abominations of this little city!"[18]

The judgments of visiting Jeremiahs did little to stem the speculative trade in land and the rapid construction of new homes, public buildings, and even new neighborhoods. The latter reflected a general desire by the wealthy to rise above the river and set themselves apart from commerce. Richmond's Common Hall, the government organized when the city was incorporated in 1782, met in the Henrico County Courthouse; this courthouse and the adjacent Henrico County Jail were the city's first public buildings. The men elected to Richmond's first Common Hall were local merchants, several of whom served for long periods.[19]

Especially prominent were Richard Adams, his sons, and his son-in-law, William Marshall, who served from the early 1780s until 1819. Adams, who built his home above the town on Richmond Hill, at the northeast edges of Major Mayo's grid, owned much of the land in that high section that came to be called Church Hill after St. John's Church, which was located there. The speculative hopes of Richard Adams were raised by his expectation that the new state capitol would be placed on these heights. He offered to donate land to that purpose, but the General Assembly chose an alternate site on Shockoe Hill. Two other long-term members of the Common Hall were merchants of more modest means. David Lambert, elected in 1785, served for twenty years, and Robert Mitchell sat on council from the 1780s until he retired in 1806. Not all of the members of the Common Hall were merchants. Dr. William Foushee, an Edinburgh-educated practitioner from the state's Northern Neck, was mayor in the 1780s and sat on the Common Council for almost twelve years.[20]

In 1783, John Marshall—a young Fauquier County lawyer, delegate to the legislature, and

Revolutionary veteran—married Mary Willis Ambler and moved to Richmond. Elected to the House of Delegates from Richmond in 1787, Marshall was among the first to build a substantial house with outbuildings on Shockoe Hill. While the house was under construction, from 1788 to 1790, Marshall served as a Henrico County delegate to the June 1788 Virginia Convention and as a Richmond city delegate to the General Assembly. Richmond was one of the few places in the state where his Federalist politics would not bar him from election.[21]

From 2 to 27 June 1788, the Virginia Convention met in Richmond to consider the adoption of the federal constitution constructed in Philadelphia the previous summer, and the group ratified that document on 27 June. While delegates from nearby counties in the Piedmont and Southside Virginia voted against the Constitution, Richmond and Henrico delegates aligned themselves with the Tidewater in voting for it.

Political debate was lively and frequent throughout the consideration of the Constitution and the development, in the 1790s, of the two political factions known as Federalists and Democratic-Republicans. Most Virginians supported the policies of Thomas Jefferson, who advocated an agricultural republic and, before his presidency, looked with skepticism on commerce, industry, and cities. But Richmond aligned with the policies of the Federalists, who appeared to them to represent continuity and commerce. Tavern fights with serious gouging and maiming resulted from political arguments. Schoolboys disrupted classrooms to cheer, jeer, or throw their hats up for favorite candidates. Neither the young city nor the young republic had yet established that factions might share political power peacefully.

If political stability was not yet assured, Richmond was still connected to a larger world of products and philosophies. Public buildings reflected the rationality and balance of the European Enlightenment, while a new concern for organized benevolence and sociability could be seen in the creation of the Amicable Club, formed by prosperous city men; a Masonic Order, formed by men of many classes; Ezrat Orchim, or "Help for Visitors," established by Temple Beth Shalome; and the Female Humane Society, founded by women from prominent families. Particularly, the Female Humane Society gave Eliza Ambler Carrington, who had earlier complained of the dearth of stimulation in Richmond, an opportunity to use her excellent mind and education in pursuit of civic improvement. Just as evangelical religion

The newly built state capitol rises above both nature and the cluster of modest habitations to its east in this watercolor by Benjamin Henry Latrobe. The long dirt road in the foreground suggests the distance from the real to the ideal in the republican capital. **View of Richmond from the Banks of the James River** *(1798), watercolor, courtesy of the Maryland Historical Society, Baltimore*

offered women of middling circumstances a voice at the center of that social world, enlightened benevolence encouraged Richmond women of high status and education to become purposeful and active through the provision of organized aid and protection to other white females.[22]

While post-Revolutionary forces encouraged private charity, a new abundance of products offered buyers greater quantities and more fashionable choices than ever before, emphasizing display as a measure of status. William Waddell's store "at the sign of the Thirteen Stars" offered paste shoe buckles and knee buckles for gentlemen and ladies. Other stores sold imported hoops and stays from France, as well as muslins, drab silk for men's summer coats, lute strings, artificial flowers, kid gloves, hair powder, and ladies' riding hats trimmed with feathers.[23]

Also visible as a sign of confidence in the city's future were the public buildings constructed or planned in the 1780s and 1790s. In 1785, Thomas Jefferson wrote to Madison that in the "Maisonquaree of Nimes" he had found the Roman model that he had long been seeking for the Virginia state capitol. He linked this architectural style with his aspirations for the nation: he described it as "very simple" but added that "it is noble beyond expression and would have done honor to our country as presenting to travelers a morsel of taste in our infancy, promising much for our maturer age." Work actually started on the capitol before Jefferson returned to Richmond with his plans, but he prevailed. The capitol, finished in brick in 1792 and stuccoed in 1798, stood alone on Shockoe Hill above the town and did raise the city's sights and its image. In 1787, a Masonic Hall was built, sponsored by an assortment of citizens ranging from Attorney General Edmund Randolph, the first Grand Master, to Gabriel Galt, the keeper of City Tavern, who donated land acquired through his marriage to Elizabeth Ege. The following year, driven by a vision of a New World intellectual utopia, French immigrant Quesnay de Beaurepaire laid the cornerstone for his Academy of Arts and Sciences. The new state penitentiary, designed by Benjamin Henry Latrobe, reflected Enlightenment ideas of character reformation through solitary confinement followed by group labor.[24]

In this age of revolution, it was scarcely surprising that every group desired to extend the benefits of liberty and equality to themselves. Those Richmond women who had the opportunity promoted female education as well as the protection of widows and orphans. They argued that their roles as the mothers of republican citizens demanded that they acquire an education, and in the 1780s the gap between male and female literacy began to close.[25] Census evidence shows that women without husbands slipped into poverty rapidly, and aid to widows and orphans was a well-placed concern, not a sentimental gesture. Jane Allegre, a typical widow, put herself and her daughters to work as mantua makers, one of the few occupations open to women. Children without families were frequently taken into the large households of prosperous merchants or artisans, where their status may have been ambiguous. Boys were often

Richmond's new public buildings and statuary reflected the simplicity and dignity in the new nation's republican principles. The penitentiary (top left), begun by Benjamin Henry Latrobe, was designed to encourage reformation rather than exact vengeance. Jean-Antoine Houdon's statue of Washington displays a leader of natural dignity and power—the republican model of a virtuous citizen, but spared the Roman garb. The capitol (bottom left), designed by Thomas Jefferson, was intended as a model for the balanced and rational proceedings of government. **George Washington** (1788), statue by Jean-Antoine Houdon, and **Virginia State Penitentiary** (c. 1810), hand-tinted aquatint by J. Wood, from the Valentine, Richmond, Virginia; **Capitol of Virginia** (c. 1840), watercolor by unknown artist, courtesy of estate of Joseph Stewart Bryan

apprenticed to a craft, but girls without property or family often became domestic workers, with all their hopes fastened on a respectable marriage. Young women such as Martha Hutchings, who lived with the family of flour inspector Samuel Ege, Jr., were kept busy with daily tasks and the care of young children.[26]

The Age of Revolution ended in Richmond in 1800, late on a hot August Saturday, with one more reach for liberty and freedom. There had been no hint of a thunderstorm earlier in the day, and people tried to complete their business before the heat of late afternoon made all exertion an effort. In late afternoon, clouds gathered, and in the early evening a torrential thunderstorm broke over Richmond and the surrounding countryside, swelling the creeks and small rivers. When the sun returned the next day to a brighter and cooler landscape, a curious and alarming story had reached the genial governor, James Monroe, in Richmond. From farms and plantations on the outskirts of the city came an account of a planned slave revolt aimed at Richmond and deterred only at the last minute by the storm, which made it impossible for the conspirators to ford the creeks. As details of the scope and intentions of the conspiracy trickled into the city, Monroe, not a man to become unduly alarmed, called out the militia and sent them to arrest and interrogate all those whose names were mentioned as part of the conspiracy.

In the following days, the entire town learned that Gabriel, the slave of Thomas Prosser, Jr., had organized a wide-ranging and complex conspiracy to invade Richmond, take guns from the state armory, seize the state capitol with the assistance of its free black night watchman, hold the governor captive, and negotiate for the release of all slaves. In addition to his plantation, Brookfield, Thomas Prosser owned a dwelling in Richmond at Fourth and Clay. Gabriel was often in the city, and many citizens remembered him as the powerfully built young black man who had bitten off part of a white man's ear in a fight the year before. As testimony was collected, it emerged that Gabriel had spent months gathering recruits for his army.[27]

At their trials, conspirators outlined their plans and their goals. They had intended to set fire to Rocketts, "that part of town being of little value," and draw out the whites to fight the fire so that blacks might enter the capitol and armory to capture guns and ammunition. Slave Ben Woolfolk testified that he and fellow slave Gilbert intended to purchase a piece of silk for a flag, on which they would inscribe "death or Liberty," and they further intended to kill

DOCUMENTS

RESPECTING THE

INSURRECTION OF THE SLAVES.

(CONTINUED.)

Trial of Martin, property of Thomas H. Proffer. Witness John and Ben.

BEN. Martin enlisted under Gabriel, but Gabriel said he was too old. Then Martin said he would run bullets, and keep them in bullets: *Guilty.* Executed on Monday: Valued at 300. dollars.

Trial of Charles, on the testimony of Patrick and Ben.

Patrick. Charles asked him at Gregory's tavern if he was a man. He said he wanted to meet him Saturday or Sunday. He wanted to talk with a man. He would pay him well.

Ben. Charles wanted to be a captain, Gabriel said he might be a serjeant, he was too trifling a fellow. Charles cursed mightily about it. Charles was to meet Gabriel on a certain day at Mr. Gregory's tavern, where there were 29 arms, where he was to be furnished with arms. He told Gabriel after he agreed to make him a captain, that he would raise him 30 or 40 arms. *Guilty.* To be executed on Monday. Valued at £. 100.

The slave Gabriel's conspiracy, which aimed to take control of Richmond and bring about a slave insurrection based on the principles of the American and French revolutions, was electrifying news in the city. The conspirators were first betrayed by other slaves, then arrested, hanged, or deported. The air crackled with rumors of more slave revolts, and fear of black conspiracy became part of the city's heritage. Excerpt from article published in the Richmond Recorder, 1803, from the Valentine, Richmond, Virginia

Advertisements for runaway slaves appeared regularly in newspapers. The runaway pattern that eventually emerged in Richmond was apparent in these earlier advertisements, which were published in the Williamsburg Gazette on the eve of the American Revolution. The majority of runaways were young men, and few of them attempted to reach the northern states, especially before the 1830s. From the Valentine, Richmond, Virginia

RUN away from *Hampton*, on *Sunday* last, a lusty Mulatto Fellow named ARGYLE, well known about the Country, has a Scar on one of his Wrists, and has lost one or more of his fore Teeth; he is a very handy Fellow by Water, or about the House, &c. loves Drink, and is very bold in his Cups, but dastardly when sober. Whether he will go for a Man of War's Man, or not, I cannot say; but I will give 40 s. to have him brought to me. He can read and write.

NOVEMBER 2, 1775. JACOB WRAY.

all whites except "Quakers, Methodists, and French people" unless "they agreed to the freedom of the blacks." According to another witness, Gabriel asserted "[t]hat if the white people agreed to their freedom, they would then hoist a white flag, and he would dine and drink with the merchants of the city on the day when it should be agreed to."[28]

Many hours of testimony were taken from arrested free blacks and slaves, but Gabriel, who hid aboard a commercial vessel in the James for ten days, gave no statement between his arrest and his hanging. His plans are known only by the testimony of others involved in the plot, and their statements reveal the web of communication and movement between blacks in Richmond and the surrounding countryside. Conspirators told of meeting under bridges, after church, and at fish barbecues held by slaves on Sundays. Gabriel and his lieutenants, who included his brother, made exaggerated claims about the number of weapons they had fashioned and perhaps about other aspects of the conspiracy in order to recruit members. They framed their conspiracy in the language of republican liberty familiar from the American Revolution and from the daily discourse in Virginia's legislature. In an age of revolution, they saw their bid for liberty as an extension of the American Revolution. White Richmond was quick to see it as a parallel to the recent slave revolt in Haiti, a briefly successful effort led by Toussaint L'Ouverture.[29]

The impact of this conspiracy on white Richmond can scarcely be overestimated. It sent the Virginia legislature into secret session, intently searching the globe for a site to which to send black Virginians. The echoes of "Give me liberty or give me death" had been in the air in Richmond ever since Patrick Henry's speech at St. John's Church. The meanings of virtue and liberty had been debated in the Virginia statehouse, in the newspapers, in taverns and dining rooms. Any illusion that blacks had paid no attention or had heard the debate as an abstraction could no longer be maintained. Gabriel's Conspiracy was liberty's shadow, and it darkened all the republican architecture and aspirations in the little capital city.

CHAPTER FOUR

Rocky Road to Richmond

Each spring, when shad ran upriver to spawn, those fishermen who vied successfully for the best spots on the rocks and islands in the James River were rewarded with a panoramic view of the city from the river as well as the largest catch of fish. From their vantage points, they could see to the east a cluster of weathered frame buildings, occasionally relieved by brick or stone, and beyond, sloping to the river, the dock called Rocketts Landing. An open area contained the town market, where well-dressed gentlemen with straw baskets inspected the produce. Nearby, washerwomen and housewives knelt to wash clothes in the river and spread trousers, petticoats, and bits of linen to dry on the grass of the town common. This was the site of the old colonial village, still a busy, crowded, and cluttered area of shops, taverns, piled merchandise, dockworkers, and tobacco hogsheads. It housed a newer population of dancing masters, seamstresses, and free black artisans, all hoping to improve their fortunes by selling their services in the growing city.[1]

Just to the left was Shockoe Creek, dividing the old mercantile village from the ambitious heights of Shockoe Hill. The new capitol, which crowned the hill, surveyed with republican equanimity the tangled underbrush and steep ravines dropping south toward the river. On these heights, the homes of state officers, city magistrates, wealthy merchants, and lawyers were rapidly arising, imparting a new appearance of solidity to a roughly graded area still crisscrossed with gullies. Flat boats and barges poled along the James River canal past the Virginia Manufactory of Arms, the Haxall and Chevallié flour mills, and David Ross's iron foundry. Barges carried coal downriver from the Chesterfield pits, while flour mills on both sides of the James shunted water through mill races. A turning basin for ship traffic, dug in a wooded area south of the capitol, drew a cluster of businesses to its rim.

Part of the city's rugged terrain was utilized in pleasure gardens like the Haymarket Gardens and Jackson's Gardens, which offered landscaped walks as well as refreshments and, at Falling Gardens, public baths. A wagon-rutted road that brought country produce into the city ran between the governor's house and the capitol down to Main Street; legislators crossed that road daily to reach the five-gallon bowl of toddy at the governor's house. A mile to the

Rocketts Landing, just below the town, was a busy port that drew ships up the James to deliver merchandise and collect tobacco, wheat, and varied produce stored and milled nearby. "Rolling roads" for tobacco made irregular patterns through the town, coming from all directions toward their common destination at Rocketts. **View down James River from Mr. Nicholson's House above Rocketts** (1796), watercolor by Benjamin Henry Latrobe, courtesy of the Maryland Historical Society, Baltimore

west, at Buchanan's Spring, Richmond's foremost lawyers competed at the Quoits Club, or Barbecue Club, and relieved their thirst with a claret punch.[2]

The 1800 federal census confirmed that the city had more than doubled its population—from 2,000 to 5,700—during the previous decade, and only a small part of that increase was due to the 1793 annexation of one and a half square miles northwest of the capitol. Many of the new residents were free blacks from Virginia's countryside or artisans from northern cities. Carpenters, plasterers, and bricklayers worked to meet the demand for new buildings. Slave craftsmen were often more valuable hired out in town than utilized on rural farms, and free

When David Ross purchased this gristmill from Samuel Overton in 1789, he installed a millrace that made an island of the eastern portion of this tip of land. Later known as Brown's Island, the site was central to Richmond's industry for two centuries. **Sketch of the Lower End of the Falls of James River, Richmond, Virginia** *(1796), by Benjamin Henry Latrobe, courtesy of the Maryland Historical Society, Baltimore*

blacks were apprenticed to trades during this period of rapid building. The structures built ranged from wooden frame buildings sixteen feet square to the imposing buildings of brick and stone, organized as small in-town plantations.

Beyond the city's western boundary, not far from Buchanan's Spring, John Mayo built a grand house he called the Hermitage. There he entertained members of an elite militia company, the Richmond Light Infantry Blues, and guests such as Mr. and Mrs. John Wickham, to whom he served tea and ice cream. The city's foremost black musicians, fiddler Sy Gilliat and flutist London Briggs, dressed in the knee britches and vests of their youth in colonial

Williamsburg, were hired to play at Mayo's parties and at various dances and fancy balls in the town.[3]

The shadow of Gabriel's Conspiracy was apparent in the organization in 1800 of a Public Guard, a paid state force that would guard the new armory, capitol, and penitentiary against slave insurrection. Rumors of black conspiracy continued to alarm the city periodically. The city and state moved to limit the increase in the population of free blacks and to restrict black freedom of movement. In 1806 Richmond's city council passed the first of many ordinances designed to control the movements of hired-out slaves, and in the same year the Virginia legislature revoked the liberal emancipation law adopted in 1782 and required newly emancipated slaves to leave the state. The Virginia Abolition Society ceased to exist.[4]

For many young white men, law seemed the career most likely to provide political and economic success. The commonwealth's capital had a stellar collection of lawyers, and many aspirants to the bar's loftiest levels. Bushrod Washington, the nephew of the first president, was a Richmond lawyer who, like his fellow Federalist John Marshall, was known for the hospitality of his house and table as well as his modest demeanor. Washington, Marshall, and the legal scholar George Wythe drew small armies of law clerks and young lawyers to Richmond for the opportunity to study near them and to observe such rising attorneys as John Wickham, William Wirt, and George Hay.

Charles Copland was one of those who came to Richmond with little money but great expectations. After Christmas in 1788, he moved from Charles City County to Richmond to practice law and built a modest house on Shockoe Hill. "My poverty made it needful that I should use economy in forming this establishment and therefore the house that I put on the lot was framed in Charles City . . . and the frames were brought to Richmond by water." Copland also rode his only horse into the countryside to cut firewood rather than buy it in town.[5]

Bushrod Washington and John Marshall departed for the United States Supreme Court, and the elderly George Wythe was murdered by his nephew, but new talents rose to take their places. Ambitious young men could best display their powers of analysis and rhetoric in the courtroom, where an outstanding performance might be noticed by important politicians in their party. They might also stand about the courts to listen for rumors of foreclosures and buy up property. Law was not always lucrative for its practitioners in Richmond, but it was at the center of activity in the early years of the republican city.

In 1807, national politics and local ambition came together in the treason trial of Aaron Burr. When Burr, former vice president of the United States, was arrested in an apparent filibustering expedition to the Louisiana Territory, he was brought to Richmond to be tried for treason in a Supreme Court circuit presided over by Chief Justice John Marshall. The trial featured prominent Richmond lawyers, including William Wirt for the prosecution and John Wickham for the defense. Wickham was considered the most able man at the Richmond bar and Wirt one of the best legal orators.[6]

The Burr trial promised to provide Richmond not only with legal precedents but also with the wit and debate for which the city had a highly developed taste. The oratorical merits of Wickham and Wirt were as well known as the speeds of the quarter horses at the race track. Interest in the trial was heightened by the aura of political conspiracy that surrounded it. That a vice president of the United States might conspire with the Spanish or attempt his own empire did not seem unlikely in the climate of Europe's Napoleonic Wars. Richmond and the untested republic were fearful and bitterly divided, and the city's political factions suspected each other of treasonous affection for one European power or the other.

William Wirt, styled a "Whip Syllabub Genius" by his Federalist rivals because of his frothy and too-palatable oratory, was a self-made man who understood the advantages of public attention to his talent. For a brief moment in his early career, his ambition seemed stymied at the Richmond bar and he considered a move to Kentucky. To a friend he confided, "In Virginia I will never resume the practice of law — I know the labor and the little profit of bushwhacking it. . . . [I]n Kentucky every upstart pettifogger makes a fortune in a few years."[7] Yet the next year he published a witty and satirical account of Richmond's striving new families, *Letters of the British Spy*, and began a career of writing, more worshipfully, about Virginia's patriotic forefathers — a move that served his legal career as well as a political office might have.

John Wickham came to Virginia from Long Island and, overcoming the stigma of Loyalist sympathies during the Revolution, began a brilliant career at the bar; as a nineteenth-century lawyer he retained much of the formality and sense of natural authority characteristic of the eighteenth-century gentleman. Wickham shared John Marshall's Federalist sympathies, and while neither bore any political affection for Burr, the ex–vice president's trial was an opportunity to further the Federalist project of an "independent judiciary" in which judges became arbiters of issues, determining which were political and which were legal, thus removing some decisions from popular influence.[8]

The political theater of Burr's trial began when Burr was brought into the city. John Marshall examined him privately at the Eagle Tavern while the Virginia *Argus* fumed that there was "no good reason . . . in a free country . . . [for the methods of] the Spanish Inquisition. The public is much excited and wants to view the proceedings." Marshall's political error was then reversed, and the rest of Burr's examination was held at the capitol with a large audience. Burr was charged only with conspiracy, not treason, and Marshall briefly admitted him to bail. A few days later the *Argus* had more reason to fume. "It is reported, and we are sorry to say, that the fact appears indisputable that Colonel Aaron Burr and the Chief Justice of the United States dined together at Mr. Wickham's since his examination and since his honor had himself solemnly decided that there were probable grounds to believe him guilty of a high misdemeanor against the United States. . . . We . . . confess our astonishment that men, whose intellects are so penetrating as those of Mr. Wickham and Mr. Marshall, did not perceive the extreme indelicacy and impropriety."[9]

In the months leading up to the trial, Burr was treated as a celebrity, and Richmond matrons sent food to the rooms where he was eventually under house arrest. William Wirt did yeoman work for the prosecution and for Thomas Jefferson in attacking Burr as a "snake in the Garden of Eden." The eventual verdict of "not proved" was a triumph of both Marshall's ability to shape the law and Wickham's ability to present a case as if the court were a gentleman's club and its proceedings a matter of sorting things out among gentlemen. Still, Wirt had his reward. Jefferson complimented him on his "correct views" and suggested that Wirt enter Congress and assume leadership of the Republican Party there.[10]

Richmond, fond of courtroom theatrics, was even more fond of the theater itself. On the night after Christmas in 1811, more than six hundred people — among them many of the city's foremost citizens and their guests, members of the state legislature, and visitors to the city, as

The influential and precedent-setting chief justice of the United States Supreme Court, John Marshall, began his career in Richmond, a city he found congenial to his Federalist sympathies. As part of his Supreme Court duties on the circuit, in 1807 he presided over the treason trial of ex–vice president Aaron Burr, held in Richmond. Though on the Court for thirty-five years, Marshall never moved from Richmond, and he remained engaged in the city's concerns. **John Marshall** (c. 1825), artist unknown, from the Valentine, Richmond, Virginia

John Wickham, a Long Island Tory, was suspected of British sympathies during the Revolution but became the most famous and successful lawyer in Richmond from the 1780s until his death in 1839. Highly successful as a courtroom speaker, he remained an eighteenth-century gentleman in the more open sphere of the nineteenth-century bar. **John Wickham** (c. 1825), attributed to John Wesley Jarvis, from the Valentine, Richmond, Virginia

well as free blacks and slaves—attended the theater to see *The Father, or Family Feuds*, a translation of Diderot by Louis Girardin, a French émigré who conducted an academy for boys at Eighth and Cary streets in Richmond. The afterpiece was *Agnes and Raymond, or, The Bleeding Nun*. The wealthy sat in boxes and chatted back and forth, the middle classes sat in the pit, and poorer whites and blacks sat in the galleries on long uncushioned benches without backs. All members of the audience felt free to comment on the performance and to be as loud and clever as their near seatmates would permit.

As the play ended and the theater prepared for the afterpiece, a stage manager brushed a theater curtain with a lighted chandelier. Flames moved rapidly up the curtain, and the cry of "Fire!" caused the tightly packed audience to rise up and move, with mounting panic, toward the exits, which were soon blocked. Those in the pits escaped more easily than those in the boxes, which all led to a narrow stairway with a single door. Seventy-two people died in the

Despite prohibitions on theater-going by the growing number of evangelical Protestants in the city, many English actors and acting companies found a receptive audience in Richmond. Among the city's favorite actors was the erratic Junius Brutus Booth, whose dramatic private life paralleled his roles on the stage. His sons, Edwin Booth and John Wilkes Booth, were favorites of the Richmond stage, although Wilkes Booth was considered an immature actor. **Junius Brutus Booth** (c. 1830s), by R. M. Sully, from the Valentine, Richmond, Virginia

fire, including the newly appointed governor of Virginia and twenty free blacks and slaves. Fifty of the dead were women, most of them trapped in the boxes and hindered by their fashionable clothing.

The week between Christmas and New Year's Day was customarily a slave holiday, and most work was suspended. Gilbert Hunt, a slave blacksmith, had just sat down to dinner in the kitchen with his wife, a slave in the George Mayo household, when Mrs. Mayo entered and, greatly agitated, asked Hunt to run to the theater, where a fire had broken out, and rescue her daughter Louisa. According to his later account, Hunt rushed to the scene of the fire and, unable to enter the building, looked up and saw Dr. James McCaw at an upper window. McCaw dropped a dozen women out the window to Hunt, who caught them in his arms before breaking the fall of McCaw himself. Louisa Mayo was not among those rescued. Gilbert Hunt later noted that the young Louisa Mayo "was teaching me my book" at the time of her death.[11]

The Richmond theater fire was sensational news all over the nation and a boon to Protestant evangelicalism, which was quick to point out, in tract and sermon, the hand of God in the destruction of the theater. Until the fire, many of Richmond's prominent families had resisted evangelicalism. The tragedy of the theater fire gave evangelical ministers within the Presbyterian and Episcopalian churches an opening into these Richmond churches. Men like Presbyterian John Holt Rice and Episcopalian William Meade denounced the stage, the racetrack, and the dance floor and advanced their vision of a church that emphasized a personal salvation and promoted missions.

The BURNING of the THEATRE in RICHMOND, VIRGINIA, on the Night of the 26th December 1811,
By which awful Calamity upwards of SEVENTY FIVE of its most valuable Citizens suddenly lost their lives, and many others, were much injured

The theater fire of 26 December 1811 claimed at least seventy-two lives of every rank and station and inspired sermons nationwide on the moral dangers of theater-going. The establishment of Monumental Church, which was placed on the theater site as a memorial to the city's dead, marked the beginning of the separation of the Presbyterian and Episcopal congregations, which had combined their resources for many years. The Monumental Church became Episcopalian, the Presbyterians sought other quarters, and both denominations became more evangelical. **The Burning of the Theater in Richmond** *(1812), by B. Tanner, courtesy of the Valentine Museum, Richmond, Virginia;* **Monumental Church** *(1870s), from the Valentine, Richmond, Virginia*

The provinces of education, philanthropy, morality, and family became domains in which the city's white women exerted influence and extended their social and physical space in the city. Yet the novelty of female organization made the early Female Humane Society dependent on the status and authority of the members' husbands. Soon these socially prominent women were reinforced by the new evangelical woman, and the rationales of both varieties—civic and moral—were blended in their public activities. Increasingly, women were considered morally superior to men and the spiritual teachers of their children. Women began to substitute moral authority for family prominence when they acted publicly in behalf of others, and this move broadened the range of women who might participate and lessened the importance of husbands.

By 1815, Baptist women in Richmond had formed a mission society that raised money for education and for missions abroad. Evangelical women sponsored bazaars and fairs, Juvenile Societies, and Female Mite Societies. While clergymen and tract writers in Richmond urged white women to restrict their sphere of activity to the home, where they might reign supreme, evangelical voluntary associations continued to connect women with public participation and fostered a sense of purpose and organization.[12]

Few civic leaders early on were attracted to evangelicalism, but many of their wives were. Evangelicalism sometimes divided elite churches and families. When individuals adopted the evangelical worldview, they were no longer seen at many social functions. They retreated from the city's social rounds and joined men and women from less socially prominent denominations to attempt conversion of the slaves, to distribute food and Bible tracts, and to raise money for missions. Occasionally such women found it necessary to fall back on patriarchal authority. Female societies caused a celebrated fight at St. Paul's Episcopal Church, whose minister questioned the propriety of the Female Charitable Association's sponsoring a fair to raise money for missions. The father of Magdelena Carrington answered in print, threatening the clergyman with a lawsuit if he did not retract his statements. The minister lost at least this battle with the ladies of the church.[13]

Within months the tragedy of the theater fire was driven from the forefront of the public mind by the outbreak of war with Great Britain. The European wars that raged intermittently

THEATRE.

"THE GREAT AND TERRIBLE DAY OF THE LORD."

BY COMMAND OF THE KING OF KINGS;

AND AT THE DESIRE OF ALL WHO LOVE HIS APPEARING. (b)

AT THE THEATRE OF THE UNIVERSE, (c)

ON THE EVE OF TIME (d) WILL BE PERFORMED

THE GREAT ASSIZE,

OR DAY OF JUDGMENT. (e)

THE SCENERY

Which is now actually preparing, will not only surpass everything that has yet been seen, but will infinitely exceed the utmost stretch of human conception. (f) There will be a just REPRESENTATION of ALL THE INHABITANTS of the WORLD, in their various and proper colors; and their customs and manners will be so exact, and so minutely delineated, that the most secret thought will be discovered. (g) "For God shall bring every work into Judgment, with every secret thing, whether it be GOOD, or whether it be EVIL." ECCL. xii: 14.

THIS THEATRE will be laid out after a new plan, and will consist of

PIT AND GALLERY ONLY;

And contrary to all others, the Gallery is fitted up for the reception of Persons of High (or heavenly) Birth, (h) and the PIT for those of low (or earthly) Rank. (i) N. B.—The Gallery is very spacious, (k) and the Pit without bottom. (l)

To prevent inconvenience, there are separate doors for admitting the company; and they are so different that none can mistake that are not wilfully blind. The Door which opens into the GALLERY is very narrow, and the steps up to it somewhat difficult; for which reason there are seldom many people about it. (m) But the Door that gives entrance into the PIT is very wide and very commodious; which causes such numbers to flock to it that it is generally crowded. (n) N. B. The strait Door leads towards the right hand, and the broad one to the left. (o) It will be in vain for one in a tinselled coat and borrowed language to personate one of HIGH BIRTH, in order to get admittance into the upper places, (p) for there is One of wonderful and deep penetration, who will search and examine every individual; (q) and all who cannot pronounce SHIBBO-LETH, (r) in the language of Canaan, (s) or has not received a white stone and a new name; (t) or cannot prove a clear title to a certain portion of the LAND of PROMISE, (u) must be turned in at the left door.

THE PRINCIPAL PERFORMERS are described in Thess. iv: 10; 2 Thess. i: 7, 8, 9; Matt. xxiv: 30, 31, and xxv: 31, 32; Daniel vii: 9, 10; Jude 14 to 19; Rev. xx: 12 to 15 &c. But as there are some people much better acquainted with the contents of a PLAY BILL than the WORD of GOD, it may not be amiss to transcribe a verse or two for their perusal:—

"The Lord Jesus shall be revealed from Heaven with his mighty angels, in flaming fire, taking vengeance on them that obey not the Gospel," but "to be glorified in his Saints. (v) A fiery stream issued and came forth from before him. Thousands of thousands ministered unto him, and ten thousand times ten thousand stood before him; the Judgment was set and the Books were opened. (w) And whomsoever was not found in the Book of Life was cast into the Lake of Fire." (x)

ACT FIRST of this grand and solemn piece, will be opened by

AN ARCHANGEL WITH THE TRUMP OF GOD.

"For the Trumpet shall sound and the Dead shall be raised."—1 COR. xv: 52.

ACT SECOND.

Procession of Saints

In white, with Golden Harps, accompanied with shouts of Joy and Songs of Praise. (y)

ACT THIRD.

AN ASSEMBLAGE OF ALL THE UNREGENERATE.

THE MUSIC will chiefly consist of CRIES (z) accompanied with WEEPING, WAILING, MOURNING, LAMENTATION and WOE. (aa)

TO CONCLUDE WITH AN

ORATION BY THE SON OF GOD.

It is written in the 25th of Matthew, from the 31st verse to the end of the chapter; but for the sake of those who seldom read the Scriptures I shall here transcribe two verses.—"Then shall the King say to them on his Right Hand, "Come ye blessed of my Father, inherit the Kingdom prepared for you from the foundation of the world." Then shall he also say unto them on his left hand, "Depart from me ye cursed, into everlasting Fire, prepared (not indeed for you, but) for the Devil and his angels."

AFTER WHICH THE CURTAIN WILL DROP.

Then! O to tell!

John v : 28, 29	Some rais'd on high, and others doom'd to hell!
Rev. v : 9 ; xiv : 3, 4	These praise the Lamb, and sing redeeming Love,
Luke xvi : 22, 23	Lodged in his bosom, all his goodness prove:
Luke xix : 14, 27	While those who trampled under foot his grace,
Matt. xxv : 30 ; 2 Thess. i: 9	Are banished now, forever from his Face,
Luke xvi : 26	Divided thus, a Gulf is fixed between,
Matt. xxv : 46	And everlasting closes up the scene.

"Thus will I do unto thee, O Israel; and because I will do thus unto thee, prepare to meet thy God, O Israel." Amos iv : 12.

TICKETS FOR THE PIT, at the easy purchase of following the pomps and vanities of the Fashionable World, and the desires and amusements of the Flesh, (bb) to be had at every Flesh-pleasing Assembly. "If ye live after the flesh ye shall die." Rom. viii: 13.

TICKETS FOR THE GALLERY, at no less rate than being converted, (cc) forsaking all, (dd) denying self, taking up the Cross, (ee) and following Christ in the Regeneration. (ff) To be had nowhere but in the Word of God, and where that word appoints.

"He that hath ears to hear, let him hear." "And be not deceived God is not mocked. For whatsoever a man soweth, that shall he also reap." Matt. xi: 15. Gal. vi: 7.

N. B. No money will be taken at the door, (ll) nor will any Tickets give admittance into the gallery but those sealed by the Lamb. "Watch, therefore, be ye also ready for in such an hour as ye think not the Son of Man cometh." Matt. xxiv: 44

(a) Rev. xix : 10; 1 Tim. vi : 15. (b) 2 Tim iv : 8; Titus ii: 13. (c) Matt. xxiv: 27. (d) Rev. x : 6, 7; 1 Cor. xv : 51, 52. (e) Heb. ix : 27; Jude xv; Psalm ix : 7, 8; Rev. vi : 17; 2 Cor. v : 10. (f) 1 Cor. ii : 9. (g) Matt. xiii : 36; xxv : 32; 1 Cor. iv : 5; Rom. ii: 12, 16. (h) John iii : 3, 4; 1 Pet. i : 23; Rom. viii : 14. (i) James iii : 14, 15; Rom. iii: 8. (j) Luke xiv : 21. (k) Rev. iv : 1, 2; xix : 20. (l) Matt. viii: 13. (m) Matt. xxv : 35. (n) Matt. vii: 21, 22, 23; xxii : 13; Jerem. xvi: 20, 21; 2 Tim. ii: 19; John x : 14. (o) Judges xii: 6. (r) Isaiah xix : 18; Zeph. iii: 9. (s) Rev. ii : 17; 2 Cor. xiii: 5; Gal. iii: 29; Heb. ix: 1, 8, 9. (u) Heb. iii: 17, 18, 19; Rom. xiii : 9; Psalm ix:17. (v) 2 Thess. i: 7, 10; Matt. xxiv : 31. (w) Dan. vii: 10. (x) Rev. xx: 12, 15. (y) Rev. xiv: 2, 3; xv: 2, 3, 4. (z) Matt. 2, xiii: 42, 50; xxv: 32, 41; 1 Cor. vi: 9, 10. (ee) Luke xviii: 29; Psalm xxii: 19; Rev. xii: 16, 17. (bb) Luke xii: 28; Matt. xiii: 49, 50; Rev. i: 7; Ezek. ii: 10. (cc) James iv : 4; 1 John ii: 15, 16, 17; 1 Tim. v : 6; Eph. ii: 2, 5. (dd) Matt. xviii : 12; viii: 18 to 22. (ee) Luke xiv: 23; xvii: 28 to 33. (ff) Luke ix : 23 to 27; xiv: 27. (ll) Matt. xxv: 28, 29. (ee) Acts viii: 18 to 21. (ee) 2 Cor. i: 22; Eph. i: 13, 14; iv: 30. (oe) Rev. vii: 3; Rev. iv: 30.

The evangelical attack on the worldly temptations of the theater in Richmond in one instance took the form of a mock playbill that was actually a cautionary sermon. Nineteenth-century evangelical Protestantism was inherently suspicious of the theatricality and facade that developed in commercial centers. Broadside from the Valentine, Richmond, Virginia

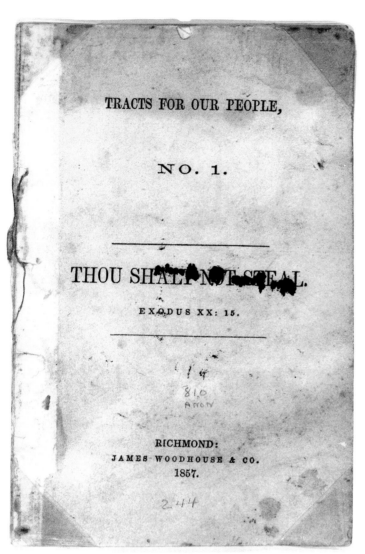

TRACTS FOR OUR PEOPLE,

NO. 1.

THOU SHALL NOT STEAL.

EXODUS XX: 15.

RICHMOND:
JAMES WOODHOUSE & CO.
1857.

Domestic slavery in Richmond households meant a high level of management by the mistress of the house and constant vigilance. Access to the larder and to other supplies was controlled by the housewife, whose systems of delegated daily tasks ideally left little unstructured time. If structure and threats were not sufficient to prevent pilfering, religious instruction was an added admonition. Tracts for Our People *was a series of religious instruction booklets to be used by the mistress to reinforce standards of proper behavior by the slaves. From the Valentine, Richmond, Virginia*

from the early 1790s affected every American town and city that traded with Europe, and Richmond was among them. American vessels were stopped and searched, and crew members were often "impressed" or taken by British ships. Protests of American neutrality did not stop these practices or allow American ships to bypass the naval blockades of trade ports. When the British ship *Leopard* searched the American vessel *Chesapeake* off the Virginia coast in 1807, Richmond was ready to declare war on England. James Monroe presided over a mass meeting at the capitol to organize a boycott of British goods and promote domestic manufacture. It was agreed that Fourth of July celebrants would wear only clothes of American make and consume domestic liquors. In a series of acts designed to limit American involvement in European trade and keep the nation out of war, President Jefferson persuaded Congress to place an embargo on American trade to Europe. Although New England cities complained most loudly about the effects of the Embargo Act, Richmond was also badly hurt by its inability to ship tobacco or flour to Europe. Coal exports from the Midlothian mines also suffered, and merchants struggled to find new markets.[14]

Although both England and France attempted to curtail American trade with the other and refused to recognize American sea rights, it was Britain with which the nation went to war in 1812, and the Chesapeake area near Norfolk and Hampton became the scene of British warship harassment and invasion. Several times rumors that the British were marching or sailing on Richmond sent citizens out of town; but the real effect of the war was to persuade many Virginians of the necessity for more manufactures. Even Thomas Jefferson, who had long advocated an agricultural republic, concluded, "We must now place the manufacturer by the side of the agriculturalist."[15] This was a very congenial view to a Richmond often at odds with Jefferson, and at the end of the war the city contemplated its prospects for commerce and industry with enthusiasm. The city's commercial hopes rested on its position at the fall line between the Piedmont and Tidewater, on the James River and Kanawha Canal, and on a myriad of water-powered industries. Richmond was poised to develop its cotton goods production, tobacco processing, flour milling, and small arms manufacture, although the region could not expect to rival cities that were nearer the Atlantic coast and enjoyed natural harbors and a much earlier investment in ships and trade connections.[16]

While Richmond had no lack of schemes for investment or ideas for new manufactures, many important conditions for industrial expansion, including transportation, were inadequate. A committee of the state legislature expressed the need carefully, creating a bridge from republican virtue to the infrastructure of enterprise. "Public virtue is the spring of all political action and political action must be taken by Virginia to build canals and turnpikes and assure that American trade and manufacturing be enhanced so that the nation need not depend on Europe for products." A Richmond entrepreneur expressed it more energetically: "*Capitalists*! We invite you to settle among us! Here is fuel for the employment of your capital. Richmond is destined to be great." Richmonders enthusiastically purchased stock in a variety of navigation, railroad, and turnpike companies; a majority of the James River Company stock was purchased by city residents and city government in the expectation that improved transportation would strengthen the city's ties with the regions to the west and south.[17]

In 1814, the Richmond Cotton Manufactory advertised for "Men, Women, Boys and Girls of various sizes" to work in the plant, promising "comfortable houses" and "a school

The War of 1812 left even Jeffersonians believing that Americans should not be hostage to European manufacturers. Richmond had many ambitious entrepreneurs eager to advertise their diverse wares. The castings of this iron foundry suggest the uses of iron in a region dominated by farms and plantations and serviced by local businesses. Richmond Union Foundry broadside in a letter from David Burr to John Hartwell Cocke dated 13 April 1822, Cocke Family Papers (no. 640), Special Collections Department, Manuscripts Division, Alderman Library, University of Virginia, Charlottesville

and books" for workers; white apprentices were welcome. This cotton manufactory's utopian vision was short-lived. It soon began employing black women, as the tobacco factories hired black males. Nationwide problems of inadequate industrial labor supply, which New England met with women and children, were resolved in Richmond by the use of slave labor.[18]

Another obstacle to commercial growth was a shortage of local capital and a bank loan policy that favored certain Richmond and Virginia families who were the bank's directors. The Bank of Virginia and the Farmer's Bank, both located near the capitol, were the state's chartered banks and had competition only from the Bank of the United States branches at Norfolk and Richmond. The directors of the state banks included influential members of the Richmond and Virginia merchant, planter, and legal elites who belonged to a group, part legend and part reality, known as the Richmond Junto. The Junto was a very loose alliance, significant mainly for the name it gave to the interconnected interests between state and city leaders and between public policy and private banking. After 1816 a new Board of Public Works could use state money to acquire as much as two-fifths of any company approved by the General Assembly; the board could sell shares and distribute dividends. The state invested the special funds from the Board of Public Works in bank stocks, thus further tying these banks to the economy. Loans from state banks to Richmond residents fueled speculation in suburban land and contributed to a financial panic in 1819.

The most important Junto associates in Richmond were Judge Spencer Roane; Thomas Ritchie of the Richmond *Enquirer*; and their mutual first cousins, Dr. John and Judge William Brockenbrough. It was not in the interest of Richmond's Common Hall, whose membership was now drawn from the local merchant elite and professional men, to challenge these interlocking family networks. Banks were the most lucrative clients of Richmond lawyers, merchants depended on them for transactions and consistent interest rates, and land speculators of all backgrounds hoped for bank loans.[19]

An analysis of Richmond's strengths and limitations was offered in 1817 by the writer of a newspaper essay who signed himself "Mechanic," a term that suggested republican pride in artisans and small manufacturers. He wrote, "Richmond, which was so lately an object of pity to her own citizens, a bye-word of contempt to others, is rising from the bed of sloth into

RICHMOND UNION FOUNDERY.

On the Canal, Corner of B and 5th streets.

Nearly opposite the Va. Manufactory of arms.

THIS ESTABLISHMENT IS CONDUCTED BY THE SUBSCRIBER, WHO SOLICITS ORDERS FOR

Castings of Iron for Machinery of all kinds;

Particularly for Flour, Grist and Saw mills; the superiority of which for durability, cheapness, and saving friction, should recommend it to every Mill owner.

The Subscriber will also furnish Steam Engines complete, on the most approved plans, or castings for the separate parts; Threshing Machines, Iron Tobacco Presses, and Screws; Kettles and Stills, of any sizes; Bark Mills, Plaster of Paris and Corn Crushers; Patent Corn Shellers, Plough Irons; Fire place Backs, Jambs, Facings and Hearths; Stoves, and Grates: Scale and Window weights; Railings for enclosing buildings, yards, graves, &c. Cart and wagon Boxes; Fire Dogs and every variety of Iron castings.

Also, Brass, Copper & Composition Castings, viz.

Bells for Churches, Academies, Taverns, &c. Coach hinges and Caps; Brass mounting for Grates, Railings, Furniture, &c.

Wrought Iron Machinery and Smiths work in General.

Orders received by the Subscriber at the Foundery, by Mr. Francis Follet, Petersburg, and Mr. Vincent Lea, Norfolk, to whom articles will be forwarded for delivery when requested.

DAVID J. BURR.

JULY, 24th, 1821.

As one of the new nation's largest cities, Richmond received contemporary information, goods, and fashions. Richmond was among the cities to which craftsmen in the young republic were drawn by the existence of a market for their products. Richmond craftsmen could supply luxuries for local consumption as well as simply functional items. Silversmiths, cabinet-makers, portrait painters, and pewterers all found clients in Richmond, although many were likely to move to the next town when the supply of local buyers appeared to be exhausted. Sign advertising shop of pewtersmith Joseph Danforth, painted white pine, 1814, from the Valentine, Richmond, Virginia

activity and reputation." "Mechanic" blamed both the bank system and the lack of encouragement by the state for Richmond's slow development of manufactures. Implicit in the essay was a criticism of the incorporated monopolies emerging from the state legislature, which were believed to thwart entrepreneurial initiative and capital investment by white skilled labor. Ending on a note of optimism, "Mechanic" claimed that immigrants from the North and from Europe had designed and built much of the city, and he urged a new influx of such craftsmen to develop manufactures.[20] For an evanescent moment after the War of 1812, sentiments of nationalism had seemed to pervade the republic and overwhelm regional differences, but by the end of the second decade of the nineteenth century, fissures appeared in the national unity and optimism. In an 1819 recession, land values in Richmond, driven up by speculation, plummeted, and to add to the town's woes, an embezzlement scandal involving city treasurer John Seabrook created inadequate revenues and caused the Common Hall's members to divide among themselves for the first time.

The fundamental flaw inherent in a republic based politically on individual liberty and economically on chattel slavery became more apparent each year. By 1820, Richmond residents read the political news from Washington more apprehensively in the city's fiercely partisan newspapers. Voters in Richmond supported Federalist candidates while the party existed, but after 1816 it no longer put forward presidential candidates. The lack of two warring parties may have made some people believe that the United States had reached the millenium of political harmony, but those who looked closely could see the jostling for position as new southern factions and alliances formed around the emerging figures of Henry Clay, John C. Calhoun, and Andrew Jackson.

At the national level, Congress began a debate over whether the Missouri Territory should be admitted to the Union as a slave state. Richmond's city fathers shared with Thomas Jefferson the sense that this issue was "a firebell in the night." In many ways, the city's efforts to encourage commerce and remain competitive with northern cities were at odds with Virginia's drift toward more cautious and conservative social and political views and the development of an ideology to match them. The 1820 census confirmed for Virginia that it was no longer the preeminent state in the union and no longer the most populous. Virginia's dynasty of presidents

Like Sallie Gladman—Edward Valentine's nurse, shown in the daguerreotype—those black slave women assigned to care for the children of a white family were often idealized as "mammies," both before and after the Civil War. The true affection that these black women felt for their charges made them a part of the family, but it did not free them from the bondage of slavery. Some remained in the household until death, while others were sold or traded away when the child was ready to enter school. From the Valentine, Richmond, Virginia

was ending in a series of squabbles and factions. As Tidewater plantations grew less profitable agriculturally, the most valuable property on the plantation was often the slave laborers, who were increasingly subject to being hired out in cities or, more likely, sold to new cotton plantations in the Lower South.

The Missouri Compromise and the political sensitivity to slavery that followed it served as a sharp reminder of the limits to Richmond's dreams of factories rising in the air, just as Gabriel's Conspiracy had served to indicate the limits to the rights of man. Despite all its natural advantages for commerce, Richmond was surrounded by plantation agriculture and slavery. The defense of slavery and the control of slaves and free blacks came to dominate much of the debate over Virginia's relative decline. A somewhat contradictory combination of republican uneasiness over slavery, evangelical zeal, and a desire to strengthen slavery by removing free blacks led to Richmond's interest in an African colonization scheme developed by Virginia congressman Charles Fenton Mercer, who had been a law clerk in Richmond at the time of Gabriel's Conspiracy. Free blacks' interest in the scheme was a commentary on their frustration at the limits placed on their advancement.

Mercer came to believe that since blacks could not share in the republican experiment, the races must be separated, beginning with the free black population. In 1816 he founded the American Colonization Society to send free blacks and emancipated slaves to colonize and Christianize West Africa. Richmond's free blacks noted the formation of the Washington-based society and held a mass meeting in which they expressed interest in colonization but suggested the western part of the United States as a site, describing Africa as an alien land. When it became clear that the society's colony would be in Africa, two of Richmond's free blacks, Lott Cary and Colin Teage, both elders in the Baptist Church, volunteered as African missionaries.

Born a slave in New Kent County, Cary was hired out as a tobacco worker in Richmond and, like Teage, joined the Baptist Church, where he learned to read and write in a religious evening school run by William Crane, a white Baptist shoemaker from New Jersey. Cary became a preacher and later bought his freedom and that of his family with money from overtime work. In 1820, before sending the two men as missionaries to the colony of Liberia, the Baptist Board of Missions organized Cary, Teage, their families, and several other Richmond free blacks as the Providence Baptist Church, with Cary and Teage as ministers.

Cary and a small group of white evangelical businessmen formed a trading company to exchange African commodities for manufactures from Richmond. Cary tried coffee, camwood, and goods exchanged in trade with Africans. Profits were elusive, but Cary remained adamant that Liberia offered blacks both liberty and a field for missions. His urgings persuaded some free black Baptist families in Richmond to go to Liberia, and in 1823 the white Baptists who had worked closely with Cary formed a Richmond auxiliary of the American Colonization Society to support them.

The pull of Liberia was not entirely evangelical. Gilbert Hunt, the slave blacksmith who was heralded as a hero in the Richmond theater fire, bought his freedom from his master in 1829 and migrated to Liberia in 1830. Hunt apparently hoped to make money as a blacksmith there, but he found the economy unready for his skills. After a year he returned to Richmond, where the colonization society's secretary referred to him as "a complete croaker" for his negative assessment of Liberia. By then, the state's colonization society had ceased to offer Richmond's free blacks a vision of political and economic possibility in Liberia.[21]

The small flurry of African colonization activity in Richmond reflected uneasy questions about the progress of the republic and the city. The return of the aged Marquis de Lafayette to America and to Richmond for a tour of the scenes of his Revolutionary youth provided more evidence of the tension between Revolutionary themes and slavery. Lafayette's tour of the United States in 1824 and 1825 provided him with ceremonial honors and gave rise to general

Lott Cary, a hired-out slave working in a Richmond tobacco factory, purchased his own freedom and that of his family through overtime work. Cary realized that neither his freedom, his conversion experience, nor his entrepreneurial abilities would ever provide him with full citizenship in the United States. With the financial assistance of Richmond's African Baptist Missionary Society, he and other Richmond blacks left in 1820 for the colony of Liberia on the western coast of Africa, where he was a Baptist minister and leader of the colony until his death. **Lott Cary,** date and artist unknown, courtesy of the First African Baptist Church, Richmond, Virginia

celebration. That celebration was as much for the young republic as for Lafayette. In lauding Lafayette, Richmond praised its own patriotic citizens, its heroic veterans, and its beautiful and virtuous women. In Virginia's capital, as in other American cities, the prominent and the would-be prominent vied to entertain the aging veteran and thus authenticate their own claims to history and status.[22]

For Lafayette's benefit, certain of the city's school children, drawn from the best of the numerous private academies, were chosen to recite poetry and declaim while young ladies gave speeches of welcome and displayed their musical talents. Edgar Allan Poe, a student at Burke's Academy for Boys, was part of the cadet corps that welcomed Lafayette, while the pupils of Harmony Hall school presented the general with a life membership in the Virginia Bible Society. Edgar Poe was placed by his foster father, John Allan, in schools well-known for their academic attainments and scholarly headmasters. A variety of private schools offered young men excellent preparation; between 1816 and 1869, boys without tuition could attend a Lancasterian school, based on an English model of tuition-free education in which students taught each other. However, families were often unwilling to send their sons to a charity school.[23]

Few of the female seminaries and boarding schools in Richmond dared advertise, as did Reynolds' Female Seminary, that they offered Greek, Latin, Italian, Spanish, "all kinds of history, geography, globes, maps, English composition, moral philosophy, chemistry, astronomy, botany, mineralogy, music, drawing, embroidery, and wax works." Most still promised a broad range of subjects, often taught by one or two women instructors in rented rooms above shops. Schooling was a private business and one in which women teachers competed successfully with men. The curriculum may have represented what was taught in "a real, honest, old-fashioned boarding school where a reasonable quantity of accomplishments were sold at a reasonable

The Marquis de Lafayette was a popular officer in Washington's Virginia army, but nothing could match the enthusiasm with which he was greeted on his return to Richmond in 1824. For local residents, his presence confirmed and extended their story of heroic origins. Although Lafayette was pained by the continued presence of slavery, he remained the genial guest of the city and the nation. **Marquis de Lafayette** (1824), by Edward F. Peticolas, from the Valentine, Richmond, Virginia

price and where girls might be sent to be out of the way and scramble themselves into a little education without any danger of coming back prodigies." [24]

Still, the growth of female academies in Richmond reflected both a republican belief in the education of women who would instruct their children for citizenship and an increase in the number of families who could afford some education for their daughters. Richmond's Female Academy, established by the legislature and opened in 1807, offered a curriculum equal to that of boys' academies and advertised for young women from across the state to board. An 1818 school announcement made the argument for female education, noting, "The study . . . deemed so necessary to sons . . . [is] almost everywhere denied to daughters." Yet, the printed notice continued, the education of women favored public morals, private happiness, and female self-reliance in "the full power and splendid attractions of knowledge." In antebellum Richmond, this idea was imperfectly realized and often viewed with suspicion, but it remained a powerful argument for female education because it combined the unassailable verities of the era: republican duty, domestic morality, and individual attainment. [25]

By the time of Lafayette's visit, Richmond had grown large enough to parade its civic culture, made up of military units, academies, social clubs, and governmental offices. All the

Richmond had dozens of academies and schools for young women. Some represented impoverished widows' short-lived efforts to support themselves; others had a longer existence and were designed to teach young women both the decorative skills of needlework and music and the more classical curriculum available to young men. The photograph above shows the Richmond Female Institute in 1897; below it is a Berlin-work picture made in 1850 by Mary A. Driscoll at St. Joseph's Academy. From the Valentine, Richmond, Virginia

presentations and rituals, dinners, toasts, and sporting pastimes enacted in honor of Lafayette placed the city's leaders, merchants, and an urban gentry of planter-related families on display. On his first full day in Richmond, Lafayette was entertained at a horse race, where the winner was promptly renamed Virginia de La Fayette. This race was followed by a lavish early afternoon dinner at the Jockey Club, the special preserve of several of the city's leading gentlemen, who had inherited the gentry tradition of breeding and racing horses. Well into the 1820s, most Richmond clubs remained the province of men with the leisure and money to pursue avocations. Jockey and cricket clubs and library, literary, and debating societies were all fashionably exclusive and provided men with an opportunity to advance their careers under the pretext of fellowship and sport.

The city's official day for Lafayette began with a procession from the Eagle Hotel to City Hall, where John Marshall spoke on behalf of veterans. Lafayette then greeted the ladies and reviewed the troops, after which a public reception was held on Capitol Square and Lafayette shook hands with all who were permitted to enter. Newspapers had cautioned, "No intoxicated or colored person will be permitted to enter the Square."[26]

Passing through the city streets later, Lafayette recognized in the crowd one of those barred from Capitol Square, a man who had served as his spy in the camp of Cornwallis. The general drew James Lafayette forward—the same hired-out slave once known as James Armistead and now a free man in New Kent County. Lafayette's spontaneous embrace of James gave visibility to a group not included in the hierarchy of celebration—the city's free blacks, long resident in the town and maintaining their numbers at a tenth of the total population.[27]

As Lafayette's procession approached the Union Hotel, where a dinner with government officials and his revolutionary compatriots was to be held, it paused under a double arch covered with evergreen wreaths; a young lady was stationed at the base of each arch. The young women who waited upon Lafayette, forever known as "Lafayette girls," were deemed the most attractive in town, often on the basis of their family status and youth. For their part, they did their best to appear as the softly rounded, pale and slim-waisted ladies that were judged romantic and fashionable.[28]

Richmond's theaters grew more restrictive in their seating arrangements, confining blacks to limited areas, just at the time when blackface minstrelsy began to appear on stages. This enormously popular form of theater permitted white men to sing and dance on stage in a way that was possible only when they were in disguise. Richmonders supported "the Ethiopian burlesque" with enthusiasm. Broadside, 1848, from the Valentine, Richmond, Virginia

Reflecting on Lafayette's return to the city after more than forty years, the Richmond *Enquirer* noted dolefully, "Our City has improved with less rapidity than many of those he has visited to the North—but we have some objects still that are new to the illustrious stranger. Our capitol, our square, the statue of Washington, the bust of LaFayette himself, our Canal may attract some of his attention."[29] Three of the five objects listed looked back to the Revolutionary Era; only the canal pointed to Richmond's future. Despite these evocations of a common white Revolutionary past, there was much dissatisfaction among Richmond whites over the state's suffrage system. Virginia's Revolutionary constitution, which in 1776 had been heavily weighted to favor the Tidewater, had not been modified to extend the franchise in the ensuing decades. By 1829, when a reluctant Virginia General Assembly called a constitutional convention to consider the system of freehold suffrage and county representation, Virginia had the lowest percentage of eligible voters in the Union. Suffrage based on property meant that Virginia cities were underrepresented in the legislature, while the county unit system of representation overrepresented the Tidewater.

Both the cities and western counties sought redress at the 1829 convention in Richmond, which drew considerable interest from outside the state as a last meeting of Virginia's old Revolutionary heroes, now elected as delegates. Crowds gathered in Capitol Square to see James Monroe, James Madison, and John Marshall, as well as former senator John Randolph of Roanoke and current senators John Tyler and Littleton Waller Tazewell. The glance backward was significant, because any possibility for real change in the convention had been lost weeks before, when the General Assembly decided to elect delegates based on the 1810 census, already twenty years old and not at all reflective of the changes in Virginia's population patterns.

Richmond delegates offered sharply contrasting views at the constitutional convention. Benjamin Watkins Leigh, a Richmond lawyer and a son-in-law of John Wickham, was the most articulate spokesman of the conservatives, who feared extension of the suffrage. Leigh spoke scornfully of democracy and predicted it would lead to "rapine, anarchy, and bloodshed." He asserted that those white Virginians who "labour for their daily bread" could never have enough "political intelligence" to participate in government. Early in the convention, John Marshall introduced a memorial from Richmond's white artisans and mechanics protesting the property qualifications for voting in Virginia. They asserted that it was difficult for urban commercial and manufacturing classes to purchase property and that they "felt with full force their degraded condition." They would not, they promised, continue to countenance a "privileged order" based on the "patrician pretensions of the landholder." Nevertheless, the convention, fearful that non-property holders would vote to increase the taxes on slaves, voted down almost all the reforms introduced. The unhappy commercial and mechanical classes were left with little satisfaction at the conclusion of the 1829 convention, and the city's call for commerce and industry may have had a hollow ring to their ears.[30]

"Rocky Road to Richmond," an Irish fiddle tune that had casually been adapted to local place-names and circumstances, used rising and plunging notes to musically describe the rut-filled roads leading to the city, but its cheerful energy belied its complaints. Sy Gilliat played such tunes as dance jigs at house parties where the city's prominent families gathered in the early nineteenth century. As Richmond filled in its ravines, smoothing the physical landscape in anticipation of economic growth, the political landscape grew unexpectedly rocky.

CHAPTER FIVE

Richmond's Great Expectations

I n 1848, Samuel Smith, a white shoemaker in Richmond, carefully addressed a large wooden crate to William Johnson, Arch Street, Philadelphia, Pennsylvania. Calling for a mule-drawn dray, in the early morning he accompanied the box from his shop on Main Street, distinguished by a large painted red boot sign, down the city's ill-paved streets toward the Adams Express office at Eighteenth and Main, below the Exchange Hotel. The dray rumbled past the Old Market, where wagon drivers from the countryside sold their produce to stallkeepers or haggled with slaves from Shockoe Hill and Church Hill over the price of vegetables. Mist hovered over the river as other slaves, lunchbuckets in hand, stepped around the dray and its bulky cargo on their way to the tobacco factories strung out along the James River. A few women, sleeves rolled up, applied brooms to the trampled-dirt space in front of a cookshop or eating house, anticipating the first morning customers.[1]

At the Adams Express office, Smith watched as the box was unloaded to be sent to the depot and placed in a freight car of the Richmond, Fredericksburg, and Potomac Railroad; the box would be transported by rail to Aquia Creek, then by water and rail to the Philadelphia office of Adams Express. Samuel Smith returned to his modest residence, where he was arrested a few months later for attempting to box up two more slaves and send them from Richmond to freedom in Philadelphia. The northern-born shoemaker served a seven-year prison term for his part in the Underground Railroad before he was released and returned to the North. His earlier cargo to Philadelphia was more fortunate. Henry Brown became the famous "Box" Brown, among the best known of runaway slaves and the subject of a memoir widely circulated in the North.

Henry Brown met his wife, who was also a slave, in Richmond, and together they were able to rent a small home, where they lived with their two children. Brown and his wife paid her owner for her time through his overtime work at the tobacco factory and her work as a washerwoman. Through their joint efforts, they were able to live much like a free black couple might. This happy illusion died when her master sold her to another man who then sold her South, along with her children. Brown vowed to find someone who would help him escape to the north; he found Samuel Smith, who was paid eighty-six dollars to ship him to Philadelphia. Supplied with a bladder of water to pour on his neck if the box grew overheated,

Henry Brown's wife and children were sold away from him, and with no family ties, he determined to escape to the North. Samuel Smith, a white shoemaker, boxed him up with a bladder of water, and Brown was delivered to Philadelphia via stage, rail, and water. **The Resurrection of Henry Box Brown at Philadelphia** (1850) courtesy of the Library of Congress

THE RESURRECTION OF HENRY BOX BROWN AT PHILADELPHIA.
Who escaped from Richmond Va in a Box 3 feet long 2½ ft deep and 2 ft wide

Brown climbed into the container. Arrows noted "This End Up," but the shippers followed their time-honored practice of ignoring these directions, and Brown spent part of the trip on his head. It is not clear whether the money that Brown paid Smith to help him escape was for the risks Smith took or simply for the cost of shipping him North.[2]

Brown's family life in Richmond exemplifies the effort of urban slaves to create private domestic space and to acquire contacts as well as discretionary cash. The lives of free blacks and urban slaves were braided together through kinship, living patterns, work patterns, and ties of affection. While slaves used earned money in a variety of ways, ranging from church donations to gambling, more than one slave family used those resources to fashion a private life and to buy relatives out of slavery. Amanda Cousins, a free black seamstress, raised the two children of a relative on her earnings, while Gilbert Hunt used his extra earnings as a blacksmith to purchase his freedom. Slaves hired in the city were seldom closely supervised, and hired slaves or slave artisans often found ways to earn spending money through "overwork."[3]

The story of Henry Brown's escape from Richmond illustrated everything that Richmond feared about the dizzying pace with which the city was growing in the mid-nineteenth century. Richmond had at last achieved the commercial growth and industrial production it had long sought. Between 1850 and 1860, the city's population grew by one-third, and prosperity brought more northern workers, European immigrants, and hired-out slaves to the city. Property-owning shopkeepers, merchants, and manufacturers, who did well in these flush times, sought ways to display their enhanced status, while less fortunate artisans began to believe that their difficulties were caused by competition with black labor. Richmond's antebellum industrialization brought together a diverse group of residents and created, between them, a contest for space, for money, and for autonomy.[4]

Even before the city's industrial expansion, rural slaves were hired in the town, and town slaves were hired to others than their masters. It was possible for slaves to find their own employment by the year and pay the master or mistress in one lump sum. This flexibility proved profitable but immensely confusing. The Richmond Police Daybook for 1834 to 1843 is entitled "A Record of Robberies," but the vast majority of the entries relate to slave runaways and often to the difficulties in locating a missing slave through a hierarchy of subcontractors. One example noted: "July 7, 1837: Harriett [from Amelia County] states that she was enticed off by Jordan or Jordan Harris who belongs to Major John Foster who resides on the adjoining plantation . . . to her master's. . . . Jordan was hired out for the present year to Frederick Hobson at Farmville and Hobson hired him to Reuben Seay of Powhatan who is engaged in blowing rock on the river."[5]

There were patterns to runaways. Women with children or old people seldom attempted escape. Young men ran to get away from slavery, while young women hid with friends or relatives in the city to negotiate better working conditions. One runaway advertisement illustrated the filament of connection that lay over Richmond like a sheer spider's web: "RUNAWAY! A girl named Ellen, about eighteen . . . , hired to Mr. Greery, the tailor. Her mother, Judy, is hired to Mrs. Broome. Her father, Joe Dawson, is hired to Mr. Wallace, the grocer living in Cary Street. The father must know where she is and should produce her."[6]

The layered story of two other runaways, Jenny and Kitty, is told in terse notations scribbled on small slips of paper as the legal executor of a will traipsed around Richmond asking about the missing young black women. "Jenny staying with Kitty who says she is hired to Saunders but he denies it. Kitty—18 to 20 years." Then: "Jenny—19—bad, daughter of Charles and Molly—is with her Aunt Kitty who is kin to Saunders. Jenny hired to Mr. Pargot on Main

These picturesque views of antebellum Richmond also depict the activity of the busy James River canal, which was finally completed as far as Lynchburg. The wagon roads from south of the city, the flour mills and foundries near the river banks, the public buildings, and the numerous church spires all belie the image's calm and suggest a less pastoral world of factory bells, coal cinders, clanking wheels, and flour mill dust. Above, **Richmond, Virginia, from Hollywood** (1854), by William Mac-Leod, and below, **From Manchester** (1852), by Smith Brothers, from the Valentine, Richmond, Virginia

Street." Finally: "Kitty—a girl—Jacob Ege (Saunders)." It took the executor some time to discover, first, where Kitty and Jenny were, and second, where they were supposed to be. That these two young slave women had been living with a free black relative in Richmond as runaways from nearby domestic hire reinforces the notion of lack of control in urban slavery and affirms the complicity of free blacks in assisting slave runaways.[7]

It also suggests the core of an urban black female culture that existed by its wits and relied on assistance from all of its members. Richmond's free black households were predominantly female-headed and included other free and slave women or children or both. If these rural slaves hired out in Richmond are an example, the ability of slaves to create a private landscape over the city and countryside had not lessened since Gabriel's Conspiracy. Some whites suspected the extent to which slaves interpreted and lived in a world beyond white knowledge, but few were prepared for the news of a slave revolt in rural Southampton County, Virginia, in which a slave preacher led a band that murdered fifty-five whites.

The rebellion led by Nat Turner in Southampton County in August 1831 forced Virginia at least momentarily to confront and debate slavery. The legislative session that met in the fall of 1831 and carried on into early 1832 in Richmond was remarkable in the South for its open discussion of slavery, a discussion that the Richmond newspapers carried in full. Virginia, which had provided so much political leadership for the Revolution, could find no creative solution for its division over slavery, and Richmond too was divided between forms of emancipation, although the general sentiment expressed in letters to the newspapers was for an end to the legal institution of chattel slavery.

When the assembly voted 16–15 to table the report of the special committee on slavery rather than vote on the issue, the *Richmond Constitutional Whig* expressed both its satisfaction that a majority of the House of Delegates had rejected perpetual slavery and its hope that "when public opinion is more developed . . . and means are better devised," gradual emancipation might begin. For the first time, delegates to a legislative session had publicly proclaimed slavery to be "a pernicious evil," a "curse," and "inherently disgusting," and many in Richmond believed that sentiment for emancipation was building.[8]

Instead, after the Nat Turner crisis, Virginia and Richmond turned back to old systems of controlling black actions. In the city, the corporate response to Nat Turner's fearful rebellion was to legislate more controls on slaves and free blacks, but the personal response was to continue as before, with little monitoring of urban slaves. Various other remedies and rationales were offered, including new support for African colonization, attacks on northern abolitionism, and a reinterpretation of Virginia's past to explain and justify the present.[9]

The southern sectional self-consciousness that gained political ground in the 1830s was partly expressed through the creation of a heroic and sentimentalized past of Revolutionary heroes and pastoral plantations where all lived in harmony. The yearning for an idealized past expressed a fear for the future apparent in the work of the Richmond gentlemen—often lawyers—who wrote novels and poetry for publication or for serial printing in the newspapers. Most of that writing was conventional at best, but one local youth proved to be an exception.

To the first great flowering of American literary genius, antebellum Richmond contributed the foster child Edgar Poe. When Poe's actress mother died, Frances Valentine Allan took him home. The child first lived with the family in rooms above John Allan's tobacco wholesale business; later, when the fortunes of this Scottish-born foster father improved, the family moved to a large house at Fifth and Main. Poe's relation to the city had the same layers of ambiguity that his relation to the Allan family did—he was never formally adopted, never completely a part of either, yet shaped by both.

Poe was an exotic plant in Richmond, a lush orchid amid the magnolia and laurel. Nevertheless, he truly was of Richmond and the South, and at the heart of his vision was an artist's intensification of the regional sense of being haunted by the past and inadequate to the standards of the fathers. Poe's actor parents and his status as a foster child made his social position particularly insecure, a fact well known to his foster father's slaves. In one letter to Allan, Poe complained, "You suffer me to be subjected to the whim and caprice, not only of your white family, but to the complete authority of the blacks."[10]

Poe's uncertain social status caused him not to question local values but rather to embrace them as fully as any Richmonder did; he contributed to the growing southern defense of slavery just as that defense was becoming truly vigorous. The *Southern Literary Messenger*, the South's only literary magazine, was edited and published in Richmond, and for almost two

Although he set only two of his famous stories in Virginia, the life and career of Edgar Allan Poe were deeply entwined with Richmond, where he was raised and educated as a tobacco merchant's foster son and where he later edited the Southern Literary Messenger. **Edgar Allan Poe** *(c. 1860), by Flavius Fisher, from the Valentine, Richmond, Virginia*

years—from March 1835 to January 1837—Poe was editor of the magazine. In his reviews of books on the South, he described the system of permanent bondage as civilized and moral. Poe asserted, "Nothing is wanting but manly discussion to convince our own people at least, that in continuing to command the services of their slaves, they violate no law divine or human. . . . [W]e believe (with our esteemed correspondent Professor Dew) that society in the South will derive much more of good than evil from this much abused partially-considered institution." [11]

Other Richmond writers began early to idealize the Revolutionary generation and cast a sentimental haze over the past. In the 1830s, as Virginia began to defend slavery as a positive good, the term "southern chivalry" appeared for the first time. Romances and histories greatly inflated the number of "Cavaliers" who came to colonial Virginia and likewise diminished the count of indentured servants. James Ewell Heath, who assisted Thomas Willis White—owner and publisher of the *Southern Literary Messenger*—wrote *Edge Hill: or, the Family of the Fitzroyals* (1828), a plantation novel that involved a sentimentalized faithful slave based on the local legend of James Armistead Lafayette, the slave who served as a Revolutionary spy. Such early novels already looked backward nostalgically to a past when blacks had better manners and when relations between the gentry and their slaves took the form of a mutually polite paternalism. [12]

Samuel Mordecai, much-quoted author of *Richmond in By-Gone Days*, participated in this tradition when he noted, "Besides the pride of station, there was a strong attachment generally on the part of servants to their masters and mistresses, and this descended to the next generation and was mutual. The changes which have been brought about in the breaking up of families, by death, misfortune, remote intermarriages, etc., have greatly diminished the number of these respectable domestic establishments." [13] Mordecai's delicate phrasing avoids placing responsibility for the breakup of slave families directly on white owners, but his belief that slave auctions undermined the old paternal relationship was an uneasy thought that occasionally occurred in Richmond.

When Richmonders wrote about their region, they were likely to use the literary forms familiar to them from popular English novels. John Esten Cooke, a Richmond lawyer, modeled the characters in *Ellie*—an 1850s novel of white poverty in Richmond—on the factory waifs of Charles Dickens. The astringent qualities of advice books caused young ladies to prefer the romance novels of Sir Walter Scott. The idea of a "reigning belle" whose very presence drew all the swains of the region became an important part of the image of young white women. The girl so designated became an unofficial "queen of love and beauty" before marriage carried her off to domestic realities and a chair at the edge of the dance floor. Richmonders were also fond of Jane Austen, although Constance Cary Harrison, in a novel of antebellum Virginia life, described young boys who enjoyed reading Walter Scott but "pooh-poohed Miss Austen as rather a dull old thing, who wrote about people you could see just by driving around the county."[14]

Caught between a mythologized past and an uncertain future, Richmond discovered the uses of "chivalry" just as the city began a commercial and industrial expansion that made it among the most diverse and prosperous of antebellum American cities. In these decades, the Tredegar Iron Works and a number of small foundries began the work that made Richmond a center of southern iron manufacture by 1840. At the same time, the number of tobacco factories, often seen as an entrepreneur's dream because they cost little to start up, began to expand. With competition keen, tobacco merchants might fail or be absorbed into a larger firm. The number and size of tobacco factories fluctuated through the 1840s and 1850s.[15]

The success of New York's Erie Canal in connecting eastern port cities with western products encouraged state-financed canal building in other states. The Virginia legislature invested in the James River and Kanawha Canal, although no canal in the United States passed a longer distance through more mountainous terrain than the proposed route from Richmond to the Kanawha River, which connected with the Ohio River. In 1832, the James River and Kanawha Company was chartered as a joint-stock enterprise in an attempt to revive the flagging state effort at connecting Richmond with the Ohio River Valley. Laborers were imported

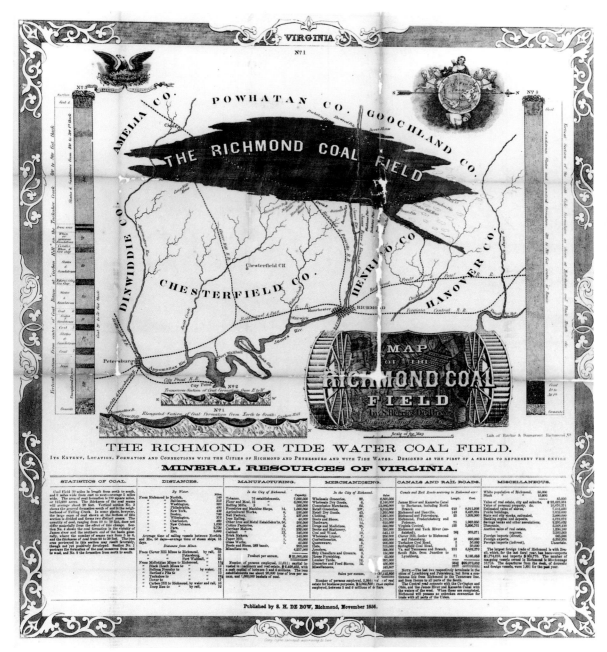

Even as the Richmond coalfields advertised their proximity to Richmond, Petersburg, and the Tidewater ports, their importance was overshadowed by the increasing use of a hard-burning coal found near Scranton, Pennsylvania. This anthracite coal was suited to new methods of iron and steel production, but it was expensive for Richmond to import this new coal, so Richmond industries often found it cheaper to continue old methods. Map of the Richmond coalfields, 1858, courtesy of the Virginia Historical Society, Richmond

from Germany and Ireland to work on the canal, and both free blacks and slaves were hired for the project. That the canal would ever be built across the mountains was a fantasy as compelling and unreal as Christopher Newport's vision of golden cities or the Pacific Ocean just beyond the Appalachian range; that it was built as far as Lynchburg was at least a spur to the local economy.[16]

In the 1830s and 1840s, railroad construction overtook and surpassed canal construction just as the Richmond city council made a major commitment to the canal route to the west. Fewer Richmond citizens invested in the state-sponsored Richmond, Fredericksburg, and Potomac Railroad, which began its first twenty-mile run into the city in 1836. The rail

The 1850s were a period of great prosperity for Richmond's flour mills. The quality of the best flour, which was resistant to mildew and insects, made it very popular with Brazilian markets. In turn, the Brazilians brought coffee to the Richmond docks for national distribution. This 1865 photograph shows the Dunlop Flour Mills. From the Valentine, Richmond, Virginia

lines installed in the 1840s and 1850s provided access to local agriculture but failed to connect Richmond with any major city or other transportation network. During this period the city began construction of a waterworks to replace its springs and wells. The new system employed pumps, more than a mile of street mains, and a million-gallon reservoir. In a year, the system had almost three hundred subscribers.[17]

The late antebellum era saw significant immigration into the city from Ireland and Germany, more hired-out slaves, new homes and factories, and an uneasy jostling for place among the many groups and individuals who made up the growing city. This striving for position was apparent in strikes of white labor against the introduction of black labor; the growth of separate black churches and rival temperance organizations; parades and public appeals by Whigs and Democrats; a third-party movement; a state constitution that enlarged the voting base; and an exponential growth in clubs and societies that were ethnic, religious, and social. Richmond in this era was a laboratory testing the hypothesis that a southern city might continue to grow as other nineteenth-century American cities grew—with new hotels, railroad construction, parks, factories, and agricultural fairs—while maintaining a labor system based on slavery. Before the Civil War interrupted its progress, Richmond showed remarkable ability to adapt.

In diaries, memoirs, and letters written in Richmond during this period, two new terms appear, carefully bracketed by quotation marks—"saloon" and "upper-tendom." A visitor to Richmond wrote: "[I]t was now the height of the ambition to get a 'place' on Shokkoe Hill, which . . . belongs exclusively to 'upper tendom.'" The city chronicler, Samuel Mordecai, commented: "Lager has raised its head and gone ahead of all the other beverages. . . . The number of 'saloons' that bear its name is scarcely exceeded by that of clothing shops, kept also by Germans." New words describe new realities or at least new perceptions of reality. Upper-tendom was not upper-class; it contained an element of striving energy consistent with the machine age. Saloons were places where workers met, especially Irish and German immigrant workers, in new neighborhoods or crowded into old ones. The power of ambition drove the city as much as the power of steam and water, and the city was full of new faces who had come to Richmond to see what its prosperity might mean to them.[18]

Richmond's prominent citizens—merchants, mill owners, lawyers, and government officials—lived in imposing homes on Shockoe Hill or Church Hill. Their families married, attended school, studied law, danced, and took the waters together at the mineral springs. On average their households had four children, similar to prominent families in northern cities, but the homes of these southern civic leaders were usually crammed with domestic slaves and hired servants. Almost half of those who owned domestic slaves found it necessary or economical to hire additional free labor in the household. There were also visiting relatives—perhaps a nephew studying law or an aunt helping out during a convalescence—and boarders, young men working for the head of the household. These patterns of visitation continued a rural tradition and assured country cousins of an introduction to the opportunities of the city. Whether permanent or temporary, their residence in an established household was of benefit to the boarders.[19]

The difference in wealth between the city's traditional elite and the aspiring citizenry was not that great, but the heights and valleys of the city remained symbols of class distinction even as the financial fortunes of Shockoe Hill's old families declined. The children and grandchildren of John Wickham and John Marshall, a numerous tribe, had divided their patrimony into tiny portions. They were important citizens and, for the most part, had comfortable livings, but they and other old Richmond families had to share the industrialized city with new money and new families.[20] Linden Waller reminisced in old age about his antebellum youth: "In old times the boys of Shockoe Hill and the boys of the valley or Butchertown used to fight rock battles, usually on Friday or Saturday afternoons. The boys on the hill were called Hill Cats. Those in the valley Butcher Cats. The former were the sons of the gentlemen, the latter the lower class of the valley."[21]

Richmond's late antebellum prosperity rested on a workforce that was predominantly black and European-born. As Richmond's population grew, new neighborhoods grew up connected to the city's industries. The Shockoe Creek neighborhood, low-lying and near the tobacco warehouses, was home to many of Richmond's free blacks and to industrial slaves who found their own lodging. German and Irish immigrants clustered first in industrial neighborhoods, often living next to free blacks and boarding-out slaves. Many immigrants opened grocery or clothing stores, while free blacks and slaves started small "cookshops" where workers could purchase a quick hot meal. In 1842 William Thalhimer arrived from Germany via Petersburg and opened his first dry-goods store, on Seventeenth Street; after five relocations, the expanded store finally found a home on Broad Street.[22]

Germans moved to the new neighborhoods of Union Hill, Navy Hill, and Oregon Hill, while the Irish moved into Oregon Hill and Fulton. Oregon Hill was a by-product of the growth of nearby Tredegar Iron Works, defined more by iron worker occupation than ethnicity. In 1851, an ex-resident returned and noted that Oregon Hill had "risen from the bosom of the forest" in the 1840s and that as a result, property that "could have been purchased for a mere song is now commanding exorbitant prices." On Union Hill, across Shockoe Creek, Germans built rather more substantial homes and a Sons of Temperance Hall. In the 1850s, a central section of the city around Second, Third, and Fourth Streets attracted both Germans and free blacks.[23]

The saloon in antebellum Richmond grew out of the taverns, grog shops, grocery stores,

This goblet, which was presented to the Virginia Gesangverein, or German Singing Society, in 1860, indicated the extent to which German and other immigrant groups had re-established in Richmond many of the social and cultural institutions from their countries of origin. From the Valentine, Richmond, Virginia

and tippling houses that had always been an indispensable part of city life. Saloons provided more than the furtive tippling house but less than the old-fashioned tavern. As hotels replaced taverns for genteel lodging, saloons became the place where men could gather to eat and drink and exchange information. Grocery stores and saloons took on new functions as German and Irish grocers offered credit during periods of layoff, translated for their countrymen, and acted as cultural mediators for greenhorns.

As the saloon filled one social need, the evangelically based temperance movement, whose members were dedicated to abstaining from alcohol consumption, filled another. The temperance movement did not just draw from rising mechanics and their employers. It found adherents in Richmond among black church members and women of both races, organized into auxiliaries. Richmond had over a thousand avowed temperance advocates by 1834. In the 1840s, a new and more secular temperance group, the Washingtonians, opened their society to all who pledged abstinence and promised to reform, whether they were church members or not. In Richmond, in one instance more than eight hundred people took the Washingtonian pledge and held "experience" meetings in which they chronicled their fall and rise.

The Sons of Temperance, by contrast, used an evangelical model that stressed individual conversion and responsibility. In the 1850s, Sons of Temperance divisions attracted skilled workers, both native-born and immigrant, and among the state officers were two Richmond newspaper editors and a Richmond attorney. Sisters of Temperance and youth divisions were also organized. Temperance offered an entering wedge into respectability and social status by redefining the true gentleman as "moderate, sober, and stable," and it provided fellowship for such gentlemen. Temperance Halls constructed in the city hoped to provide a social alternative to the saloon.[24]

Church societies and associations were a central part of the antebellum sorting-out process by which individuals and families defined themselves, especially as part of an emerging middle class. This identity was available to black participants and was highly influenced by women. The organization of immigrant-based churches and synagogues in Richmond was paralleled by the organization of black churches. From 1840 to 1860, at least five black churches were organized in Richmond. The first and largest, First African Baptist, was organized in 1842, and with over two thousand members it served as a little government unto itself. Its members were subject to being called before the deacons for infractions of rules against drunkenness, fighting, adultery, or bad debts. All of these churches, black and immigrant, produced benevolent and fraternal organizations, like the free black Union Burial Ground Society, organized in 1848, and the German Sick Assistance Association, established in 1841.[25] An important product of evangelicalism, temperance, and benevolence was the rise of an identifiable "respectable" black middle class.

To join one of the African Baptist Churches meant to submit to its discipline and to identify with its doctrines so closely that they became the central narrative of a life. In an 1847 memoir, Fields Cook, a young slave tobacco worker in Richmond, described his feelings as he struggled against conversion: "I went on the dancing florrer which thing I had not done for a long time before and while I stood on the floorer I all at ounce felt such a guilt and shameful feeling come over me that I could not hold myself still and the very first chance I got to slip away from my partnor I done so to go out of door and there I stood looking up toward heaven which appeared to frown vengeance on my head." God, he said, had hooked him, and his soul struggled futilely like "the great rock fish [that] runs off with the line until he is overcome . . . and then taken into the canoe."[26] Cook's conversion experience was the most important event of his life. For the "better sort" of slaves and free blacks, conversion established standards and behavior that set them apart from nonreligious blacks and cut across other distinctions of labor.

Although nearby Petersburg employed black women as tobacco stemmers, the number of women employed in the tobacco factories or cotton mills in Richmond was in steady decline in favor of black males. In 1860, while the percentage of black artisans in Richmond—especially those in the building trades—had dropped below that of earlier decades, half the plasterers in the city and almost one-fifth of the bricklayers were free blacks. Free blacks dominated barbering as well. Increasingly, slaves were hired by the year rather than purchased. Slave hiring was particularly characteristic of tobacco factories but was also common for railroads, canals, and a wide range of businesses, from taverns to blacksmiths.[27]

In tobacco processing, where it was possible to set up a factory in an old church or any dilapidated building, entrepreneurs depended on the cheap labor of slaves and free blacks to provide a profit margin. A thousand new slave workers found employment in the tobacco factories in the 1850s. Competition from the southern cotton fields and from Virginia's agricultural revival in the fifties made hiring slaves more expensive, but it was still more profitable than purchasing them. Much of the time the city ordinances that restricted black activity were not enforced, and daily life proceeded on the basis of what was convenient for employers. While the number of slaves in the city increased, German and Irish immigration caused the white population to grow faster.

Some white citizens were uneasy with the loss of control inherent in urban slavery, but it was too profitable for owners or employers to give up. Schemes that promised to limit black freedom of movement in the city or to prevent slave runaways were occasionally tested. One was the Society for the Prevention of the Abducting and Absconding of Slave Property, an organization of Richmond businessmen who insured each other from the loss of slave property by contributing to a general fund. The owner of a runaway slave would be compensated for his loss from the fund if a detective hired by the society and sent North failed to find the missing slave.[28]

Schemes for an end to reliance on northern products also had a certain popularity, especially among those who advocated southern economic independence from Yankee abolition-

Gilbert Hunt, a slave blacksmith in Richmond, was a hero of the 1811 theater fire, where he caught a dozen women thrown from the burning building. In 1829 Hunt purchased his own freedom through overtime work and left Richmond for Liberia. He returned in a year and lived another generation in the city as a free blacksmith and deacon at First African Baptist Church. This photograph was made in 1859, shortly before his death. From the Valentine, Richmond, Virginia

Richmond's antebellum barbershops were staffed and often owned by free mulattos. Because the barbershop was a center for information, barbers often heard about sympathetic northern shipmasters or the possibility of a police raid; some barbers passed such news on, helping slaves to escape. **Barbershop in Richmond,** *engraving by Eyre Crowe, published in the* London Illustrated News, *9 March 1861, from the Valentine, Richmond, Virginia*

ism. In the 1830s and 1850s, the *Southern Literary Messenger* imagined trade routes connecting the South and a line of steamers running from Virginia to Europe. The *Southern Planter*, published in Richmond, claimed that most of the northern products used in Virginia might be purchased within the state. In late 1850, the Southern Rights Association, a group of businessmen, lawyers, and politicians, organized in Richmond to petition for an end to the sale of northern goods. Their leader, Daniel London, a young dry-goods merchant in the city, suggested that a license should be necessary to trade in northern merchandise and a fine levied for the

CONSTITUTION

OF

THE UNION BURIAL GROUND SOCIETY.

Whereas, we, a portion of the Free Persons of Color of the City of Richmond, feeling a deep interest in the welfare of our race and the importance of advancing in morality, and believing as we do that the formation of a society for the interment of the dead will exert its due weight of influence—we have organized ourselves into a body for the erection of a Burial Ground, and have adopted the following Rules for the government of said body, viz:

Article I. This Society shall be called the "Union Burial Ground Society."

Article II. The land which was bought by Peter Roper for the benefit of the Society, is conveyed to three Trustees chosen by the Society.

Article III. The ground shall be laid off in sections, say fourteen by fourteen feet, and all sections numbered.

Article IV. Any free person can have a section for the sum of ten dollars.

Article V. Each member of the Society shall have and hold a certificate with the number of his section, with a right to inter any person he may think proper; and this certificate at his death, shall entitle his heirs to the same privilege.

Article VI. This Society shall have an interest in some one of the banks of the City fifty dollars, for the purpose of keeping in repair the said land.

Article VII. The certificates shall be printed in blank form—which blanks shall be filled by the Trustees; also a number of the section.

Article VIII. The Officers of this Society shall consist of a President, Vice President, Treasurer, Secretary and nine Managers.

Article IX. The President shall preside in the meetings of the Society; in case of his absence, the Vice President shall fill his chair; and in the absence of both, the members present shall appoint a president pro tem.

Article X. The President shall have power to call a meeting whenever the interest of the Society may require it.

Article XI. Five of the Managers with the President and Secretary, shall form a quorum to do business.

Article XII. The Treasurer of this Society shall be a responsible married man—one who holds real estate—and he shall give his notes for the amount of money or certificates which he may receive.

Article XIII. The Secretary shall keep a regular record of the proceedings of the Society; also, a regular list of the names of the members, with their payments opposite their names; and he shall also keep a number of sections.

Article XIV. The election of officers shall take place annually.

Article XV. There shall be one section appropriated for the burial of strangers.

Article XVI. All alterations or amendments to this Constitution shall be made known at least three months previous to the annual meeting, and be sanctioned by at least two-thirds of the members present, before adopted.

Adopted January 23d, 1848.

NAMES OF THE MEMBERS.

Gilbert Hunt,	Samuel Harris,
Samuel Scott,	James Anderson,
Alpheus Roper,	Ebenezer Roper,
Peter Roper,	Nelson Vanvaul,
James Lightfoord,	John Loney,
Isaac Gwynn,	Sally George,
Tarlton Mose,	William Clayton,
James Booker,	Peter Price,
Braxton Smith,	Archibald Goode,
Richard Brooks,	James Boasmin.

TRUSTEES OF THE BURYING GROUND:

William Lightfoord, James Ellis, Benjamin Harris.

use of northern ships. The association suggested sending two steamers direct to Liverpool; others wanted European capital investment and direct trade with Belgium and the Netherlands. Southern rights, in this context, meant economic independence.[29]

The rhetoric of southern self-sufficiency and independent European trade, with Richmond as the industrial hub, was simply one of the "castles in the air" that boosters and southern nationalists liked to design. Richmond could scarcely afford to advance its canal and railroad ventures to their destinations without outside capital, and steamships were surely beyond

The Union Burial Ground Society established one of several African American cemeteries that were located near a cluster of free black settlements in northwest Richmond. Religious, fraternal, and social organizations proliferated among Richmond's antebellum free blacks and slaves. Leaders in antebellum black organizations were typically artisans, tradesmen, and tradeswomen. Courtesy of the Virginia State Library and Archives, Richmond

To produce the popular plug tobacco of the era, workers would open a hogshead of tobacco and moisten the tobacco leaves. Then the stem was removed and the leaf was twisted and dried. The dried twists were squeezed in a press into a small, compact plug, which was boxed up and shipped out for sale. **Interior of the Seabrook Tobacco Warehouse at Richmond, Virginia,** engraving published in Harper's Weekly, 11 November 1865, from the Valentine, Richmond, Virginia

Just west of the city's boundaries lay a section of land covered with scrub pines and black-berry bushes. Acquired by the city in 1851, it was transformed into a site for a state fair, featuring an annual exhibition of the best in agricultural and mechanical arts. The state fair was an effort by Richmond to draw Virginia into the spirit of progress, optimism, and competition so charac-teristic of the northern states. **Fair Grounds of the Virginia State Agricultural Society** *(1854), lithograph by Ritchie & Dunnavant, Richmond, Virginia; from the Valentine, Richmond, Virginia*

them. Northern capital was needed and so were northern artisans, especially those with a nest egg and an interest in inventing new devices and procedures.

The iron industry in Richmond illustrated the dilemma of industrial growth. Iron production began in earnest in the 1830s, when extension of the James River and Kanawha Canal and three railroad lines began to connect Richmond's coal mines with the iron foundries of the Shenandoah Valley and southwest Virginia, while providing an obvious new market for iron rails and bridge work. By the 1850s, Richmond was the iron producer for the South. The largest and most important of the iron companies was the Tredegar Iron Works, which began as a small foundry, forge, and rolling mill between the James River and the Kanawha Canal. In 1841 the young company, injured by the recession of 1837, called in Joseph Reid Anderson as a commercial agent to attempt to drive the company forward.

Anderson, a young man of modest origins from the Shenandoah Valley, was shrewd, ambitious, and well qualified to run the company. He is a primary example of Richmond's tendency to attract new business leadership from its countryside and then to enfold the successful entrepreneur into the city's highest social and political circles. Anderson first secured federal military contracts for Tredegar to supply chain cable, shot, and shell; then, with a view to fur-

One of the first important industrial sites in Richmond, the Virginia Manufactory of Arms (above, to the left), had a balanced and classical appearance. Iron production grew up around it, especially the Tredegar Iron Works (above, to the right), which in the 1830s began its rise to become the South's primary producer of iron. **View from Gamble's Hill** (1857), lithograph by Edward Beyer published in The Album of Virginia (Berlin: Loeillot, 1857), from the Valentine, Richmond, Virginia

ther contracts, he acquired the equipment necessary for Tredegar to make heavy ordnance. Under Anderson's direction Tredegar soon developed a reputation for quality cast-iron work. Anderson's government contracts brought the company out of recession, and he sought customers in the North and South. He was particularly successful in providing iron for southern railroad construction.

Anderson had a preference for slave labor in heavy construction, a preference he formed while supervising the Shenandoah Valley Turnpike construction in 1839–40. He first brought slaves into the Tredegar mill in 1842 and put them in subordinate positions in the puddling mill. In 1847, Anderson attempted to use slaves as puddlers at the Armory furnace, a facility adjacent to Tredegar that he and his family had just acquired. His action precipitated a strike of white Tredegar and Armory puddlers, heaters, and rollers, who feared that they would be replaced once the slaves acquired skills.

On Saturday, 22 May 1847, workers from both mills told Anderson of their intention to strike. Meeting again on Sunday, they asked for an increase in the price per ton they were paid and resolved not to work until slaves were removed from all positions at the Tredegar and Armory mills. Two days later, perhaps anticipating Anderson's harsh response, they added a resolution noting that they had not raised a mob and did not wish to injure employers but wanted an end to "the employment of colored people in the said Works." The same day, Anderson addressed them through the newspaper as "my late workmen" and said he had not intended to use black puddlers at Tredegar, only at Armory, but now he was forced to do so and all workers who had fired themselves by striking must vacate company-owned housing.[30]

The Richmond press supported Anderson and said any restriction on the use of slave labor would soon destroy the value of slave property. After firing the workers, Anderson took them to court, charging that they had formed an illegal combination "pregnant with [abolition] evils." The stunned and dispirited strikers could only plead innocent of unlawful combination and express regret if they had violated the law. The mayor then dismissed the case. The swift and merciless rout of the strikers was an object lesson to all in Richmond.[31]

The replacement of white workers with black at Tredegar led the city's white mechanics to fear that they would soon become mere competitors of slaves. At pains to separate themselves from antislavery, they declared, "[W]e do not aim to conflict with the interests of the slave owners, but to elevate ourselves as a class from the degrading positions which competition with those who are not citizens of the commonwealth entails on us." These workers sought to be equal members of a white republican society and feared the degradation of status that black competition and connections would bring. They believed that "[t]he mechanic arts are the poor man's inheritance . . . the star of hope to his sons[, enabling them] to stand as fair a chance as any other man to become rich and influential citizens." This was the old rhetoric of the republican artisan, but it had lost its self-confident tone.[32]

Ultimately, the economies of slave labor could not compensate for the inadequacy of the region's raw materials base and production methods. Virginia foundries continued to use charcoal fuel and outmoded techniques, and as a result their production costs remained high. To substitute, Tredegar began to import Pennsylvania pig iron and coal, of a consistently higher quality than the coal produced near Richmond and the iron ore from the Shenandoah Valley. Tredegar also sought skilled northern workers, and by 1860 the mill was dependent on both labor and raw materials from outside the area.[33]

The iron industry was one of four enterprises that dominated Richmond through the

Foundries in Richmond hired significant numbers of slave ironworkers and attracted significant numbers of British and German immigrants as well. In this 1860 photograph, immigrant workers stand outside the Samson & Pea foundry. From the Valentine, Richmond, Virginia

nineteenth century and that reached their peak of profit in the years just before the Civil War. The others were the slave trade and the processing of flour and tobacco. The 1860 census listed almost 1,700 men in iron and metal shops, with sales of $2.3 million. Tredegar claimed half of the employment and sales; the rest was distributed among almost sixty small shops. Flour production was concentrated in a few large mills, which required expensive machinery but fewer workers. By contrast, antebellum tobacco factories used hand labor to process tobacco and needed workers more than machinery. Only tobacco grossed more money than slave trading in the 1850s. Richmond was an important slave market in the upper South, and slaves from the countryside brought to Richmond were usually sold to the South and Southwest.[34]

In 1859, Richmond's seven flour mills and a few others in surrounding counties produced nearly as much as the more than fifty mills in Baltimore. Richmond's largest flour mills, handed down through the Gallego and Chevallie families, found new markets in Latin America after Abram Warwick became manager in 1837; Warwick's mills dominated the Brazilian and Australian markets because their flour maintained its quality in the tropics. Richmond flour mills also enjoyed economies of production. The Gallego mill, it was claimed, occupied the largest physical plant in the world. The fleet of schooners and brigs that carried Richmond's flour around the world returned with enough coffee to make Richmond, in 1860, the nation's largest coffee market.

Tobacco processing in Richmond was spurred by rising prices for tobacco in Europe and

The sale of slave family members away from each other was generally condemned in Richmond, but owners often resorted to it. Either publicly, by auction, or privately, in an office, friends and family could disappear. Margaret Ann Brooks, the daughter of Albert Royal and Lucy Goode Brooks, was sold to Tennessee in 1858 and was never heard from again. **After the Sale: Slaves Going South from Richmond** (c. 1853), by Eyre Crowe, courtesy of the Chicago Historical Society; Margaret Ann Brooks photograph courtesy of Charlotte K. Brooks

by the popularity of a new flue-cured bright leaf tobacco grown in the Piedmont near Richmond. In the early nineteenth century, a handful of tobacco factories in the city produced plug or pipe tobacco, and most of the leaf left the city unprocessed. But tobacco-processing factories grew rapidly, and by the 1840s Richmond had become the largest tobacco production market in the world, with fifty factories, including two cigar manufactories, and related manufacturers like box makers and label printers.

The tobacco factories furnished another example of the growing class division between manufacturing workers and owners or managers. As in the Tredegar Iron Works strike, slave labor was the spark for a confrontation in which owners demonstrated that their first allegiance was to the maintenance of property and production. The tobacco company overseers were native-born white men who were often young and inexperienced. In 1852, a seventeen-year-old black tobacco worker struck and killed a nineteen-year-old overseer who had decided to whip him for an infraction of the rules. At first the slave, Jordan Hatcher, was condemned to death; then, after appeals for clemency by prominent citizens, his sentence was commuted to sale and transportation outside the state. Large crowds of angry and resentful white workers gathered before the governor's home to protest this action, understanding that the governor's commutation had sanctioned the property rights of owners at the expense of white labor.[35]

The petitioners who urged commutation of Jordan Hatcher's sentence were men of influence and standing in Richmond—men who lived high above the tobacco factories where dramas of slave punishment and resistance were played out. Outside the factories, other dramas of establishing place and boundaries were played out on the streets. For those young white men who were not busy with Sunday schools and church societies, military organizations and volunteer fire brigades, which paraded and drilled, offered an opportunity to spend time with other young men. Richmond revived its military units, and new ones were formed in and after the 1830s due to new middle-class involvement. To the early militias, the Richmond Blues and Richmond Greys, were added a half dozen more units and a junior division, each with its own uniform and officers. Irishmen formed the Montgomery Guard and the Hibernian Guard, while Germans formed the Virginia Rifles. The city's various military organizations all joined forces to sponsor dances and parades.[36]

A revolution in women's wear took place as expensive European-made fabric and clothing gave way to domestic production and the advent of the dry-goods store, which sold cloth and sewing accessories. While quality of fabric and skill in construction varied greatly, fashion magazines and papers were available to a wide range of women, and in terms of style, the advent of the sewing machine further blurred class distinctions. Left, Valentine and Breeden sewing notions sample, 1842; top right, upper-class dress of brown brocaded silk, trimmed with brown silk fringe, c. 1855; bottom right, working-class dress of plaid cotton, c. 1860. From the Valentine, Richmond, Virginia

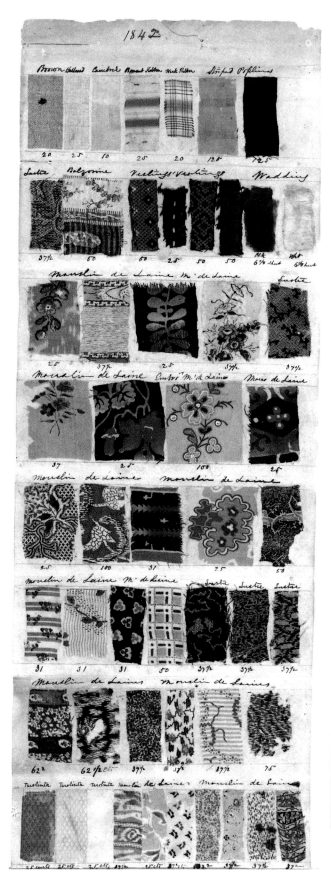

The city's volunteer fire companies provided another opportunity for both camaraderie and service. They attracted white mechanics and clerks, who elected officers, hosted picnics and dinners, and paraded with banners on their decorated engines. The engines were pulled by slaves who had permission to answer the fire bell. Crowds of young men, called "runners," followed the fire companies to fires. More boisterous than the militia units, and with less social status, fire companies often fought among themselves and occasionally turned the hoses on bystanders. This rowdiness threatened the safety of the town as well as the reputations of firefighters, and in the late 1850s the firefighters petitioned to eliminate the slave firemen and to become paid city employees. By 1858, they had effectively achieved this status.[37]

More ambivalent were the social boundaries surrounding the city's slave traders, some at the margins of respectability, others important businessmen and members of the Common Council. The sale of supplies to traders leading coffles or trainloads of slaves southward was important to the city's economy. Both buyers and sellers lodged and dined at local hotels; local government taxed dealers and slave pens; and local businessmen, for a percentage of the hire, served as agents for slave owners who rented their slaves out by the year.[38]

The highly public and often ritual-based style of so many city organizations was reflected in city politics. Once the Whig Party was formed, in the early 1830s, Richmond became a Whig city, usually in opposition to the Democratic Party of Andrew Jackson and Martin Van Buren. Despite Thomas Ritchie's nationally influential position as the Democratic editor of the *Richmond Enquirer*, city government remained in the hands of Whigs who were interested in promoting Richmond's commerce and industry within a stable union. They saw the influx of immigrants into the city as proof that slave labor could coexist with white artisans. City Democrats were so sparse they were called "the Spartan band."

In the 1840s, Whigs and Democrats vied for popular support, enlisting as many enthusiastic partisans as would appear for rallies, processions, barbecues, and speeches. The Whigs built a log cabin in the city and held their meetings there, imitating the Democrats' appeal to the common man as voter by stressing the humble origins of the Whig candidates from Virginia, William Henry Harrison and Henry Clay. In late 1844, after Clay's presidential defeat, women who met at the First Presbyterian Church organized the Virginia Association of

Ladies for Erecting a Statue to Henry Clay. They justified their political activity on the basis of their roles as mothers of citizens, but that republican language now encompassed the role of Richmond women in the processions and public rituals of the second-party system, both as symbols of the new American domesticity and for their demonstrated skills as social organizers. In the generation since the virginal and decorative "Lafayette girls" were the primary female presence in public and political ritual, Richmond women had acquired a more substantive presence. In an intensified market economy, where greater weight was given to private benevolence, women's political activity developed naturally from the charitable and religious societies through which Richmond women had chipped away at the barriers separating them from public participation.[39]

Another group of Richmond residents was also concerned with the barriers that separated them from public participation. In 1850 a Virginia Constitutional Convention, brought about by those who remained dissatisfied with the modest changes of 1829, finally established white male suffrage and made most state offices elective. A reluctant city council accepted the popular desire to drop property qualifications for voting, encouraging the emergence of new-style candidates with a working-class constituency. One of them, Martin Meredith Lipscomb, a bricklayer and rousing stump speaker, won a race for city sergeant in 1854. Lipscomb said he won because he went out and met the people "in their republican gatherings."[40] His supporters celebrated his victory by parading through the streets waving torches, blowing horns and whistles, and banging pots. Lipscomb was the first of many self-made and working-class politicians to arrive on the public stage with a message delivered in the language of republicanism and democracy, which exalted artisans and echoed the words of "Mechanic." Yet that world had changed irrevocably since 1817, and the working men elected to city council, although often ridiculed by the newspapers for their lack of education and style, were the shrewd survivors of an economic revolution that had dealt less generously with other artisans.

For the second time in the short history of the young republic, the national party system began to break down. Again, Richmond had been loyal to the party that disappeared. For Richmond, the fragmentation of the Whigs was more ominous than the earlier decline of the Federalists. When the Whig effort to remain a national party despite regional divisions over

In 1858, the remains of President Monroe were brought from New York to Hollywood Cemetery by honor guards from both New York and Richmond. The camaraderie and warm sentiments exchanged at their banquet would be replaced within three years by serious efforts on both sides to fill all the gravesites in Boston and Richmond with each other's bodies. **Grand Banquet Given to the Seventh Regiment and the Richmond Volunteers, in the Warwick Mill, by the City of Richmond, Virginia,** engraving published in Frank Leslie's Illustrated Newspaper, *31 July 1858, from the Valentine, Richmond, Virginia*

slavery failed, city politicians feared that Richmond's prosperous alliance of slavery and industry would be lost with the emergence of hot-headed sectionalists in the North and South. In the nation's widening division over slavery and the constitutional issues of states' rights, the city's businessmen feared both northern abolitionists and southern fire-eaters.

The American, or Know-Nothing, Party of the 1850s—a national anti-immigrant and nativist movement—could not replace the Whigs in Richmond on the basis of opposition to immigrants. Richmond had courted immigrants and the newspapers had praised them. Richmond's American Party represented not so much an anti-immigrant stance as a desperate attempt by local Whigs to stay distinct from Democrats and remain part of a national party coalition. The only attacks on the foreign-born came from the occasional suspicion that they might be sympathetic to abolition.[41]

The American Party faded quickly in Richmond, and the new Republican Party left many Richmond Whigs with no place to go. As the crisis of the union approached at the end of the decade, the city had just experienced its own political upheaval. In 1860, there were three times as many voters in city elections as there had been in 1850. City council elections had become a lively area of debate, with colorful candidates, mass appeals, and newspaper coverage. But just as the city might have reflected with some satisfaction on its thorough-going transformation into a northern-style industrial city, with politics to match, John Brown's attack on the federal armory at Harpers Ferry reminded Richmond again of its geographic position.

In October 1859, Gov. Henry Wise received word that the national armory at Harpers

Members of Richmond's militia companies were dispatched to Harpers Ferry in October 1859 in response to John Brown's attempted raid on the federal armory there. Militia companies grew in number during the 1850s as Irish and German Richmonders formed new companies based on ethnicity to rival the old Richmond Blues and Richmond Greys. Photograph from a daguerreotype of the Richmond Greys, 1859, and shakoe with epaulets, both from the Valentine, Richmond, Virginia

Ferry was under siege from a mixed group of abolitionists and free blacks. The governor sent militia units to Harpers Ferry, where they were too late to participate in the capture of Brown and his supporters. Richmond newspapers reported rumors of abolitionist-inspired slave revolts and of a general northern conspiracy against the institution of slavery in all the southern states. The *Richmond Enquirer* predicted secession, and Governor Wise again ordered up militia units, this time to protect Virginia against the armed abolitionists rumored to be approaching Harpers Ferry.

More substantial were the concerns reflected in legal restrictions on slave activity, which culminated in "An Ordinance Concerning Negroes," enacted in 1859. This ordinance reflected the realities of urban slavery while attempting to suppress them. Blacks were to carry passes or free papers at all times; slaves were not to rent rooms or houses, hire themselves out, buy medicine or liquor, join or attend secret societies, own guns, or gather in groups. They were not to ride in carriages or walk in Capitol Square or near the city spring or City Hall. The legal code even included elaborate regulations of behavior on the sidewalk in order to reinforce white authority: "A negro meeting or overtaking, or being overtaken by a white person on a sidewalk, shall pass on the outside; and if it be necessary to enable such white person to pass, shall immediately get off the sidewalk."[42]

Concurrent with this furor, the Virginia Association of Ladies for Erecting a Statue to Henry Clay finally received the statue of Henry Clay for which they had contracted in 1846. They requested and received permission to place it on the public square in front of the capitol portico. The monument to the Great Compromiser was dedicated with military bands, American flags, and patriotic speeches on 12 April 1860 before a crowd of 20,000. Just a year later, Richmond prepared to leave the union that Clay had worked to hold together. With all its bustle and diversity and its affinity with a national urban culture, Richmond was about to become the backdrop for a southern drama played out on a grand stage.

CHAPTER SIX

Confederate Richmond

In the late afternoon and early evening of 12 April 1861, clusters of men milled about near Main and Franklin, at Twelfth and Thirteenth streets, where the city's newspapers had their offices, close to the busy slave auctions at the Odd Fellows Hall and Lumpkin's Jail. In the crowd were dusty, sunburned farmers who rode into the city from nearby counties. They talked with pale, bewhiskered men in slouch hats who jabbed the air with a cigar or spit tobacco emphatically to punctuate their opinions. Any activity within the newspaper offices caused the crowd of men to press forward in the expectation that a bulletin might be posted. At the office of the *Richmond Whig*, a coastal survey chart of Charleston Harbor was pinned up with battery positions marked.

Several of the town's most esteemed citizens could be seen uncharacteristically loitering in the streets. Members of the statewide convention, which had been in session since February, came out of the nearby Ballard and Exchange Hotels to see if they could purchase, from the free blacks and slaves who sold them, a small, half-page newspaper extra. They sought some information on the confrontation in the Charleston, South Carolina harbor where Pres. Abraham Lincoln's policy toward secession would be tested as Lincoln weighed his responsibility to defend the federal Fort Sumter against the possibility of pushing the Upper South states, especially Virginia, into the Confederacy.

Delegates to the convention, in its third month of deliberation on the issue of Virginia's secession from the Union, approached the crowded streets warily. The mood of the crowds had shifted rapidly in the past few days, and the convention's reluctance to ratify secession now had many of those on the street corners muttering against them. An alternative convention, called the "People's Convention" or "Spontaneous Convention," had been organized by ex-governor Henry Wise and other southern rights fire-eaters impatient for secession. Scheduled to meet in Metropolitan Hall on the next Tuesday, 16 April, it threatened to declare itself empowered to take Virginia out of the Union by virtue of popular opinion if the duly elected convention did not cease its debating and act.

Newspaper extras arrived on the streets to confirm the rumors that Confederate forces had fired on the Union soldiers and officers at Fort Sumter. Williams C. Wickham, a delegate to the convention from nearby Henrico County, read of the attack with grim dismay. Wickham was a strong Union man who had voted against secession. From a family that had long been

Federalist or Whig, Wickham was both a planter and a railroad investor and saw Virginia's future in commerce and in alliances with northern businesses. Wickham still hoped for some signal that this encounter was another false alarm; forty years of firebells in the night with no conflagration had bred a certain cynical optimism into most Americans, especially southern Unionists.[1]

The city of Richmond had long resisted the more extreme manifestations of southern states'-rights politics, slow to lose its conviction that sectional differences could be worked out within the Union. Despite the collapse of the Whig Party, political competition continued at the state level, and confidence remained that the national political system would provide enough leverage to protect Virginia's interests. While much of the South seemed fearful that the region would lose its political and economic power within the Union, bustling Richmond had just finished a decade of growth that made the residents optimistic, despite the doleful political forebodings of the city's newspapers—forebodings that had grown more intense since John Brown's raid on the federal armory at Harpers Ferry some sixteen months before.

The election of 1860 further frayed the bonds that held the Union together. At the Democratic National Convention, delegates from the lower South withdrew and nominated John C. Breckinridge of Kentucky for president, while northern Democrats, meeting in Baltimore, nominated Stephen A. Douglas. Unhappy with both candidates and with sectional politics, Upper South moderates formed the Constitutional Union Party and nominated John Bell of Tennessee. The founders were Unionist Whigs who wanted a conservative but national party that avoided slavery agitation. Bell carried only the states of Virginia, Kentucky, and Tennessee, but in Richmond he was the choice by a margin of two to one. The city's voters showed themselves to be overwhelmingly ex-Whigs opposed to secession. In fact, those northern and southern cities with strong commercial ties to each other voted in 1860 for the "moderate" candidates, Douglas and Bell. They rejected Lincoln and Breckinridge, whom they saw as purveyors of a rending sectional politics.[2]

Abraham Lincoln, the candidate of the Republican Party, won the election but without a single southern electoral vote. South Carolina immediately drafted an act of secession, and by the end of the year had left the Union, followed by six other states in the Lower South. Virginia and the other states of the Upper South hesitated. An editorial letter in the *Richmond Daily*

Examiner for 3 December 1860 expressed their fear: "For the first time since the union was formed we have seen a president nominated and elected, so far as the popular voice is concerned, by a sectional party—a party founded in hostility to the institution of slavery which exists in nearly half the states in the union."[3]

In the view of most Richmond business and professional men, any breakup of the republic would be financially disastrous and politically unwise. The only part of the secessionist argument that acted as a siren call upon their reason was the prospect that Richmond might become the cotton-manufacturing center of a new southern nation. It was pleasing to contemplate the spindles of Lowell and Manchester silenced as northern artisans moved south, but for most citizens the vision was not ultimately convincing.

In this crisis, there was a curious divergence between Richmond's citizens and its newspapers. The newspapers' rhetorical defense of slavery had helped create and support a closed social and intellectual system in the South. Certain editors were deeply and personally invested in these arrangements, while most businessmen had conducted their enterprises with little concern for ideology or justification of the South's institutions. In the months after Lincoln's election, Richmond was the center of intense activity to prevent dissolution of the Union, even as newspaper editors—especially John M. Daniel, editor of the *Examiner*, and George W. Bagby, the new editor of the *Southern Literary Messenger*—urged that Virginia follow South Carolina out of the Union. Bagby argued that a defense of slavery was a defense of republican institutions and described the South as an idyllic world threatened by Yankee aggression.

At a special legislative session in January 1861, Governor Letcher summarized the situation more gloomily: "Surely no people have been blessed as we have been, and it is melancholy to think that all is now about to be sacrificed on the Altar of Passion." Letcher believed secession to be legal, but he also believed it to be a mistake. The Virginia legislature took two actions: it called for elections to a special convention to decide the issue of secession and sponsored a Peace Convention in Washington to attempt to reach a compromise. Secession provoked the immediate crisis, but the efforts at finding a compromise revolved around the core issue of slavery. The Peace Convention failed, and the Richmond papers labeled the delegates "traitors."[4]

With two of three opposed to secession, Richmond's delegates to the Secession Convention reflected the balance of opinion in the state. George Wythe Randolph, grandson of Thomas Jefferson, favored secession, while Marmaduke Johnson and William H. McFarland were Union men. Convened in early February, the convention did not vote until 4 April, when it voted against secession. A few days later, all the factors—complex loyalties of region and nation, questions of the state's economic identity and future, and the role of slavery in Virginia—narrowed to the question of whether or not Lincoln and the federal government would attempt to re-provision a small island garrison off the South Carolina coast. As the Secession Convention awaited Lincoln's decision, the newspapers, which inflamed passions through their editorials, subjected delegates to intense pressure. Described in the *Richmond Examiner* as a "curly-haired poodle almost overcome with dignity and fat," convention delegate Marmaduke Johnson shot at editor John Daniel on the street. Daniel returned the fire, and Johnson was placed under a peace bond.[5]

On Saturday, 13 April, news of the firing on Fort Sumter and its surrender to a Confederate military force spread through the city. A large and restless crowd of armed men, encouraged by members of the People's Convention, moved up the canal bank to the Tredegar Iron Works and raised the Confederate Stars and Bars. The Fayette Artillery gathered for a one-hundred-gun salute, then the crowd pushed onto the capitol grounds to replace the American flag, despite reminders by Governor Letcher that Virginia was still in the Union. That evening, bonfires, impromptu parades, illuminated houses, and firecrackers expressed the enthusiasm for secession, and Confederate flags were displayed in windows and flown from flagstaffs.

The secession convention still hesitated. On Monday, 15 April, President Lincoln called for eight thousand Virginia men to put down the rebellion. The People's Convention met on Tuesday and gave the elected state delegates one more day to vote to leave the Union. The delegates did so and thus kept ex-governor Wise and his allies from fomenting open rebellion. Over ten thousand Richmonders poured into the streets on 19 April for a massive torchlight procession, with bands playing, crowds singing, southern flags flying, and Roman candles and rockets blazing in the night sky. In the enthusiasm and emotion of the moment, those who had reservations kept them to themselves. Two days later, the false alarm known as "Pawnee

Sunday" demonstrated the high pitch of emotion and perhaps the overwrought nerves of the city. Bells tolled as the rumor spread that the Union gunboat *Pawnee* was on its way up the James to bombard the city. Thousands of Richmond men armed with ancient sabers, blunderbusses, and kitchen knives moved toward Rocketts to defend the city against a nonexistent enemy. Local politician Martin Meredith Lipscomb, later implicated as a Union spy, guided a heavy wagon to the Virginia Armory, where he loaded up several ornamented brass guns that had been in place there since Lafayette's visit and put them in front of the post office.[6]

The Confederate government, organized in Montgomery, Alabama, sent its vice president, Alexander Stephens, to urge Virginia into the Confederacy and to offer Richmond the capital. Before the end of April the Secession Convention had ratified the Confederate constitution and invited the government to Richmond. Virginia's central importance in the history of the nation gave legitimacy and continuity to the Confederacy, and Richmond's finance and industry provided the means for waging war. In 1860, Richmond was the nation's twenty-fifth largest city, but it ranked thirteenth in manufactures. Richmond had four major banks, with a combined capital of $10 million. Its fifty-two tobacco factories grossed $5 million in 1860; its flour mills engaged in international trade, and one of them was considered the largest such mill in the world. Central to the Confederacy were the productive capacities of the Tredegar Iron Works and the city's other, smaller iron-manufacturing companies. Five railroad lines entered the city. For a city of two and one-half square miles with 38,000 inhabitants, of whom 14,275 were slaves and free blacks, Richmond had disproportionate resources and capacities.[7]

To this city, early on the morning of 29 May 1861, came the Confederate government in the form of a train from Petersburg carrying Jefferson Davis and his family and entourage. Governor Letcher and Richmond mayor Joseph Mayo went to Petersburg to ride into Richmond with them. As guns were fired and the crowd cheered, Davis made his way to temporary headquarters in the Spottswood Hotel, and Richmond became the capital of the Confederacy.

The history of Richmond as the capital of the Confederacy is not the history of battles, except as those battles pressed on the city or filled the streets with prisoners and wagons of wounded men. Nor is it the history of military strategy or rivalries in the Confederate cabinet. It is the story of what happened to Richmond and its people—how a war effort much

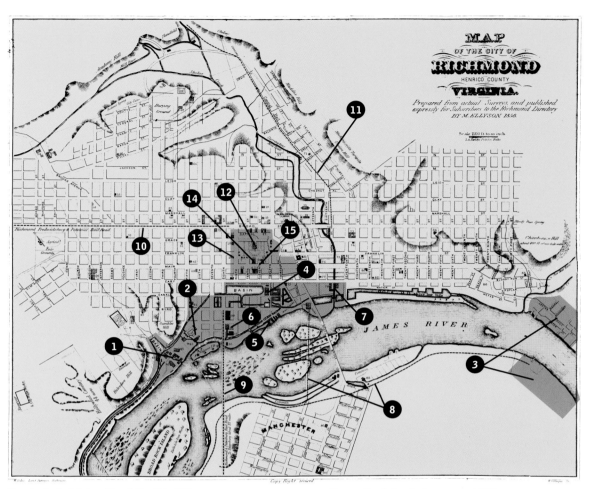

Despite its proximity to the North and to Washington, Richmond made a logical Confederate capital because of its industries and transportation networks. When the war began, many existing buildings were converted to support government offices and the Confederate Congress. **Map of the City of Richmond** *(1856), by M. Ellyson (from the Valentine, Richmond, Virginia), with information from Richard M. Lee, General Lee's City (McLean, Va.: EPM Publications, 1987).*

Purple: Industrial and Logistical Facilities

1 Tredegar Iron Works	7 Talbotts Foundry
2 Virginia Manufactory of Arms	8 Richmond and Danville RR
3 Confederate Navy Yard	9 Richmond and Petersburg RR
4 Gallego Mills	10 Richmond, Fredericksburg, and Potomac RR
5 Columbia Mills	11 Central RR
6 Franklin Paper Mill	

Green: Confederate Government Offices

12 Virginia State Capitol (meeting place of Confederate Congress)
13 Mechanic's Hall (Confederate War and Navy Departments)
14 Former U.S. Customs House (offices of President Davis and Secretary of State)
15 Grouping of Confederate Quartermaster, Commissary, and Ordnance offices on Main and Bank streets; some on Cary Street

more demanding and encompassing than anything imagined in the spring of 1861 altered the city's landscape. It is the story of some residents' great and creative ingenuity and the weight of accumulated distresses that pressed others down. It is the story of a city inundated with new people—soldiers, refugees, runaways, grifters, patriots, prostitutes, and correspondents from European newspapers. All competed for space, for food, for news. As in other wartime cities, people tried to continue their lives, but inevitably, all became caught up in the crisis of the war and found their lives deeply changed.

Wartime necessity called for the talents and labor of every Richmond resident, including white women and African Americans, traditionally barred from activity in the public sphere, from civic accomplishment, and from most wage labor. In the next four years, women worked in munitions factories, hospitals, offices, and stores. The skills of slaves and free blacks made the war effort against an industrially advanced North possible. A polyglot crowd with a thousand diverse private concerns mingled on the streets as never before. Yet this wartime intensity and change did not represent a marked difference from the past. Those who were now asked to come forward and do their best for the Confederacy, in the absence of white males, could not have been as successful as they were had it not been for their earlier efforts to assert and establish themselves in the antebellum city.

During the chaotic summer of 1861, Americans tried to sort themselves into two nations. As flags were designed, uniforms sewn, and troops drilled, Richmond drew refugees from the North as well as Confederate congressmen and their families from the South. Some families left for the North, while others from the federal armory at Harpers Ferry came to work in the newly reopened Virginia Manufactory of Arms. Many residents of border states—especially Maryland—moved southward, and some came from farther north. J. B. Jones, a journalist and editor, was living in New Jersey when Fort Sumter fell; he left immediately for the Confederacy.

Three different governments now contended for power and space in Richmond. The Confederate government exercised a certain imperial reach, and the city council made every early effort to be accommodating. In the first flush of southern patriotism, the Virginia legislature played gracious host and offered buildings, offices, and homes to the Confederacy. Jefferson Davis and his family were invited to use the handsome Clay Street structure known as the Brockenbrough house as the White House of the Confederacy, and Davis accepted this offer. As time passed, the Virginia legislature and its delegates to the Confederate Congress—soon to include former Unionist Williams C. Wickham—occasionally opposed that body, but they seldom supported the city in its efforts to care for its own residents before meeting Confederate needs, and Richmonders could not go home in a huff when they felt the Confederacy infringed on their state and local rights.

The Union embargo of the Virginia coast prevented badly needed tools and replacement parts from reaching the city. The countryside around Richmond was often the scene of battles, which prevented farmers from entering the city with produce, but by far the greatest obstacle to a dependable distribution of goods was the disorganization and overlapping functions among Confederate bureaus and Richmond city government offices. The struggle between governing entities and the ultimate lack of centralized control or authority in the city caused several important enterprises to seek their own self-sufficiency. Chimborazo and Winder hospitals and Tredegar Iron Works, for example, created small farms within the city to provide for their own workers' needs, because they could not depend on government distribution or private sellers for their foodstuffs or supplies.

The war at first appeared to be an economic boon to the city. It brought wealthy southerners who spent money for lodging and food. It brought contracts to local businesses to produce goods for the Confederacy. The value of all space and all objects increased rapidly. Business and industry expanded, although lack of access to raw materials, inflated currency and, to a lesser extent, lack of manpower always hampered them. These limitations grew more severe as the war progressed. However, Richmond had two important advantages that persisted almost until the end of the conflict. One was the urban black work force; the other was the agricultural production of the surrounding countryside. Virginia farms and plantations, now often run by women and slaves, produced grain and foodstuffs in abundance until the last year of the war.

Order and calm were the war's first casualties. Public spaces in the city took on new uses, and within months the overcrowded city had been divided into spheres of war. The tents of training encampments filled the parks and fairgrounds, and commandeered federal, state, and private buildings provided offices for Confederate departments. The capitol building was divided between the Confederate Congress and the Virginia General Assembly and also housed a Virginia Constitutional Convention, which was trying to adapt the 1850 constitution to the altered circumstances, and the governor's office. The U.S. Customs House became the Confederate Treasury, and the Mechanic's Institute was turned into the War Department Building. Members of the Confederate Congress and the five cabinet-level departments of the executive branch vied for living quarters. Military officers, attachés, job seekers, and businessmen filled the hotels and boardinghouses of the city. A slim, string-bound city directory justified its publication by declaring, "The immense amount of business arising from the prosecution of the war has been distributed among a large number of departments, bureaux, etc., which are located in so many different places that persons having business at some of them are unable to find them, except by persistent inquiry."[8]

Families of Confederate officials found homes near the capitol or on Church Hill. Laborers moved into crowded shanties along Shockoe Creek and the James River, while reinforcements for the demimonde found Locust Alley brothels and upstairs gambling dens. New and expanding industrial plants sprawled across the landscape. Captured Union soldiers occupied warehouses, slave pens, and islands in the James River; railroad tracks laid in new streets connected previously independent lines. The Medical College of Virginia became a hospital, and its staff and students found their every resource tested.

Both North and South believed the war would be of short duration—a conviction reinforced by the Confederate victory at Manassas, Virginia, on 21 July 1861. This skirmish between unprepared troops on both sides seemed to confirm the Confederates' confidence in their ability to send the Yankees running, but the casualties brought into the city by ambulance, stretcher, and train chilled much of the euphoria. The casualties of First Manassas quickly overwhelmed the existing hospitals, and the sick and wounded were put up everywhere—in homes, hotels, barns, and churches. The Confederate Surgeon General, Dr. Samuel Preston Moore, sought even more space. The newly constructed almshouse was rented from the city as a hospital; tobacco factories and the empty St. Charles Hotel were also utilized. Seabrook's Warehouse, which lay on a railroad line from the Manassas battlefield, became a receiving hospital.

In time, there were hospitals in Main Street saloons and Manchester and Union Hill Temperance Halls. There were special hospitals for gangrene and smallpox. A prison hospital named Castle Thunder, in a tobacco company building on Cary Street, included a section for mental cases, and a hospital in the Engineering Bureau at Nineteenth and Cary cared for black laborers working on fortifications.[9]

The Confederate government initially ordered the construction of five general hospitals in Richmond; Camps Winder and Chimborazo, the largest, were located on vacant land at the east and west edges of the city. Both became self-sufficient enterprises with wooden barracks or houses, gardens and groves of trees, pastures and canal boats. Set on a flat plain of forty acres high above the James River, Chimborazo had good drainage and fresh spring water and could easily receive supplies from the James River. Opened in October 1861, it quickly became a village of the wounded, keeping goats and cattle on nearby Tree Hill Farm and gathering

On the eastern edge of Richmond, on the high, flat plain called Chimborazo, the Confederacy produced a near-miracle of self-sufficiency and high recovery rates at the Chimborazo Hospital (seen in the background of this photograph). Dr. James McCaw, the surgeon in chief, was aided by white women hospital matrons and nurses; by slave and free black nurses, both male and female; and by male orderlies, who included slaves and convalescing veterans. Photograph by Mathew Brady, courtesy of the Library of Congress

produce from its own garden. The hospital had five separate divisions, each with its own laundry, kitchen, and bathhouse; it had a central bakery and dairy. Located on the grounds were five icehouses and a "Russian bath house." Nearby tobacco factories were converted into soup kitchens for Chimborazo, and the hospital even had its own trading boat, *The Chimborazo,* which traveled the Kanawha Canal, gathering provisions.[10]

In charge at the hospital was Dr. James McCaw, who had been chief surgeon at the Medical College of Virginia before the war. He was responsible for many of the creative adaptations that permitted the hospital to overcome the shortages created by constant warfare in the surrounding countryside and the inefficiencies of the Confederate Quartermaster General. In 1862, faced with a shortage of hospital staff, the Confederate government authorized the hiring of females as matrons and ward attendants. While women had long been the home caretakers for sick and injured family, a military hospital was thought to be an improper place for respectable women because of its masculine atmosphere and intensely physical work. As in other areas, wartime necessity soon overcame these reservations, and white women joined the black men and women already engaged in hospital work.

Phoebe Yates Pember, an intelligent and resourceful young widow from a well-known South Carolina family, was typical of the women hired. Pember, a matron at Hospital Num-

No.	Date of Admitted	Names.	Rank.	Co.	Regiment.	Nature of Disease.	Furloughed. Date. Time.	1865 Returned Duty.	Transferred. When. Where.	Died.	Remarks.
	Dec. 17	Chas. Scott.	Private	2nd	Rich. Howitzer	Syphilitic Psoriasis.		Feb. 7th/65			
	" "	W. B. Smith.	Captain	K	24th Va. Cav.	Chronic Diarrhea.		Jan. 16th			
	" 18	" Bowling.	Private	A	2nd Md. Inf.	Apoplectic Tendency.			Feb. 16/65 Chimborazo		
	" "	Jas. Davidson.	"	D	7th N. Car.	Pneumonia.			Jan. 21st Charlotte N. C.		
	" "	R. J. Crawford	"		Mosby's Batt.	Haemorrhoids.		Feb. 10th			
	" 24	Stiles Kennedy	Surg.		8th N. Carolina	Purunculus.		Jan. 3rd			
	Jan. 3	E. W. James.	Med. Purveyor's Office.			Delirium Tremens.		" 14th		Died April 29/65 Jan. 12 Discharged.	
	" "	Jno. Crumley.	Private	K	59th Virginia	Chronic Diarrhea.					
	" 7	Chas. Brady.	"	F	2nd Va. Reserve	Typhoid fever.		Feb. 1st/65			
	" "	Willis Lawhorn.	"		Lawhorn's Arty.	Intermittent fever.		Jan. 16th			
	" "	Isaac Hall.	"	I	20th S. Carolina	Chronic Diarrhea.		" "			
	" 9	Jno. Quinn.	"	C	2nd Md. Cav.	Diabetis Mellitus.				Mch. 5/65	
	" "	L. T. Dickenson.	"	A	1st "	Dyspesia.			Feb. 15 Gordonsville		
	" 10	Chas. Fiege	"		2nd " Inf.	Intermittent fever.			" 18 Chimborazo		
	" 12	Townley Roby.	Sgt.	E	1st Cav.	Typhoid		Feb. 14th			
	" 13	Isaac Eve.	Private	A	60th Va.	Int.			" 15 do		
	" "	R. B. Beery.	Sgt.	"	" "	" "			" 16 do		
	" 15	J. M. King.	Captain	C	13th La.	Amputation of right leg.	Feb. 22 60		Jan. 18th Ex. Board Off.		[Pris.]
	" 16	W. T. Hixson.	Private	B	20th Ga.	Pneumonia.	Feb. 18 60				
	" "	Young Harris.	"	E	9th "	Int. fever.		Feb. 4th/65			
	" "	W. H. Wilkes.	"		Huger's Arty.	Pneumonia.			Feb. 17 Chimborazo		
	" 18	W. R. McKnew.	Asst. Sur.	1st	Md. Cav.	Remit. fever.			Jan. 27th Stewart Hos.		
	" 20	N. J. Milhardo.	Sgt.		Signal Corps.	Chronic Diarrhea.		Jan. 31st			
	" "	Wm. Couch.	H. S.	Med. Pur. Off. A. N. Va.		Perineal abscess.		Feb. 1st			
	" "	Thos. A. Smith.	Private	2nd	Rich. Howitzer	V. S. right leg.	Jan. 24th 60				Dover Mills Va.
	" 22	E. W. James.	"		Med. Pur. Off.	Delirium Tremens.	Feb. 7th				
	" 23	J. R. Herbert.	Lt. Col.	2nd	Md. Inf.	Dyspesia	" 8th 60				[Pri.] S.O. 33 Par. X Hd. Qr. A. N. V.
	" 24	Chas. Dooley.	Private	1st	Rich. How.	Rheumatism.	Mch. 20 60	1	Feb. 15 Emory Henry		
	" 31	G. T. Jenkins.	"		1st Md. Batt.	Debilitas.			Dec. 13 Howards Grove		
	" "	H. M. Adams.	"	C	48th Miss.	V. S. Right side of lower maxilla					
	Feb. 1st 2nd	F. A. Dickens.	"	A	6th Va. Cav.	foot.		Feb. 17th			
	" "	R. J. Harris.	"		33rd N. Car.	left side of lower maxilla		Feb. 4th	Camp Winder.		

Throughout the war, contagious diseases and exposure-related illnesses filled the hospitals with soldiers. Casualties were brought from nearby battlefields to Richmond hospitals, but even between military encounters, the hospitals stayed full with the deadly effects of camp life. Patient registry courtesy of the Eleanor S. Brockenbrough Library, The Museum of the Confederacy, Richmond, Virginia

ber 2, kept a diary of her hospital years and sometimes recorded her annoyance with the Richmond ladies who thought she had sacrificed her status by her work. In 1861, Sally L. Tompkins rented a house at Third and Main, which she equipped at her own expense and opened as a hospital. She became famous for her patients' rate of recovery, and President Davis appointed her a captain in the Confederate army.

Sarah Rice Pryor, assigned to work with nurses on a twelve-hour day shift, was given "the promise of night service should I be needed," and observed, "Efficient, kindly colored women assisted us. Their motherly manner soothed the prostrate soldier, whom they always addressed as son." Neither white matrons and nurses, nor slave nurses, nor hired disabled veterans attempted the more strenuous and difficult nursing work at the hospitals. That work—lifting, washing, clothing, and carrying patients—was done by hired black men, both slave and free.[11]

Prisons filled almost as rapidly as hospitals after First Manassas and expanded regularly after each major battle within a wide range of the city. The prisoners were put in converted warehouses and factories. The warehouse and ship chandlery belonging to the estate of Luther Libby became Libby Prison. As the number of prisoners increased, only officers stayed in buildings, while enlisted men tented on Belle Isle. Richmond was at first seen as a way station for prisoners of war, but bureaucracy, war conditions, and lack of anywhere else to send them

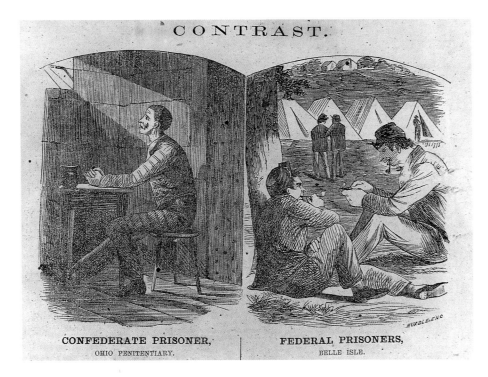

CONTRAST.

CONFEDERATE PRISONER,
OHIO PENITENTIARY.

FEDERAL PRISONERS,
BELLE ISLE.

The tents of Union army prisoners covered Belle Isle in the James River. As the war progressed, the number of prisoners grew, and conditions deteriorated in all prison camps. Food and clothing were inadequate, and disease spread through polluted water and over-crowding. Each side attempted to portray the other as abusing prisoners' rights, but the real factors determining prison conditions were the availability of housing and food resources in the region and the midwar cessation of prisoner exchanges. **Contrast,** engraving published in the Southern Illustrated News, *10 October 1863, and* **The Prisons at Richmond—Union Troops Prisoners at Belle Isle,** engraving published in Harper's Weekly, *5 December 1863, from the Valentine, Richmond, Virginia*

kept Union soldiers crowded in Richmond, where prison conditions soon threatened their health and the health of all the city's nearby residents. This situation persisted for the duration of the war; in late 1864, there were at least 6,000 Union soldiers on Belle Isle in the James River and 270 officers in a single large room at Libby Prison.

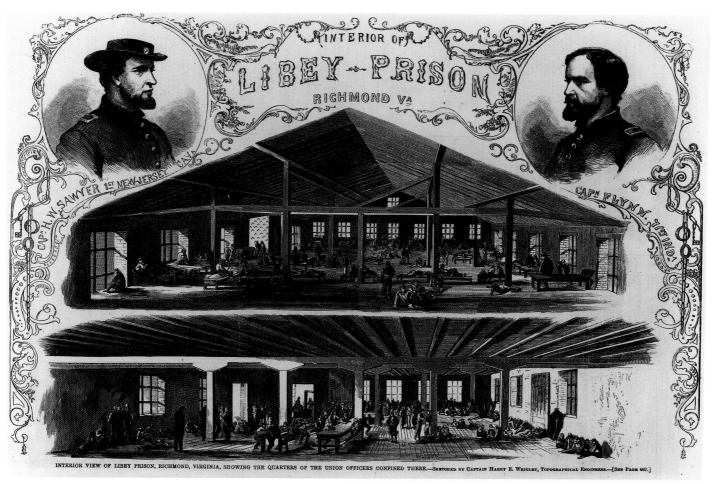

INTERIOR VIEW OF LIBEY PRISON, RICHMOND, VIRGINIA, SHOWING THE QUARTERS OF THE UNION OFFICERS CONFINED THERE.—Sketched by Captain Harry E. Wrigley, Topographical Engineers.—[See Page 667.]

This ship-chandler warehouse converted to a prison was where Union officers were held. In one celebrated escape effort, a small group of officers dug a hole under the wall, over time, and eventually tunneled their way out. In general, however, only death or the end of the war could break the daily deprivation and tedium. **Interior View of Libby Prison,** *engraving published in* Harper's Weekly, *17 October 1863, from the Valentine, Richmond, Virginia*

Factories and railroads, like the hospitals, had to rely on ingenuity and self-reliance. The Richmond and Danville Railroad operated its own sawmill for cross ties and bridge timber and hauled the logs with its own wagons and teams. The company opened a foundry for iron and brass castings, prepared car grease and oil in the company's shops, and even bought sides of beef and pork to cure for employee consumption.[12]

Richmond was a terminus for five railroads, but their differing gauges meant there was no central depot and no connections between the lines. Heavy wartime traffic soon made every junction point a clutter of desperately scarce freight cars; these cars often sat for days or weeks before their contents were transferred to other lines. Local hotel owners and cart drivers resisted when wartime imperatives dictated that the railroads connect, accustomed as they were to transporting goods and housing weary travelers who had to debark when the train line ended in front of their establishments.

At the Tredegar Iron Works, before Virginia's secession the industrious Joseph Reid Anderson won contracts to supply cannon and munitions to Lower South states and to provide machinery for the Manufactory of Arms. Although it was hampered by shortages of materials and never operated at full capacity, Tredegar soon combined with the renovated armory and other iron foundries to form an almost self-sufficient industrial city on the banks of the James. Anderson's enterprises, with a workforce of nearly 2,500 men (including 750 blacks), owned or controlled two coal mines, a tannery, shoe-making shops, a sawmill, a firebrick factory, a farm and herds, nine canal boats, and a blockade runner.[13]

Given the superior manpower and industry of the Union, the Confederacy was willing to experiment with any weapon or device that promised to make the odds more equal. Confederate ordnance, which went from being the worst supplied War Department Bureau to the best, was considered an area of spectacular success. Richmond's Tredegar Iron Works was one of eight large arsenals, and Richmond armories and carbine manufactories were supplemented by new installations and related industries that developed in other southern cities. With Richmond as the prime beneficiary, the Confederacy promoted an industrial impetus for southern towns from Danville to Macon.

In the course of the war, Tredegar developed a large, rail-mounted cannon; naval mines; a rifled cannon; and an ironclad vessel, the CSS *Virginia*. The *Virginia* was born when iron plates fashioned at Tredegar were attached to the hull of the USS *Merrimac*, scuttled earlier at Norfolk by the retreating United States Navy. Tredegar also supplied the guns and shot, and the foundry worked overtime to get the vessel into the water in early March 1862. At federally controlled Hampton Roads, rumors abounded about the infernal machine from Richmond. One New York journalist described the fearful anticipation, noting, "The cry of '*Merrimac*' was sounded like that of 'wolf' and every puff of smoke approaching Sewall's Point was thought to be the Confederate monster." Once in the James, the *Merrimac* did promptly steam to Hampton Roads, where it disabled several Union ships and engaged in its famous four-hour battle with the Union's ironclad *Monitor* while Union shot "rattled on the armor of the *Merrimac* like peas on a drum and fell harmless into the water." The Confederates destroyed the now-legendary *Merrimac* or *Virginia* on 11 May 1862, fearing that the vessel's heavy draft might cause it to fall to the Union as the *Monitor* approached up the James.[14]

As well as a city of hospitals, factories, and prisons, Richmond became a city of the dead, most visibly at Hollywood Cemetery, where the two acres set aside for Confederate dead filled before the end of the Peninsular Campaign in the summer of 1862. Confederate Secretary of

War George Wythe Randolph, once a city council member and a Richmond delegate to the Secession Convention, made his old compatriots on the council furious by preempting their powers and granting the Hollywood Cemetery Company the right to bury on adjacent city land. The city protested that graves were about to occupy the best site for a needed new water reservoir and that it had already granted the Confederacy the right to as much land as it needed at Oakwood Cemetery. This grant, plus the purchase of privately owned lots adjacent to Hollywood Cemetery and convenient to Winder and Jackson hospitals, allowed for the burial of thousands. Grass disappeared beneath clumps of reddish-brown soil from the constant work of gravedigger's spades. Other cemeteries were as busy. The Hebrew Cemetery set aside a section for war dead. Funerals for enlisted men became perfunctory and burials continued into the night. Gravediggers at Shockoe Cemetery went on strike because of overwork; black workers briefly replaced them, but the white laborers returned to physically wrest back their jobs.[15]

When the theater of war moved briefly away from Richmond after First Manassas, the city proceeded with war preparations and with elections to the Confederate government. The inauguration of Pres. Jefferson Davis took place on Washington's birthday, 22 February 1862, at the foot of the Washington monument in Capitol Square. The young man whom Richmonders called John Booth and whose stage name was J. B. Wilkes or Wilkes Booth may have been present in the crowd, just as he contrived to be present at Harpers Ferry in 1859. That month Booth played Richmond for the last time, in *The Virginia Cavalier*. Old residents remembered that the Booth family often had difficulty confining their histrionics to the stage. They recalled how John Booth's father, Junius Brutus Booth, playing in Richmond in 1824, had attempted to murder the stage manager with a dagger the morning after a performance of *Othello*.[16]

A few days after his inauguration, President Davis declared martial law within a ten-mile radius of Richmond and charged Gen. John H. Winder with enforcing it. Many of those whom Winder hired as special police were street toughs, refugees from Baltimore who became known locally as the "Plug-Uglies." Most of their previous experience with the law had been at the other end of the policeman's nightstick, and their new positions improved neither their manners nor their morals.

Richmond and Confederate authorities also tried to control the flow of information into and out of the city. All the newspapers in the Confederacy sent reporters to the Confederate capital, and many European correspondents visited the city as well. Attempts to censor their dispatches met with mixed success. Confederate military officers complained throughout the war that reporters revealed too much about military positions and strength, while reporters asserted that they were being censored for having pointed out errors and ineptitude among the officers.

After martial law was declared in March 1862, John Winder, commandant of Richmond prisons as well as commander of the Department of Henrico, arrested several suspicious persons and placed them in the prison called Castle Godwin. Various political suspects, deserters, and disorderly soldiers were added to their numbers until, in late 1863, 250 prisoners were transferred from Castle Godwin to the former tobacco factory on Cary Street known as Castle Thunder.[17]

Winder's police were intended to supplement local efforts to catch spies, but they failed to catch or even seriously monitor the activities of certain Unionists in the city; chief among these were Elizabeth Van Lew and her household, in their imposing home on Church Hill. Van Lew had long been opposed to slavery, confiding her thoughts to occasional sympathetic visitors from the North and from Europe. As a young woman in the 1850s, she worked to buy and then free slaves, sending Mary, the daughter of the family's hired cook, Caroline, north to school. Mary, later the wife of Wilson Bowser, worked as a table girl in the Davis household and reportedly sent information to Van Lew, who forwarded it, via slaves and free blacks, to the Union lines.[18]

A number of Richmond residents as well as visitors were suspected of Union sympathies, and arrests—like that of John Minor Botts, a local Unionist—occasionally occurred. In retrospect, such actions appear arbitrary rather than consistent with a logical pattern of apprehending spies. It was difficult for authorities to know when Whiggish Unionism or northern birth translated into subversive or treasonable action. Accusations of spying sometimes redressed old political grievances, and rumors gained credibility easily. The city government was simply not competent to function as an intelligence-gathering network, and the Confederate government did not do much better in ferreting out spies. It was difficult enough, in most cases, for both entities to contend with the enemy outside the city.[19]

An early example of this difficulty could be seen in the responsibility for fortifying Richmond. City councilman Thomas Wynne, chairman of the Committee on Defense, had solicited funds from both the city and the Confederate governments to build a ring of forts and embankments around the city. But numerous delays forced the Confederate government to take over the project from the city, and these fortifications reached a state of near completion only after Richmond came under siege in the spring of 1862.

The Union army threatened Richmond directly at the end of May 1862, at the climax of the long Peninsular Campaign, which had been designed to end the war by capturing Richmond. As Union armies grew closer, plans were made to evacuate the capital. Government archives would go to Lynchburg or Columbia, South Carolina. Confederate Treasury Secretary Christopher Memminger ordered that a locomotive and car be kept ready to carry off the contents of the treasury. Railroad bridges were planked to permit artillery to escape the city, and emergency tracks at last connected the Virginia Central, Richmond and Petersburg, and Richmond, Fredericksburg, and Potomac Railroads so that their equipment could move south.

When Confederate guns at the Drewry's Bluff fortifications, seven miles south of the city, fired on the federal army, a young woman in the city recalled: "It was so near that the first guns sent our hearts into our mouths, like a sudden loud knocking at one's door at night." The Confederate bombardment turned back the Union forces, led by the *Monitor*, while women in the city made bandages, scraped lint, and prepared beds.[20]

The wounded arrived in overwhelming numbers and filled the streets, churches, and hotels as well as the hospitals. "Two of us girls," wrote Constance Cary Harrison, "tramped down Main Street through the hot sun over burning pavements from one scene of horror to another." After viewing streets of powder-blackened, dying youths, bandages stiff with blood and thick with flies, they climbed the steep steps to the top of the capitol, where they "looked down on the city that could not sleep and . . . listened to the voice of the river." But the sounds of a city completely overtaken by war covered the comforting and familiar roar of the water.[21]

Two Richmond women of opposite convictions showed equal determination in pursuit of their Civil War goals. Elizabeth Van Lew (left) spied for the Union, while Sally Tompkins (right) set up a hospital for wounded Confederate soldiers. Had Richmond been accustomed to taking women's activities seriously, Van Lew might have been arrested and Tompkins given the charge of all the hospitals in the city. From the Valentine, Richmond, Virginia

Mayor Joseph Mayo and a fifteen-member city council presided over the wartime city. The venerable Mayo had been mayor since 1853 and put a high premium on order. The city's free black and slave residents cordially disliked him for the alacrity with which he had them whipped for minor public offenses. City ordinances and the commonwealth's legal system codified public whippings, a standard plantation punishment, as customary for free blacks or slaves in the city. For the master, whipping was better than incarceration because it did not cost the master the slave's time. Free blacks, who did not have the rights of citizens, were also subject to this punishment and to forced labor on the Confederate defenses.

Unpopular legislation passed by the Confederate Congress and the Virginia General Assembly included taxation and military conscription acts. White men were liable to a military draft if they did not volunteer; free blacks were drafted for military work, while impressment laws forced slaveholders to send their slaves to the military. Free blacks registered in February 1862, as Jefferson Davis was inaugurated, and they were called up for 180 days of labor. The Confederacy also sold Confederate bonds and further taxed the incomes, licenses, fees, and profits of businesses and professions.

The councilmen who attempted to sort out the layers and levels of responsibility and power in the Confederate city were business and professional men of moderate views and solid

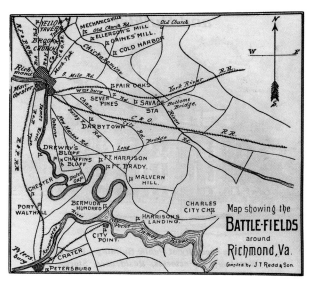

As the war entered its fourth year, Richmond became the symbolic focus of the struggle between two armies. The city was long spared a direct assault but found itself increasingly isolated and increasingly surrounded by the destruction and carnage just beyond its borders. Hill Directory Company's battlefields map, 1905, from the Valentine, Richmond Virginia

local accomplishments. With few exceptions, they represented neither the Virginia aristocracy nor the artisans and workers of Richmond's industries. They did their earnest best to govern the city, but the Virginia state government and the Confederate executive and legislative departments often overruled or ignored their attempts to defend the city's prerogatives and to maintain law and order.[22]

Although the city council was ultimately successful in its efforts to exempt from the draft vital city workers such as firemen, police, and superintendents at the waterworks and gas works, the council was never able to maintain a volunteer home guard to keep order in the city. As the war progressed, the need for such an organization became more apparent. Winder's detectives, who supplemented the police force, behaved with such coarseness and corruption that they were released from their jobs, but they were not replaced. The city police, known as the City Battalion, and the Public Guard, a military unit under the governor's command, were inadequate by the spring of 1863, when after two winters of war, hunger stalked the poor and middling people of Richmond.

The late winter bore uncommonly hard on laboring women with few resources as food became particularly scarce. In February 1863, the Confederate Congress legalized the impressment of food by army agents. The military was required to pay a "fair price," but they often set that price by prewar standards, while farmers gauged the price in inflated dollars. Impressment emptied the markets, and scarcity drove prices higher. It was at the end of winter—always the hardest time to acquire food—that the women's problems came to a head. On 13 March, an explosion at the Ordnance Laboratory on Brown's Island killed sixty-nine women working there. A few days later, the city waterworks failed, and many families had to use an old well on Capitol Square. A group of women from Oregon Hill invited others to a meeting at Belvidere Hill Baptist Church on the evening of 1 April. Viewing themselves as citizens of Virginia, they planned to plead with the governor to intervene and lower prices to the levels set by the Confederate government.[23]

Early on the morning of 2 April, large numbers of women and children from the city and surrounding counties converged on the Capitol Square. At the governor's mansion, they demanded "bread or blood" and were told that Gov. John Letcher was at work. The crowd gathered in the square began to move toward Cary Street. When asked where they were going, one emaciated girl said, "to get food." The Bread Riot of April 1863 was aptly named, for despite efforts by the Richmond press and Confederate politicians to deny it, there was much hunger and malnutrition in the city. Storefronts on nearby Cary Street had food on display, and to these shops they moved as a body, breaking windows to grab loaves of bread and sacks of foodstuffs. The women carried rusty pistols, clubs, knives, and bayonets. Men soon joined women in taking shoes, sacks of flour, bolts of cloth, and even jewelry; they also took sides of beef from government wagons. By the time Mayor Mayo and the local police arrived to read and enforce the riot act, it was difficult to discern who were the original protestors, who were opportunistic looters, and who, in the large crowd, were mere bystanders. Governor Letcher and President Davis arrived to plead with the crowd, but when that availed little, Davis ordered the Public Guard to begin firing into the crowd in five minutes. After a long stunned minute, the women dispersed. In the arrests and trials that followed, older and poorer women, considered ringleaders because of their condition, received longer jail sentences than younger women or those of good family. The very disadvantages that drove women to steal for bread sent them to prison.[24]

The Bread Riot did cause a greater effort to identify and feed the poor. The grievances of the women and children who assembled on Capitol Square came from the inflationary spiral that drove prices for even common foodstuffs far beyond their ability to pay. The Young Men's Christian Association (YMCA) began to distribute food from a depot on Bank Street. At Sixth and Clay Streets, and on Cary Street between Tenth and Eleventh, "free markets" were set up where city residents who were deemed eligible by a committee could exchange paper vouchers for food.[25]

A scarcity of basic goods drove food prices up and was particularly hard on urban laborers without resources. A group of women who met in a church on Oregon Hill resolved to present their grievances to the governor, but after some people broke shop windows and stole goods, the women were ordered to disperse or be fired upon. Although the press portrayed the women as non-natives, the laboring families of Richmond were indeed severely malnourished. Engraving published in Frank Leslie's Illustrated News, 23 May 1863, courtesy of the Virginia State Library and Archives, Richmond

Families in the highest social circles of Richmond society also experienced hardship and loss but exhibited varying sensitivity to the plight of less fortunate families. One woman marveled to a friend about the high price of cake and champagne, but other women organized a Soup Association to feed poor families. Varina Davis wrote of food substitutes that families she knew used: for coffee, parched sweet potato parings or parched corn and wheat; for tea, sassafras with boiled sorghum. President Davis gave more and more civilian employees access to a military commissary, which considerably improved the standard of living for those eligible. Prices there remained at peacetime levels. Although the federal blockade of the Virginia coast made some items scarce, many families in the city received food from rural relatives and friends. Young people continued to have their parties, but some were called "starvation parties" and featured only water.[26]

Businessmen attempted to stave off the effects of inflation by selling their goods at the current or a future market price, while the government attempted to hold merchants to prices agreed upon earlier. Inevitably, speculators and hoarders appeared. Few merchants could resist the urge to hold back their production in anticipation of rising prices. Companies with military contracts began to feel that the prices for which they had agreed to supply grain or iron were now too low.

Among those who contracted with the army were slave owners, many of whom determined that the most profitable use of their skilled slaves was to hire them out in the city's booming industries before they were conscripted to dig fortifications. The Confederacy utilized slave labor intensively in munitions, ironworks, food processing, hospital work, railroad and roadbed construction and repair, and mining. By the end of the war, Major Anderson of the Tredegar foundry was negotiating with the Confederate army to recover black craftsmen impressed by the military as laborers.[27] In the city, the old problem of control over hired slaves grew worse. Hospital surgeons, housewives, and factory owners all complained that slaves frequently disappeared at will into a private world. Because they often returned with medicine, food, or tools, some independence was tolerated, but uneasily.

In the world's first industrial war, the skills of Virginia's slaves and free urban blacks, especially in Richmond, were crucial to the Confederacy. Those with experience in manufacturing, transport, or hospitals were seldom moved from their work, but free black day laborers were commandeered and removed from their neighborhoods, often to become unpaid labor—slaves, in effect—on military fortifications around Richmond. An observant young printer's apprentice, Ernest Walthall, noted that to justify this action, free blacks were told that they were protecting their own homes and property. Conditions for such unskilled and unprotected workers—the least likely to own property—were extremely bad, and many died or returned to Richmond sick.[28]

Neither the master nor the slave failed to see that the former's power did not protect the latter from impressment, but the Confederacy at least accounted to the master for his slave. Some slaves slipped toward Union lines. By the midpoint of the war, runaway slaves included more than just those forced to dig trenches on the edge of the city. Several white families returned from an evening out to discover that trusted household slaves had departed with clothes, silver, and money.

An act of the General Assembly "To Provide for the Enrollment and Employment of Free Negroes in the Public Service" empowered Robert E. Lee to ask for able-bodied male free Negroes to work on fortifications near Richmond. Lee asked the judge to deliver the laborers through the sheriff and promised to compensate the sheriff. In another letter Lee advised, "let the slaves of your country remain at home, but use all Diligence in bringing the quota of Free Negroes called for . . . to this place."[29]

Confidence in the Confederacy and perhaps the sheer inability to imagine a society without slaves kept the price of that property high. In October 1862, Albert Brooks, a free black who had bought his liberty, purchased his wife and three youngest children from Daniel Von Groning, a German tobacco agent. The rates had not fallen since the original agreement between the Brooks family and Von Groning, who had bought them four years earlier in response to the desperate request of Brooks's wife, Lucy, after her master died and the children were to be sold. With Von Groning's cooperation, Albert and Lucy Brooks maintained their household through the Civil War. The three oldest boys—Prince Albert, David Burr, and Walter—were not included in the purchase and worked in tobacco factories as slaves until the end of the war. The man for whom David Burr Brooks was named, city council member David Burr, was a local merchant who had long been treasurer of the Richmond-Manchester Colonization Society. That voluntary association suspended its work after the Civil War began, but others formed to meet new circumstances.

Richmond citizens now took up two kinds of private charity. One helped needy local residents, and the other aided ill or wounded soldiers in the city. Both groups began by taking food and firewood to the poor or treats and books to the soldiers. Mary Chesnut and Emma Mordecai wrote of taking ice cream and lemonade from Pizzini's Confectionery to the hospitals. It was expected that wives of government officials would visit the hospitals, but few did so regularly.

Organizations formed by women reflected their class standing; and the Richmond women who formed the Ladies Gunboat Society in April 1862 were women of very high status. As McClellan's Peninsular Campaign pressed upon Richmond in 1862, they met to raise money and collect scrap iron for a gunboat, to be called the *Lady Davis*, to protect Richmond. These women had access to the Confederate Navy officers and the managers of Tredegar only because of their husbands' importance and their vaunted patriotism. Their enterprise appeared to collapse for lack of money and lack of means to move scrap iron to Richmond, although their female correspondents had collected thousands of pounds at various sites. Records of the Ladies Gunboat Association reveal a struggle for decision-making power between Richmond women and members from the Lower South whose husbands were well placed in the

For most of the war, President and Mrs. Davis felt it necessary to hold receptions for cabinet members, officers, and other visitors. On New Year's Day, the custom of open house gave the public a chance to file past and see how the Confederacy had remodeled the home once owned by the Brockenbrough family. **Davis and Varina at Reception** (c. 1878), by William L. Sheppard, from the Valentine, Richmond, Virginia

Confederate government. This internal conflict mirrored, to some extent, the career-building jealousies operating among military officers and bureaucrats in Richmond. Mary Boykin Chesnut displayed a keen awareness of this atmosphere in her well-known diary of life in the high social circles of the Confederacy. In order to write about it, she adopted the style of Thackeray's *Vanity Fair*, a novel of manners in which scheming and social climbing are the central activities.[30]

The wives of Confederate cabinet officers were the chief diarists of the war years, and the writings of this inner circle constituted a Greek chorus to the tragedy of the Confederacy. They contributed little, however, to an understanding of those women without similar status who lost male relatives on whom they were financially dependent. With husbands, sons, fathers, and brothers gone, some Richmond women were desperate for paying work. Many worked in government agencies, factories, and hospitals; some kept boardinghouses, farmed, and cooked; some were speculators, smugglers, entrepreneurs, and prostitutes. Whole families of women with all their men gone struggled to survive in Richmond. Fannie Walker was an eighteen-year-old "copying clerk" in the Bureau of War—the only woman there—while her mother and sister were matrons at Howard Grove Hospital and her aunt worked for the Treasury Department.[31]

Constance Cary Harrison came to Richmond with her widowed mother when the Union army approached their home in Alexandria, Virginia. Her mother sought paid employment in the Confederate Treasury Department. Treasury was the first to hire white women, followed by the post office and the War Department. In time, all Confederate departments employed white women. Many genteel but impoverished women applied for each job, and Treasury Secretary Christopher Memminger said that each vacancy "brought a hundred applications." Hiring was usually based on financial need, and testimonials from Confederate congressmen, clergy, and military were almost necessities in a woman's search for employment. The post office interviewer gave preference to refugees over local women because he believed them to be more needy.[32]

At the midpoint of the war, after the Bread Riot, after the Confederate retreat from Gettysburg and the fall of Vicksburg, most citizens remained staunch supporters of the Confederacy, but an element of fear and a sense of real scarcity entered into the townspeople's calculations. President Davis grew less available for local officials or for citizens. Within Confederate agencies, bureaucratic bickering and departmental jealousies grew. Employees often seemed more concerned with their own advancement or that of a department chief than with the conduct of the war. It became more difficult for citizens to acquire passports to travel outside Confederate lines or even outside Richmond. In the almost inevitable search for scapegoats, speculators held a high place and immigrants were often labeled as speculators in certain prints. The articles and cartoons in *Southern Punch*, *Southern Illustrated News*, and the *Southern Literary Messenger*, the favorite reading material of the city's upper classes, regularly characterized German immigrants as unpatriotic and German Jews, in particular, as avaricious and disloyal.[33]

Early in 1864, over one hundred Union soldiers escaped from Libby Prison; this escape and an attempted Union raid on Richmond that followed on its heels set the tone for a year of war in which the city felt more vulnerable from within and without. The captured Yankees used spoons as shovels to dig their way out of the downtown prison. A few weeks later, the Armory Battalion, supplemented with clerks and boys, stopped a Union raiding party only two and a half miles from the city. Papers taken from the body of a Union officer, Col. Ulric Dahlgren, indicated that the Yankees had planned to release Union prisoners from Belle Isle and assist them in burning the city. Richmonders briefly considered hanging all the Yankees caught in the raid but decided against it.

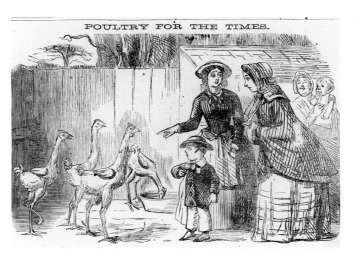

POULTRY FOR THE TIMES.

Southern Punch, *published in Richmond, was quick to find scapegoats for shortages and reversals of fortune. In the cartoon at far left, captioned "Shameful Extortion!," a profiteering cloth merchant smiles as the black woman exclaims at the high price of even the plain, old-fashioned calico. The* Southern Illustrated News, *another Richmond publication, also made humor of the shortages — here, in its depiction of the strange, scrawny poultry offered for sale. The vendor explains, "You'll find they go very far. Two cuts on the neck, two on the back, two leg joints besides the heads, which is good for soup. We pulls their feathers every month for the furniture men." From the* Valentine, Richmond, Virginia

Turning to local problems, the city council and the General Assembly devised creative means to find and distribute supplies for the city. Gov. William "Extra Billy" Smith was particularly resourceful and briefly successful in his acquisition of blockade runners and the services of the York River Railroad to bring corn and rice to the city. The assembly made belated efforts to centralize the sale and distribution of staples like cotton and salt, selling cotton yarn to be carded at home and establishing state control over privately owned salt works. The city council enlarged its concept of the needy to include those in military service and dependents but would not increase the city's bonded indebtedness. Instead, the council took short-term loans from banks to buy food from the countryside.

In the final year of the war, men were pressed into service with little regard for deferments. When a city militia or reserves were called up to defend the city, every workplace emptied—from the post office to the Armory. In that last year, the city sold its railroad stock to reduce its large deficit and, near the end of the winter, was considering tripling the tax rate and eliminating gas and water subsidies.[34]

Springtime marked both the beginning and ending of the war. Each April provided a moment to assess the Confederacy and southern patriotism in Richmond. The cheers, parades, and illuminations of April 1861 swept all hesitation aside. April 1862 saw Richmond calm and confident, though threatened by McClellan's Peninsular Campaign; by the next April, the threat came from within, as the Bread Riot punctuated the war in the city. From that time, distress and need in the city commanded a larger proportion of attention from all three levels of government. April 1864 saw even greater shortages. The grinding and merciless Wilderness Campaign enabled the Union to make feints toward the city, which were deflected at great cost. The city reluctant to join the Confederacy had in fact *become* the Confederacy—and Lee ex-

Mayor Mayo called up a citizen guard when Richmond appeared to be threatened in the spring of 1862, but as the war progressed it became increasingly hard to find a sufficient number of volunteers. Broadside from the Valentine, Richmond, Virginia

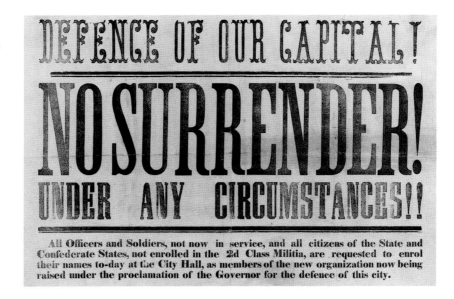

hausted his army in its defense.[35] Another year of death, privation, everyday courage in some quarters, tireless self-concern in others, and belated attempts at rationing and central control flowed inevitably to the final April of the war, when a break in Lee's lines allowed Union soldiers to pour toward Richmond.

CHAPTER SEVEN

Reconstruction Richmond

The war ended for Richmond on 3 April 1865, when, after a day of rumors, hasty packing, and maneuvering for space on trains, carts, and carriages, the Confederate government left the city, followed after nightfall by the Confederate army. The retreating army torched warehouses of tobacco and cotton, arsenals of munitions, railroad trestles, and, finally, Mayo's Bridge, which connected Richmond with Manchester. They set charges to explode Confederate gunboats and powder magazines. Although Mayor Mayo and other citizens protested that the fire might destroy the entire city, the Confederate commanders believed they had no choice but to destroy supplies, and they had little time or patience for civilian complaints. With the Confederate army gone, the fire spreading, and shells exploding at the burning arsenal, the residents, prison escapees, and refugees who gathered in the streets became a looting mob—some drunk from the broken casks of liquor spilled in the gutters but others soberly determined to get for themselves something tangible with which to barter against an uncertain future. The uncontrolled fire and mob prompted the aged Mayor Mayo to seek out the Army of the Potomac under Gen. Godfrey Weitzel, moving into Richmond from the east, and surrender the city.

The otherworldly chaos of the evacuation fire, with its frenzied activity highlighted by burning buildings and reflected in the shattered window glass on the streets, gave rise to many legends in Richmond. One often-repeated story was that Mrs. Robert Stanard, a noted Richmond hostess, dressed in an elegant gown and sat outside while her mansion burned to the ground. Richmond's best people, the legend suggests, did not participate in the wild night and early morning but faced the destruction of the wit and beauty of the Old South with elegant stoicism and calm defiance. But there were other legends of the fall of Richmond too. One story preserved in Virginia folk narrative asserted that blacks "took Richmond" before the Union army entered. In this account, blacks claimed the streets for their celebration of freedom after the Confederate army left, filling the air with a mighty roar. They were there to greet black cavalry troops and musicians who marched into the city as part of the Union army.[1]

Weitzel's Third Division marched to the center of the city. A few longtime Unionists joined black Richmonders in cheering the Union troops, but most white Richmonders stayed indoors, more angry and outraged than terrified. Right after raising the United States flag in

In this well-known image by Currier and Ives, Confederate troops evacuate Richmond, heading south over Mayo's Bridge after setting fire to supplies, records, and munitions, while explosions light the smoky night landscape. For many years, this image hung in the parlors of many white Richmond families. **The Fall of Richmond, Virginia, on the Night of April 2nd 1865,** by Currier and Ives (1865), from the Valentine, Richmond, Virginia

Capitol Square, the Union troops attempted to contain the fire and destruction. They worked with civilians in bucket brigades, set backfires to work against the blaze, and arrested looters as well as a few Rebels too eager to say what they thought of the Yankees.

It was a strange and anticlimactic ending to the war for Richmond, which had long been the tangible symbol of Confederate resistance and the elusive object of Union military strategy. Union soldiers saw fire, debris-ridden streets, and the shabby homes of working-class whites as they entered the city from the east and passed through riverfront and factory districts. For their part, Richmonders had to acknowledge the discipline and order of the Union troops and reluctantly abandon their predictions of rape and pillage. For both sides, the first task was an intensely cooperative one, especially since arms now passing water buckets may have been pointing rifles just a day before.[2]

Richmond's symbolic importance in the four-year struggle drew, like a magnet, the president of the United States and commander in chief of the Union army. Abraham Lincoln had

Lincoln's walk through Richmond just a day after the entry of the Union army emphasized the symbolic importance of the Confederate capital to the Union as well as to the South. His presence became part of the emancipation story for Richmond blacks, while he was pointedly ignored by most whites. **President Lincoln Entering Richmond, 4 April 1865,** engraving published in Harper's Weekly, 4 February 1866, from the Valentine, Richmond, Virginia

been the guest of the Army of the Potomac as it approached its final campaigns, and he was in Petersburg on 3 April. Lincoln apparently shared in the sense of unreality that the last days of the war seemed to provoke on both sides. That night he said to Adm. David Porter, "Thank God I have lived to see this. It seems to me that I have been dreaming a horrid dream for four years and now the nightmare is gone. I want to see Richmond."[3]

The next day, 4 April, Lincoln came upriver by ship and barge and docked at Rocketts Landing. Hailed by former slaves as a Messiah, he walked uphill from the river and over the streets of Richmond to the capitol and the White House of the Confederacy. Later he toured the city in a carriage, and Richmond's black population thronged the streets and square to see the tangible evidence that the faraway events about which they had privately speculated for four years had actually taken place.[4]

The evacuation fire made Richmond's position as the desolate center of a defeated nation all too apparent. Photographs of gaunt chimneys standing amid heaped rubble quickly became enduring symbols of the Confederacy in defeat. The fall of Richmond and the subsequent surrender of the Army of Northern Virginia marked the end of the armed rebellion, but it was not clear whether all of the old order really lay in the ruins of the Confederate capital's commercial district. All Richmonders, black and white, understood that something would rise from the ashes.

For most of the remainder of the nineteenth century the city's direction was vigorously contested. On one side were those who sought to reaffirm and reclaim the political and social order of antebellum Richmond; on the other were those who saw the disruptions of war and emancipation as their opportunity to redress old grievances and enact a new order. It was not only the government and the burnt district that were being reconstructed, but some portion of the city's social and economic base as well. Richmond's prominent citizens preferred to model the future on the past and to continue social relations and industrial growth on their antebellum basis. The times, however, would not permit an easy continuity.

In the days and weeks after the fall of Richmond and the surrender of the Confederate armies, events proceeded at a pace almost too rapid for Richmond residents to absorb. The surrender of Lee and his army, the murder of President Lincoln, the surrender of Confederate

Despite the occupation of Richmond by U.S. Army troops, few people left the city and many entered. Black and white refugees sought families, food, and information in town. Many refugees sought out Union officers to learn what rules prevailed. Others were determined never to acknowledge the presence of the occupying forces. Photographs of Richmond ruins, 1865, from the Valentine, Richmond, Virginia

The White House of the Confederacy (above) and most of the Confederate public buildings became quarters for Union army officers or enlisted men. Richmonders were forced to seek rations, passes, pardons, and rules from the rooms once at the center of the Confederacy. Photograph, 1865, from the Valentine, Richmond, Virginia

armies in North Carolina, and the collapse of the Confederacy were paralleled in Richmond by changes of equal rapidity. General Weitzel was replaced by Gen. O. C. Ord within ten days. Ord was joined by Gen. Marsena Patrick as provost marshal and Gen. Henry Halleck as senior officer for Virginia and North Carolina. These officers understood federal reconstruction policy to be lenient toward the South, in an effort to mend the Union, and were personally inclined to seek some rapprochement with the Richmond citizenry. They asked for an oath of loyalty to the Union from whites and labor contracts from blacks as a prerequisite for receiving government rations and services.

The evacuation fire had consumed more than twenty blocks of the commercial district, including banks, warehouses, groceries, brokerage houses, offices, and print shops, as well as smaller iron works. Severely damaged industrial facilities included a stove foundry, a machinist's shop, two carriage factories, two paper mills, a tin shop, a pottery, two tobacco factories, and several flour mills. State and local court records were destroyed. The rubble-clearing began immediately and the rebuilding soon after. Both black and white men sought jobs cleaning up the burnt district and salvaging usable materials. War and fire had badly damaged the city's transportation network, and it received early attention. The Union army quickly made a pontoon bridge across the James to Manchester to replace Mayo's Bridge. Telegraph lines were restored immediately, and two railroad bridges were replaced within fourteen months. Four of the five railroads terminating in Richmond had resumed some operation by the end of April.[5]

Francis Pierpont, who had acted as governor of those sections of Virginia described as "loyal" or "restored" during the war, was recognized by the new president, Andrew Johnson, as governor of all Virginia in early May, and he moved his government to Richmond that month. Food for the city's residents and for the rural people, black and white, streaming into the city was a primary requirement. The beleaguered city council, which had struggled with massive problems and overlapping authorities during the war, now faced more of the same, with armies in gray replaced by armies in blue. Shortly after the fall of the Confederacy, Richmond's market revealed the pinch of scarcity, exhibiting only "a few cabbages, a few pecks of sweet potatoes, a pair of live chickens tied together at the legs, a goose or duck in a box with its head sticking out, . . . a woman in rags with a sallow complexion and a basket of eggs, . . . a mulatto boy with a string of rockfish, hard peaches in a bag, a box of wild grapes."[6]

During the first week of occupation, the Union army supplied enough rations for the entire city. Refugees from the countryside, ex–Confederate soldiers, and the curious entered the city seeking food, friends, family, and information. Private northern charities soon supplemented the army rations with flour, soup, and garden supplies. Five weeks after federal troops entered the city, a white woman refugee expressed the ambivalence that many in Richmond felt toward the Union army and its activities: "I am in 'Yankeetown'—for we are surrounded by troops. . . . I am afraid they will succeed by their leniency and kindness in winning over the Southern people and healing their wounds. . . . [L]ast night the sweet notes of their music was almost melting my soul into forgiveness while I was struggling against it. We will be intermingled with 'those people' so much so as even to feel that we are one People." The courteous behavior of Union officers that involuntarily conciliated some white Richmonders did not extend to the freedmen, who had few northern advocates in the occupied city for two months. At the end of May, the Bureau of Refugees, Freedmen, and Abandoned Lands, an agency established by Congress and under the regional direction of Gen. Orlando Brown, began its relief operations. Yet cooperation between the Freedmen's Bureau officers and the officers of the occupation did not develop until Gen. Alfred Terry, more sympathetic to blacks, replaced General Ord in mid-June as commandant of Richmond.[7]

Ord's transfer was due in part to the policies that he, Patrick, and Halleck had instituted shortly after the federals occupied Richmond. It soon became clear that the army's desire to keep down the Rebels did not mean that they intended to elevate the blacks. In the over-crowded capital city of a defeated rebellion, the Union army feared civil disorder almost as much as further rebellion, and their Provost Guard acted in much the same manner as the Richmond city police, randomly harassing, beating, and arresting blacks on the streets of Rich-mond in an effort to keep them from congregating. Blacks were prevented from entering the Capitol Square, and at the end of April, after the army complained that the presence of black troops made freedmen harder to control, all black units were temporarily removed.

Appeals to General Patrick from black leaders in Richmond proved unavailing, and early in June, two months after the fall of Richmond, Governor Pierpont reappointed Mayor Mayo to office. "Old Joe Mayo" was a particular bane to the black residents of Richmond because of his enthusiasm for sending every black person on the streets without a pass to the whipping post for thirty-nine lashes. This reinstatement of Confederate city officials made it appear as if nothing had changed in the social and political relations between the races. Only blacks had to apply for and exhibit a pass showing that they were vouched for as local residents. When Union forces and local police arrested hundreds of blacks without passes, including children, one group of black residents wrote an embittered letter to the *New York Tribune*, concluding, "All that is needed to restore slavery in full is the auction block as it used to be." Other black men and women took depositions concerning abuses of the pass law and drafted a petition that a delegation carried to President Johnson.[8]

As a result of that meeting, Governor Pierpont removed Mayor Mayo from office, and President Johnson ordered the transfer of Generals Halleck, Ord, and Patrick. General Terry, replacing Ord, struck down the city's vagrancy law on which the pass system was based and announced that the army would treat all inhabitants as equals under the law. At the end of July,

Secretary of War Stanton instructed southern commanders to discontinue the pass system and not to hinder black freedom of movement. Although but briefly noticed in the turmoil of the time, the prompt and organized response of Richmond blacks to the policies of the Union army in the first few months of occupation may have prevented an early reenactment of the antebellum civil codes that controlled free blacks. Freedmen were unwilling to settle for that status and understood the importance of precedents in determining their future in the city.[9]

In asserting their new status, black men and women claimed new roles and created a new history of emancipation, with its own holiday celebrations and pantheon of heroes. Black men formed militia units like those so popular in the antebellum city and exercised the privilege of parading, with weapons, on days that were significant to them. One of those saluted by a black militia unit was Elizabeth Van Lew, the white Richmond woman who had aided the Union cause as part of a spy network. The militia under William Evins borrowed the American flag presented to Van Lew by Gen. Benjamin Butler in order to march with it. According to Van Lew, the militia "stopped before our house in a body, thanked me for it, called me the Goddess of Liberty and Minerva, etc., etc., and appropriated it." Many whites resented the drilling, parading, and horn-blowing of the black militia units, and the press feared that "the rougher element of the Negroes might be preparing for a war of the races." But William Evins pointed to the real meaning of the black militias when he wrote to Van Lew thanking her for the "lonement" of the flag, under which "we ma[r]ched like men."[10]

The black militia who "ma[r]ched like men" might have honored Elizabeth Van Lew for her wartime heroism, but her later agitation for the right to vote on the basis of paying a property tax attracted little support anywhere in the city. The end of the Civil War marked no dramatic turning point in the lives of Richmond's white women. What the war did was to accelerate tendencies, already in evidence in the antebellum era, toward organizing for monument building, education, temperance, health, and benevolence. While white women had proved themselves to be strong, resourceful, and competent, and many had worked for wages for the first time during the war, there was very little sentiment for further exhibitions of female capabilities. An editorial in the *Richmond Enquirer and Examiner* made this point explicit: "Women often commit the mistake of claiming for their sex what does not belong to them. They claim to have as much sense as men but this is not true. They claim to have as much integrity of character, but this is not so. Women have far less principle than men. They are far less reliable. Their moral nature is less solid. . . . But the strength of woman lies in her practice of that highest of all moral achievements . . . [:] SELF-RENUNCIATION." However, those women who found themselves alone after the war, without money or family, did not have to be reminded of the need for self-denial. In 1867, all of the residents of the city's almshouses were white women, with the exception of one black female, only recently eligible for admission.[11]

For many black women in Richmond, freedom's first steps meant walking away from domestic labor for someone else. The day after Union troops entered Richmond, one Richmonder noted grimly, "A few thousand negroes (mostly women) are idle in the streets, or lying in the Capitol Square, or crowding about headquarters at the Capitol." Emancipation for them meant sorting out families, determining whether they would take paid labor and, if so, under what conditions. While black women continued their benevolent societies and formed political auxiliaries, it was in their everyday domestic and work lives that the politics of emancipation were primarily worked out. Scattered evidence suggests that most chose traditional marriages, with clearly gendered divisions of tasks and responsibilities. These marriages were more common where the black male head of household was a skilled laborer or propertyholder and an officer in trade and church societies. Households that depended on women's domestic or factory labor were less likely to provide men for Reconstruction politics.[12]

The early leadership among freedmen came largely from black families active in the churches and secret societies of antebellum Richmond. Some of them were free-born blacks, and others had acquired their freedom through self-purchase. Some postwar leaders, such as the Reverend J. H. Holmes, the first black pastor of the First African Baptist Church, and the Reverend John Jasper, pastor of Sixth Mount Zion, remained enslaved until Emancipation. The prominence of many men had less to do with their shade of color or antebellum status than it did with their ability to support their families and free their wives from employment outside the home. In secret societies, tobacco factory workers held leadership posts out of proportion to their numbers in the population, but few men married to domestics were elected to office.

By 1867, outlines of Richmond's memorialization of the Confederacy had emerged. The South was portrayed as an invaded country, and Confederate women were often depicted as passive mourners, but in life they expressed their grief in a more active fashion as they made Hollywood Cemetery the Confederacy's most important burial ground. **Hollywood Cemetery, Richmond, Virginia— Decorating the Graves of the Rebel Soldiers, May 31, 1867,** engraving by W. L. Sheppard, published in Harper's Weekly, 17 August 1867, and masthead for the Southern Opinion, *from the Valentine, Richmond, Virginia*

The family of Albert Brooks illustrated the tendency to assign status through wealth and its corollary, respectability. Brooks was described as "of unmixed African ancestry," while his wife, Lucy Brooks, appeared almost entirely European. During the war Lucy Brooks was purchased by her husband and ended her labor for others. Already established as a respectable matron and church member, she worked in the late 1860s with her sewing circle and a group of Quakers to found an orphanage for black children. In Richmond, evangelical religion and benevolence, marriage and a paternalistic household, steady wages or profits, and education were the characteristics of a black middle class that appeared after Emancipation but began its formation years earlier.[13]

Some African Americans who entered the city soon after the Union troops differed from white "carpetbaggers" in that they were native Virginians who were familiar with the area. Peter Randolph, the Baptist minister who came to Richmond from Boston at the close of the war, was freed in Virginia and and moved North, while others who returned to the region had been runaway slaves. Randolph returned to take the pulpit at Ebenezer Baptist Church. For the first generation of emancipated blacks in Richmond, religious conviction was reinforced by the dramatic manner in which their freedom had been achieved. Emancipation seemed both the fulfillment of biblical prophecy and the affirmation of the sacred worldview that had sustained many of them through slavery.[14]

A few freedmen, on the other hand, identified openly with the southern cause and exhibited hostility to Yankees and black soldiers. Lomax Smith, for example, was a free mulatto barber who had told Mayor Mayo in 1859 that he would go to Harpers Ferry and "shear the ears" of John Brown. In 1866, when Smith's daughter tried to marry a black Union soldier, Smith had the Richmond police arrest a black preacher who was willing to perform the ceremony. When Smith's house was burned that year, in an apparent act of arson, the *Richmond Enquirer* urged aid for him and described him as a black man who knew that the southern gentleman was his best friend.

Few blacks shared Lomax Smith's enthusiasms, but black barbers, caterers, hack drivers, and others who depended on white patronage for their living found it difficult to be active politically without losing their livelihood. Albert Brooks, who owned a hack (or taxi) service

Chief-Justice Chase

President Davis

Judge Underwood

E. Fox
W.A.Parsons
J. Freeman
L Carter
J.R. Fritchet
C.P. Fritchet
W. Van Lew
J.Cox
F.Smith
H.L.Wiggand
J. E. Frazier
L.Tabb
J.B.Willis
L. Boyd
B.Wardwell
Thos.Lucas
A. Brooks
L.Lipscomb
L. Lindsey
A Lilly
J.Morrisey
J. Turner
Wilburn
Dr W.Scott

The grand jury that was convened to consider evidence against Jefferson Davis, imprisoned ex-president of the Confederacy, included several newly enfranchised black citizens, among them Albert Brooks. Wartime Unionists were also on the jury, but Davis was not indicted because the federal government decided that such a trial would inflame the restive South. From the Valentine, Richmond, Virginia

and had many white connections, was deeply involved in early Reconstruction politics. He carried a Richmond petition for universal black male suffrage to Congress in 1867 and served on the Richmond jury chosen to hear evidence for an indictment of Jefferson Davis. Although charges against Davis were reduced and then dropped, Brooks's travel to Washington to petition Congress caused the *Richmond Whig* to hint that his hack license might not be renewed as a result of his activities. At that point Brooks withdrew from overt action and concentrated on obtaining an education for his children.[15]

WHILE both black and white Richmonders sought to influence policy in local, concrete ways that affected their daily lives, most of the nation's attention was drawn to the more abstract national questions of the status of the southern states and the method of their reentry into national politics. The struggle between President Johnson and Congress for control of Reconstruction occupied national politics while the Union's military forces occupied the South. Little national thought was given to the economic reconstruction of southern banks, industry, and agricultural production. It was assumed that outside capital, mostly northern, would invest where it was profitable. Local opinion generally held that the results of the war vindicated Richmond's antebellum commitment to commerce and industry, and it was reasonable to assume that the city could regain and surpass its former position, now that the South seemed convinced of the benefits of "progress."

Almost all of the physical damage done to Richmond in the war was confined to the fire on the night of the evacuation. The war's larger economic costs for Richmond and for the South took longer to tally. A series of dismal statistics describe the southern losses: The white South had lost two-thirds of its assessed wealth and one-quarter of its white men of military age. Nearly half of the livestock and farm machinery of the agricultural regions was destroyed. Southern agricultural and manufacturing capital declined by 46 percent; when the loss of slaves is counted, the decline was 74 percent. Southern per capita commodity output fell from almost equal to the North's in 1860 to only half of the North's in 1870. Southern per capita income dropped from two-thirds of the North's to less than two-fifths.[16]

Yet there were signs of hope in Richmond. The city had grown in population and industrial capacity during the war. The Tredegar Iron Works was not destroyed in the fire because Major Anderson armed his employees and drove off the Confederate torchbearers. Richmond rebuilt rapidly during Reconstruction, faster than most southern cities. It lost little of its wartime population and, in the 1870 census, maintained its prewar rank as the second largest city in the South. Richmond had prospered with the ambiguities and contradictions of urban slavery, and the city's urban leaders had expectations for similar adjustments under the new system. To implement those adjustments, they needed political control of the city. In the former capital of the Confederacy, as elsewhere in the South, southerners were generally willing to accept their military defeat and the end of slavery but were generally unwilling to grant civil and political rights to the freedmen. Reconstruction was a different event from city to city and state to state in the South. Partly because Richmond experienced less mob violence than cities such as Mobile and New Orleans, Virginia's official Reconstruction ended as early as 1870. But events in Richmond, while less violent, were intensely political.

Between 1865 and 1867—the period in which Pres. Andrew Johnson, a southern small farmer, controlled the southern states' reconstruction and readmission to the Union—a southerner much like him in background was the leading white radical in Richmond. The sympathies of Union loyalist James W. Hunnicutt, a white Primitive Baptist preacher and the longtime editor of the *Fredericksburg (Va.) Christian Banner*, initially lay more with Virginia's yeomen than with freedmen. Hunnicutt was outraged in 1861 with what he perceived to be the secession conspiracy of Henry Wise and others of Virginia's planter class. He established the *Richmond New Nation* in 1866 and promoted a "revolutionized" Virginia, with public schools, manufacturing, and confiscation of the lands of the powerful planters he called "negro-oligarchs."

But most of Virginia's Unionists (referred to as "scalawags") and carpetbaggers—the postwar migrants who organized Virginia's Republican Party—were mindful always of the South's need to build a Republican Party connected with the national party. They were wary of extreme positions that might alienate prewar Whigs, seen as potential allies, or discourage northern capital from investing in the South. While certain highly visible Republicans in Richmond were radical or "ultra" in their desire to change social and political institutions, most, black and white, were moderate, and some were inclined to make few changes at all. Radicals advocated restructuring of the tax system, redistribution of land, and massive expenditures for public education. These goals allowed others, who focused on political rights and local schools, to position themselves as centrists by contrast.[17]

White Republicans in Richmond were often men who were native to the city or to Virginia. Many of them had been Whigs or, briefly, Know-Nothings before the Civil War, and a healthy fraction were German immigrants. They had made their fortunes or established their shops before the Civil War, and that conflict caught them just as they entered city politics. Half lived in the crowded center city of Jefferson Ward. The 1867 annexation of large tracts on all sides of the city, from which Marshall Ward was formed, created more white working-class voters in the same year that the franchise was extended to black male voters and Congress took control of Reconstruction from President Johnson.

After 1867, the contest for political control of the city centered in the wards and in the distribution of black and white voters. The customary pattern in older southern cities was for slaves to be domiciled in or near the master's house. In Richmond's old genteel neighborhoods, servants still lived in the alleys and outbuildings until late in the century, while a majority of black workers lived near factories and stores. The 1870 census showed a relatively even distribution of blacks among the five large wards of the city, clustered in the north above Leigh and Jackson streets and in the low ground east of Shockoe Creek Bottom. Jackson Ward was formed in 1870, largely from land acquired in the 1867 annexation; the ward held enough black voters to elect one or more black councilmen. Jackson Ward was a classic gerrymander to contain black voting power, and over time it did encourage black residence in that neighborhood. Political power was now the most widely distributed it had ever been in Richmond, and the possibilities for faction were almost infinite. Over the next generation, in the process of testing alliances, white Richmond voters repeatedly had to decide whether racial or class interests were more important.

For most blacks, the Republican Party was the party of emancipation, associated with the fall of Richmond and Lincoln's walk through the city. Blacks were mindful of the importance of commemorating Emancipation but disagreed on which date to honor. Some celebrated on 6 April 1866, to mark the first anniversary of Richmond's fall, but others favored 1 January, the anniversary of the Emancipation Proclamation. Marchers on 1 January 1866, some 2,000 strong, were organized by societies; they marched in ceremonial dress to the capitol, where they and a crowd of 15,000 observers heard James W. Hunnicutt and black speakers. The parade to Capitol Square, an area from which blacks had been banished, was an important symbol of a world turned upside down. The city's municipal officers opposed the celebration, but permission was granted by federal authorities. Although the celebration's organizers had issued a letter avowing their peaceful intent, a subsequent fire at Second African Baptist Church was generally believed to have been retaliatory arson.[18]

The passage of the Reconstruction Act of 1867, which granted Congress power over the defeated Confederate states, encouraged freedmen in southern cities to enter horse-drawn streetcars rather than staying in their traditional place on the cars' platform. On 11 April 1867, after a rally at the First African Baptist Church, blacks attempted to integrate Richmond's streetcars. When they left the platform and took seats inside, four blacks were arrested while an angry black crowd observed. Two weeks later, three members of a black militia unit, the Lincoln Mounted Guard, refused to move from streetcar seats and were arrested. Within a month

Northern benevolent and missionary societies followed the Freedmen's Bureau into Richmond and opened schools for black learners of all ages wherever space could be obtained. This school was held in Chimborazo Hospital. **The Misses Cookes' School-Room, Chimborazo Hospital,** engraving published in Frank Leslie's Illustrated Newspaper, 17 November 1866, from the Valentine, Richmond, Virginia

the cars were segregated entirely, with four of six cars reserved for white women and children. Black riders could use two cars, and white men could board any car they pleased.

This system of segregation was later modified and continued informally throughout the 1870s and 1880s in its original intent, which was to separate white women from black passengers, especially black men. In public settings, especially those frequented by both men and women, separation of the races was customary. While some efforts were made to breach the barriers in public accommodations, tradition held firm in established activities. In theaters, railroad cars, and boats, the traditional antebellum physical separation between free blacks and whites now prevailed during Reconstruction despite protests, written complaints, and lawsuits by freedmen. Blacks had also been customarily excluded from inns, hotels, and restaurants and segregated or excluded from public services such as cemeteries and almshouses.[19]

In the newer realm of public education in Richmond, free black schools preceded free white schools, and the systems remained separate. Schools for black children and adults were quickly established, with teachers from the American Missionary Association and the Freedmen's Bureau. Even during the brief period in 1869 when "radicals" gained control of the city's Common Council and established a school system, they approved separate school systems for the two races. Publicly funded education, new to Richmond and the state, had only modest support in many areas, and an attempt to place both races in the same classroom would have meant a white boycott and the collapse of the school system. Richmond's black delegates to the Constitutional Convention protested that this was a dangerous precedent, but as northern aid to black schools fell off and the Freedmen's Bureau closed its operations, Richmond's black citizens turned their attention to maintaining existing schools rather than gaining access to white schools.[20]

In at least one sphere, it was blacks who chose to remain apart from whites. Black Baptists, the largest denomination, and some black Methodists remained separate from their white counterparts. Peter Randolph, pastor of Ebenezer Baptist, explained why he and his fellows formed the all-black Shiloh Baptist Association of Virginia rather than accept the invitation of white Baptists to join with them: "I think I voice the sentiment of my brethren when I say, that we chose rather to grope our way in the dark, than to have thrust upon us the kind of preachers we had had in the dark days of slavery. . . . Besides, we knew that our white brethren denied our manhood. . . . If we were poor and ignorant, we wanted to be consistent."[21]

In January 1867 the Virginia General Assembly failed to ratify the Fourteenth Amendment to the Constitution, passed by Congress in June 1866, which granted citizenship to freedmen. When the South rejected this amendment, Congress took control of Reconstruction in March 1867 and required each Confederate state to adopt a new constitution and then to reapply for admission to the Union. Republican nominating conventions met twice in Richmond in 1867. The conventions, rallies, debates, and party formation of the period provided platforms for issues of taxation, education, manufactures, and urban growth.

James Hunnicutt and his radical allies, many of them black delegates, dominated the Republican state conventions in 1867. In December of that year, when the state Constitutional Convention met to draft a new constitution so that Virginia might be readmitted to the Union, Richmond was represented by five Republicans, including the fiery James Hunnicutt and two other white men long resident in Virginia — Judge John Underwood, a northern-born farmer, and James Morissey, born in Ireland. The two black delegates were Lewis Lindsay and Joseph Cox, both considered radicals. Cox favored disfranchising all Rebels except poor whites, and Lindsay said that public buildings, places of amusement, and schools should be open to all. While the Virginia constitution that emerged was a compromise, moderate Republicans — who hoped for the party to create an alliance of planters, urban businessmen, and blacks, with white propertied elements in control — feared that Hunnicutt's rhetoric and influence would drive away prospective members and were determined to eliminate his presence. In early 1868, Clerk of the House McPherson rescinded Hunnicutt's government printing contract and thus killed his newspaper and his livelihood.[22]

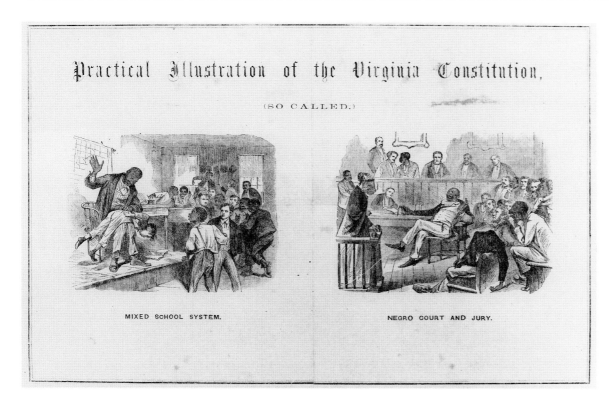

Practical Illustration of the Virginia Constitution,

(SO CALLED.)

MIXED SCHOOL SYSTEM.

NEGRO COURT AND JURY.

Each Confederate state was compelled to write a new state constitution before reentering the Union. This political cartoon illustrates the deepest fear of Virginians: that their long-assumed superiority based on race would be gone if freedmen were enfranchised. Courtesy of the Virginia State Library and Archives, Richmond

The radicals' strength convinced many former Democrats and former Whigs to form the Conservative Party in order to battle the Republicans. Late in 1868, as Virginia's draft constitution was making its way through the federal Congress, Alexander H. H. Stuart promoted a compromise in which political rights for blacks would be traded for a general amnesty for all ex-Confederates. In the subsequent political maneuvering in Washington, Virginia Democrats saw the possibility of common ground with conservative Republicans. Blacks played only a small role in the reorganization of the Republican Party and the drawing up of a new gubernatorial slate in the spring of 1869.[23]

Gilbert Walker, a conservative Republican from New York who was acceptable to Virginia Democrats, was elected governor in July 1869, and in 1870 an Enabling Act passed by the General Assembly gave him the power not only to fill vacant offices but to appoint new officials and to dismiss appointees or even elected officials. In Richmond, Walker's appointment of a new city council precipitated the most violent confrontation of the Reconstruction period. The Walker-appointed council selected the Conservative Henry Ellyson as mayor and appointed a known foe of blacks as police chief. The Republican mayor George Chahoon, a young radical from New York, and his black and white supporters refused to vacate the city government.

Chahoon had appointed Ben Scott, the militia captain who had drilled black Confederates and two years later had led the effort to integrate streetcars, as the head of a contingent of black police, and they, along with other police, refused to give up their guns and badges.

The Conservatives deputized civilians and firemen and surrounded Chahoon at the police station, cutting off food, water, and gaslights. A series of skirmishes took place between blacks and deputized police in which one of each side was killed. After being driven from the police station, the Chahoon forces appealed to the courts, and both sides packed the courtroom on the second floor of the capitol building on the day the decision was to be handed down. The courtroom gallery collapsed under the weight and fell into the House of Delegates below. Sixty people were killed and hundreds injured.

Two days later, the court announced a decision in favor of Ellyson, who was installed as mayor until regular elections could be held in May. In that election, the ballot boxes from the Jefferson Ward precinct, in which Chahoon had the largest majority, were stolen, and the remaining ballots gave the victory to Ellyson, who refused to serve under such circumstances. Another election was held and won by a Conservative Party member who was an Irish Catholic native of New Jersey and a Confederate veteran.

Republican and military rule in the city of Richmond ended with confrontation, disaster, and election fraud. When Reconstruction ended, white Richmonders believed they had repelled the threat of black equality and its attendant social chaos. But the diminished horizon for Richmond blacks meant, for Richmond itself, the loss of a particularly articulate, alert, and ambitious group; the city needed just such people in its working population as it attempted to rebuild after the Civil War and, more important, to find a profitable place in the new industrial nation.[24]

In the years before 1873, when a severe economic downturn halted growth for the rest of the decade, Richmond modernized its infrastructure, not only improving the quality of urban life but also creating a base for later development. Considering the desperately narrow tax base and the number of poor Virginians entering the city for work, a significant amount of renovation and construction was accomplished. The city also extended the horse-drawn streetcar line, rebuilt bridges, and began a constitutionally mandated public school system. Before the war, the city had been dependent on special licenses, taxes, and fees for revenue; now the city instituted a property tax and expanded the use of bond issues to finance postbellum public improvements.

An 1870 municipal war between conservatives and Republican city officials led to a siege of Republican forces, several deaths, and a disputed mayoral election. So many men packed the capitol's court gallery to hear the legal decision that the gallery collapsed into the House of Delegates. **The Richmond Calamity— Citizens and Firemen Removing the Wounded, the Dying and the Dead, from the Ruins,** engraving by W. L. Sheppard, published in Frank Leslie's Illustrated Newspaper, 14 May 1870, from the Valentine, Richmond, Virginia

Richmond expanded water, gaslight, and fire department services and promoted a professional police force in the years following the Civil War. The thirty-year-old waterworks west of Richmond had proved inadequate during wartime, and residents were forced to drink the amber water of the James River. Despite postwar efforts—repairing the pumps and enlarging the reservoir—the waterworks still did not meet the needs of the city, so the city planned and constructed a new reservoir, which was completed in 1876. The city gasworks suffered from worn-out equipment and high costs of production. Although money was invested in modernization, the gasworks remained only marginally profitable. The city council also established a uniformed and armed police force of 120 white men and 8 sergeants and agreed in principle to a modernized fire department, although it was unwilling to buy fire engines.[25]

Richmond's advantages before the Civil War had been excellent waterpower, a navigable river, and nearby natural resources. Although the iron ore and coal deposits of the region were not of the highest quality, they were adequate for the needs of the metal industries that first developed in the city. Wheat and corn were converted to flour and meal with river power, tobacco was processed with local labor, and all were distributed through railroads, canals, or shipping on the James. But with the exception of tobacco processing, all of these initial advantages fell short of the demands of the late-nineteenth-century economy.

Richmond's postwar economic difficulties existed on several levels. The need to rebuild and the cash-poor nature of the regional economy were obvious. Less apparent was the nation's shift toward a larger-scale economy, in which the city's advantages were not sufficient to make it more than a regional center. There were difficulties in even that effort: the quality of the area's natural resources was far from high; the James River's rocks and constant silting made dredging for a deepwater port very difficult; and Richmond's five railroads dominated trade with the countryside but did not connect it with other cities in a more comprehensive regional trade system.

These trends were not immediately clear following the war. Production resumed quickly in most industries, and tobacco manufacturers regained their old markets to the north. Richmond appeared a better prospect to many investors than did most of the South. Within a year, three banks had been set up, and the Tredegar Iron Works had attracted enough northern investment to resume production. The confidence of Richmond's businessmen was expressed in an editorial that urged, "Vote for Richmond's quota to the subscription stock of the Chesapeake and Ohio road, and Richmond will become the rival of Cincinnati. 'Now's the day, and now's the hour.'" Although Richmond voters affirmed this vision and subscribed to railroad bonds in 1868, the Virginia legislature—unlike those in Georgia, Alabama, and the Carolinas—chose to pay off the state's prewar debt at high interest rates rather than invest their limited resources in modernizing railroads. When Virginia railroads went into default and receivership in the early 1870s, the state sold most of its stock. National companies bought the lines and financed the consolidations and mergers, which took place with an eye to national markets. In this national reorganization, Richmond lost much of its former function as a point of exchange.[26]

While the city was apparently making a rapid economic recovery in the late 1860s, the James River seemed determined to show the city's limitations. Attempts to clear the river of wartime debris and to deepen the channel only demonstrated that natural rock formations in the river and a rapid silting process would make it impossible for newer ships with deeper drafts to come upriver to Richmond. Although some damage to the James River and Kanawha Canal was repaired and the city council appropriated funds for canal improvements, railroads replaced the canal and river as a central means of transporting goods.[27]

By the time that the Panic of 1873 halted economic growth, the Main Street business district was substantially rebuilt, and Broad Street had expanded its dry-goods stores, hotels, and saloons. The new buildings were better built than their predecessors; most of them were made of brick, masonry, and stucco, often with ornamental lintels. Iron fronts that were bolted to the inner frames of buildings permitted the installation of larger show windows. Four or five stories high, with flat roofs and sheer fronts, these buildings looked functional and made Richmond look modern and competitive.[28]

The Panic of 1873 and the subsequent depression affected the entire nation but was particularly hard on the South, where cotton prices fell by almost half until they were little higher than the cost of production. Tobacco, rice, and sugar also suffered severe declines in price. Tobacco farmers recovering from the war lost the gains they had managed to make, and local

Cutting and selling wood on the city streets was one of many small enterprises by which residents contrived to earn a living in the post-war years. Richmond's economic recovery was rapid enough to draw new people looking for employment. From the Valentine, Richmond, Virginia

banks, which often had inadequate capital to begin with, were unable to provide them with loans. Flour mills suffered less; they continued to regain markets until the 1880s. Gallego and Haxall-Crenshaw rebuilt larger mills after the evacuation fire and an 1874 fire at the latter.

The depression was a genuinely devastating setback for Richmond's economic aspirations, but neither the Panic of 1873, Reconstruction, nor the Civil War upended the structure of wealth in the city. At the end of official Reconstruction, half of those who had been the city's wealthiest citizens in 1860 remained in that category. The newly wealthy—almost all from Virginia or Richmond—resembled in family background, occupation, and economic interest those whom they had displaced. Freedmen were at the other end of the economic scale. Faced with lack of capital in the postwar years, black tobacco factory workers attempted to organize both a producers' cooperative and a home-building society. But neither their Tobacco Manufacturing Society or the Building Aid Society ever acquired sufficient capital to establish a cooperative factory or build a home. The obstacles to such enterprises were too great. More successful was the Freedmen's Savings Bank, in which some seven thousand Richmond blacks opened accounts.[29]

The depression slowed commerce and drove many merchants into bankruptcy. Artisans were laid off or failed to get contracts. Black artisans, who had fewer resources than white artisans, were hit especially hard. The depression caused the Freedmen's Bank to fail, and with it went the hard-earned savings of many small depositors. The venerable Tredegar Iron Works, which had survived the evacuation fire, was forced into bankruptcy. In 1880 the South's per capita income was only one-third that of the rest of the nation, and the region was farther behind in agricultural and industrial production than it had been in 1870.[30]

Even if Richmond had lost its antebellum industrial advantages, it had made a creditable economic recovery in an era of great turmoil. But the economic collapse of 1873 and 1874 overwhelmed an economy that had appeared to be rebounding from the war. Few people entered the city for the rest of the decade. Another event of 1873 prefigured one direction that the city would take in the next decades. The newly organized Southern Historical Society acquired an all-Virginia executive committee and moved from New Orleans to rent-free space in Richmond's capitol; from here, its memorial activities and publications would make post-Reconstruction Richmond the center of Confederate commemoration and memory.

CHAPTER EIGHT

Sorting Out the New South City

Ten years after the end of the Confederacy, Richmond unveiled and dedicated a statue of Stonewall Jackson. Begun with money from English donors and completed with funds from the Virginia state legislature, the statue was the first in the Confederate capital to honor a Confederate hero, and it drew many veterans and some of their families to the city. Tattered Confederate flags flew beside fresh American ones, and downtown the city erected a Grand Arch; a stone wall was painted on the arch, and atop this wall lay a saber, a Bible, and a Confederate cap. Above these artifacts the Angel of Peace was ascending and pointing to the pinnacle of the arch, which held a cross. At the base of the arch was inscribed, "Warrior, Christian, Patriot."

The decorations had a homemade quality that only added to the pride and enthusiasm of the crowds gathered for the dedication. White Richmonders opened their homes to veterans, while soldiers who had been cared for in the Confederate hospitals held reunions with their nurses. In the first decade after the Civil War, sentiments of shared grief and comradeship united ex-Confederates and their families, and a sense of mutual impoverishment intensified those feelings.[1]

In the years that followed, more Confederate memorials and monuments found sites in the city, Confederate reunions developed patterns that became traditions, and in the same decades, ethnic political alliances and labor unions reached their local peak of power and influence. Late-nineteenth-century Richmond witnessed a continuation of the process, between the races and among classes, of testing the post-emancipation world and contesting for space in the city. The city's traditional leadership sought to maintain political control and to reaffirm its status, while immigrants, shopkeepers, factory workers, and freedmen sought more access to urban politics and space.

A quick trip to Richmond during this period might convince a visitor that southern roles had strangely reversed after the war. Despite the requisite Confederate soldier placed on every courthouse square, the South was now devoted to progress, whereas Richmond, the old industrial city, had no peer in collecting documents, building monuments, and planning memorials to the Confederacy. Southern editors and urban boosters heralded the dawn of a New South — one that they claimed was dedicated to emulating the north's achievements in industry — while Richmond became the cenfer of the Lost Cause, a cluster of enterprises devoted to interpreting and preserving the history of the War between the States. But the visitor who stayed in town a few days would find that this first impression had been hasty and that the ritualization of the Confederate past was productively linked with the New South vision of economic growth.[2]

Richmond was the region's dominant city, far ahead of Petersburg and Norfolk but not connected with either of them in a regional system of trade. The 1867 annexation of large tracts to the west and east was only part of the reason for the city's remarkable growth between 1860 and 1890, when it more than doubled in population. The old industries of plug tobacco, iron, and flour continued in those decades; later, in the 1880s, cigarettes became an important new commodity and related paper products, chemicals, dyes, and spices were developed. At the same time, though Richmond's growth in population and production was real, other cities that were better placed for the new national trade systems grew faster.

Atlanta, placed at the intersection of trade routes from the Ohio River Valley to the Atlantic and from New Orleans to Richmond and Washington, found that its superior location was not diminished by the Civil War. Near the end of the nineteenth century the population of Atlanta reached and passed that of Richmond. Birmingham—scarcely a crossroads when Richmond iron was rebuilding after the Civil War—surpassed Richmond in iron production in 1878, only seven years after the city was established. These two cities were part of the physically new South, well connected with new railroads and better positioned than Richmond to take advantage of the post–Civil War national economy. The southern entrepreneurial prizes of the late nineteenth century seemed to favor the Piedmont, and while Richmond was at the Piedmont's edge, it was tied to an older industrial structure that had been hard-pressed to remain nationally competitive even before the Civil War brought a brief but intense stimulus to all forms of production.

The antebellum flour centers, including Richmond, Baltimore, and Wilmington, all suffered as the wheat belt moved west and large milling centers were established on the Great Lakes. The growth of a flour industry in South America removed a major market for Richmond's products. In iron and steel, both Pittsburgh and Birmingham benefited from new technology and from planning that envisioned national markets.[3]

Richmond drew little of the new European migration entering northern and midwest-

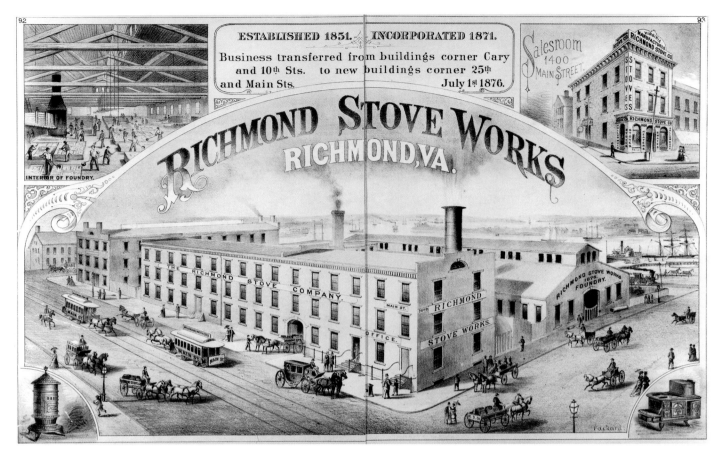

RICHMOND STOVE COMPANY,
2501 to 2519 Main Street, RICHMOND, VA.,
MANUFACTURERS OF

COOKING STOVES AND RANGES,
Heating Stoves, Stove Hollow-Ware and Furniture,
Fronts, Grates, Fenders, &c.
GOODS UNSURPASSED IN QUALITY.
SATISFACTION GUARANTEED.

Richmond had a wide variety of small industries in the late nineteenth century. Some were by-products of iron-making and tobacco processing, while others were the product of local inspiration. Selling southern patriotism and domestic efficiency, Richmond Stove Works combined a Lost Cause icon and a New South product in its new Lee Stove of 1889. Above, **Richmond Stove Works,** *lithograph published in F. W. Beers Illustrated Atlas of Richmond (1876); below,* **The New Lee Stove,** *published in Picturesque Richmond. Richmond, Virginia, and Her Suburbs (Richmond: J. L. Hill Printing Co., 1891). From the Valentine, Richmond, Virginia*

ern cities, but after the Civil War, rural Virginians and many from North Carolina were drawn to Richmond as if by a magnetic force, settling near the old industrial center of the city along the James River and Shockoe Creek. White industrial workers lived in narrow frame houses on Oregon Hill, Gamble's Hill, and Fulton, and walked to their factories. Black industrial workers remained in the crowded bottomland and walked to tobacco factories in the oldest parts of the city.[4]

The new Confederate memorials on the landscape did not indicate a change of heart in the city's long desire for industry and growth; the monuments to the Confederacy contributed to the city's real estate speculation and suburban development. Richmond's central role in the Confederacy and its willingness to help provide support for a Confederate archive encouraged ex-Confederates to move the recently formed Southern Historical Society from New Orleans to Richmond in 1873. The same local energy and purposefulness that expanded old businesses and began new ones characterized the vigorous efforts to memorialize the Confederacy, collect its artifacts, and write its history. In their advertising and in city directories, city businessmen at every level found it useful to mention their service to the Confederacy.

When Confederate general Jubal Early maneuvered the Southern Historical Society to Richmond, the Reverend William Jones was installed as secretary-treasurer, with offices in the state capitol building. Jones, a Baptist minister and former Confederate chaplain, became the high priest of the Lost Cause. The society began collecting records of the war and establishing an agreed-upon version of the war's causes and battles. As editor of the Southern Historical Society papers, Jones allowed a wide range of opinion over battle tactics, but not over the cause of the war, which was identified as a constitutional struggle over the states' right to secede from the Union. He acted as censor of textbooks and opinions not sympathetic to the Confederate view and promoted ex-Confederates for public office.[5]

Hollywood Cemetery, which since the 1840s had been intended to be a romantic and natural setting with paths and carriageways through a picturesque landscape, boasted the graves of Virginia-born presidents John Tyler and James Monroe. It also contained the city's first Confederate memorial, the product of a heartfelt effort to honor the war dead. The Hollywood Memorial Association, organized by Richmond women, first sponsored a grave-cleaning project in Hollywood Cemetery, purchased stones for each grave, and constructed a paved walk. In 1869, a large stone pyramid—a starkly eloquent statement of waste and grief—was dedicated there through the efforts of the Memorial Association. Although Richmond had several cemeteries of historic note that contained the remains of both notable citizens and Confederate war dead, Hollywood Cemetery became the cemetery of record, reflecting and evoking the city's past. Hollywood supplanted old-fashioned burying grounds like Shockoe Cemetery, which held many of the city's early illustrious citizens, such as John Marshall and John Wickham.[6]

Hollywood Cemetery was designed to be a place of thoughtful reflection in a parklike setting. Modeled after Mt. Auburn Cemetery near Boston, it contained paths, benches, and panoramic vistas of the James River, as well as mausoleums. The Hollywood Memorial Association, organized by Richmond women, commissioned this monument to the Confederate dead buried in the cemetery. Designed by engineer Charles Dimmock, the monument was completed in 1869 and represents a part of the nation's first phase of Civil War monument-building. From the Valentine, Richmond, Virginia

Memorial societies were part of the realm of sentiment, which women controlled, and in this role women acted as arbiters of tradition and chief mourners in the Lost Cause. What was new about these societies was the forward role that women took in choosing memorial sites, contracting with sculptors, and raising money, often in conflict with Confederate veterans engaged in their own memorial activities. The memorial societies and monument associations provided space for a new assertiveness and independence by white women and affirmed their class status through their own efforts, without the sponsorship of male or religious authority, and sometimes even in opposition to it.

The death of Robert E. Lee in October 1870 provided the stimulus for the formation of two new organizations—the Ladies' Lee Monument Association and a veterans' organization, the Association of the Army of Northern Virginia, both centered in Richmond. The Lee Monument Association was formed from the governing board of the Hollywood Memorial Association and hoped to be as successful as that group had been in raising money for a memorial. But this group of women from prominent families had to contend with the ambitious founder of the veterans' organization—the unreconstructed Confederate general Jubal Early—who tried very hard to wrest control of the Lee Monument Association from the women's group and once threatened to gather a band of veterans and blow the statue up if a Frenchman was permitted to design it. In 1877, Early's group was asked to turn over its funds to a state governing board, and in 1886 the men's and women's associations were combined. Gov. Fitzhugh Lee and the Common Council ultimately sided with the ladies of the Lee Monument Association, who kept control of the finances, the placement, and the design.[7]

As factions within the city's elite and within the state government rallied to affirm their past and assure their future, others became determined to show that they too were in the real tradition of American patriots and had as much claim to the material rewards of labor and citizenship. In the decades when Confederate reunions and monuments were disputed between sexes and classes, Richmond also experienced other white class conflicts as well as serious efforts at cross-racial alliances. In April 1870, black workmen in Richmond organized a branch of the Colored National Labor Union, which had been formed in Washington in January, with Fields Cook as a delegate from Richmond. The Richmond branch appointed twenty-four honorary vice presidents, mostly older craftsmen and younger ironworkers, but the group also included two Baptist ministers. Concurrently, the Mechanics' Trade Union, a white local craft union that resembled an older mutual benefit association, aroused suspicion among merchants in the city by becoming politically active and inviting a speaker from the National Labor Union. His speech was called "communistic" in the local press and was represented as an attempt to stir up class feeling among white workers where none had existed before.[8]

In the late 1870s, Richmond entered a period of growth in which industrial diversification compensated for the lackluster performance of certain older firms. The Gallego and Haxall flour mills, once world-renowned, lost much of their international and national markets late in the century, and the old triumvirate of tobacco, flour, and iron declined in the city's total manufactured product. The growth of Richmond Cedar Works and Richmond Chemical Works typified the expansion of the wood products and chemical industries, and C. F. Sauer and Company, begun by a young German immigrant, joined several other coffee and spice manufacturers and distributors in the city. Many of these enterprises derived from long-term Richmond commercial specialities, but at least one was in the best tradition of American entrepreneurship. Mann S. Valentine, in search of a nutritious drink for his ailing wife, created a beef marrow extract that became the basis for the Valentine Meat Juice Company. Founded in 1871, the company was so successful that a new plant was needed by 1877. Although the company made other products as well, it was known worldwide for the blood-bracing qualities of its meat juice.

Richmond tobacco experienced the fortunate combination of a popular new product, an available new technology, and a ready supply of quality raw material. Cigarette production—only a small part of the tobacco industry until the 1880s—soared when a new mechanism for rapid production was introduced. That mechanism was the Bonsack machine, which James A. Bonsack developed in response to a prize offered by the Richmond tobacco company Allen and Ginter. But Allen and Ginter failed to adopt the technology for its Richmond cigarette factory and let the mechanism go to James B. Duke of Durham, North Carolina, who improved it and used it to parlay his way to controlling most of the tobacco industry in the South. The growth of the cigarette industry provided employment for thousands in Richmond, even though the Duke tobacco trust dominated production.[9]

Mass production of cigarettes meant increased need for packaging, box design, chemicals, and dyes. Having long been a center for southern publishing, Richmond expanded its print and paper production to include advertising, specializing in the multicolored cigarette cards depicting languorous ladies or mustachioed baseball players. By the 1890s, over half the city's production encompassed such varied industries as agricultural implements; blank books and paper boxes; boots and leather; bricks, brooms, and woodenware; candy and confectionery; construction trades; drugs, chemicals, and bitters; fertilizer; furniture and mattresses; and tinware and plumbing.

The nature of the industrial work force changed rapidly as factories, especially the cigarette- and cigar-making branches of the tobacco industry, hired white women, first as hand rollers and then as machine operators. In a culture that claimed to elevate them, the hiring of white women for factory work made it important to describe cigarette-rolling as women's

Through his search for a nutritious drink for his ailing wife, Mann S. Valentine—a Richmond businessman and amateur scientist—created a beef marrow extract in 1871 that became the basis for the Valentine Meat Juice Company. For the Paris Exposition of 1878, Valentine had this display cabinet made out of Virginia woods. In 1892, Valentine donated his family home and his collections of art, Indian artifacts, family books and writings, and Richmond memorabilia as a museum for the history of the city. From the Valentine, Richmond, Virginia

Prizes, giveaways, and tobacco pack inserts were an important part of cigarette advertising. These women in baseball uniforms combined the two most popular themes in cigarette cards — sports and sex. Provocatively posed to display the curve of the thigh, the cards were meant to appeal to the late-Victorian gentleman smoker and perhaps to parody women's increasing interest in vigorous exercise through sport. From the Valentine, Richmond, Virginia

work and industrial labor as "light work" for their "nimble fingers," but the reality was that white women needed employment and would work for less than white men. White "female operatives" hardly existed in Richmond before the Civil War but now found factory employment in clothing, cotton goods, and paper bags and boxes as well as in tobacco.[10]

The plug tobacco industry and stemmeries, which had used primarily male slave labor, now employed black men, women, and children. The small shops of artisans and craftsmen in which black Richmonders had long worked were in decline, and those that survived attempted to exclude blacks from craft unions. In factories, a hierarchy of labor developed in which workers were separated by race and sex through task assignments, with black women and men consigned to lower-paid and more arduous work. Black and white men might interact in separate tasks, as in iron-making, but the work environment of black and white women was strictly segregated. The persistence of black skilled labor in Richmond—an unusual pattern for southern cities—was finally undermined as mechanization and changing patterns of production provided an opportunity to exclude skilled blacks while unions ignored or segregated them.[11]

The expansion of the industrial working class, changes in its composition, and the enfranchisement of the freedmen were central factors in Richmond workers' effort to organize and to negotiate their wages and working conditions. The National Labor Union did not survive the economic hard times of the 1870s, and other attempts at labor organization in the 1870s and 1880s met with mixed success. Usually the gains were temporary and efforts to unite black and white workers, as in the Amalgamated Iron and Steel strike of 1882, did not succeed.

Then the Knights of Labor, the nation's first mass labor union, organized assemblies in Richmond. The Order of the Knights of Labor was one large union of skilled and unskilled, black and white, men and women, farmers, and people from small business. After a visit to Richmond by Knights of Labor grand master Terence Powderly in January 1885, more local assemblies of the Knights were organized. Twelve "colored assemblies" in Richmond and Manchester appeared in two months, indicating that blacks had been ready to create assemblies before the Order was ready to accept them. Black women tobacco workers formed assemblies, as did white women workers in tobacco and box factories. By mid-1886, the Knights had supported the coopers in a successful boycott of convict-made barrels, and a wave of strike actions

Tobacco remained central to Richmond's economy after the Civil War, but the product and the labor force diversified, while the production was mechanized. The manufacture of plug tobacco by hydraulic presses remained dominated by a black male workforce. Tobacco stemming, seen as black labor, was mechanized and employed more black females. The mechanization of cigar making — traditionally a craft — was, in Richmond, an opportunity to employ white women. The labor force reflected the city's growing segregation. The top photo shows women manufacturing cigars; the photo at bottom left, tobacco stemmers; and the photo at bottom right, employees and machinery in a nineteenth-century tobacco factory. From the Valentine, Richmond, Virginia

The Knights of Labor, a national union open to unskilled workers, to women, and to blacks, held its national convention in Richmond in 1886. The white women delegates shown at left affirmed their solidarity, respectability, and maternity. The presence of white women was not an issue, but the active participation of black men in the convention and racial confrontations in the city caused some white craft unions to draw away from the Knights. Despite the national and local setbacks that the Knights experienced in 1886, Richmond maintained assemblies of the Knights of Labor as long as the national union lasted. Women and baby photograph courtesy of Catholic University, Washington, D.C.; **Knights of Labor Convention, Richmond, 1886** (top left), engraving published in Frank Leslie's Illustrated Newspaper, 16 October 1886, courtesy of the Virginia State Library and Archives, Richmond; John Taylor Chappel photo (top right) from the Valentine, Richmond, Virginia

and boycotts had forced recognition of the union. The Knights opened a cooperative soap factory and planned a cooperative building association.

Public reaction to violent labor confrontations elsewhere in the nation emboldened Richmond employers to resist the Knights of Labor. In June 1886, the Old Dominion Iron and Nail Works announced their intention to cut wages by 10 percent and to introduce the Bessemer Process of steel production, which would eliminate numerous jobs. Baughman Brothers, a nonunion print shop, brought an injunction against the Knights and prepared a civil suit for damages.

In this climate, the national convention of the Knights of Labor met in October in Richmond. As black delegates from New York made a calculated attack on the color line, they were refused seating in restaurants and theaters. Gov. Fitzhugh Lee, who was scheduled to address the convention, refused to be introduced by a black delegate. Here, in public and in high relief, was the issue that would divide and conquer the Knights of Labor in Richmond. The Knights were unable to maintain racial unity in strikes, and employers saw that they could pit white and black laborers against each other.

Powderly and the Knights of Labor were caught between a genuine desire to treat black members as brothers and sisters and the realization that insisting on equal treatment for blacks could destroy the union in the South at a perilous moment in the union's effort to maintain national stature. Indeed, the Knights had to cancel a fancy-dress ball at the end of the Richmond convention, and the only onlookers at a labor parade were the city's blacks. By the end of the two-week convention, during which the local newspapers had repeatedly criticized the Knights' racial egalitarianism, local white laborers seemed less inclined to align with blacks than they had been earlier. Although the Knights of Labor continued to exist as a biracial union in Richmond until the Depression of 1893, membership dropped rapidly over the next year as Richmond businessmen, supported by the newspapers and the Law and Order League, countered union activity through injunctions and lawsuits.[12]

In the mid-1880s, when the Knights of Labor was organizing assemblies in Richmond, the politics of the city exhibited many of the characteristics of the ward-based alliances then dominant in northern and midwestern cities. Jackson Ward, a political entity designed to con-

1 Clay Ward   5 Jefferson Ward
2 Jackson Ward   6 Marshall Ward
3 Monroe Ward   7 Manchester Ward
4 Madison Ward

tain as much of the black population as possible in one voting district, became the center of black community and political life even while the area was still home to many Irish and German families. The Virginia-born children of antebellum immigrants supported two daily German-language newspapers and two branches of the Irish National League; along with the city's Italian families, they found centers of political and social activity in the Catholic Church, the saloon, new and revived militia companies, and work-based organizations. Even as ethnic whites continued to live and vote in Jackson Ward, black voters continued to make up more than 20 percent of the electorate in every ward. The gerrymandered creation of Jackson Ward meant that black members of city council would come only from that ward, but it also meant that Richmond continued to have at least one black city council member for a generation after the official end of Reconstruction. The politics of ethnic negotiation created alliances between black, German, and Irish ward politicians, who competed with business leaders for city council seats until late in the century. City politics in the 1880s and 1890s featured an important

Many of Richmond's factory operatives and laborers saw the saloon as the "working man's club." The city's many saloons were centers of political debate and organization as well as shop talk. They also offered work information, held mail for men with no fixed address, and often provided a free lunch. The women and children crowded into ramshackle housing often felt that too much of the paycheck was left at the saloon. Temperance organizations, which set up men's lodges or coffee bars, tried to maintain the private social space of saloons while eliminating the alcohol. Photographs of exterior of Giannotti's Saloon, corner of East Broad and Ninth streets, c. 1889–90, and tenement housing both from the Valentine, Richmond, Virginia; photograph of interior of Otto Gragnani's shop, Old Brook Road, early 1900s, courtesy of the Catherine Szari Collection, Richmond, Virginia

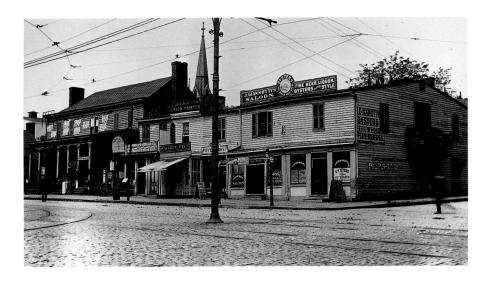

alliance between James Bahen, an Irish immigrant grocer and saloon keeper in Jackson Ward, and John Mitchell, editor of the city's black newspaper, the *Richmond Planet*. Mitchell, the son of slaves and only twenty-one when he became editor of the *Planet*, worked with Bahen, a fellow alderman and personal friend, to deliver the vote for the Republicans.[13]

Their saloon-based ward politics caused them to be called the "Whiskey Ring" and aroused the ire of those who did not want "white rum-keepers" to represent Jackson Ward. The saloon played a central role in city politics until after the turn of the twentieth century, and not all the "rum-keeper" politicians were white. Both Ben Scott and R. A. Paul, vigorous activists in city politics and captains of black militia, were saloon proprietors. The Whiskey Ring was opposed by the "Post Office Gang," which was largely made up of Republican appointees to federal jobs and which claimed more respectability. Both groups garnered black and white votes through the 1880s and 1890s.[14]

Voters were not neatly divided into Republican and Conservative or Republican and Democratic camps, nor were the parties themselves united. In this politically fluid period, alliances were made and broken, and each faction courted others, with little regard to race. As early as the Republican split of 1869, the Conservatives garnered some black votes, and they continued to do so as they evolved into the Democratic Party. Most black voters began and remained Republicans, and some white Virginians, such as ex-Confederate officer John S. Wise, believed the Republicans offered the best hope for the region. Confederate general William Mahone soon made common cause with the Conservatives but split with them over the increasingly controversial issue of Virginia's state debt. While other southern state legislatures were refusing to pay some or all of their antebellum debt, Virginia's conservatives, or Bourbon Democrats, were willing to divert funds from the new public school system to make payments on the debt.

A convention of Mahone supporters, called Readjusters for their willingness to readjust the state debt, met in Richmond in 1879 and formed a political alliance of white and black in an effort to lower the debt and keep the conservatives out of power. For four years, with the pivotal aid of the black vote, Readjusters controlled the state legislature, scaled down debt, saved Richmond's fledgling school system, and offered black leaders state jobs in the customs

The seventeenth-century diary of William Byrd I records the instructions he gave to an African worker for setting powder to explode rocks at the falls. Two hundred years later, quarrymen still broke rock in the region. As long as Richmond remained a city of diverse midscale enterprises, there was a market for extractive industries, such as this quarry, in the nearby area. From the Valentine, Richmond, Virginia

house or post office in return for their support. In 1883, Mahone's alliance lost the legislature, and Richmond's black voters lost much of their power to promote their interests at the state level. The Mahone supporters then became Republicans just in time to watch a Democrat, Grover Cleveland, enter the White House.[15]

At the city level, it took longer for conservative forces to defeat the ethnic and labor coalitions that united black and white in a viable opposition. In May 1886, a labor reform slate took control of the municipal government in Richmond, but this tumultuous year of strikes, lockouts, and shutdowns across the nation reverberated in Richmond and, along with the divisive Knights of Labor convention, broke the reform momentum.

In the next year, plans for placement of the Robert E. Lee monument and for an electric streetcar system began to change the physical landscape of the city and to shift attention from the old wards to new suburban sections. With that change in perspective and geography came a heightened attention to the racial division of space in Richmond, which developed just as other southern cities began to enact laws that segregated transportation and other public facilities. Prior to the late 1880s, segregation of public space, unlike public institutions, was often both tentative and negotiable in southern cities. In Richmond, as long as black artisans in tobacco, iron, and especially the building trades continued to work, they shared space

MAP OF THE
RICHMOND TRACTION CO.

Rival streetcar companies, especially the Richmond Traction Company and the Richmond Passenger and Power Company, fought in the city council and the state legislature for exclusive rights to build new lines or to control old ones. For the first time, residential development was driven by transportation rivalries. Richmond Traction Company map, 1898, from the Valentine, Richmond, Virginia

intermittently with white craftsmen. Often both groups lived in neighborhoods close to the factory and gathered in the same saloon after work. The uncertain nature of public segregation in Richmond was well illustrated by an Irish saloon in the working-class Fulton neighborhood, which simply drew a curtain down the middle of the bar when black and white drinkers reached a certain critical mass.[16]

In 1887, an enthusiastic city council authorized the Richmond Union Passenger Railway Company and a young New York engineer, Frank Sprague, to develop an electrical railway system. At that time the Richmond City Railway Company owned 190 horses and mules, which pulled rail cars over four and a quarter miles of track in the downtown business district. Other American cities were experimenting with electric streetcars, but Richmond was the first to attempt a complete system that reached out to growing residential areas beyond the downtown, extending from Church Hill in the east to the new Reservoir Park recently established at the city's western boundaries. Sprague used a four-wheeled car connected to an overhead wire called a troller, so the cars were called trolleys. The trolley line began operation in May 1888 with twelve miles of track and twenty-three cars; eventually the track was extended to eighty-two miles, and much of the new track ran to new suburbs.[17]

Improvement in transportation was one part of a reordering taking place as American cities came of age with American industry in the late nineteenth century. The World's Columbian Exposition in Chicago in 1893 reflected, in its emphasis on urban architecture, Americans' desire to make their growing cities civil and livable. New city plans included parks, suburban development, the expansion of public water and sewers, and the extension of new public services like electricity and telephones. Richmond was still the second largest city in the South, and its civic boosters proclaimed, "Richmond! Star of the South in the Provincial and Confederate days; in these [days] well-named the electric city."[18]

The price of industrial progress and the need for improved city services could be seen in the lower sections of the central wards of the city, where garbage piled up, flies swarmed, streets remained unpaved, and the bloated body of a dead work horse, still in blinders, might lie in the street for days. Most of the city's wells and springs had been contaminated by cesspools and privies, and canal water had become "foul and pestilent." As for Shockoe Creek, at the center of the city, the Board of Health commented, "In the summer its current is sluggish, and loaded as it is, by the contents of several public sewers and the refuse from many slaughter houses emptying into it . . . [,] its course seems to breed disease." The Committee on Streets stated that "in effect, Richmond is traversed in its whole breadth, and almost at its center, by an open sewer."[19]

Residents were increasingly dependent on a city water supply, not on the springs and wells that had once dotted the landscape nor on access to the river. The city had constructed new pumps and holding tanks in 1876, but the pumps were straining their capacity from almost the first day, and with inadequate holding tanks, water in the pipes remained muddy and was unfit for drinking. A new pump house, finished in 1882, removed the water shortage problem but did not remove the amber tint in the water. Water rates were high and were equally divided among users, which did not encourage water conservation. Only the gradual introduction of water meters after 1883 brought water consumption under control and made it economical for citizens to install more water closets, taps, and bathtubs.

Long bothered by coal smoke, poor paving and lighting, and the effluvient pollution of Shockoe Creek, the genteel residential section of the city moved westward from the neighborhoods around the state capitol. The transition was slow, and many downtown pleasures persisted. Grace and Franklin streets and parts of Gamble Hill lingered as residential areas, while on Church Hill, to the east, Richmonders continued to construct new middle-class residences. The Old Market on Seventeenth Street and the New Market at Sixth Street remained lively places, with farmers from the countryside and their produce, butchers, fish mongers, and hucksters haggling over price and calling their wares. In the diversity of their offerings, general stores were overwhelming to the senses. The aroma in Christian and White's Grocery on Main Street was "a marvelous mixture of coffee being ground, pickle in open barrels, spices, sweets . . . , vinegar, flour, ham and every pleasant odor under the sun." Oysters in season lay open in containers with long-handled dippers, hams hung from the ceiling, and pickles, flour, and crackers were displayed in barrels.[20]

Downtown citizens strolled to a restaurant for dinner after dances, and children played games in the streets and on Capitol Square. Boys rolled and smoked cigarettes in alleys and under bridges. The appearance of the city lamplighter was the children's signal to go home for supper, after which, in summer, they gathered in the streets again and played until well after dark. The favorite spots for babies and their nurses were Monroe Park, Capitol Square, and the pavement in front of St. Paul's Episcopal Church. Two department stores, Thalhimer's and Miller & Rhoads, anchored a commercial expansion on Broad and Grace streets, which catered to the woman shopper and offered employment to young white women. Meanwhile, the great tulip poplars on Franklin Street were "slowly dying from the wounds at their roots and the electric wires in their branches."[21]

New houses marched westward on city streets, representing the first line of residential movement from downtown. Streetcar companies bought suburban tracts and placed amusement parks and picnic sites at the end of trolley lines as an inducement to purchasers. The city of Richmond also acquired land for parks as early as 1875, purchasing Chimborazo, scene of the Civil War hospital, and Libby Hill in the east end. The most popular of the amusement parks was Forest Hill Park in Manchester (later south Richmond), which was served by the Richmond, Manchester, and Woodland Heights Line. Other city parks on the new trolley lines were Reservoir Park (later called Byrd Park), Ginter Park, Jefferson Park, Gamble's Hill Park, and Lakeside, which lay seven miles from Richmond. Bicycles and roller skates, adopted

In late 1915, a group
of children watched as
an oak tree reported to
be three hundred years
old was cut down on Park
Street near Harrison. As
utility pipes and wires
attacked their roots
and branches, the old
downtown trees died, and
more families considered
moving to the newer and
greener suburbs. From
the Valentine, Richmond,
Virginia

with enthusiasm by both children and adults, were well suited for the city and its parks. Young women rode bicycles for exercise and organized groups to cycle to parks, where they cooked chafing-dish suppers on the picnic grounds, extending their sphere of activity in the city while they kept physically fit.

Built by wealthy tobacco merchant Lewis Ginter, the streetcar suburb called Ginter Park represented a model of spaciousness and handsome houses. Ginter was not part of the traction wars; he ran his own Lakeside Line trolley cars to the suburb. From the Valentine, Richmond, Virginia

The *Richmond Dispatch* noted in 1891 that "men of means seeking villa sites; mechanics desiring cheap lots; people who delight in roominess and ample acreage have . . . encircled Richmond and Manchester with built-up suburbs."[22] Fares of a nickel, still too high for many workers, made the streetcar the transportation system of an enlarged middle class that included bank cashiers, insurance agents, teachers, and builders. Many of these houses displayed a new architecture of late Victorian exuberance, which contrasted with the austere flat fronts of downtown and the cramped, close-in frame subdivisions built by or for mechanics. Middle-class houses featuring the curves and dramatic flourishes known as the Queen Anne style of architecture were promoted by developers like Lewis Ginter and James Barton, who developed both streetcar lines and suburbs.

Ginter Park, an elegant northern suburb, was reached by Ginter's Lakeside line, and Barton Heights was built by Barton's Northside Land Company, which built a streetcar viaduct across Bacon Quarter ravine, a longtime obstacle to northern expansion. The Fan District, an eclectic assortment of housing west of Monroe Park, was built between the 1880s and 1920s, primarily in architectural styles that were part of a national suburban architectural trend designed to evoke a preindustrial past. In these suburbs, women shaped the landscape more than they had ever done downtown, forming garden clubs and taking responsibility for communal sections of the neighborhoods.[23]

In the late-nineteenth-century reordering of Richmond, middle-class women extended their domain beyond suburban landscapes. If the suburbs were, in part, a response to the declining quality of central city life, so were the new organizational activities of women, both black and white. The forms of these activities were as varied as the women engaged in them and at first seemed to have little connection. The Young Women's Christian Association formed a Richmond branch for white women in 1887 and developed a particular concern for rural girls entering the city for work. YWCA members met trains, provided employment referrals, and offered classes, clubs, libraries, and sports. Their concern began with shielding young women from a "life of sin," but it soon extended to surveying the working and living conditions of women and their families.

While women of the YWCA sought respectable boardinghouses and documented sanitary facilities in factories, the Association for the Preservation of Virginia Antiquities, founded in nearby Williamsburg in 1889, sought to preserve certain of Richmond's many historic sites. The 1890s also saw the national emergence of hereditary patriotic societies, such as the Daughters of the American Revolution and the United Daughters of the Confederacy, and a woman's club movement that began in Richmond with the Progressive Literary Association, organized by Jewish women in 1888.

At the same time the decade saw, in 1894, the beginning of diploma programs for Richmond nurses. Women graduates organized a settlement house, in which they offered classes on sanitation and nutrition and from which they went out to work in factories, kindergartens, and homes. Kate Waller Barrett, whose husband was a minister in Butchertown in the 1890s, began her work with the unmarried mothers commonly seen as "fallen women." In 1895, a Richmond Mother's Club was formed by Rosa Dixon Bowser and other black women. The grim realities of Jim Crow meant that from its inception this black women's club was involved with political and legal issues for all black women as well as civic and personal concerns.[24]

Another form of shaping and explaining the Richmond environment began in 1897 with the publication of the first book by a young city native. Ellen Glasgow, the daughter of a Scotch-Irish ironmaker and an old Tidewater family, resisted from an early age the image of the southern female and the southern past presented in Richmond, but she remained in Richmond for her five-decades-long writing career. At the heart of many of her novels was a tension between romanticism and realism that reflected her own conflicts and those, she believed, of her native state and city. Her novelistic weapons of social realism and irony did not entirely vanquish sentimental tendencies, and in this divided self she remained true to her personal vision of Virginia and Richmond.[25]

The wide aisles of the new department stores, the city baseball diamond, the Queen Anne houses rising on Church Hill, the patriotic and civic societies, the streetcar, and the parks were, like the electric railway system, evidence of a new urban culture and a new style of daily life. It was characteristic of Richmond that a national trend—in this case, a trend toward suburbanization and city beautification—would find a regional expression that combined Confederate memory and entrepreneurial aspiration. In June 1886, newspapers announced that "several prominent local officials, and property-holders in the neighborhood of the Allen lot" had met with a committee of the Lee Monument Association. The "Allen lot" was held by Otway Allen,

The front parlor of the middle-class home was the public face of the house and reflected Victorian propriety in its "terrible little gilt chairs and horsehair sofas and antimacassars," according to Richmonder Robert Cutchins. In the sedate atmosphere of the parlor, magic lantern slides entertained families with views of distant and exotic places or events in history. Dominoes, tiddlywinks, jackstraws, and jigsaw puzzles also amused the family, but many families banned card-playing because of its association with gambling. Parlor of the home of Dr. and Mrs. William B. Gray, 817 East Marshall Street, c. 1882, from the Valentine, Richmond, Virginia

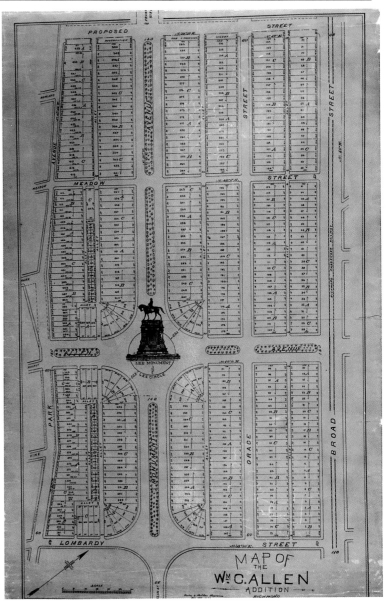

The dedication of statues and memorials to fallen heroes, as in this 1890 gathering for the unveiling of the Robert E. Lee statue on Monument Avenue, brought thousands of veterans and their families to the city for parades, speeches, and an atmosphere of reunion and renewal. The placement of the monument and the design of the adjacent area assured that the Allen property's value as a site for suburban development would appreciate. From the Valentine, Richmond, Virginia

a prominent citizen whose membership in the exclusive Westmoreland Club and in Confederate organizations aided his efforts to place the statue on his land. In arguing for this suburban site, Gov. Fitzhugh Lee stressed the increased city tax revenue from the monument's placement in a suburban area sure to be annexed; he made little reference to Confederate memory. After a year of planning and heated discussion — and Allen's donation of eleven of his fifty-eight acres for proposed avenues and a monument circle — the decision was made to place the monument on this lot, a flat field just outside the city's western boundaries. A small annexation in 1892 brought the area, which contained the Lee Monument and was developed as Monument Avenue, into the city.[26]

On 29 May 1890, the Lee Monument was dedicated in Richmond. The celebration that accompanied the placement and unveiling of the statue of Lee on horseback was elaborate, ritualized, and very well attended. Although donations had come from all over the South, Richmond's citizens played a central role in the commemorative ceremonies, which featured most of the white citizenry involved in transporting the statue through the streets. Infants and toddlers were taken from the nursery to touch the ropes that pulled the statue; one of four ropes was especially for young ladies, and pieces of the rope were kept as souvenirs and passed down in families. At the dedication ceremonies, the main speaker was Archer Anderson of the Tredegar Iron Works family, who pointed out that the unswerving devotion to duty practiced by Robert E. Lee and other Confederates now had to be applied to the battle for southern industrial development. John Mitchell, writing in the *Richmond Planet*, had another view. He believed that the Rebel flags and Rebel yells "told in no uncertain tones that they still cling to theories which were presumed to be buried for all eternity." Mitchell said the ceremonies "handed a legacy of treason and blood" to the future.[27]

The Lee Monument's unveiling marked the beginning of the period in which these rituals would be conducted by the United Confederate Veterans, a group organized the year before. In the 1890s, Confederate reunions in Richmond became increasingly commercial, usually linked with advertising campaigns. At the annual meeting of the United Confederate Veterans held in Richmond in 1896, souvenirs and relics were for sale, and ten-dollar discounts were available for veterans on the purchase of a piano or at the Great Reunion Sale of Millinery. In earlier times, visiting veterans had been taken into people's homes. Now hotel and restaurants merely offered discounts, although remnants remained of the old spirit; for example, Miss Sally Tompkins inserted a notice that read, "All the veterans who were nursed at the Robertson Hospital during the war are cordially invited to be entertained during the reunion at 600 East Main Street." During the 1896 reunion, white musicians at the Richmond Academy of Music turned out to offer the veterans a minstrel version of the sunny and carefree Old South. Polk Miller gave his production of "Old Times Down South," assisted by Judge Farrar as Johnny Reb. Also on the program were the Imperial Quartette's plantation melodies, Tony Miller's old-time banjo pickers, and Mr. E. H. Clowes's character rendition of "De Old Battered Banjo I Played When a Boy."[28]

The Old South and the Lost Cause came to be enshrined in more than monuments and

COLORED PEOPLE'S
CELEBRATION
At RICHMOND, VA.,
October 15th, 16th, and 17th.

"The chief object of this gathering is to establish a National Thanksgiving Day for Freedom, to be annually observed by the Negro Race.

The following is an outline of the programme for the occasion:

On the 15th the people will assemble at the Exposition Grounds. Welcome addresses by the Governor and Mayor. Speeches by Prominent Colored Men. The appointment of a committee to select and recommend the day to be annually celebrated by the colored people throughout the country.

On the 16th, grand parade to the Exposition Grounds, composed of **all organizations of colored people.** The report of the committee and the adoption of the day.

On the 17th, and last day, general speech-making and praise to God for the blessing of freedom. Fire-Works at night.

Each day there will be on the grounds all kinds of amusements and attractions, such as are exhibited at Expositions, &c.

Speakers from all over the country. Hon. B. K. BRUCE, Hon. JOHN M. LANGSTON, Hon. J. C. PRICE, D. D., of North Carolina, and Rev. W. W. BROWNE, President Savings Bank, Richmond, will be among the noted speakers for the occasion."

The R., F. & P. R. R. CO.
WILL SELL
Round-Trip Tickets at Specially Reduced Rates,

And visitors from on its line can attend the celebration and return home on the same day, if desired.

Agents of the Richmond, Fredericksburg and Potomac Railroad Company will cheerfully furnish information as to rates and schedule of trains for this occasion.

C. A. TAYLOR,
Traffic Manager.

As white Richmonders claimed space and time for Confederate memorials and rituals, the city's black residents debated which day should be celebrated as their day of emancipation. The store above was decorated for Emancipation Day in April 1888, the month that marked the fall of Richmond. Just two years later, shortly after the Lee Monument ceremonies, a series of articles in the September and October issues of the Richmond Planet debated the issue, and an attempt was made to move the celebration to October and to make it both a holiday excursion and a parade of black Richmond's accomplishments. Emancipation Day photograph from the Valentine, Richmond; broadside courtesy of the Virginia State Library and Archives, Richmond

minstrel shows. A cluster of museum enterprises began in the city in the 1890s. It was suggested that a central museum for the whole South be established in Richmond to serve as a repository for Confederate records. As a result, the Confederate Memorial Institute, a museum and archive, was undertaken with an initial donation from a wealthy Confederate veteran; the balance was made up largely from Richmond donors and Richmond city government. In 1892, Mann S. Valentine, a local businessman and amateur scientist and brother of the sculptor Edward, donated his family home and his collections of art, Indian artifacts, family books and writings, and Richmond memorabilia as a museum for the history of the city. One block away, the White House of the Confederacy, which had been used as a public school in the years after Reconstruction, was rescued from demolition and turned over to the Confederate Memorial Literary Society to become a Confederate museum.

The closer Richmond moved toward the twentieth century, the more it seemed both a city of archives and icons, the "holy city" of the Confederacy, and an American industrial city, reflecting the prosperity and problems of mass production. The Lost Cause as a form of civil religion for the South was especially evocative in Richmond. Yet the political influence of the Lost Cause zealots was probably not as great as its acolytes imagined. Both politicians and businessmen found the Lost Cause to be a malleable concept, adaptable to new circumstances.

Members of the Bryan family, influential newspaper publishers, were among the most active preservers and promoters of the Lost Cause in the city. Their lives reflected the harmony between that concern and New South development. Confederate veteran Joseph Bryan

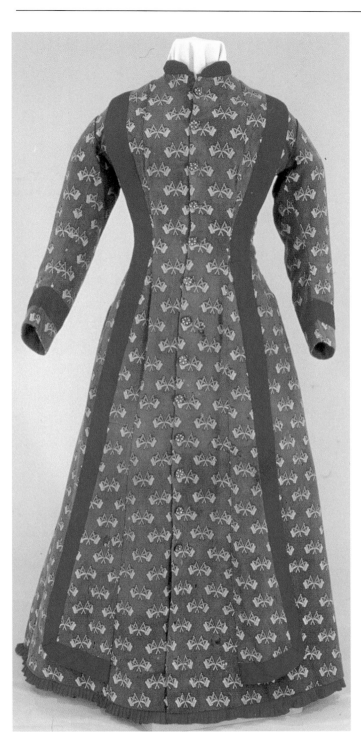

Much of the South's desire to memorialize the Confederacy and to ameliorate the condition of veterans was centered in Richmond. The Confederate flag–embossed material in this dress (left) was sold by the yard to benefit the city's Confederate Soldiers' Home (right). From the Valentine, Richmond, Virginia

organized a railroad holding company, the Richmond and West Point Terminal Railway, and was president of the Richmond Locomotive Works, which he expanded from a small shop to a major employer with federal contracts. He purchased the *Richmond Times* and there installed the first Mergenthaler Linotype machine south of the Potomac. In 1890 Bryan and his wife, Isobel Stewart Bryan, were among the founders of the Confederate Memorial Literary Society, and they helped to secure Lee's wartime home in Richmond for use as the headquarters for the Virginia Historical Society.[29]

Even as they trumpeted the arrival of an industrial South, Richmond editors were still challenged to duels as a result of what they printed. Although newspaper stories and light verse had provoked duels and a shooting in Richmond in the 1870s and 1880s, New South urban boosters saw dueling as an archaic relic that they hoped to leave behind. It was scarcely part of the plan for attracting business investment to the South. But as late as 1893, the secretary of the Richmond Democratic Committee, offended by an article in the *Richmond Times*, challenged newspaper owner Joseph Bryan to a duel. Bryan refused, saying that he was a Christian, a law-abiding citizen, and that he considered that method of settling differences absurd and barbarous. Made by one of the city's preeminent leaders in preserving the past and envisioning the future, the statement said that dueling was not to be a part of the New South or the new century.[30]

Readers of palms and tea leaves, clairvoyants, crystal ball gazers, and self-appointed experts often do a brisk business in pointing out portents and signs near the turn of a century. Richmonders who were looking for omens of the new century might have found them in three public events enacted on the city's streets at the turn of the century. An industrial parade celebrated economic progress and national reunion, while a streetcar strike and a streetcar boycott emphasized weakened labor organization and segregated public space.

When the Spanish-American War began in 1898, the city was proud to offer to the nation, beyond army volunteers, both an ex–Confederate general and ex–Virginia governor—Fitzhugh Lee—and a shipbuilding industry ready to manufacture the most advanced naval weaponry. A year after the brief conflict, an industrial parade of Richmond's trades was held, with President McKinley in attendance, to celebrate the launching of the USS *Schubrick*, a torpedo

In the late 1890s and early 1900s, Richmond celebrated its commercial and industrial growth with a series of trade parades. The early parade entries were homemade, small, and varied—much like local business was during that era. From the Valentine, Richmond, Virginia

boat built at the Trigg shipyard. The happy blend of Old South tradition and New South production that Richmond offered to the nation was never more apparent than during the Spanish-American War.

It was not lost on Richmond or American sensibilities that the breach between the North and South was almost closed when Fitzhugh Lee wore the blue uniform of the United States Army. The Spanish-American War signified a nation reunited, not least because the national policy of not granting citizenship to the dark-skinned residents of newly acquired territories seemed to confirm the southern experiment in second-class citizenship.[31]

The electric streetcar served as a focus of labor and race struggles in 1903 and 1904—the first a strike of white streetcar workers, and the second the last major effort by blacks to integrate the city's public transportation. The fact that the poorly run Richmond Passenger Power Company was owned by outsiders, yet enjoyed more access to the city council than Richmond citizens did, made it the target of much local hostility.

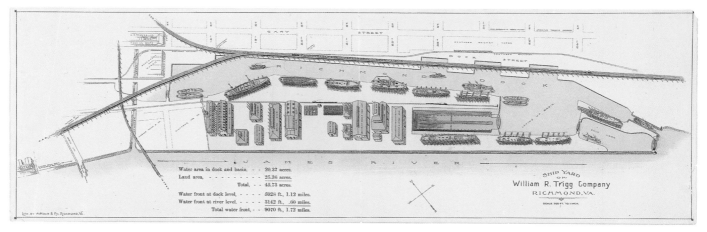

Water area in dock and basin, - - 20.37 acres.
Land area, - - - - - - - - - - 25.36 acres.
Total, - - 45.73 acres.

Water front at dock level, - - - - 5928 ft., 1.12 miles.
Water front at river level, - - - - 3142 ft., .60 miles.
Total water front, - - 9070 ft., 1.72 miles.

SHIP YARD
OF
William R. Trigg Company
RICHMOND, VA.

At the turn of the twentieth century, Richmond was proud of its shipbuilding industry and its contribution to the nation and the U.S. Navy during the Spanish-American War. Because the nearby ship lock was now too small to accommodate modern warships, a system of sluice gates and movable barriers was built at the shipyard to launch ships down the James River. **Ship Yard of William R. Trigg Company, Richmond, Va.** *(date unknown), lithograph by A. Hoen and Co., Richmond, from the Valentine, Richmond, Virginia*

In 1902, after several years of wage reductions, trolley motormen and conductors struck for a wage raise and were granted it. When car men went on strike in June 1903, transit officials resisted and asked for help from the business community, declaring that it was time to confront and defeat the unions. City merchants were divided; some merchants supported the strikers, but there were those who helped the transit company keep the trolleys running until professional strikebreakers arrived from Baltimore. Workers pelted the trolleys with mud, eggs, and filth, and, in Fulton, piled debris on the tracks. Shots were exchanged on Lombardy Street, cars were ambushed, and a later riot in Fulton brought two deaths.[32]

Violence caused the mayor to call in the state militia, and although the strike had broad support in the city, the presence of the militia kept the cars running and broke the strike and the union. This was Richmond's last major strike for twenty years. While union activism declined in Richmond, the number of skilled white male union members grew among the new and relatively conservative American Federation of Labor trade unions, especially in the metal and construction trades. A Tobacco Worker's International Union, with a biracial work force, organized blacks and whites into separate locals. The TWIU attempted to maintain white dominance in the union, but their experience in the Knights of Labor and their sheer numbers encouraged black locals to press their own agendas. In the early decades of the twentieth century, Richmond's labor movement remained visible but divided by race and dominated by skilled craftsmen.[33]

The year after the streetcar men's strike, Virginia passed a law permitting segregation of the state's streetcars. The Virginia Passenger and Power Company became the only company in Richmond to enforce a segregated seating system. In the *Richmond Planet*, John Mitchell called for a streetcar boycott. "Let us walk," he proclaimed, adding that "A people who willingly accept discrimination . . . are not sufficiently advanced to be entitled to the liberties of a free people."[34]

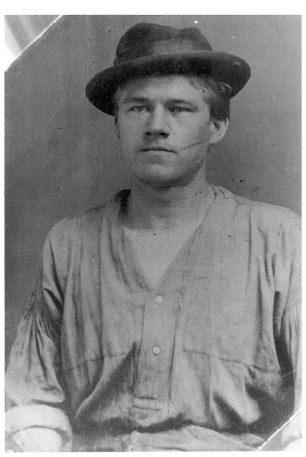

Henry Carter Osterbind (bottom left) grew up in this house at 621 South Belvidere and followed his father, German-born Anton Osterbind, into the Tredegar Iron Works. He was followed less than a generation later by his own son, Carter Clarke Osterbind (bottom right, man at left). Ties of friendship and family in the workplace, an informal system of apprenticeship, and the possibility of advancement within the work setting mediated the hard labor involved in iron-working. Henry Carter Osterbind in hat and work shirt (tintype, c. 1870–1875) and Henry Carter Osterbind and his son Carter Clarke Osterbind at Tredegar (photograph, c. 1910), courtesy of Mary Geschwind; 621 South Belvidere photograph from the Valentine, Richmond, Virginia

The boycott, which began in April 1904, was maintained for almost a year before numbers dwindled. Richmond's streetcar boycott was one of twenty-five in southern cities at the turn of the century, and none were successful. In 1906, the Virginia General Assembly passed a law requiring, rather than permitting, segregated streetcars.

Early in the twentieth century, it was apparent that the white cultural solidarity of the Lost Cause did not hamper the business coalition in Richmond. Instead, the institution of a

John Mitchell, long-time editor of the Richmond Planet and city councilman from Jackson Ward, grew up in the decades just after the Civil War, when Richmond's blacks voted and ran for office and Richmond Colored Normal had the resources and the teachers to turn out a well-educated and ambitious generation of post-emancipation black citizens. In his lifetime he witnessed, rallied against, and chronicled the contraction of possibility for black Richmonders. From the Valentine, Richmond, Virginia

PROCLAMATION.

To the Citizens of Manchester:

In view of the riots and resistance to law in our sister city of Richmond, caused by evil-doers taking advantage of conditions resulting from the Street Railway Strike, and being officially informed that the Virginia Passenger and Power Company will today commence running its cars in the City of Manchester, I hereby call upon all the good and law-abiding citizens of this city to aid me in the preservation of law and order. Any obstruction to the running of said cars, or the destruction of its property, or throwing missiles at or shooting at its cars is a very grave offence against the laws of this Commonwealth and will subject the offender to severe punishment.

This is a government of law and order and there can be no personal liberty without obedience to law. I shall expect and require the good people at this time, as in the past, to maintain their reputation for respect and obedience to law, which reputation we should be proud of and suffer no man or set of men to destroy by lawless acts.

As your Mayor, I shall see that the laws of this State are fearlessly executed and enforced. I confidently demand and expect your co-operation in upholding the laws and preserving the peace.

HENRY A. MAURICE,

July 2, 1903.   Mayor.

Wm. W. Lumpkin, Printer, 1006 Hull street.

SOLDIERS FIRING INTO ROCKETTS BOTTOM LAST NIGHT.

After the defeat of the Knights of Labor, Richmond's working class was on the defensive. Frustrations with conditions in the city came to a head with the strike of streetcar workers in 1903. Streetcar tracks were ripped out in Fulton and other working-class neighborhoods, and protesters attacked cars. The Virginia State Militia was called in to quell the disturbances. Workers lost this battle, which was Richmond's last major strike until 1922. Courtesy of the Virginia State Library and Archives, Richmond

civil religion created a surface harmony among whites that muted class issues and helped to maintain racial separation at a time when these class divisions were deep and sharp in other American cities. The Lost Cause was too flexible politically and economically and too valuable as a commodity not to be reinvented and revived as occasion demanded.[35] Still, it was Richmond's modern electric streetcar, more than its Confederate monuments, that sped up the process of creating new suburbs that sorted the city out by race and economic class, demonstrating once again that the modernizing technology in the New South was in harmony with the Lost Cause.

CHAPTER NINE

The Prism of Progress

Thinking back on his early years, a businessman reflected, "The night I arrived in Richmond is as vivid as if it were last night. Passing over the present James River Bridge, the train at eight o'clock pulled into the old Byrd Street Station, then the only entrance of the [Atlantic] Coast Line to Richmond. The sight of the lighted city as I crossed this bridge was somewhat dazzling. I did not know anyone in the city. I was a stranger in a strange land and my sensations, when I got off the train were mingled fear, misgivings and joy." [1]

The young man stepping off the train in Richmond at the end of the nineteenth century was, like thousands before and after him, from out in the Virginia countryside. Richmond was growing, although not as rapidly as its major New South rivals, Atlanta, Nashville, and Louisville. Southern cities at the turn of the century were experiencing the rapid growth that northern cities had earlier undergone, and Richmond offered the attractions of a regional retail and commercial center with a diversifying industrial economy and a proud history. Louis Powell, who saw the limitations of rural life, came to Richmond to attend a business college and to make his way in the world of commerce. Others came to study law, work on the docks, or become live-in maids, schoolteachers, typists, or telephone operators. Except in the hardest of hard times, rural Virginians came to Richmond steadily, especially in the early part of the twentieth century. They brought with them a resupply of rural values, beliefs, and pastimes that kept Richmond from drawing too far from its countryside.

It was possible to come to town from the country and, with respectable connections and good manners, to make one's way upward. Friends he made in a Baptist men's Bible study class helped Louis Powell find a position as a clerk. The migration of "country cousins"—stock figures on the stage but an ever-present reality in Richmond—proved an invigorating infusion into the city's commerce and produced many of its innovative entrepreneurs and civic leaders in each generation. Near the turn of the century, the rural migrant in the train station or on the docks at the James River, clutching a bulging suitcase and the remains of a packed lunch, was the intermediary figure between the Old South's rural values and the New South's urban vision. [2]

New people might enter Richmond on one of six major rail lines, six steamship companies, or a narrow gauge line from Farmville. Rail and river lines carried coal from western

Virginia to Norfolk, and fertilizer materials, ice, lumber, railroad ties, and grain to the city for processing or use. Tobacco remained the major industry; more than ten thousand employees were engaged in the manufacture of cigars, cigarettes, and cheroots. Iron, woodworking, and milling industries followed tobacco as employers, but the nature of such work was changing at the turn of the twentieth century even as iron and milling declined in importance. Manufacturing companies mechanized and subdivided labor processes, intruding on the traditional work systems of craftsmen and their helpers and substituting new workers, often women, in nonskilled or repetitive tasks. New employers—department stores and telephone companies—hired chiefly women, while office work was an expanding source of employment for both men and women.[3]

By the late nineteenth century, many of these migrants were single women. Women who had worked on isolated family farms without pay and without prospect of inheritance viewed the hard labor of factories as a decided improvement in their circumstances. Cash wages, the company of other youth, dance halls, and the colorful abundance of the notions counter in the department stores balanced the equation, at least for a few years.[4]

The prospering members of a new managerial and entrepreneurial elite scaled the social barricades in Richmond as they did in other southern cities, but only to a small extent did they replace the old antebellum families of Richmond. In truth, they rose because the city had grown and there was more room at the top. Few of them were true outsiders, and most of them had enough Virginia forebears that, with selective kinship emphasis, they could join the United Daughters of the Confederacy, the Lee Camp of United Confederate Veterans, the Colonial Dames, and, ultimately, the city's private clubs and country clubs. Social organizations such as the Westmoreland Club, the Richmond Club, and the newer Commonwealth Club played an important role in determining social status in the city. James Branch Cabell, Richmond novelist and essayist, asserted that nothing could rival a membership in the Richmond German, the city's exclusive social dance club.

Ellen Glasgow noted that the key to the city of Richmond was golden—that "anybody from anywhere who could afford to give a larger party became automatically . . . a 'social leader'"—although there were still some "authentic antiques [among the] varnished reproduc-

By the turn of the twentieth century, Richmond's black and white middle classes had both expanded. Customs of racial separation, recently contested by blacks, were now codified in city and state statutes. While the black and white middle classes shared many values, their lives seldom touched. Train excursions and picnics for black youth took place in separate railroad cars and on black-owned land. Only young whites skated at Reservoir Pond. From the Valentine, Richmond, Virginia

tions scattered to the far end of Monument Avenue." Glasgow described middle-aged members of the Westmoreland Club who murmured, over the punch bowl, that many of those dancing the minuet at the Colonial Ball would not have been accepted in society just a few decades before.[5]

It is a common perception that Richmond changed little between the late 1880s and World War I. Local memories and memoirs often evoke quiet streets, a slower pace, and the pleasures of civility. A long period of race and class conflict that began in Reconstruction ended with white political victory. The new century saw racial segregation established by

Jefferson Davis long lagged far behind Generals Robert E. Lee and Thomas "Stonewall" Jackson as a symbol for the Lost Cause in Richmond. When Davis was reburied in Hollywood Cemetery in 1893 (above) and an elaborate monument, very different from those of the military heroes, was unveiled in 1907 (left), it moved the Lost Cause beyond claims of valor and heroism and signaled a reassertion of the political and constitutional views that Davis represented. From the Valentine, Richmond, Virginia

law and the electorate, black and white, severely reduced. A powerful form of social control existed in the Lost Cause explanations of history, which dominated textbooks and promoted conformity to a narrow range of acceptable behaviors and opinions. For many, this world was comprehensible, comfortable, and complete. For others, the city offered employment, but little else could be taken for granted.[6]

While Richmond's industry remained spread along the James River, the city's core was still shared by black and white workers. Downtown saloons offered free or at-cost lunches to men, but not to women, who carried their lunches to Byrd Street Depot, Capitol Square, or a couch in the nearest lavatory. A few women ate lunch at tea rooms or walked to the YWCA. Men and women who worked in offices were likely to walk home for lunch, and housewives usually planned the main meal of the day to be the noon or early afternoon dinner. The financial district on Main Street was the domain of white men, while the south side of Broad Street was a shopping area for white women. The continuing presence of important banks and financial services became assured when, in 1914, the new Federal Reserve Commission chose Richmond over Atlanta for a regional center. The north side of Broad Street held small shops patronized by black Richmond and saloons patronized by men.[7]

Although most white workers could look forward to upward mobility, to acquiring skills and property in the city, this pattern was a less realistic prospect for black workers. Most Richmond blacks lived in rental housing in overcrowded neighborhoods lacking city water and sewer connections, with poorly lighted and unpaved streets. The income of blacks was less than one-half that of whites. The spread of suburbs encouraged residential segregation. While white residents moved to the edges of the city, black households moved only to areas turning commercial or abandoned by whites. White population grew faster than black and, by 1920, comprised almost 70 percent of the population. The movement of rural blacks to the city was countered both by the movement of many urban blacks to the North after 1910 and by the city's annexations, which added white residents in 1906 and 1914 and the town of Manchester in 1910.[8]

The steady influx of new people into the city prompted charitable and religious societies to press for better living and working conditions. Particularly concerned about working girls and struggling families, organizations such as the Ladies' Hebrew Benevolent Society, the Richmond Exchange for Women's Work, Sheltering Arms Hospital and Retreat for the Sick, and the Richmond Mother's Club began to assess the need for housing, health care, education, and recreation in Richmond and to attempt to provide solutions. Even the more elite and selective groups, like the Richmond Women's Club and the United Daughters of the Confederacy, became active in civic improvement, education, and, as a by-product of their educational goals, benevolence.[9]

Women's organizations like the white YWCA (the South's first branch, founded in 1887) and the black Richmond Mother's Club sponsored boardinghouses, special courses, day care and kindergarten, and investigations of factory conditions. Black and white women's groups petitioned the city school system to include medical inspections in schools, to award prizes for gardens in black and white neighborhoods, and to establish homes for unwed mothers or "delinquent" girls. The YWCA sponsored a 1911 survey of working and living conditions for women; this survey is notable for its depiction of the grim existence in tobacco factories. Tobacco factory women, one-third of whom boarded out on Seventeenth and Eighteenth streets and on Fourteenth below Main, lived in dark, uncarpeted rooms shared by two to four women, with poor bath facilities and limited wardrobe space. In one tobacco factory, black women stood and fed stemming machines ten hours a day in thick dust with no ventilation. White women, who worked the same hours, sat on boxes as they performed different tasks from those assigned to the black women, often in a separate, but no more wholesome, space.[10]

The YWCA survey became part of the factual basis on which efforts to end child labor and to reduce working hours for women were grounded. The moral and physical vulnerability of young women in the city was a common theme that united many reform groups. The enactment of special legislation for women reinforced traditional values while promising a more efficient work force. This was a major concern of Lucy Randolph Mason, secretary of the YWCA, and one she carried into her later work with labor unions. The founding of the Phyllis Wheatley branch of the YWCA in 1914 began to provide for black women in factories some of the housing and programs that the white YWCA had been developing since 1887.

The rapid pace of urban growth and industrialization, the attention focused on suburbs at the expense of older sections of the city, the lack of sanitation and health programs, and inadequate public education were viewed with dismay by a growing national urban middle class who began in the 1890s to organize a wide-ranging coalition to reform and repair the cities. Their movement, called Progressivism, sought to bring to government and society new ways to solve problems through efficiency and the application of specialized acquired knowledge. This era saw an amazing number of organizations formed with social progress as their goal and remedial reform as their tactic. But what this progress meant varied widely from group to group and sometimes within groups as well.

Richmond's Progressive movement belonged not only to a national urban middle-class

By the 1890s, genteel young white women in Richmond rode bicycles, ice-skated, and played tennis. The ideal woman was now robust and vigorous. Soon the YWCA offered a more regimented route to physical fitness through calisthenics and gymnastics, and white schools and settlement houses taught folk dancing. From the Valentine, Richmond, Virginia

organizational pattern but also to a southern context of promoting racial separation. Many southern Progressives believed that black participation in politics was partly responsible for the corruption and disarray of city life. Better schools, closed saloons, and clean elections all seemed to require eliminating black voters and segregating the city through statute. The movement called Progressivism moved forward with a variety of visions, most of them seen through the prism of race. One version was civic or business progressivism, which sought greater efficiency and focused on city government and policies; another was a social progressivism, which moved from traditional benevolence to educational efforts and on to legislative reform. Other forms of Progressivism were found in Richmond's black middle class—a group that was small in numbers but diverse and energetic in strategies.[11]

This new black middle class was composed of teachers, lawyers, businessmen, and ministers, who founded literary and debating societies, established Masonic lodges, and organized balls and dances. They were indeed a vanguard, as most of Richmond's black wage earners were unskilled or industrial laborers after the decline of black artisans. The small size of the black middle class and the fact that black women's earnings were needed after marriage meant that black professional and laboring women, who were also women with families, were called upon to play forward roles in community improvement plans, while white women with similar roles were less likely to be employed.[12]

Among Richmond's black citizens, opinion was deeply divided over the appropriate strategies for maintaining a political presence in the city. Virtually abandoned by the Republicans and alternately courted and defrauded by the Democrats, blacks might adopt the strategically accommodationist tactics of William Washington Browne and Giles B. Jackson or the more confrontational stance of the early John Mitchell. The differences among these leaders, and among dozens of others, were more tactical than philosophical.

William Washington Browne came to Richmond as a Methodist minister in 1882 but soon devoted all his time to the Grand United Order of True Reformers, the temperance society that he had earlier brought to the city. Browne was essentially a businessman who believed that the pledge of sobriety and the development of black institutions would do the most to help the black race. In 1888 the True Reformers incorporated the nation's first black-owned and -operated savings bank; in 1898 they purchased land in Westham and built an incorporated Old Folks Home. A lawyer named Giles B. Jackson served as attorney for the Order of True Reformers and drafted its original bank charter. His talent for diplomacy and public relations helped him to successfully produce an exhibit of black achievement at the Jamestown Ter-Centennial in 1907, and in 1908, with the poet and educator D. Webster Davis, he published *The Industrial History of the Negro Race*.[13]

The young black men and women who received their education in federal- and northern-sponsored Freedmen's Schools, and at Richmond Normal and High School in its first, expansive decades, were particularly confident and knowledgeable. White Richmonders called them "new-issue" and claimed that this post-emancipation generation was responsible for disrupting harmonious race relations in the city. An enduring white fantasy, reaching back to James Lafayette and the American Revolution, continued to assert that the generation of black Richmonders just past had been more content. Whites often explained the emergence of Jim Crow laws by the decline in "old-time darkies" and the deterioration of cordial relations, which they blamed on black education.[14]

Yet even the preaching of John Jasper, the elderly former slave and longtime minister of Sixth Mount Zion Baptist Church, praised God's power to confound white authority, a theme that many whites failed to recognize. Jasper, whose sermons were popular among white Richmonders, was seen as an "old fogy" by younger, educated blacks, but he maintained a loyal following among those who had shared his experiences. His most famous sermon, "The Sun Do Move," asserted that if God could free the slave, he could certainly cause the sun to move, as the Old Testament affirmed.[15]

It was Jasper's emphasis on the miraculous and his emotional expression of it as a folk preacher that made better-educated blacks impatient. Jasper's death in 1901 occurred as whites were displacing blacks in many skilled occupations and as whites stopped patronizing black businesses. The black middle class of entrepreneurs and professionals, even the younger ministers, believed in knowledge and self-help, believed that science and education could help them find a way through the maze of Jim Crow legislation that brought them up against successive dead ends. In the new century, efforts at separate black businesses and institutions paralleled Progressive reforms in schools, saloons, and factories. The social sciences gained ground on the old-time religion; but it was a social science that rationalized racial separation.

Through the late nineteenth century, black voters were challenged at the polls or threatened and intimidated; frequent and varied vote-counting frauds also took place. Many Progressive reformers, New South businessmen, and Democratic politicians believed that voting restrictions promised an end to the messy ward politics of Richmond by limiting both the black and the white franchise. For these Progressives, disfranchisement was a reform that would result in a more democratic and "pure" system. One Richmond-based Progressive theorized, "If we could get a clean electorate and a clean ballot, then we may at once achieve an ethical and intellectual freedom."[16]

The early years of the twentieth century represented the nadir in postbellum race relations in Richmond, as in much of the rest of the nation. The city council election of 1900 demonstrated how far white Richmond Democrats would go to suppress black votes. In that election, blacks managed to surmount internal divisions to offer a slate of candidates, but white Democrats added bogus and similar-sounding names to the registration list and stuffed ballot boxes during the election.[17] In the same year, the General Assembly passed legislation requiring segregated passenger trains. An attempt was made to divide the public school tax base by race, so that black schools received only black taxes. In 1903, the city council abolished Jackson Ward as a political entity and thereby eliminated the possibility of a black councilman.

At the state level, the 1902 Virginia Constitution, which imposed a poll tax and other restrictions on voting, severely reduced the number of voters. Although some blacks in Richmond continued to pay the poll tax and vote, their political bargaining power was gone. In addition, the new requirements for voting constricted the white working-class vote. A generation of negotiated politics was at an end, and the early twentieth century saw the completion of the segregated city.

This was a victory for the southern urban business progressives. Their agenda for civic efficiency and order was to limit or end black voting; extend segregation to all public spaces and public transportation; segregate housing and neighborhoods through zoning; and annex adjacent land and suburbs as the supreme expression of "growth." The great goal of the city's businessmen was secure investment, which required a stable workforce in a predictable environment. The great fear was of disorder—strikes, riots, racial clashes. City planning seemed to offer a form of social engineering that would provide racial and class control while it provided sufficient public services and trained personnel to attract business and industry.[18] This agenda evolved slowly, beginning with the Depression of 1893, which brought a pause to real estate development, now acknowledged as an important part of the city's economy. No banks failed in Richmond, but the loss of business orders proved the final blow to the old Haxall-Crenshaw flour mill and many other smaller companies in the city.

While the city council and Board of Aldermen had enthusiastically promoted suburban growth for a decade, their commitment now waned. New and expanded city services and the construction of an expensive and waste-ridden new city hall caused the city's debt level to rise, and consequently the city council began to investigate "waste and mismanagement." Although the chamber of commerce at first applauded the council's efforts to cut costs, white businessmen soon saw an austerity program as an impediment to New South expansion. They replaced the council's "retrenchment" theme with the new watchwords "efficiency" and "planning," which seemed to promise more city services for the same money. Efficiency was seen as a strategy that would control and regularize city life without raising taxes.[19]

Business progressives blamed the bulky and unwieldy two-house city council system, with its weak mayor, for Richmond's governmental inefficiencies but, unwilling to risk a major restructuring, sought only a partial management reform in the creation of an Administrative Board in 1912. A modest labor resurgence on the Administrative Board led to criticism from conservatives, while others felt the change did not go far enough. A new city charter, adopted in 1918 with the support of the city's growing white middle class, eliminated the Administrative Board and gave the mayor more power, but the essential structure of Richmond city government remained unchanged. In this, Progressive Richmond differed from those American cities that risked more in this period, experimenting with city managers and other forms of professionalized management.[20]

Business policies carried out through city government included annexations of surrounding territory, recruitment of business enterprises, and improvement of certain city services, especially the police and fire departments, public schools, and streets and transportation.[21] With little in tax money, Richmond counted on growth through annexation and took into its boundaries many of the streetcar suburbs, begun and built in the previous two decades, that lay north, west, and south of the city. Among them were Wright's Park, a white neighborhood with advertisements that coaxed: "[Come] where the air is pure and wholesome. . . . Why continue to 'bottle' yourself up in the congested city? Come with us out in the open and begin to live." Nearby Oak Park, one of the few black suburbs under development, echoed the same theme. "There are few parts of the world which offer the colored man . . . better and safer opportunities . . . fresh air, good water, sunshine . . . success, prosperity, and happiness." Black lawyer Giles B. Jackson, in a 1911 letter to the developer reproduced in the promotional pam-

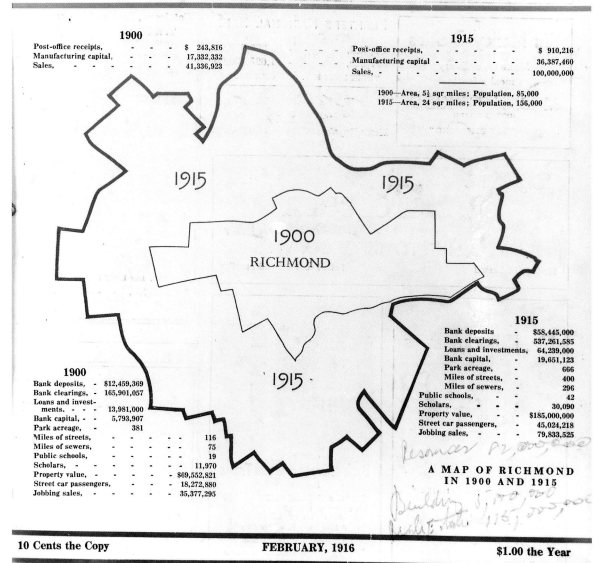

RICHMOND

PROSPERITY

PUBLISHED MONTHLY BY THE CHAMBER OF COMMERCE

1900

Post-office receipts,	- - -	$ 243,816
Manufacturing capital,	- - -	17,332,332
Sales,	- - - - -	41,336,923

1915

Post-office receipts,	- - - - -	$ 910,216
Manufacturing capital	- - - - -	36,387,460
Sales, -	- - - - - -	100,000,000

1900—Area, 5½ sqr miles; Population, 85,000
1915—Area, 24 sqr miles; Population, 156,000

1915

1915

1900
RICHMOND

1915

1900

Bank deposits,	-	$12,459,369
Bank clearings, -		165,901,057
Loans and investments, - - -		13,981,000
Bank capital, - -		5,793,907
Park acreage,	-	381
Miles of streets,	- - - - -	116
Miles of sewers,	- - - - -	75
Public schools,	- - - - -	19
Scholars, -	- - - -	11,970
Property value,	- - - -	$69,552,821
Street car passengers,	- - -	18,272,880
Jobbing sales, -	- - -	35,377,295

1915

1915

Bank deposits	-	$58,445,000
Bank clearings,	-	537,261,585
Loans and investments,		64,239,000
Bank capital,	-	19,651,123
Park acreage,	-	666
Miles of streets,	-	400
Miles of sewers,	-	296
Public schools,	- -	42
Scholars,	- -	30,090
Property value,	-	$185,000,000
Street car passengers,	-	45,024,218
Jobbing sales, -	- -	79,833,525

**A MAP OF RICHMOND
IN 1900 AND 1915**

10 Cents the Copy   **FEBRUARY, 1916**   **$1.00 the Year**

Most members of the Richmond city government in the Progressive Era believed that the city must expand in order to remain prosperous. They encouraged suburban investment and incorporation into the city through extension of city services. Annexations in 1906, 1910, and 1914 quadrupled the size of Richmond and represented the streetcar city at its zenith. Annexation map published in the February 1916 issue of Richmond Magazine, *from the Valentine, Richmond, Virginia*

phlet, predicted success for the suburb because, he noted succinctly, "the segregation act has so congested the area occupied by colored people in which they are compelled to reside" that they will be glad to have a suburban option.[22]

The act to which Jackson referred was a 1911 city council ordinance that laid out the most elaborate and comprehensive racial zoning code in the nation, the first major attempt to control property values using government power to separate racial groups. After the United States

CUSTOM BUILT SIX

THE result of long experience in designing and developing a six-cylinder car. Away back in 1906 our designers developed a six-cylinder motor and have constantly since adhered to it. For eleven years KLINE KARS have been on the market, and thousands will testify to their quality. Our constant aim has been to build one model with different types of bodies (bodies custom built in our own factory), believing concentration builds better cars at a lower price. All KLINE KARS are built from the best standard units which gives to owners service in the entire United States and most foreign countries, and around these we build a custom made car in our own factory which makes them

*"Not only the best at the price,
But the best at any price."*

Kline Car Corporation

FACTORY:
RICHMOND, VIRGINIA
U. S. A.

THE WILLIAM BYRD PRESS, INC., RICHMOND, VA.

"The Ace of the Highway"

In the first few decades of the twentieth century, the automobile remained a sport and a luxury. Women men, and sometimes families took part in the rallies, tours, and races from town to town over roads that were often scarcely more than wagon ruts. The early automobile was individually crafted, and companies like the Kline Car Corporation of Richmond, in operation from 1912 to 1923, were able to compete with other makers until centralization and mass-production techniques made them noncompetitive. From the Valentine, Richmond, Virginia

Kline Kar Berliner
1913

Supreme Court declared such laws unconstitutional in 1917, Richmond and other southern cities found devices by which to reenact portions of the law in the 1920s.[23]

Racial zoning codes were an example of the way in which Progressive reforms provided varying perspectives depending upon their advocates. This was apparent when men moved to politicize reforms initiated primarily by women, as in the antiliquor crusade and the historic preservation movement. The origins of antiliquor efforts lay in the antebellum temperance movement, the Richmond Women's Christian Temperance Union (WCTU), and the subsequent Anti-Saloon League. In September 1882, local church women met in the YMCA parlor to organize the first local of the WCTU. Their first action was "the establishment of a Coffee House in a suitable location for street car drivers and others"; then they "visited the First African Church and formed a Union. We have not received any report so do not know how they are progressing." Their zeal for temperance led them to cross racial lines, and their concern with the results of drunkenness led them to investigate infant mortality, factory conditions, venereal disease, and prisons; many later became active in the suffrage movement. They gathered signatures on petitions and distributed literature in jails and schools, train stations and fairgrounds. They established browsing rooms for workers on lunch breaks, sponsored public meetings, and organized parades in which young children marched for temperance in special regalia.[24]

Temperance was a respectable framework for such activities among Richmond WCTU women who were predominantly the wives of clerks, skilled workers, and small proprietors. More than half of the leadership was from this group, whose commitment to temperance was in part an aspect of their identification with middle-class status and values.[25] In 1901, their tactics and perspective began to take second place to a more political agenda for temperance. That year a Virginia branch of the national Anti-Saloon League was organized, and the single-minded energy of Methodist minister James Cannon, Jr., began to push the antiliquor movement into Virginia politics and away from the social concerns of women.

Cannon edited an antiliquor newspaper, the *Richmond Virginian*, and pressed for an alliance with the Democratic party machine. Democratic opposition to his overtures sent Cannon not to Virginia Progressives but to a grass-roots drive for local option on liquor and, in 1914, a successful statewide referendum to restrict the sale of liquor. A once-reluctant Democratic machine came to support antiliquor forces, but the city of Richmond resisted until the last vote. By aligning the antiliquor movement with conservative politics, without tying its fate to social reforms, Cannon narrowed its range to issues of control over alcohol and focused successfully on obtaining political support for prohibition. Prohibition was a particularly appropriate reform for the South because it reaffirmed traditional values while promising cleaner politics and social progress. But some of the social justice aspect of antiliquor efforts may have been lost when the WCTU became an appendage to the political agenda of Cannon and the other ministers.[26]

The Association for the Preservation of Virginia Antiquities (APVA) provided another example of divided tactics among Richmond Progressives. Founded by prominent Virginia women in 1889, it was dedicated to preserving the state's surviving material culture—as much that of colonial and Revolutionary Virginia as that of the Old South and the Confederacy. In its first generation of activity, the APVA bought land and artifacts associated with Jamestown and Williamsburg and, in Richmond, acquired the home of Chief Justice John Marshall and a modest structure known as the Old Stone House, once the home of the Ege family and probably the city's oldest building.

With its acquisition of buildings for use as museums, its tablets and memorial plaques, the APVA continued the tradition of genteel women who were extending their domestic sphere while remaining in charge of memorialization and ritual. But the APVA's use of historic buildings was metaphoric and selective. Older buildings that were not associated with their political perspective were merely "unsightly" and might be removed with impunity. The APVA's Gentlemen's Advisory Board used the structures explicitly to bring the past into the political present and to shape the political future. The Marshall house was used to extol John Marshall's views on the rule of law and the sanctity of contract, in contrast to the Readjustors and the biracial ward politics of Richmond. Speakers for the APVA later supported the Constitution of 1902 and noted that Virginia had been most powerful when limited voting and social deference prevailed. APVA history stressed legal conservatism, state sovereignty, and limited democracy. As professional men became dominant in the organization, women's importance as guardians and custodians of the artifacts diminished.[27]

Two other reforms or, in common parlance, "crusades" begun by women maintained a high degree of female control and direction. The Richmond Education Association was founded in 1900 and led by Benjamin and Lila Meade Valentine, along with Beverly and Mary Cooke Branch Munford. Although Richmond's major newspapers could not be said to be reformist, there was one area in which they crusaded for change: they shared with both southern civic boosters and reformers a sense of embarrassment over the limitations of the region's two school systems. Already below northern standards, public education suffered from lack of money and lack of a traditional base of support, and black education suffered most of all. Despite the fact that black students in Richmond had a slightly higher daily attendance record than white students, who had a nine-month school term, the 1902 Virginia constitution mandated only four months of school for black children.[28]

The educational awakening at the turn of the century became a sustained focus of southern reform; it drew northern philanthropy and provided one of the few arenas for interracial cooperation. The *Richmond Times-Dispatch* introduced an education department and reported on school conditions. A major educational funding campaign in 1905, the May Campaign, benefited both black and white schools in Richmond. At meetings of the Southern Education Board, composed of northern and southern Progressives, Mary Cooke Branch Munford found "the major interests of my life . . . education for all the people, fostering better knowledge and understanding between the races, and especially the rebuilding of my mother state, Virginia." Her wide-ranging educational efforts touched every area from kindergarten to college; the concern for black education that she and her husband felt was a concern not widely shared among white Richmonders in the early Jim Crow era.[29]

Munford's colleague in the education movement, Lila Meade Valentine, was a founder of the Instructional Visiting Nurses Association (IVNA), a group of dedicated and trained nurses who were inspired by settlement house work in other cities to establish their own Nurses' Settlement House in Richmond. The IVNA taught health and nutrition, visited homes with contagious diseases, placed nurses in factories, founded a home for working women, and reached into every corner of Richmond to nurse and nurture. A year after the Phyllis Wheatley branch of the YWCA opened, African American nurses joined the IVNA.[30]

Lila Meade Valentine—
founder of the Richmond
Education Association,
founder of the Instructive
Visiting Nurses' Associa-
tion, and president of the
Equal Suffrage League—
was part of a generation
of Richmond women
whose interconnected
associations formed
a formidable phalanx
for social reform in the
early 1900s. From the
Valentine, Richmond,
Virginia

With the triumph of Jim Crow in politics, Richmond's black leaders emphasized the development of separate businesses and institutions and a pragmatic philosophy of self-help,
which stressed the dignity of labor and the importance of saving. "Labor, all labor is noble
and holy," wrote Daniel Webster Davis, a Richmond poet, pastor, and chronicler of black life.
He was echoing a theme familiar from the 1880s and the Knights of Labor campaign. Black
Richmonders sought to counter the intense racism of the period by emphasizing achievement
and protesting negative images. Richmond hosted Negro Fairs in 1910 and 1915, and in 1915 the
city's blacks sent a delegation to the mayor to protest the showing of *Birth of a Nation*, a film of
stunning technical and dramatic achievement in the infant art but one that portrayed the Ku
Klux Klan as saviors in the Reconstruction South.[31]

For black women, their concerns as women and their concerns as members of a racial
community were inseparable. Maggie Lena Walker was the best known of Richmond's many
black women involved in businesses and service. Her wide-ranging activities demonstrated
her desire both to work with other black women and to extend the benefits of that work to
the entire black community. In 1899 Walker took charge of a failing beneficial society, the Independent Order of Saint Luke. After getting a predominantly female board and a loan fund,
she expanded in a community direction with a department store, the Saint Luke Emporium,
which offered employment to black women as clerks, and a weekly newspaper, the *Saint Luke
Herald*, which discussed political topics. She founded the Saint Luke Penny Savings Bank to
encourage the habit of thrift and to make funds available for loans to black enterprises.

In a time and place where black women's virtue and morality were debated or denied by

Born in the Reconstruction era and raised in the generation when Richmond's black citizens pressed actively to expand their presence and possibilities in every area of civic and commercial life, Maggie Walker had a comprehensive vision for the black community and the black family in a local Progressive movement often divided by gender roles and race. From the Valentine, Richmond, Virginia

whites and the *Richmond Planet* asserted that "Jim Crow beds are more necessary in the Southland than Jim Crow [street]cars," Walker had to defend black women's clubs against the charge in her own community that they would lead to "the decadence of the home." "Men should not be so pessimistic and down on women's clubs," she argued. "They don't seek to destroy the home or disgrace the race." Walker's vision was never limited to club work. She maintained that black women should always be able to support themselves and described the best marriage as "the partnership of a businessman and a businesswoman."[32]

During this period when the constant mediation between tradition and modernity were particularly apparent, the tensions in the city produced a quality of literature unparalleled in the city's history. Ellen Glasgow and Mary Johnston began writing careers that led them from historic romances with ironic undertones to a direct consideration of the interplay between Virginia tradition and the roles of women. In 1913 Mary Johnston published *Hagar* and Ellen Glasgow published *Virginia*. Both were novels of southern womanhood that examined aspects of the southern lady. Published in the year Glasgow turned forty, *Virginia* was her tenth novel, but she called it her first mature work.[33] At the same time, both women were deeply involved with the movement to acquire the right to vote for women.

The path of reform, once taken, led many to consider women's suffrage a necessity. Whether the initial interest was infant health, public education, or factory working conditions, women gained knowledge and experience in their efforts to ameliorate social ills. These middle-class black and white women came to be the experts on Richmond's social conditions. They had the data and they had an agenda for the city. They also developed a new perspective

The black-run print shop, shown here, assured the presence of an alternative voice in the press or from the pulpit. From the Valentine, Richmond, Virginia

on the traditional roles of women. Their roles as petitioners and advocates for others caused them to see the limits of their own political power.

Recounting her career as a suffragist, Ellen Glasgow inaccurately claimed, "In the early autumn of 1909 I . . . [spoke] the first word ever uttered in Virginia in favor of votes for women"; actually, many Virginia women had spoken to the topic over many years. Glasgow could, however, take credit for a meeting at her home with Laura Clay, a suffragist from Kentucky, and a group of Richmond women who came for tea. "Nothing could have been more ridiculous than the timid yet courageous air with which the few bold spirits arrived, glancing round as they ascended the front steps, to assure themselves that no strayed male was watching them." Several days later, an organizational meeting "was held among carved rosewood furniture, in the charming Victorian drawing room of Mrs. Clayton Glanville Coleman."[34] The group organized the Virginia League for Women Suffrage, and the next day Ellen and Cary Glasgow asked Lila Meade Valentine, a founder of the Richmond Education Association, to head it.

The Richmond Equal Suffrage League benefited from the artistic sensibility among its leadership. In addition to the active roles played by nationally prominent novelists Ellen Glasgow and Mary Johnston, two local painters who had been trained in New York and Paris devoted much of their energy to suffrage. Artists Adele Clark and Nora Houston formed the Art Club of Richmond in the early years of the century and then established an art school that they described as "the cultural center of Richmond." As part of the suffrage campaign, Clark and Houston set up their easels at the corner of Fifth and Broad in Richmond and then addressed the gathered crowds on the topic of votes for women.[35]

The suffragists concerned themselves with more than acquiring the vote. They called for consumer protection laws and better schools, playgrounds, and parks, and said special legislation was necessary to protect women and girls in the city. The *Virginia Suffrage News* joined the Central Trades and Labor Council and other union locals in supporting a resolution against a local department store that exceeded the ten-hour day for female employees, and their pressure forced the store to change its policy.[36]

The Richmond Equal Suffrage League, upper-middle-class and respectable, was countered by the Virginia Association Opposed to Woman Suffrage, whose members were equally genteel. Similar backgrounds and shared family connections within the two groups did not

The Virginia Equal Suffrage League was dominated by its Richmond chapter, the largest in the state. Although its efforts were unavailing in the Virginia General Assembly, the league demonstrated the new power and visibility of middle-class white women. Photograph of rally, 1916, from the Valentine, Richmond, Virginia

prevent very different interpretations of women's suffrage. For the antisuffragists, votes for women appeared to disrupt the social structure from which they benefited as the wives and daughters of important men, especially if black women should also vote. Virginia antisuffragists asserted that "every argument for sexual equality is, and must be, an argument also for racial equality. There is no way around it."[37] Richmond suffragists did not raise the race question themselves and never denied that black women would be eligible to vote, but they responded to the antisuffragist claims by noting that white women greatly outnumbered black women in most parts of Virginia.[38]

Richmond provided the Virginia suffrage movement with leadership, financial support, and a large following, but the city was not a leader in a parallel "reform" of the era—the prohibition of alcohol, which excited almost no enthusiasm. Just the opposite could be said about the rural parts of the state. Both the expectations for women's suffrage and for liquor prohibition were speeded up by America's entry into World War I in April 1917. This move was not unexpected, as the European conflict had begun in August 1914 and American sentiment had slowly tilted toward the English and their allies. Factory conversions to war production included the Richmond works of the American Locomotive Company, which became a munitions factory, and Tredegar Iron Works, which produced shells and shrapnel cases. Three thousand workers were employed at a Du Pont powder plant near Sandston. Camp Lee, near Petersburg, was set up as a training center, and nearby Hopewell was built from the ground up as a factory city for war production.[39]

In many parts of the United States, World War I increased tensions between German Americans and their neighbors. Richmond, which had a large second-generation German American population, experienced some of that tension. German Catholic churches reported that it was "an unhappy period for the congregation," and the number of children in their parochial school declined. Young Dewey Gottwald volunteered for the army and was turned down because of the German origin of his name, even after his employer intervened on his behalf.[40]

This bizarre and inappropriate ethnic animosity was, in part, a result of the national effort to mobilize public opinion in support of the war. Propaganda aimed at civilians portrayed the Central Powers, or Germans, as barbaric "Huns," and the war effort was taken to homes and

When the United States entered World War I in 1917, Richmond entered into every aspect of the war effort against Germany and Austria with enthusiasm. Parades to sell war bonds—a chief means of financing the war—also portrayed the Germans, the chief Central Power enemy, as "Huns," inherently savage and uncivilized. To be depicted this negatively was a new and unpleasant experience for Richmond's Germans. In this mini-drama designed to encourage the purchase of war bonds, Miss Liberty and Uncle Sam join together against a Hun. From the Valentine, Richmond, Virginia

schools. Children carried home draft regulations, and schools held Red Cross drives and sold war bonds, or "Liberty Loans." Victory Gardens supplanted or surrounded flower gardens and produced vegetables for home canning. A class in "Patriotic Cooking" was held at Armstrong High for the black cooks employed by whites and featured quickbreads made with 100 percent wheat substitutes.[41]

During the war, women entered new factory employment. In general, white women took the jobs of white men who had joined the armed services, and black women took the work of white women and black men. This exchange of places was on a modest scale; most black women remained in domestic service, while those white women at the Du Pont plant donned "trouserettes" or "womanalls," a work garment with a bloused top and pleated pants designed to protect women both from industrial accidents and from any gender deviation.[42]

World War I brought new levels of prosperity to Richmond and also brought new levels of government involvement in the daily lives of citizens. Some of the reform impulse was weakened, especially in the area of regulating factory conditions, even as Prohibition and women's suffrage became amendments to the Constitution. Municipal and community organization for the war was so successful that it pointed city officials, civic boosters, and reformers all toward a more bureaucratic and institutional approach to their goals.

After World War I, Richmond Progressives could count widely diverse achievements. The

World War I provided both danger and opportunity for young Richmond men. In this photograph from his wartime photo album, which documents life in a segregated black military unit training in Washington, D.C., Sergeant Ammons (first name unknown) looks over his motorcycle handlebars while a companion sits in the sidecar. From the Valentine, Richmond, Virginia

city received one of the true plums of the Progressive Era when Virginian and Treasury Secretary Carter Glass made certain that a regional branch of the Federal Reserve System was located in the city. The Federal Reserve Act of 1913 provided the nation with its first efficient and coordinated banking system since the 1830s and created twelve branch banks throughout the nation. The Federal Reserve Branch drew investment banks, money, and talent to the city and helped to make Richmond a financial center.

Virginia had gone "bone dry" before the Eighteenth Amendment, which prohibited the manufacture, sale, or transportation of alcohol, was ratified with alacrity by the Virginia General Assembly.[43] Women's suffrage entered the U.S. Constitution with the Nineteenth Amendment, but Virginia did not race to ratify first, as it had with Prohibition, and did not endorse women's suffrage until 1952.[44] The Virginia Equal Suffrage League became the League of Women Voters and carried its legislative concerns into the 1920s with a progressive agenda that reflected a national and international perspective.

There was at least one melancholy chord in Richmond's march of Progressive legislation in the century's second decade. Many of the efforts at independent black-owned retail business, real estate, and finance ran hard up against white resistance or a lack of capital. After William Washington Browne's death, the True Reformers Mercantile and Industrial Association expanded to stores, hotels, newspaper and printing offices, and real estate. This network was the largest black business concern in America when the bank collapsed in 1910. A bank embezzlement scandal revealed that the business empire was overextended, with unsecured loans to its own projects.

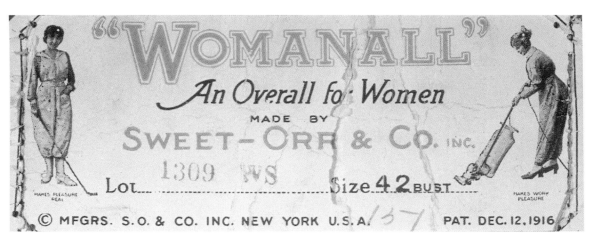

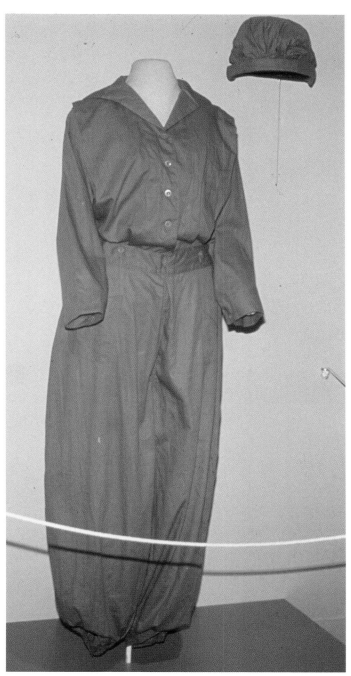

The employment of women in war-related industrial plants inspired a modification in their clothing. Although factory women donned a form of baggy overall, called "womanalls," at work, wearing pants remained a function of employment, and women did not appear in the streets in pants, nor did they usually maintain their employment for long after the war's end. From the Valentine, Richmond, Virginia

When factory workers left their jobs to join the army, their places were often taken by white women, while black women moved into the jobs of white women and black men. At the end of the war, returning veterans resumed their previous employment. From the Valentine, Richmond, Virginia

In 1921, John Mitchell's Mechanics Savings Bank of Richmond, long known by the Virginia State Banking Commission to be unstable, failed. None of the four black banks in Richmond had been able to afford to belong to an official clearinghouse, and each had a "parent" relationship with a white bank that honored its checks. Black banks depended on this relationship, which was voluntary and might end at any time. Now a portly banker in a white linen suit and panama hat, Mitchell could not criticize white Richmond as directly as he had when he was the young editor of the *Richmond Planet* and a city council man. But his lifelong refusal to ride the trolleys connected him with that era of energy and hope.[45]

Women voted for the first time in the presidential election of 1920. Rumors abounded that black women might be turned away at the polls, and a meeting of black and white women was held in the art school of Adele Clark and Nora Houston to arrange for white suffragists to monitor the polling places for illegal challenges. This brief alliance pointed toward a new decade of greater interracial efforts for social reform in the South.

In the 1921 state election, Ellen Glasgow's sometimes fiancé, Henry Anderson, ran for governor as a Republican, and she departed from her family's historic Democratic identity to support him. The Republicans believed that in order to defeat the Democratic machine and institute reforms, they had to divest themselves of the remaining black role in the party. Their platform called for an exclusively white party, while it also called for poll tax repeal, election reform, labor's right to organize and bargain collectively, better schools, and more roads. This "lily-white" Republican party was attacking the pillars on which white supremacy was based, but to correct the Democratic error, they repeated it. Their "lily-white" stance in 1921 persuaded Richmond blacks to run their own slate of candidates. John Mitchell ran for governor and Maggie Walker for superintendent of public instruction on the "lily-black" ticket.[46]

Both Maggie Walker and Ellen Glasgow had put all their energy and considerable intelligence into understanding, explaining, and changing their native city. Glasgow's mainly literary efforts and Walker's mainly entrepreneurial ones met in the arena of women's suffrage, for which both had worked hard. It was an indication of the continuing differences in the lives of black and white women that of the two most forceful, iconoclastic, and well-known women in Richmond in 1921, it was the black woman who ran for public office and the white woman who wrote in support of her fiancé. Both candidates, Walker and Anderson, lost.

The prisms through which Richmonders saw progress were, not surprisingly, prisms shaped by their own interpretations and experiences. What was surprising about those prisms was the sheer number of them. Until 1920, civic activism in Richmond was diverse, energetic, and multifocused. Each group held up a different concern and believed fervently that the light caught and reflected in their perspectives was exactly the light needed to illuminate the problems of the twentieth-century city.

CHAPTER TEN

The Up-to-Date City

In the 1920s, roller-skating boys in knickers occasionally careened through hopscotch squares and perilously close to the baby carriages in Monroe Park before veering left to the shops and stores of Broad Street, including White's Ice Cream Parlor, across from Miller & Rhoads department store. Richmond's long tradition of youthful gangs who claimed their space on the city streets continued with the Little Hickories, who had the initials "L.H." sewed on their jackets. "Little Hickories, hard to bend! Beat anything but overgrown men!" chanted the Fan skaters, heirs to generations of street games and to rock battles, the least ambiguous method of claiming urban space.[1]

The persistence of boy gangs on the city streets provided one form of continuity as Richmond entered an era in which the uses and appearance of the downtown changed in response to the automobile and a decade of expansion. The prosperity and new technologies of the 1920s altered downtowns throughout the nation, as industry moved toward the suburbs and downtowns became the site of corporate offices, financial services, and a place to buy and display the latest offerings in a national popular culture.

From suburbs to the state house, filling stations to literary salons, Richmond felt the impact of the 1920s. While the symbols of that decade became the flapper and the college boy, the flivver and the hip flask, the decade's transformations reached far beyond Jazz Age collegiates. Much of Richmond's modernizing in the twenties was a highly visible adaptation to national trends in technology and marketing. Mass-produced clothing made its final and successful assault on the seamstress and her dress form. Radios and phonograph records created and marketed a new mass music. Advertising became even more important as a business and a shaper of the culture. Many occupations became more professionalized or bureaucratic, and in these, the reign of the expert began. Perhaps most visible was the manner in which the automobile changed the spatial pattern of downtown and suburbs and freed for development many areas that weren't near streetcar tracks.

In the decades after World War I, national attention focused on the South more intently than at any time since Reconstruction. In the 1920s, the South was described as a benighted or culturally backward area; in the depression decade of the 1930s, it was characterized by Pres. Franklin Roosevelt as a poverty-stricken region that was "the nation's number one economic problem." These indictments of the region encouraged Richmonders to debate how up-to-date the city was and to issue both boosterish rebuttals and painful self-assessments. Busy factories, suburban construction, new clothing styles, and new communication and entertainment forms made the city look up-to-date and modern in a manner that deeply satisfied urban boosters in the twenties. The highly visible new technologies and popular styles were paralleled by a debate over what it meant to be urban and modern, especially in the American South. In arts and literature, in journalism and popular culture, in architectural styles, and in the rise of the expert as social worker, professor, or newspaper columnist, Richmond contributed in both decades to the national discussion over the South, while casting its arguments and programs in local terms.

In one area, Richmond continued a distinctly southern urban tradition. The city's leadership, personified by longtime mayor Fulmer Bright, remained conservative and placed a higher value on public order, tradition, and white unity than on modernizing public services and structures. During the 1930s, although New Deal programs were ultimately of much benefit to the city, the local government did not quickly pursue federal relief programs or the expansion of public involvement. The result was a central city that did not address many of its problems of deteriorating housing and inadequate city services.[2]

To the surprise of many Progressives, who had thought that city charter reforms in 1918 would result in expanded public services, the election of Mayor Bright in 1924 meant a long period of government retrenchment and private solutions for public problems. Richmond's city planning in this era was at variance with the direction of most American cities, where officials expanded services as urban rivalries intensified. Bright's long tenure as mayor was due in part to the fact that he represented the views of not just conservative businessmen but also the many working-class Richmonders who preferred a low-tax, low-service economy.

Efforts to turn attention to the needs of the central city were generally unavailing. City planning focused on designing streets, imposing a limited zoning system, coping with the automobile, and providing services to newly annexed subdivisions. A planning commission chartered in 1919 never met, but the Bureau of Design within the Public Works Department submitted a long-term request for street, sewer, and bridge construction in the central city, in-

RICHMOND MAGAZINE

JUNE, 1930   15c Per Copy. $1.50 Per Year.

NEW SUPER-SERVICE STATION OF THE RICHMOND MOTOR COMPANY
NINTH AND MARSHALL STREETS

The 1920s became the decade of the automobile in Richmond, as dealerships, gasoline stations, and repair shops sprang up to sell and service the new form of general transportation. The automobile made possible the development of suburbs not connected to the streetcar lines. From the Valentine, Richmond, Virginia

cluding a much-needed drainage system for Shockoe Valley. Still, most city funds for street and sewer construction continued to go to the suburbs, and city services were primarily promised to private developers as they surveyed the pastures and berry patches beyond the city.[3]

When the problems of the central city were considered at all, they were usually viewed as the problems of black neighborhoods. Studies described dilapidated and overcrowded housing in Fulton, Jackson Ward, and Seventeenth Street Bottom. In 1929, the Richmond Council of Social Agencies issued a report from the Negro Welfare Survey Committee, established a year earlier. Prominent black and white leaders served on the committee, and much of the report was written by Gordon Blaine Hancock, a longtime black activist and professor at Virginia Union University. The study documented the poor health among Richmond's black population and attributed much of that condition to inadequate housing. Black residents themselves named housing as their biggest problem, and the survey reported that two-thirds of rented houses needed essential repairs or alterations. While owner-occupied houses in Jackson Ward were generally well-maintained, many old brick homes had been turned into tenements for rental. Yet such conditions were hardly limited to black neighborhoods, and overcrowded residents still expressed a preference for their present conditions over their lives in the country.[4]

One reason for their preference, in the 1920s, was Broad Street, Richmond's main shopping street. Its center was a retail section that reached to Boulevard at the west end of the Fan District and to the city hall and a cluster of public buildings on the east. Richmond's renowned downtown drew shoppers from a wide section of the Upper South. To the west, Broad Street continued through successive layers of suburbs toward the foothills of the Piedmont; to the east, it dropped into Seventeenth Street Bottom, near Shockoe Creek, then ascended into the old neighborhood of Church Hill and ended at Chimborazo Park.

In 1920, when Prohibition went into effect, the saloons and taverns on the north side of Broad Street were shuttered and padlocked. Small stores of the "dollar down, dollar a week" variety appeared in their place. Across the street, Thalhimer's and Miller & Rhoads, the city's two major retailers, built new department stores, and in 1930 the city's first skyscraper, the twenty-two-story Central National Bank, was completed. Richmond got its first public library in 1924, but this library was not open to the city's African Americans. A separate facility opened

first at the Phyllis Wheatley Branch of the YWCA, then at the Rosa Bowser library branch.

The city opened its spacious and monumental Broad Street Railroad Station in 1919 on the old state fairgrounds, just a few years before the automobile, the airplane, and suburban industrialization began to remove the business traveler from the central city. City planners gave much of their attention to managing the automobile, which threatened congestion in the shopping areas, and a traffic light system went into operation downtown in 1926. In 1927 Richmond opened a municipal airport, Richard Evelyn Byrd Field, outside the city, and Du Pont announced that a $10-million rayon plant would be built near the city.[5]

After almost two decades as a novelty, the automobile became indispensable. By 1927, more than one out of every two families in urban America owned an automobile, but Richmond had paved only one-third of its streets by that year. However, this percentage actually compared favorably with other southern cities, and outside the city limits, the state imposed gasoline taxes to build and maintain state highways, while federal highways were built between major cities.

The new roads and paid vacations of the twenties enhanced Richmond as a tourist destination. Tourism was an obvious development for the 1920s because it combined new technology—the automobile—with a conservative cultural nostalgia that brought Americans to see not only Confederate records and memorials but also the many artifacts and buildings in Richmond that were related to the great men of American history. These were both genuine, like the John Marshall house, and bogus, like the small stone house once in the Ege family, which was designated as "Washington's headquarters."

Thousands of visitors came to attend the ceremonies surrounding the dedication of Monument Avenue statues to Stonewall Jackson in 1919 and Matthew Fontaine Maury in 1929 and the dedication of the Confederate Memorial Institute, known as Battle Abbey, in 1921. In 1922, more than six thousand Confederate veterans and countless other visitors came for the reunion of the United Confederate Veterans. The last Confederate reunion was held in the city in 1932, but Richmond continued to draw visitors interested in its varied historic attractions. Beginning in the late 1920s, the development of nearby Williamsburg, Virginia, as an idealized colonial village and a didactic history lesson also benefited Richmond's tourism.[6]

Along with bringing tourists, the motor vehicle disrupted the neighborhood surveillance that had monitored physical and behavioral boundaries; in particular, it removed middle- and upper-class youth from parental view. The formal and informal systems of chaperonage that had preserved a young lady's reputation based on her absence from the streets no longer functioned among the very class that saw themselves as the standard-bearers for all of society.

A cluster of movie theaters on Broad between Seventh and Ninth offered new standards for behavior as well as amusement. In December 1925, Richmonders could ponder the androgynous charms of silent-screen star Rudolf Valentino in *Cobra* or observe the dress and behavior of the flapper in the road company stage production of "No, No, Nanette" at the Academy Theater. In late 1927, the Capitol Theater announced plans for the new "talking service," which musicians correctly feared would interfere with their employment as piano and organ accompanists for the silent films.[7]

More automobiles meant that fewer repairs were made to aging trolley cars and equipment as Richmond, like most southern cities, grew in a low-density fashion, moving more and more people beyond the streetcar lines. The suburbs built around American cities in the 1920s included a popular new form of house called the bungalow, which was smaller and used space differently, reflecting changes in family life. Servants' quarters were gone, and so was the parlor, with its heavy furniture. The formal dining room now flowed into the living room and kitchen. The new homes were wired for electricity and supplied with a variety of electrical appliances, from fans to refrigerators. They were affordable for a white middle class employed downtown in advertising, banking, insurance, and corporate management. Household ser-

Richmond loved the movies and continued to find money for them even during the Great Depression. Loew's on East Grace and the Grand on East Broad were downtown movie palaces segregated by race. Theaters such as the Hippodrome served a black clientele, when possible, with films by black filmmakers. From the Valentine, Richmond, Virginia

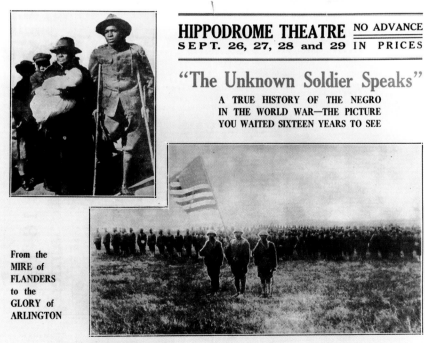

HIPPODROME THEATRE NO ADVANCE
SEPT. 26, 27, 28 and 29 IN PRICES

"The Unknown Soldier Speaks"

A TRUE HISTORY OF THE NEGRO
IN THE WORLD WAR—THE PICTURE
YOU WAITED SIXTEEN YEARS TO SEE

From the
MIRE of
FLANDERS
to the
GLORY of
ARLINGTON

vants most frequently rode the streetcar to the suburbs or lived in nearby racial enclaves.[8]

The twenties also saw the construction of affluent estates in the city's west end, developed around imported manor houses and reflecting a nationwide interest in the architecture of the English manor house. These houses reflected the desire of wealthy Richmonders—including some whose new wealth had been acquired through legal, financial, and brokerage firms in the 1920s—to create a private enclave where they could express architecturally their version of an English past and their sense of themselves as an Anglo-Saxon elite. In 1925, T. C. Williams, Jr., son of a successful tobacco manufacturer in Richmond, purchased and disassembled a sixteenth-century manor house called Agecroft in Lancashire, England. Taking the most dramatic features from the quadrangle of buildings, he reinstalled them as one structure in the city's West End. Nearby, Alexander Weddell reinstalled features of Warwick Priory, a sixteenth-century English structure, aiming at a reproduction of the ancestral home of George Washington. This structure was called Virginia House. Finally, Wilton, a pre-Revolutionary James River manor house, was moved to the West End and restored as a house museum.

With these three historic edifices as anchors for the area, Williams developed the suburb of Windsor Farms. Modeled on an English village, Windsor Farms was laid out on a common green, and owners of houses there favored Georgian styles and the architecture of William Lawrence Bottomley, who designed houses on Monument Avenue as well. An advertisement for Windsor Farms in the *Black Swan*, a promotional-pamphlet-turned-literary-magazine, pointed out, "*Restrictions* in Windsor Farms are ample to protect against the undesirable without being burdensome. . . . A special *bus* meets servants at the city car line terminals each morning and brings them to Windsor Farms in time to prepare breakfast."[9]

By the time Windsor Farms was completed, Richmond's West End had gone far toward creating a cluster of elite private educational and social institutions. The exclusive Country Club of Virginia was established there in 1910, and Richmond College moved to Westhampton in the same year, becoming the University of Richmond in 1920. St. Christopher's School for boys was founded nearby in 1920, and St. Catherine's School for girls, founded in 1890, moved to the area in 1917.

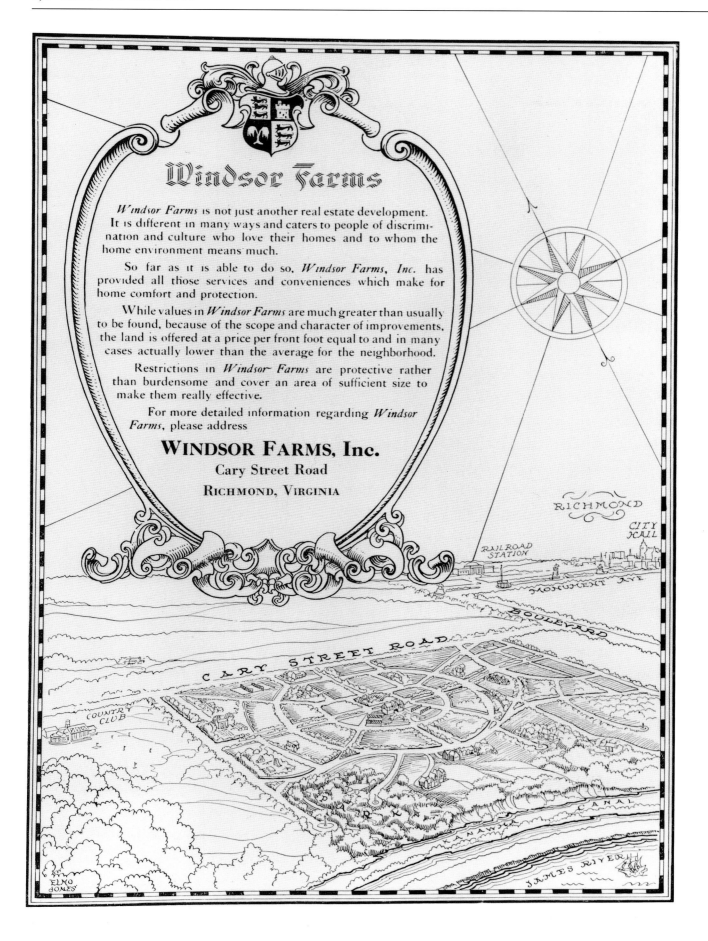

For some city residents, the enthusiastic reception of new mass-produced products and the display of new wealth evoked the demon of tackiness. When James Branch Cabell described his grandmother as an unreconstructed Confederate and a woman who ran through an industrial fortune without knowing where it went, he was not critical. In an age of brash and noisy commercialism, Cabell rather admired her opinion that any concern with money or ostentatious display was "tacky." For women like Mrs. Branch, the Lost Cause remained a secular religion and a social system. A lapse in manners or taste was equivalent to moral failure. All distasteful subjects were to be ignored. Young people's clever discussions about the "benighted" South in newspapers, magazines, and professional journals were greatly to be deplored.

Yet such discussions were a favorite topic of the day, and opinions varied as to why the South was backward. The long national revolt against the genteel tradition in literature struck Richmond with force in the early twenties, spurring the creation of literary magazines and poetry societies and launching important decades of work for Richmond authors James Branch Cabell and Ellen Glasgow. Both writers aspired to realism and determined to write without Victorian values or religion, but neither could quite give up the idealism and romanticism of the nineteenth century. They were constrained to bring at least some of the old cultural verities into new settings, and their "Tidewater Renaissance" failed to achieve a truly modern perspective because they could not quite abandon many southern truisms.[10]

Much of Richmond's literary renaissance was inspired by H. L. Mencken, who exercised his ironic wit in essays from Maryland from his *Baltimore Evening Sun* base. Mencken called the South "the Sahara of the Bozart" and had great disdain for the narrow provincialism and religious fundamentalism that he perceived in ordinary southerners. Mencken and his Richmond acolytes believed the antebellum South to have been a superior civilization before the rise of a commercial class and the entry of the lower orders into politics. This was a curious bit of posturing for Richmonders, because the city had always been commercial. Still, the second tier of literary Richmond joined the Menckenite attack on contemporary southern culture and on Prohibition.

Emily Tapscott Clark, a member of that second tier and society editor of the *Richmond News Leader*, continued the Tidewater tradition of clever amateurism in her iconoclastic cari-

Richmond's cozy avant-garde of the 1920s boasted two nationally renowned novelists. At this dinner party, Ellen Glasgow sits to the left of James Branch Cabell at the head of the table. Long united in their disdain for an insular and self-deceiving Richmond, Cabell and Glasgow grew apart in the late thirties, and each became critical of the other's style. From the Valentine, Richmond, Virginia

cature of Richmond pomposity, *Stuffed Peacocks*. At Mencken's urging, *The Reviewer*—a literary journal founded in 1921 by Clark and her friends—published some of the best new southern writing done after World War I. More important nationally than locally, the magazine appeared irregularly for several years before moving to Chapel Hill and closing in 1925.[11]

A more lasting expression of Mencken's influence in Richmond was the career of Virginius Dabney. The young Dabney, descendant of generations of southern scholars and writers, came to the *Richmond Times-Dispatch* in 1921 to work as a cub reporter. Dabney admired Mencken and respected the efforts of southern Progressives and their New South ancestors to modernize southern society. Dabney wrote eloquently and angrily against the 1920s Ku Klux Klan, Prohibition, and religious fundamentalism. As a young modern in a southern city, he saw all of these creeds as manifestations of an ignorance born of isolation and poverty. He favored more northern-style commerce and industry, accompanied by better race relations through biracial organizations, to lift the South from its low economic level. Dabney joined or helped to form many of the southern liberal and biracial organizations of the next two decades.[12]

Many of those who had taken part in the social and institutional reforms of the pre–World War I Progressive Era in Richmond became members of the Commission on Interracial Cooperation (CIC), founded in 1919. The Virginia CIC worked primarily through research and reports, products of both private and public agencies, to inform and alter white attitudes, and CIC members succeeded in making interracial work socially respectable in Richmond and Virginia. The CIC advocated antilynching legislation and better economic and educational opportunities for blacks, as well as housing reform. Few of these southern liberals in the twenties contemplated the abandonment of segregation, and blacks noted the paternalism with which whites often approached interracial cooperation. Southern liberals saw race as the primary source of inequality in the South and sought to reform the Jim Crow system, though not to replace it. Mary Cooke Branch Munford, active in the Virginia CIC and a board member for the Richmond and National Urban Leagues, argued for black control of black institutions as a precondition for progress. Paradoxically, by encouraging separate development for blacks, interracial cooperation abandoned white paternalism but supported segregation.[13]

At the other end of the analytical spectrum was John Powell, a talented Richmond musician, who formed Anglo-Saxon Clubs to promote racial separation and white dominance. Although white supremacy was legally assured in Richmond, a small but well-placed group of men organized in the 1920s to campaign for laws that would "prevent the contamination of white blood" and for complete separation of the races. In 1922, Powell, whose father had operated the Richmond Female Seminary, enlisted Earnest Cox, author of *White America*, in forming Post Number 1 of the Anglo-Saxon Clubs of America in Richmond.[14]

Cox and Powell worked to present a legislative bill requiring mandatory racial registration for every person in the state, outlawing intermarriage, and stating that only those who had "no trace whatsoever" of any blood other than Caucasian were to be considered white. Minus the registration requirement, this bill became Virginia's 1924 Racial Integrity Act—the most stringent in the nation. The next year Richmond's Anglo-Saxon Club, supported by the local newspapers, attacked Hampton Institute for permitting unsegregated seating in its performance theater. The result was a law that required racial segregation at public performances.

Along with the state's registrar of vital statistics, W. A. Plecker, Cox and Powell next turned their attention to getting a narrow legal definition of "white" through the state legislature. The *Times-Dispatch* published a series of articles about the supposed "mongrelization" of Virginia and argued that perhaps only descendants of Pocahontas could claim Indian ances-

A second Ku Klux Klan emerged nationally in 1915 and grew rapidly after World War I. In Richmond, the white supremacy movement was centered in the Anglo-Saxon Clubs begun by local musician John Powell. The Klan flourished in the 1920s and then declined; it differed from the first Klan in its new hostility to immigrants and Roman Catholics as well as blacks. From the Valentine, Richmond, Virginia

try without African admixture. Here the claim of descent from Pocahontas took on new racial purity meanings.[15] To some extent, these fears of racial amalgamation paralleled a national uneasiness that the old Americans would be overwhelmed by new immigrants whose differences were often explained as "racial," rather than ethnic or cultural.

Although the Ku Klux Klan of the twenties was never as powerful in Richmond as in other cities, it did play a role in the 1928 national election, when, aligned with the Prohibition forces of Bishop Cannon, it helped to carry Richmond and Virginia for the Republican candidate, Herbert Hoover. Much of the Klan's hostility in the twenties was directed at "foreigners," especially Catholics, and it was on these grounds that the Klan opposed the New York Catholic Democratic nominee, Al Smith, as well as a statue of Columbus in Byrd Park.

Both Powell's doctrines of white supremacy and Dabney's southern liberalism had difficulty encompassing much of the city's white working class, whose tastes and opinions seemed to belie Powell's vision of a noble Anglo-Saxon past and Dabney's expectations for a modernized and racially harmonious future. The cultural conservatism of Richmond's white working class was apparent when Richmond's churches divided over "modernism" and "fundamentalism."

Fundamentalism began as a conservative theological response to new scientific concepts of the late nineteenth century, especially the popularized version of Charles Darwin's theory of human evolution. Leading Richmond clergy tended to reject fundamentalism and to reconcile the new science with their Christian beliefs. The growing number of storefront Pentecostal and Holiness churches, all self-described as Bible-based and fundamentalist, revealed the extent to which the older evangelical churches no longer spoke to the concerns of white workers with roots on hardscrabble farms.[16]

Richmond's musical roots in rural churches, minstrel shows, and ballads were evident in the music that was popular on the city's radio stations. Radio programming began in Richmond in late 1925 when WRVA, called the Edgeworth Tobacco Station and owned by Larus & Brothers, went on the air. The white ballad singers and black gospel quartets who appeared on recordings and on the radio in the 1920s and 1930s were often urban and sometimes even professional men, but during this period in which Richmond was particularly self-conscious about southern backwardness, all such music was seen as culturally inferior.

In 1925, a railroad tunnel under construction through Church Hill collapsed, killing four men. A brakeman's song about this tunnel disaster was an authentic folk creation, but it did not correspond with the romanticized image of rural Virginians and Carolinians as isolated descendants of Anglo-Saxon pioneers, singing and speaking pure Elizabethan English. While Richmond's John Wesley Powell and Annabel Buchanan had sought out medieval ballads among the people, they disdained contemporary ballads about the deaths of railroad workers and called such music "hillbilly whining."[17] The upper-middle-class origins of both Richmond's liberals and its reactionaries made it difficult for either to seriously consider or even recognize white working-class culture, although white political unity was a central tradition in the city.

Popular radio programs included the "*News Leader* History of Old Virginia," presented by Douglas Southall Freeman, editor of the Richmond *News Leader*. Freeman, a scholar who was researching his multivolume biography of Robert E. Lee in addition to editing the newspaper, read and commented on the news for many years and had a wide range of listeners. Richmond editors had always been important opinion shapers, and the airwaves provided a new venue for their role as expert commentators.[18]

Other forms of expertise were also evolving in the city. The concentration of public health, social work, and medical teaching in Richmond encouraged attention to the urban conditions that produced illness or crime. One aspect of the modernization of the twenties was the application of national standards to occupations that had earlier been based on local standards or on a form of apprenticeship. The venerable Medical College of Virginia came close to losing its accreditation after the Flexner Report of 1913 applied national standards to regional hospitals. In 1917, the creation of the Richmond School of Social Work and Public Health by Dr. Henry Hibbs and by Dr. Orie Latham Hatcher of the Virginia Bureau of Vocations for Women reflected a desire to professionalize social work. Dr. William Sanger's reorganization of the Medical College of Virginia and the subsequent construction of a six-hundred-bed hospital did much to modernize that institution.[19]

The effects of the new standards and specializations in medicine were apparent in Richmond obstetrics. In the early 1920s, most of Richmond's babies were born at home, often with a midwife in attendance. A doctor was called in if it was believed that the birth would be difficult. Except for the administration of chloroform, little anesthesia was in use. The appearance in Richmond of the obstetric specialist and the gas called "twilight sleep" aroused skepticism. General practitioners and midwives saw no need for the specialist, and old ladies told young ones that twilight sleep robbed babies of good sense. When it became apparent that babies delivered under twilight sleep were progressing normally, the story was amended to assert that deficiencies did not show up until the second generation.

While hospital births and attendance by an obstetrics specialist became more common during the twenties and thirties, it was at a social cost. The decline in midwives and home nurses for births meant the loss of a respectable occupation for both black and white women. It meant that, for those who could afford it, childbirth was removed from the home and treated like an operation. At the same time, the greatest causes of infant and maternal mortality—poor nutrition and unsanitary environments—were not addressed by the advent of the obstetric specialist.

A study by two local doctors in the early twenties revealed a high maternal death rate in Richmond. Follow-up investigations by public health nurses were among the first "field studies" of maternal death in the nation and showed these deaths to be concentrated in poor

neighborhoods with dilapidated housing and poor sanitation. The mothers themselves had health problems. As a result of this work, the Medical Society of Virginia appointed a Maternal Welfare Committee in 1928 to set up prenatal clinics in every county of the state. Dr. Sanger also served on the Negro Welfare Survey Committee with Lucy Randolph Mason and Dr. Gordon Blaine Hancock. Although other aspects of the Roaring Twenties received more attention, Richmonders were building a public health and social welfare infrastructure that would serve the citizens well.[20]

Lucy Randolph Mason, daughter of an Episcopal minister in Richmond, was a prominent example of the women whose work with the YWCA and the Equal Suffrage League brought them to a lifelong concern for the effects of factory labor on families. As a young stenographer for a law firm, Lucy Mason refused to ride the streetcar during the 1902 strike. In the twenties, she was industrial secretary for the local YWCA and, with women like Naomi Cohn, lobbied for shorter hours for women workers and the abolition of child labor. When a 1923 Supreme Court decision voided child labor regulation, a constitutional amendment to permit such regulation was considered nationally. In *To Win These Rights*, Lucy Mason notes that on the same afternoon, two blocks apart, two different groups met to consider the amendment: J. Scott Parrish convened the chamber of commerce, while Mrs. J. Scott Parrish convened the YWCA. The chamber voted to condemn constitutional limitations on child labor, while the YWCA board adopted a resolution in favor of such an amendment. This political gender division among the city's prominent white families was common in the 1920s, as the women of the earlier Equal Suffrage League retained their sense of social purpose.[21]

Their husbands were more likely to be engaged in politics. The decade saw the rise of Harry Byrd as the leader of a powerful and conservative political organization that would control the state for fifty years—an organization based on a low-tax, low-service economy and a system of internal rewards and punishments. In the twenties, the Byrd machine developed through competent management and a restricted electorate. Many Virginians were unable to vote because of suffrage restrictions, and others did not bother. From the 1920s through 1945, only 11.5 percent of those over twenty-one voted in Virginia. In most southern states, the courthouse crowd at the county seat held much of the Democratic machine's political power, but in Virginia the state leadership in Richmond maintained control, in part because the counties had little independent political or financial power. The Byrd organization's alliance with Virginia's business and financial interests, its surface courtliness in the accomplishment of its ends, and the lack of effective opposition kept Byrd firmly in power. Those who challenged the Byrd machine seldom, if ever, prevailed.[22]

Like the rest of the nation, Richmond entered 1929 on a wave of confidence and enthusiasm. Some segments of the local economy seemed to be lagging behind, but prosperity seemed solid, and evidence for it could be seen everywhere, especially in the new office and apartment buildings, suburbs and houses that had changed and extended the city's topography within a decade. Automobile sales and construction slowed a little as buyers reached their limits on credit purchases, but this was seen as a temporary adjustment. Out in the countryside, many Virginia farmers had suffered through a decade of low prices, but when had small Virginia farmers ever been particularly prosperous?[23]

For a year after the stock market crash of October 1929, the economy of Richmond held firm. This muted response to the early depression was due to Richmond's diversified economy, its role as state capital, and its existing income disparities. Low living standards had long characterized the lives of many Richmonders, and for several years they saw little change for the worse in their income or habits. At the same time, the most prosperous Richmonders got little of their wealth from the investments whose value was dropping daily. In the middle, the state's bureaucracy and the city's office workers were seldom laid off.

The tobacco and textile industries in the city seemed almost depression-proof. Although drought-plagued tobacco farmers saw their income drop by half, the price of processed tobacco fell only slightly in 1930. Cigarette production dipped slightly between 1930 and 1932, then rose. The sales of leading brands—Luckies, Camels, and Chesterfields—dropped, but cheaper brands sold more. Many smokers bought cigarette papers and switched to "roll your own" cigarettes. The Du Pont rayon plant south of Richmond expanded as the market for synthetics increased in the nation. The value of some city enterprises, such as fertilizers and chemicals, actually rose. At the end of 1930, unemployment rates in Virginia cities were lower than those in other American cities of comparable size. Local newspapers and politicians occasion-

ally speculated that the downturn was a national illusion. But in 1931 Richmond's businesses began to feel the effects of the Great Depression.

Layoffs began in early 1931, although the deteriorating economy did not appear in retail trade statistics until the second half of the year. Service and industrial workers were among the first to lose their jobs, and the number on relief was always highest in industrial centers like Richmond. Flour milling and automobile shops were hard hit. Railroads and textile mills cut shifts; sawmills and coal mines closed. Maids were fired by families who could not afford them. By the end of 1931, construction in Richmond was down, relief expenses were up, and the Social Service Bureau was taking care of one thousand families.[24]

Social workers in the city's private and public agencies saw desertion, domestic violence, excessive drinking, begging, and prostitution all increase. Case workers, overwhelmed with requests and needy clients, became adept at juggling the city's charities with the minimal relief dole. They distributed Red Cross flour to families whose food assistance of $1.10 a week was inadequate. They doubled families up in apartments, sent sick people to clinics, and bought clothes or tools so clients could apply for work. The Family Service Society, largest of the private agencies, received its funds from the privately funded Community Chest; the Richmond Social Service Bureau, the largest of the public agencies, was administered under the Virginia Department of Public Welfare but received most of its funds from the city. Both were near the end of their resources. The Red Cross, the Salvation Army, Traveler's Aid, and a variety of religious charitable societies were equally hard-pressed.

In late November 1932, the National Unemployed Council, a radical organization intent on demonstrating the need for government intervention, entered Virginia and set up local committees in several cities; the group gained support from local black citizens who were out of work and unable, because of race, to get on the limited relief rolls. The Richmond group wanted the city to donate $750,000—a distinctly unlikely prospect—for relief in the coming winter. A hunger march on city hall ended with the arrest of the leader for marching without a permit. A nervous Mayor Bright considered the council's rallies, speeches, and protests a direct threat to city government. The police staged successive raids on their meetingplaces, and the council leaders were frequently arrested on flimsy pretexts and tried in police court, although most convictions were thrown out in the hustings court.[25]

By the time of Franklin Roosevelt's election in the fall of 1932, the ability of Richmond and other cities to provide relief was strained beyond capacity. Roosevelt, who promised a New Deal for the American people, initially found support from Virginia's senators Harry Byrd and Carter Glass. The New Deal legislative program passed by the U.S. Congress under President Roosevelt provided an important link between the New South vision of industrialization and the metropolitanism of the so-called Sunbelt South of the 1970s and 1980s, because its policies favored large farms and suburban areas.[26]

Richmond was generally up-to-date in the twenties, enthusiastic about new technologies and adopting national trends in popular culture; reflecting the reactive and nativist side of the decade as well its tentative interracial efforts. In the thirties, however, while Richmond shared the national depression, the conservatism of the Byrd organization and its Richmond allies slowed the city's participation in federal relief programs. Nevertheless, in time the city benefited greatly from those New Deal work programs that restored and rebuilt the public infrastructure. There was little construction or repair of private dwellings to match the libraries, high schools, roads, and bridges sponsored in the city by federal funds.

Virginia fiscal policy was designed to keep the state debt-free and thus creditworthy for investment. To this end, public expenditures for schools and relief were pinched, and only the highway fund remained untouched. Public opinion did not support taxes for public relief; the state appropriated money only for dependent children, called Mother's Aid, and just 4 percent of those eligible received it. Thus, because few of the unemployed were eligible for relief, neither the state nor the city was eligible for matching funds from the federal government as relief programs began to emerge from Congress.[27]

In a related area, sentiment for repeal of the Eighteenth Amendment, or Prohibition, grew stronger by the end of the 1920s. The city's newspapers briefly supported Prohibition when it was enacted but by the end of the decade felt that the noble experiment was a cultural failure. The Twenty-First Amendment, or repeal of the Eighteenth, was submitted to the states for ratification in 1933, and it carried Richmond by a four-to-one margin, winning every precinct.[28]

The repeal of Prohibition did not mean a return to the saloon culture, which had been the source of earlier political activity. Liquor by the drink remained illegal, and the chief beneficiaries of repeal were members of private clubs like the Commonwealth Club. Entertaining remained centered in the home, and, characteristic of localities with only partial repeal, Richmond maintained no respectable bars and few good restaurants.

New Deal legislation improved the working conditions of southern industrial workers and strengthened southern unions, although its assault on paternalistic southern labor relations was an opening salvo rather than a rout. The Wagner Act, passed by Congress in 1935, gave labor unions the right to organize and made Richmond a target for industrial union organizing by the Congress of Industrial Organizations, which separated by 1937 from the American Federation of Labor (AFL). The AFL was based on craft unions and drew its strength from skilled white men, at the top of the labor pyramid. The city's AFL-affiliated craft unions had shown no interest in organizing unskilled women and blacks in tobacco or textiles.

The CIO came to town to organize the industrial workers who had the lowest wages and the most precarious positions. In Richmond, this meant textile and tobacco workers, especially women. Black women were a majority of the tobacco labor force by the 1930s, but their experience with the white male–dominated Tobacco Workers International Union (TWIU), an AFL affiliate, made them skeptical of the benefits of unionization. While the TWIU organizers in Richmond failed to seek support from the larger black community, especially its ministers, the CIO organizers in Richmond held rallies in black churches and raised enthusiasm to a revival pitch.

The CIO sent seven organizers to Richmond, promised social equality in the unions, and did not ask for initiation fees. The Southern Negro Youth Congress helped lead a successful strike at two independent stemmeries, then joined with the CIO to enroll blacks in the United Cannery Workers. In August 1937, when the CIO won an election, with black support, at Larus & Brothers, the TWIU organizer, Rev. L. C. Crump, decided to "step on the gas" and push for a contract covering black workers at Philip Morris.

The TWIU had already engineered wage-hour agreements with Liggett & Myers and the American Tobacco Companies. But Lewis Evans, international president of the union, drew the line at union organization of the three hundred striking black tobacco stemmers employed by Carrington and Michaux. "We have not had a strike since 1900," he said, "and we don't want to start off with one here now." [29] This cautious approach to organizing remained characteristic of Richmond's AFL unions.

The Great Depression was particularly devastating for marginal workers and those with few resources. Richmond's African Americans were disappointed that the New Deal programs, which seemed to promise equity for blacks, were administered locally and that, as a result, few resources flowed to black neighborhoods. In this photograph, unemployed men play checkers in Sophie's Alley. Courtesy of the Virginia State Library and Archives, Richmond

New Deal Programs that combined employment, self-help, and construction left Richmond with an improved public infrastructure. The Public Works Administration (PWA), created by the Industrial Recovery Act, shared the cost of local projects and provided financing for the remainder. In six years, the PWA helped finance the most ambitious building program ever undertaken in the nation, and that program was particularly important in the urban South. Virginia was slow to take advantage of the program, because the state opposed paying the minimum wage required and was reluctant to borrow any money for construction. The PWA offered Richmond grants for a public housing project, an addition to the Medical College of Virginia, and a large, modern state library. Later, the PWA provided money for Richmond's deepwater terminal, and a WPA loan provided the money for a new black high school, to be named Maggie Walker High School.

The Civilian Conservation Corps (CCC) provided more service to Virginia than it did to any other state. Although its goal was to employ young men in soil and landscaping projects in the state's forests, the CCC also worked on restoration of historic sites and flood prevention along the James. Richmond's Battlefield Park was donated to Virginia in 1932; but because the state had no funds for its maintenance, it was turned over to the National Park Service. The CCC provided labor and materials for an extensive park system that cost Virginia very little.[30]

The Federal Emergency Relief Act contributed to an innovative Richmond program that received national attention. Organized in December 1932, the Citizens' Service Exchange of Richmond was a self-help cooperative designed to provide assistance on a work-exchange basis. The exchange used scrip to buy and sell work and had sewing rooms, shoe repair facili-

ties, and barber shops where workers invested their hours or bought services. Off the premises, its workers bartered for home improvements, firewood, and medical and dental services. While underfunded and operating on the proverbial shoestring, the cooperative had strong local support and thousands of participants, many of whom acquired new job skills.[31]

Although the New Deal programs that Roosevelt proposed and Congress passed beginning in the spring of 1933 were designed to preserve capitalism by reforming it, they quickly ran contrary to the state's tradition of a balanced budget and political conservatism, and the Byrd organization soon came to oppose Roosevelt and his policies. While Virginia's two senators lost enthusiasm for the New Deal, Richmond's two major newspapers were more

As another depression-era Christmas approached, in 1935, holiday shoppers on the south side of Broad Street searched for inexpensive gifts. Neither six years of local efforts nor two years of New Deal programs had yet significantly stimulated the local economy. From the Valentine, Richmond, Virginia

During the 1930s the Public Works Administration, an element in the New Deal strategy to combat the Great Depression by creating jobs, gave Richmond some of its most important public buildings. Here the Virginia State Library is under construction near the capitol. Courtesy of the Virginia State Library and Archives, Richmond

selective, supporting some programs while criticizing others. The *Times-Dispatch* and the *News Leader* agreed with the Supreme Court in 1935, when the Court declared the sweeping powers of the National Industrial Recovery Act unconstitutional. In this judgment the *Richmond Planet* concurred, believing that the act had been no help to the black worker. Richmond's black citizens were often denied work relief, and both public and private agencies practiced racial discrimination. The state's black-owned newspapers often criticized Jim Crow in the New Deal, and the *Richmond Planet* pointed to the Federal Emergency Relief Act and the Public Works Administration as particularly offensive. The *Planet* promoted a "buy black campaign" and, in 1936, disillusioned with the New Deal in Richmond, supported the Republican candidate, Alf Landon.[32]

While the New Deal proved disappointing in Richmond's African American community, other approaches to equal citizenship were developed in the decade. One was the systematic attempt by the National Association for the Advancement of Colored People (NAACP) to point out the inequities in segregated education through a series of court challenges beginning at the graduate school level. Alice Jackson, who watched the tobacco factory workers walk to work as a child, attended Virginia Union University and then Smith College and ended her undergraduate career with a good academic record. In the mid-1930s, when she was back in Richmond teaching English, she heard Thurgood Marshall of the NAACP speak at Virginia

Union and ask for black volunteers to apply to state graduate schools in Virginia. With the support of the NAACP, Jackson applied to the University of Virginia. The university's rejection of her in the fall of 1935 became one of the first test cases that forced the General Assembly to provide funds for black Virginians to study out of state and later was part of the structure of cases that ended segregated education in the United States. James Jackson, her brother and the first black Eagle Scout from below the Potomac, joined the Southern Negro Youth Congress and organized tobacco workers for the CIO in Richmond. Experience in union organizing and legal case–building provided more satisfaction to many Richmond blacks than did the mixed blessings of the New Deal.[33]

As a mild recovery began to assert itself in 1937, new industry located in Virginia to take advantage of its low taxes, raw materials, cheap labor, climate, and transportation. Richmond's slow industrial downturn and early recovery, compared with the precipitous decline of other factory cities, made it the nation's fastest-growing industrial center in the late thirties. By 1937, the city had exceeded all of its 1929 indexes.[34]

The opposition of the Byrd organization to taxes and New Deal programs encouraged President Roosevelt to try in 1936 and 1937 to strengthen the anti-Byrd faction in Virginia politics; but when it appeared to endanger his relations in the Senate, he abandoned the effort. From the New South to the New Deal, southern business elites favored aid to industrialists, land developers, and real estate brokers at the expense of wages and public services. Byrd's careful alliance with business and financial interests, and a certain paternalistic largesse to the poll tax–paying black voters of Virginia cities, meant that neither national Democratic strategy nor money could disrupt the state's system of government.[35]

There were other limits as well to the New Deal in Richmond. While all the legislation discouraged discrimination, enforcement of the guidelines was left to local authorities, who seldom went against prevailing practice. If black leaders were disappointed in the results of New Deal legislation in Richmond, so were those social work and public health professionals, progressive planners, and others who had long been thwarted in their desire to reform and rebuild the central city. For them, the entry of the federal government proved a mixed blessing. Federal urban policies favored construction, not renovation or repair, and encouraged suburban growth. The effects of these policies, in which run-down or predominantly black neighborhoods were written off, or "redlined," became more apparent in the late forties, after the intense and focused effort to win World War II had brought the nation out of depression and created a new boom economy.[36]

Near the end of the thirties, as the nation moved from New Deal economics to a war-preparation economy, Richmond was the center of cigarette-making, with warehouses full of Virginia Bright, Burley, Maryland, and Turkish tobacco, and the sweet scent of tobacco continued to permeate the city. In 1939, the federal government aided the tobacco industry by buying much of the 1939 bumper crop in order to sell it to Britain on credit. The beginning of World War II in Europe in that year and the Allied desire for cigarettes led to a rapid expansion in Richmond's tobacco production.[37]

The Japanese bombardment of Pearl Harbor on 7 December 1941 electrified Richmonders. The first radio announcements were quickly conveyed to every part of the city. Servicemen hastily left darkened movie theaters and living rooms to return to their bases. Families out for a Sunday drive heard the news on the car radio, and small boys ran down the street shouting into restaurants and drugstores. Yet the city was already part of the national move toward war preparedness that had begun in 1939 with the outbreak of war in Europe. In 1940, a state civil defense council was set up with Douglas Southall Freeman as chairman, and the first national peacetime conscription act required all men from twenty-one to thirty-six to register for a possible draft into the armed forces. In Virginia, the first response to that act went out from local draft boards in November 1940, and World War I's Camp Lee was renovated for service. By early 1941, a year before war was declared, Richmond's streets were crowded with servicemen on weekends, and volunteer organizations allied with city officials were sponsoring Saturday night dances at the Mosque, downtown on Monroe Square. Richmond's long-awaited Deep-water Terminal, with its 1,200-foot wharf wall and two fireproof warehouses, was dedicated in October 1940, just in time to become a reconsignment depot for the army.[38]

Although Richmond shared the nation's general aversion to another European war, there was considerable sympathy in the city for the Allied powers, especially England. In what was perhaps their first and last mutual perspective, longtime antiliquor crusader Bishop James Cannon urged a declaration of war against Germany, while one hundred of the city's most prominent citizens met at the Commonwealth Club and formed the Committee to Defend America by Aiding the Allies. Six months before Pearl Harbor, a *Richmond Times-Dispatch* poll showed that many Richmonders were willing to enter the war.[39]

The war years saw the city grow rapidly in numbers and in industrial production. A significant portion of Richmond's World War II population growth occurred when almost seventeen square miles of Henrico and Chesterfield counties, including Windsor Farms and other suburbs, were annexed in January 1942, three weeks after Pearl Harbor. The annexation turned 20,000 county residents, most of them white, into Richmond citizens. The percentage of black Richmonders, centered near downtown and in northern suburbs beyond Virginia Union University, declined to just over one-fourth of the total population.[40]

Tobacco was the city's most important industry at the American entry into World War II. The manufacture of paper and paper products ranked second; the related industries of printing, publishing, and engraving ranked third, while iron and steel manufacturing was fourth. Although many Richmond companies converted to war production, no new military industries were set up in the city. War work centered on the redirection of existing industry, the deployment and direction of supplies, and the training of servicemen. At Bellwood, near Drewry's Bluff, a quartermaster depot received and dispatched trainloads of supplies, and a reconsignment depot was established at the Deepwater Terminal. Byrd Airport, now called the Richmond Army Air Base, trained airmen.[41]

At the beginning of World War II, Richmond turned its large Du Pont nylon plant and its tobacco factories to war production. A new Du Pont plant produced rayon thread, and other factories turned to making parachutes, munitions, and gunpowder bags to fill government orders. Early in the war, Larus & Brothers packed overseas tobacco kits of Richmond cigarettes to be sent all over the world. Production at American Tobacco's Richmond plants jumped from $87 million in 1940 to $173 million in 1944. Tredegar produced munitions, while Friedman-Marks Clothing produced pea coats for the U.S. Navy. Initially, men filled the new war production and defense-related jobs in the city, but as the economy and the armed forces expanded, more women entered factories and offices as replacements for men, and it became extremely difficult to find waitresses or domestic help except for young women just in from

In wartime, women workers most frequently replaced men at factories that had always employed women or in newly established war materials plant divisions, not in heavy industries that converted directly to war production. These women welders were trained to work for the Richmond Engineering Company division that made robot bomb heads. From the Valentine, Richmond, Virginia

the country, who soon learned that there were more interesting jobs to be had. Federal efforts to establish wage policies and to override the barriers to black employment and advancement in war-related industry met with more success during World War II than in the New Deal era. But the work traditions of the city proved resilient; most of them sprang back into place once the wartime emergency had ended.[42]

At the peak of wartime production, Reynolds Metal Company and the Du Pont Company were the city's two largest industries, with employees rotating on three shifts, working several weeks without time off. Often young people would leave work near midnight, congregating in late-night restaurants and corner drugstores before returning to homes or rooming houses. The lure of factory work pulled women from low-paying secretarial work, and offices were now staffed by younger women—and more of them were married.[43]

A local chronicler astutely connected the war with a significant change in women's fashions. In addition to the many women in factory work, he noted that women worked as taxi drivers, trolley and elevator operators, draftsmen, mechanics, and barbers. Shortages and rationing of many goods forced women to appear in public without silk, or even nylon, hose, but it was the demands of factory and office work that first led them to wear flat shoes, sandals, and slacks. Fashion followed expediency, and versions of comfortable work clothes appeared on the streets. High school girls wore their father's shirts with blue denim overalls rolled to the knee. High school boys adopted short military haircuts, and both sexes experimented with peroxide bleach and even permanent waves. This departure from decorum was viewed uneasily by the young people's elders, who feared that the wartime atmosphere was rapidly eroding both class and gender distinctions.[44]

In the middle of the war, the *Richmond News Leader* announced that 34,000 servicemen visited Richmond every weekend. The military services remained segregated, as did restaurants, churches, and dances for servicemen on leave. Organizations like the Red Cross either segregated their volunteers or did not accept black volunteers. Richmond had so carefully maintained and reinforced the color line that this separation was scarcely remarked in the city, but the irony of fighting to preserve American ideals and interest, in which Jim Crow was embedded, was not lost on the young servicemen who crowded into booths and onto dance floors on Second Street, the city's black entertainment area.[45]

"Defense cash" drove the city for the war years. On "Two Street" and Broad Street and at the Mosque, stage shows, night clubs, and movies offered drama and star performances for military men and civilians with money in their pockets and very little to buy except entertainment. Shortages of most consumer items caused savings rates to grow, and shortages of materials caused the construction of much-needed housing to slow. Steep price increases for flour, meat, sugar, and lard began as early as 1939, with the outbreak of war in Europe. Richmond had no real shortages this early, but nervous housewives began hoarding, and speculators hoped to profit from their fears by driving up prices with artificial scarcities.[46]

Rationing of sugar and gasoline began in the spring of 1942, and citizens registered to receive their ration books with the invaluable coupons that would permit them to run their automobiles or bake a birthday cake. Later, a long list of staples was rationed, including coffee, cheese, meat, butter, and shoes. Limits were put on the amount of fresh vegetables each family could purchase.

Newspaper articles advised housewives how to live well and even to entertain with less food. Complainers were told, "Don't you know there's a war?" Despite widespread compli-

During World War II, cities such as Richmond, with military bases nearby, attempted to provide wholesome recreation for the thousands of young men who came into town on weekends. The young women who accompanied servicemen to church or to chaperoned social events or who volunteered in hospitals were often called "angels," a reference both to their volunteer status and their respectability. Like other wartime cities, Richmond also offered less uplifting pleasures and pastimes for soldiers, sailors, and airmen. From the Valentine, Richmond, Virginia

ance, a black market developed in gasoline and meat, a few counterfeit coupons appeared, and some domestic servants were pressured to turn over their ration books to their employers.[47]

Civilian travel by automobile and train was discouraged, and pleasure driving was banned in January 1943. The state speed limit was dropped from fifty miles per hour to thirty-five, and gas stations sold fruit and novelty items to compensate for the gas they were distinctly not selling. Retreading tires and repairing old cars kept them in business until the end of the war.[48]

While women's employment was viewed more as a patriotic duty than an opportunity for a lifetime career, many women nevertheless signed up for training programs and sought advancement at work in the hope of remaining in the workforce. But the war's conclusion brought returning veterans and a sharp social break between worker and mother. Most women returned to the home after World War II, some more happily than others. Still, their worlds, like those of the veterans, had been enlarged and altered. Even though they returned to traditional roles, they were more assertive in those roles. Teenage war brides remained in high school classes, and pants became a permanent part of women's wardrobes; women who had for years stoked coal into the furnace, done home repairs, and paid the monthly bills no longer quite thought of themselves as the "little wives." While home again became the center of many women's worlds, the boundaries of that world had expanded.[49]

Richmond remained segregated in its home-front war effort, just as the troops remained segregated in the military. Here Richmond women make bandages for the Red Cross. Black women's organizations also provided home comforts for the many black servicemen who spent weekends in Richmond. From the Valentine, Richmond, Virginia

Black and white veterans had seen a larger world. Many returned to enter college or training and to consider their city's place in a postwar world grown smaller. Black veterans had seen a world without Jim Crow, and they supported NAACP efforts, already under way, to build a legal case against segregation. As black Richmonders, especially young lawyers, tested the edges of Jim Crow in education and transportation, the southern liberal coalition of the past two decades began to fray in Richmond. The energetic Richmond editor and writer Virginius Dabney believed that desegregation efforts would simply undo the progress made toward "separate but equal."

During the twelve years of Franklin Roosevelt's presidency, Richmond and Washington were always in negotiation. The war had done more than the New Deal to provide training, travel, work experience, exposure to new worlds, and pay envelopes for those near the bottom of the economic scale. But through these decades Richmond had managed to maintain its traditions and to work its alchemy on cultural assaults and industrial change, shaping both to local perspectives. The comfortable and conservative mythologies that had guided the city's policies for decades would be put to their most severe test as Richmond carried them onto a greatly enlarged landscape at the end of World War II.

CHAPTER ELEVEN

Tollbooths and the Costs of Change

On a Saturday before Christmas in 1945, young men and women in army brown and navy blue could catch one of the last streetcars still moving along the tracks to Richmond's downtown stores. Although the war had been over for four months, many in uniform were only home on leave or had just been released from the armed forces. Christmas displays now were limited only by what the stores, especially Thalhimer's and Miller & Rhoads, the city's two largest department stores, could acquire, not by the necessity to cut back because "there's a war on." Passengers could look out at holiday decorations along Broad Street, but they could not smoke on the trolley car; a recent city ordinance made that illegal.

In newspaper ads, Thalhimer's offered "Gifts for the Lovely Lady," including a "star-studded holiday crepe dress" at $22.95, fur coats, choker necklaces, and beaded blouses. At the Miller & Rhoads Basement Store, more modest gift needs could be satisfied with pullover sweaters for women, at $4.98, and two-tone sweaters for men, at $3.98. High schoolers could pledge eternal love with engraved name bracelets for $2.60. Meat rationing had ended and there was a plentiful supply of poultry for Thanksgiving and Christmas. Holiday purchases scarcely hinted at the cornucopia of goods that would soon appear in postwar Richmond—an abundance that would offer almost every family infinite possibilities as consumers.

Newspaper announcements for entertainment still had a wartime flavor. The purchase of Victory Bonds guaranteed free tickets for crooner Frank Sinatra's concert at the Mosque on 16 December or for "She Wouldn't Say Yes," featuring movie star Rosalind Russell, at the Byrd Theater. The orchestras of the thirties, with their "big band" sound, were still popular, and in December 1945 the orchestras of Les Brown and Count Basie appeared at the Mosque; for Basie's performance the theater offered a "special section reserved for colored patrons." Bill "Bojangles" Robinson and his Concert Revue also appeared at the Mosque to a segregated audience. Robinson, a native black Richmonder, had learned tap dancing on the city's streets at the turn of the century.[1]

Shopping patterns also reflected a segregated city. The large department stores on the south side of Broad Street welcomed all customers, but only whites could try on most clothing before purchase. Black Richmonders also shopped in the black-owned businesses on the north side of Broad and on Second Street. Second Street, Richmond's premier black shopping and entertainment street, was at its commercial peak at the end of World War II. This commerce supplemented but did not challenge that of the large white-owned department stores. Not many black businesses carried the range of brand-name merchandise favored by women shopping for their households. Black soldiers, college students, touring musicians, and locals mixed at Slaughter's Hotel, Miller's Hotel, and Neverett's Place in the Eggleston Hotel. The Hippodrome movie theater, across the street from the hotels, was the venue for performers such as the Duke Ellington and Cab Calloway bands and local groups who gave midnight shows.[2]

Peace on earth had come to Richmond, and it was hoped that wartime prosperity might also stay. Cigarettes appeared to have almost limitless markets and needed no costly conversion to peacetime. Tobacco typified the expanding economy as cigarette production at American Tobacco, Liggett & Myers, Philip Morris, and Larus & Brothers, among the largest tobacco companies, absorbed returning veterans while continuing to employ women. Tobacco remained Richmond's primary industry and major employer for almost a generation after the close of World War II.[3]

World War II had done what New Deal programs could not quite manage: driven the nation's production to new levels and put money in the pockets of workers. Postwar Richmond's civic leaders hoped to use the new prosperity to make it an up-to-date American city through a variety of modifications of the physical city and its governance, including a revitalized downtown; improved transportation; adoption of the city manager plan; and, in time, annexation of surrounding suburban areas. Within a few years, the city would exchange the streetcar coin box for the expressway tollbooth.

The electric streetcars, which ran for the last time on 25 November 1949, were replaced in part by a more flexible bus system, but the most important transportation change was the rise in the number of automobiles. Nationally, car sales rose steadily after World War II and reached a sales peak in 1955; almost eight million cars were sold that year. Closely tied to suburban growth, especially in southern cities, the automobile made possible the rapid proliferation of cinderblock warehouses, burger drive-ins, and low-rise shopping malls. Richmond's first shopping mall, Willow Lawn, opened in 1956 and drew new office construction to its West

Tobacco remained the center of Richmond's economy and was celebrated with the annual Tobacco Festival, which featured a parade of business progress, a bevy of local beauties on chicken-wire-and-tissue-paper floats, a Queen of the Tobacco Festival, a football game, and some representations of Pocahontas. With the American consumption of cigarettes rising and the international market also growing, optimism prevailed. The Surgeon General's 1964 report on the health risks of smoking at first cast only a small shadow on the industry and the festival. From the Valentine, Richmond, Virginia

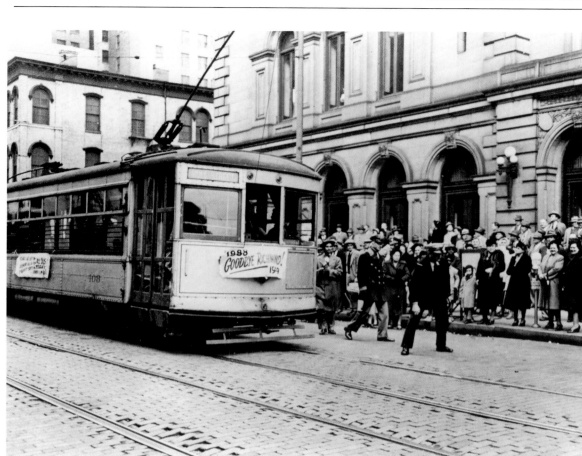

The last streetcar rumbled down Broad Street in 1949. The streetcar tracks no longer took people from where they were to where they wanted to go; buses and automobiles were seen as the more flexible alternative. The streetcar, which had long been a symbol of Richmond's civic pride and which had been the local and visible scene of battles over segregated seating and labor strikes, was replaced by the more remote freeway, with its tollbooth. These new and wide highways, which cut through central sections of downtown Richmond, offered greater speed but more isolation. Black neighborhoods, in particular, were chopped into fragments. From the Valentine, Richmond, Virginia

End setting. This became a pattern for future suburban malls and encouraged a cross-suburb work and residence pattern. Still, Richmond's downtown shopping area long maintained its reputation despite the lack of new construction in the area. In the 1950s, downtown theaters and restaurants offered the first installation of air conditioning, and they announced the news with signs that proclaimed, "It's Cool Inside!"

But there was a price to be paid for change, a price that could not be collected at the tollbooths. The city's civic elite were, as they long had been, white businessmen and lawyers who anticipated no change in Richmond's racial codes and assumed that those activities conducive to a good business climate were also good for all the city's residents. Though they were men of talent and ability, their perspectives were confined by their regional experience and their attitudes were reinforced through close association with each other and close adherence to southern racial etiquette. They had not formed political alliances with Richmond's black middle class and knew little of black expectations.

After World War II, southern cities grew even more rapidly than those in the rest of the nation, and Richmond, at first, was no exception. Its population rose to over 230,000, an increase of almost 20 percent between 1940 and 1950. Many of those who came to the city to work during the war stayed on and others joined them. The local economy continued to offer a good supply of low- to moderate-income jobs, and in the 1950s through the early 1970s, the city constructed a number of public buildings, including a civic center, a new city hall, and four library branches. Much of the outward spread of Richmond in the late forties and the fifties was the move of working-class and moderate-income families from central Richmond to bungalows and small brick homes at the edge of the city or just beyond its borders. More affluent Richmonders were beginning to move to the far West End. The area outside the central city grew by 24.3 percent in the 1960s, pushing the population of the Richmond metropolitan area to over half a million by 1970.[4]

Despite the image of pervasive domesticity for women in the new suburbs, many women did not leave the workforce after World War II, and other women entered the labor market steadily throughout the 1950s and 1960s. More of these women were married than ever before. Early marriage and early childbearing meant that the average woman was thirty-two when her youngest child started first grade. It was these women who entered the workforce to earn money for the family "extras" that kept the economic boom of those decades from faltering and made the purchase of labor-saving devices like the automatic washer a near necessity. New clerical positions opened for white women in sales and in the public sector, but black women did not move into these positions until the late 1960s. While the proportion of employed women rose, their portion of wages over the next two decades did not. The federally mandated Virginia Commission on the Status of Women reported in 1966 that women generally still held the majority of low-paying jobs and that black women earned even less than the average for women.

Southern cities like Richmond were typically smaller than their northern counterparts but had a powerful regional influence that extended far beyond the city limits. Although the postwar mechanization of southern agriculture sent many members of farm families to the city, tobacco was not mechanized until the 1960s. The tedious and labor-intensive work of tobacco culture remained much the same for several decades into the postwar period, with slow, traditional rhythms that were out of pace with the speed at which Richmond was growing.[5]

Small and midsized tract houses marched resolutely to and beyond the outskirts of the city in the postwar decades. The

GI Bill and the generally high employment rates made home ownership possible for many who dreamed of raising their

families in the privacy and greenery of the suburbs. This led, in turn, to changes in the racial

composition within the city. From the Valentine, Richmond, Virginia

Richmond's first shopping center opened in 1938. Still inside the city, but away from the downtown shopping area, the Cary Street Center (left) was the harbinger of post–World

War II expansion. The preferred solution to the transportation problem in the postwar years was the private family car, and most families acquired at least one. By the late 1950s, the inevitable

congestion that followed put ''traffic jam'' and ''rush hour'' into everyday vocabulary. From the Valentine, Richmond, Virginia

Southern cities entered the post–World War II economic boom statistically behind the northern cities in per capita income, funding for schools and libraries, and other measures of the quality of urban life; but Richmond's business leaders were optimistic that adequate planning for city growth and a more efficient city government could enable the city to catch up. Early in the postwar period, city officials acted upon two much-debated issues: the need for comprehensive planning and the structure of city government. In the first instance, the city adopted a comprehensive plan for development referred to as the Bartholomew Plan for its author, Harland Bartholomew and Associates, the nation's leading urban planning firm.

The 1946 Bartholomew Plan blamed the mix of industrial, commercial, and residential usage found in many Richmond neighborhoods for the deterioration of those neighborhoods and for residential flight to the suburbs. The plan proposed strong zoning laws to separate these functions. They advocated planned streets, improvement in the transit system, expansion of parks and school facilities, construction of a civic center, and a comprehensive housing program. The planners deplored the fact that three-fifths of the city's housing was in the low-rent category and noted that much of it was rented to blacks in low-wage domestic service. The Bartholomew Plan advocated rehabilitation of housing but did not suggest alternatives to the segregated downtown housing that was both a result of city policy and, more recently, a product of federal loan policies. The Bartholomew Plan predicted a continued low birth rate but anticipated that increased automobile usage would make the city accessible to more people living in the suburbs; it suggested the construction of east-west and north-south bypass highways through the black neighborhood of Jackson Ward in order to limit downtown streets, which had been redesigned for temporary one-way traffic, to shoppers and to eliminate some of the low-rent housing they so deplored.[6]

The planners were wrong in their predictions about the birth rate, but they were accurate, if not analytical, in predicting further migration to the suburbs. After World War II, the percentage of Americans living in urban areas grew rapidly, but urban density was lower than it had ever been, as cities spread outward on the grids and cul-de-sacs of real estate developments and on old country roads now serving as suburban arteries. For many young families, the quality of life in the city was perceived as declining, especially when the older housing stock there was contrasted with the green and private space of the suburban subdivision.

The successful conversion to a peacetime economy was aided by government programs for veterans and for the housing industry. New government loan programs and other benefits for veterans made home ownership possible for young workers who had rented or lived with their parents. The Federal Housing Administration facilitated the loans and credit with which large builders put up acres of tract housing on cheap and available land. This work was of inestimable benefit to white first-time home-buyers, but the FHA appraisal system rated old neighborhoods with black or ethnic residents as not worthy of investment. These areas were

In 1948 Oliver Hill
(fourth from right)
became the first black
member of the Richmond
City Council since 1896.
At the same time, the
system of physical segre-
gation throughout the city
remained intact. Hill and
other black lawyers in
Richmond had been work-
ing since the 1930s to
test segregation through
court cases in which
the decisions confirmed
that separate had not
been equal; by the late
1940s they had achieved
some success. Their work
became an important
part of Brown v. Board
of Education, for which
Hill was co-counsel. From
the Valentine, Richmond,
Virginia

colored in red, or redlined, and it was impossible to borrow money to improve or rebuild in them. Moreover, FHA and VA policies in the late 1940s prohibited loan guarantees for black families in white neighborhoods. These inequities had also been built into the earlier New Deal legislation, but they became more apparent in the growth years after World War II and accelerated the first "white flight" to the suburbs.[7]

Shortly after the city adopted the Bartholomew Plan in an effort to make Richmond more livable, a longtime southern Progressive tactic designed to make the city more efficient reached the implementation stage. The plan was for a new city charter that would replace the strong mayor and two-chamber council system, in place since 1918, with a city manager and a single nine-member council. It was anticipated that this structure would reduce political corruption and cronyism, and the plan was supported by the newly formed Richmond Citizens' Association, a majority of whose members lived in the prosperous West End. Through popular vote, a commission chaired by Lewis F. Powell, Jr., who was later appointed to the United States Supreme Court by President Nixon, was set up. It recommended a city manager with a non-partisan nine-member council, elected at large with no primary election. The mayor was to be chosen from among the elected council members by the members themselves and would serve mainly ceremonial functions.

In his efforts to gain popular support for the city manager plan, Powell had sought the cooperation and participation of Richmond's black citizens, including Booker T. Bradshaw, but the Richmond Citizens' Association would not place a black candidate on their first council slate in 1948, fearing the slate would be weakened. Nevertheless, black lawyer Oliver Hill ran and won a seat, becoming the first black to serve in city government since the 1890s. Hill was narrowly defeated in a bid for reelection two years later.[8]

The adoption of both the Bartholomew Plan and the city manager system reflected the ascendancy of a new, usually urban group of younger men in the state as well as in the city of Richmond. In the General Assembly they would emerge as the "Young Turks," calling for a more moderate response to integration of the races and a relaxation of the Byrd machine's rigid "pay as you go" financial policies. Embarrassed by Virginia's reputation as a "political museum piece ," they knew that the state's wealth meant it could afford more libraries, roads, and school expenditures. In its first years under a city manager system, the new council system authorized streets, buses, an airport, and a water purification plant. Although less fiscally and socially conservative than their elders in the Byrd organization, these young politicians could provide no viable alternative to the dual racial system in the state and so were caught in the middle once schools and race became central issues in the city and state.[9]

That happened in May 1954, when the United States Supreme Court delivered its opinion in *Brown v. Board of Education of Topeka, Kansas*. This decision declared that the concept of "separate but equal" facilities and institutions for black and white citizens, upheld in *Plessy v. Ferguson* (1896), was inherently unfair for blacks. Richmond lawyers had been deeply involved in the history of this legal decision, and the case itself—on both sides of the argument.

The decision in this case brought Richmond back to the center of national attention. In each of its three centuries of existence, Richmond has had a period of being driven by powerful political forces of change. First during the Revolutionary era and then during the Civil War and Reconstruction, Richmond's residents were often contentious advocates, sometimes fearful participants, and occasionally terrified onlookers, but they were in the center of events. In the middle of the twentieth century, the city was at the heart of the legal struggle over one aspect of black civil rights and was once again at the center of national events, with the city's preeminent black law firm and preeminent white law firm pitted against each other on the national stage.

Richmond lawyers Oliver Hill, Samuel Tucker, and Spottswood Robinson III were part of the NAACP's strategy, initiated in the 1930s, to undermine the legal basis of segregation in housing, transportation, and education. To bring about the legal dismantling of school segregation, the group began documenting, in case after case, that "separate but equal" had never been implemented. Hill, a lawyer in the Richmond firm of Hill, Martin, and Robinson, and the NAACP's special counsel in Virginia, brought forward a test case from Prince Edward County, Virginia, a rural county with a badly overcrowded and inferior black high school. Subsequently, the Richmond law firm Hunton and Williams was asked by officials of the Commonwealth of Virginia to work with the attorney general's office to build a well-researched and rigorous legal defense for the dual school system. These lawyers acknowledged that there was no equality in spending for the two school systems but argued primarily that the accretions of constitutional law and procedure—especially in judicial applications of the Fourteenth Amendment—as well as the lesser laws of custom and preference made segregation morally and legally permissible. The plaintiffs argued that the psychological effects of segregation could not be overcome by separate but equal facilities.[10]

As the case traveled from the federal district court to the Supreme Court, it was grouped with four other cases and became known as *Brown v. Board of Education*. Although it was not entirely unexpected, the *Brown* decision of 17 May 1954 electrified Virginia and the nation. Richmond's black middle class had watched the progress of the case closely. A history professor at black Virginia Union University commented, "A lot of us haven't been breathing [while the Court deliberated]. But today the students reacted as if a heavy burden had been lifted from their shoulders."[11]

The decision caught the state Democratic political organization and its Richmond representatives without a strategy. Governor Stanley appealed for calm, but Sen. Harry Flood Byrd soon used the term "massive resistance" to describe a strategy of total opposition to public school desegregation. The massive resistance movement was led by a Richmond newspaper, the *News Leader*, through its editor, James Kilpatrick—Douglas Southall Freeman's successor—who became the spokesman and strategist for the Byrd organization's position. In Richmond, massive resistance was not a local aberration. It was simply one of the intertwined strands in the city's history. Under political stress, romanticism and nostalgia had often overwhelmed more pragmatic and realistic considerations in the city. It may have been a sign of the city's basic 1950s optimism about the future that made this particular retreat into a mythic past shorter than other episodes.[12]

From the mid-1940s to the mid-1970s, the Richmond newspapers enjoyed a period of unparalleled influence in the state. The editorial columns of the *News Leader* and *Times-Dispatch* were powerful influences in the controversy over desegregation as well as in the debates over urban renewal. During the civil rights era, the newspapers provided the central forum for discussion of the litigious city's many legal cases. In the late forties, the voice of *Times-Dispatch* editor Virginius Dabney, who was once a prominent southern liberal, became more conservative, fearful that an attack on segregation was premature. In this he disappointed even such cautious and pragmatic Richmond black leaders as Gordon Blaine Hancock, with whom he had worked on interracial committees; Dabney's retreat gave evidence of the remaining gulf between the perceptions of the city's black and white citizens of good will. In order to justify massive resistance, Kilpatrick, an ambitious young man who had moved to Virginia from Oklahoma, reached back to the romantic lore on which the South had first constructed its cavalier image in the 1830s. He ran a three-column portrait of John C. Calhoun and described him as "a kind of Arthurian figure among southern saints, ever ready to return to the political wars if a new generation of abolitionists should threaten white supremacy and states' rights."[13]

Kilpatrick published repeated editorials attempting to resurrect and rehabilitate the doctrines of nullification and interposition. His series of editorials on the doctrine of interposition —which allowed a state to assert its sovereignty over a federal ruling it considered unconstitutional—were reprinted and sent to state leaders throughout the South.[14] Massive resistance resurrected southern theories of states' rights, not because those theories had ever been constitutionally validated but because they were a rhetorical rallying cry designed to unite southern whites. "I was on horse and the pen was a lance," Kilpatrick declared.[15] Like Lost Cause leader Jubal Early, he promised to rally the troops to battle once again when Yankee cultural choices were about to prevail. In 1956, the Virginia General Assembly, influenced by Kilpatrick, adopted the interposition resolution, but two years later it was ruled unconstitutional at the state and federal level.

In May 1955 the *Brown* decision was followed by an implementation decision which de-

As in the past, Richmond in the 1950s was deeply influenced in times of crisis by eloquent and influential newspaper editors. Virginius Dabney (left), at the Richmond Times-Dispatch, had worked to improve southern race relations in the 1930s and 1940s with his participation in South-based organizations. His thoughtful journalism on Virginia and the South gave him a national reputation and a Pulitzer Prize. At the Richmond News Leader, editor James Jackson Kilpatrick (right) vigorously promoted a philosophy called "massive resistance," which involved the ultimate threat of closing Virginia's schools rather than integrating them. While Dabney did not support integration, his editorials counseled moderation, and he did not accompany Kilpatrick into the massive resistance camp. From the Valentine, Richmond, Virginia

clared that integration should proceed "with all deliberate speed" and left that process in the hands of state and local school authorities. Virginia deflected black applicants under a 1956 state system called the Pupil Placement Board, which did the work of local school boards in avoiding integration. Gov. Lindsay Almond set the tone when he declaimed, "Let there be no misunderstanding, no weasel words on this point: We dedicate our every capacity to preserve segregation in the schools." In the fall of 1958, nine schools that were likely candidates for integration were ordered closed, and a system of tuition grants was arranged for students.[16]

Early in 1959, state and federal district courts declared the school closings illegal, but Virginia's massive resistance was really ended by the powerful urban press in Norfolk, Roanoke, and Washington, and the business community, both of which had turned against it. The image Virginia presented to the nation and the world was a threat to continued industrial and commercial development. A delegation of business leaders persuaded Governor Almond to reverse his position and adopt a new strategy. At last, even Kilpatrick announced to a Rotary Club that it was time for new strategies.

This more moderate direction was in harmony with the vision of the Richmond School Board, which, under the chairmanship of Lewis Powell, had sought during this period to keep the schools open but to minimize integration. Richmond was the home of the most active and articulate spokesmen both for segregation and for integration, and the Richmond school board emerged as a cautious entity, determined neither to close schools nor to facilitate massive desegregation. Schools in Richmond illustrated well the inequities of "separate but equal." Buildings, facilities, supplies, and teachers' salaries in black schools did not approach the standards of white schools, and black teachers were more subject to hiring and dismissal on a nonprofessional basis.

In the late fifties, the Richmond School Board, besieged by lawsuits, realized that some accommodation had to be made in the quality of black education and began a program of building new schools and upgrading old ones. Two new white high schools were built, and integration was begun in the existing high schools. This construction, it was felt, would minimize the impact of token integration. Beginning in September 1960, small numbers of middle-class black students enrolled in previously all-white schools—usually on the basis of court orders—but by 1964, ten years after the *Brown* decision, desegregation of the public schools had not advanced significantly. The power of the Pupil Placement Board ended in 1963 when Richmond lawyers Samuel Tucker and Henry Marsh won a court order abolishing the apparatus of the placement system. The board was replaced by a "freedom of choice" plan that gave the power of placing students to the local school boards, not individuals.

In 1956, several of the city's black citizens formed the Richmond Crusade for Voters to help blacks register and to get them to the polls. Led for many years by William Thornton, the group endorsed candidates, registered voters, and provided transportation to the polls. In 1967, another of the Crusade's founders, William Ferguson Reid, became the first black since Reconstruction to serve in the General Assembly. As the Crusade for Voters gained black support, its relations with the Richmond Citizens' Association—whose desire for "efficiency" and "progress" reflected the concerns of established white businessmen—became more oppositional.[17]

Following the February 1960 sit-ins in Greensboro, North Carolina, which began a new stage in the civil rights movement, many of Richmond's black citizens, including college students and certain church groups, became determined to open the lunch counters and restaurants of the city to both races. Grievances centered around downtown shopping and included restrictions on trying on clothes. Lunch counter sit-ins and an economic boycott that involved "selective buying" were launched against Thalhimer's and Miller & Rhoads until the stores agreed to serve blacks on the same basis as whites.[18]

The emphasis on racial division and legal confrontation in the city obscures the extent to which black and white Richmonders continued generations of cultural exchange and shared values while maintaining separate institutions. Music in the city demonstrated the rural and religious background of both black and white working classes. The crackle and buzz of the

WE SERVE COLORED
CARRY OUT ONLY

Several years after the Supreme Court determined that school segregation was unconstitutional, but before efforts at compliance in Richmond, southern black college students launched a movement to integrate department store lunch counters and restrooms in southern cities. Sit-ins and picketing at Richmond's major department stores by well-dressed and articulate black students and highly respectable black Richmonders led to several arrests but also gave segregationists pause. Agreements to desegregate downtown facilities followed rapidly. Photographs at left, 1960s, from the Valentine, Richmond, Virginia; photograph of sign, above, courtesy of Dr. Thomas Bridge, Petersburg, Virginia

little kitchen Philco or the car radio—where the random movement of the dial brought a babble of voices and musical sounds that were on separate wavelengths but open to any listener—was available to any class or color.

Black gospel music, which had deep roots in both rural Virginia and the city churches of Richmond, continued to flourish, to be broadcast and recorded. Some versions of urban blues and gospel style added instruments; this black music, designated "race music" when it was recorded in the 1920s and 1930s, was called "rhythm and blues" by the late 1940s. Rhythm and blues was urban, aggressive, youth-oriented black dance music. Honky-tonk, which emphasized lyrics and sang about the problems of life, became an important urban influence in white country music after World War II. Honky-tonk reflected the social changes in white working-class life. Like rhythm and blues, it used electrified instruments and was not particularly nostalgic for a lost rural past.[19]

Richmond's radio stations and jukeboxes provided the region with gospel, country, dance bands, and popular tunes. Many Richmond residents and rural Virginians who came to the city to shop on Saturdays attended the Old Dominion Barn Dance (cast shown in bottom photograph) at the Lyric Theater on Saturday nights. The Barn Dance was broadcast on WRVA, Richmond's first and most powerful radio station. In 1949, Variety magazine dropped "hillbilly" and "race" as musical categories and replaced them with "country and western" and "rhythm and blues." Faster than the charts acknowledged, popular music was exchanging influences and creating new forms soon to emerge as "rock and roll." Courtesy of the Valentine, Richmond, Virginia

More sentimental and reassuringly repetitive in its performances was the Barn Dance broadcast on Richmond's WRVA, one of the early stations to move to 50,000 kilowatts. On Saturdays, WRVA broadcast the Old Dominion Barn Dance live from the Lyric Theater, which was packed for each performance with white city residents and rural people in town to shop. The featured performer was Sunshine Sue Workman; Sue, her husband John Workman, and their regular cast provided a stage family for the audience to adopt. The Old Dominion Barn Dance, a family show, resisted new directions in country and popular music. "Elvis," as one station employee put it, "hit the Barn Dance like the atomic bomb." [20] But Elvis represented the fusion of black and white rural music that met in cities and permeated a new youth culture made possible by postwar prosperity.

American postwar prosperity, the spread of lookalike suburbs, and access to national network television programming encouraged the growth of a national youth culture in which young Richmonders were enthusiastic participants. New styles of dress and music that set teenagers apart from both adults and children coexisted with the traditional ways in which youth in the city were introduced into adulthood. Both black and white parents looked with concern on the youthful enthusiasm for honky-tonk, doo-wop, rhythm and blues, rock and roll, or the Liverpool sound.

Clockwise from upper left, "The Leftovers" making music, 1959; Neverett's Place, Eggleston Hotel, 1950s; John Marshall High School Cadet Corps Christmas Ball, 1949; buying Beatles tickets at Capitol Theater, 1964. From the Valentine, Richmond, Virginia

WRVA also produced the Sabbath Glee Club, perhaps the first identifiable black programming on Richmond's white-owned stations. Sponsored by Larus & Brothers Tobacco Company, the show featured male singers who worked in the factory. WRTD, owned by the *Richmond Times-Dispatch*, carried a program for black audiences called "Colored Richmond Is on the Air." Other stations, such as WMBG (later WTVR), also sponsored programming aimed at a black audience. WANT, which went on the air on 4 May 1951, was the first black-run radio station in Richmond.[21]

Further indications of Richmond's postwar cultural advance included the reestablishment in 1956 of the Richmond Symphony, which had been a victim of the Great Depression. The Virginia Museum of Fine Arts, constructed in the late 1930s with money from federal New

Deal agencies and collections from donor John Barton Payne, expanded its collections and exhibitions under the able directorship of Leslie Cheek, Jr., and with important donations from the Mellon and Lewis families. In 1946, the Virginia Historical Society acquired Battle Abbey from the Confederate Memorial Association and enhanced access to its important collection of Virginia-related manuscripts, books, and objects.

When WRVA-Richmond became "the South's first television station" in 1946, a television set cost as much as a good used car and was designed like a liquor cabinet. Only seven thousand sets were sold nationally that year; half a million had been sold by 1948. In 1950, AT&T linked television stations in major markets and thus brought reception to half the nation's population, spurring the sales of television sets. Each new postwar house seemed to have a car parked in its carport, and the blue light of a television set could be seen through the picture window. In contrast, much of the downtown in many American cities seemed shabby.[22]

Nationwide, one important response to this downtown decline was a federally sponsored program of urban renewal and highway construction. The city of Richmond moved more slowly than other American cities to take advantage of the Housing Acts of 1949 and 1954. Although city government had used planning throughout the twentieth century as a way to maintain racial separation, control city politics, and promote suburban growth, Richmond's ancient reluctance to become involved with federal projects—and those projects' inevitable trailing strings—caused the city fathers to be reluctant about forming such a partnership with Washington.

Slowly, urban renewal came to be seen as a mechanism for keeping offices, department stores, industry, and white neighborhoods in the central city. Reading the Bartholomew Plan through the lens of business progressivism and New Deal precedents, city officials reasoned that shabby neighborhoods had to be removed in order to renew the center city. Rehousing strategies were secondary to this concern. The city envisioned using its newly acquired power of eminent domain for slum clearance rather than revitalization of existing neighborhoods. Bartholomew's suggestions for widening streets were utilized not only to relieve congestion and achieve a more accessible business district but also to bulldoze through working-class

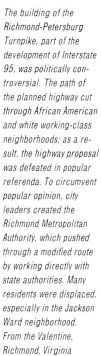

The building of the Richmond-Petersburg Turnpike, part of the development of Interstate 95, was politically controversial. The path of the planned highway cut through African American and white working-class neighborhoods; as a result, the highway proposal was defeated in popular referenda. To circumvent popular opinion, city leaders created the Richmond Metropolitan Authority, which pushed through a modified route by working directly with state authorities. Many residents were displaced, especially in the Jackson Ward neighborhood. From the Valentine, Richmond, Virginia

black and white neighborhoods. The price of progress was paid first by those neighborhoods divided by highway construction or leveled by slum clearance.

Jackson Ward was the preeminent target of highway designs, which sheared, tucked, cut, and divided the historic black neighborhood. Plans for an urban expressway had been discussed since 1946, but vigorous citywide resistance caused the city to shift to the state the responsibility for building the Richmond-Petersburg toll highway, approved by city council in 1953. Its construction later in the decade was coordinated with plans for a new civic center and

The year 1970 saw Richmond in the same social and political turmoil as the year 1870 had. Race and the control of space in the city were issues in both years. In the 1950s and 1960s, black Richmonders living in the neglected central city (right) were displaced, despite their protests, by highways and publicly financed projects like the Coliseum (above), finished in 1970. That same year, a federal court order to integrate schools through school busing drew angry resistance from white families. From the Valentine, Richmond, Virginia

the master plan for the Medical College of Virginia. The highway construction cut through Jackson Ward and forced 10 percent of the city's black population to seek new housing. A decade later, a Downtown Expressway, designed to link the central city with its southern and western suburbs, cut through the white and black working-class neighborhoods of Oregon Hill, Randolph (Sydney), and Byrd Park. Public housing projects were built to house some of those displaced, but there was a stigma attached to life in the "courts" or projects; low-income people often viewed public housing facilities as a last resort, although they were safe and viable living places until the late sixties.[23]

While the nature and financing of urban renewal was debated, economic revitalization remained the basic objective of city officials and planners. The social costs of demolition were never taken into account, nor was the prospect of mixed-income housing construction or restoration seriously considered. One example was a 1963 redevelopment plan effort to survey large sections of Jackson Ward in order to declare much of the housing dilapidated and substandard. This effort met with resistance from a loose coalition of black residents, white property owners, and preservationists, who knew the houses to have architectural and historical merit. The Richmond newspapers editorialized that dispersal of so many black residents was threatening white neighborhoods, since so few housing options were available to those displaced. A divided city council defeated the redevelopment plan, and this defeat marked the last battle by the Richmond Citizens' Association, which was replaced by Richmond Forward, a new group with similar but slightly lower goals.[24]

In contrast to the leveling contemplated for black neighborhoods, an independent 1965 plan for Monument Avenue clearly aimed at that neighborhood's restoration. In their report putting forth a design for Monument Avenue, the Richmond City Planning Commission deplored the eclipse of the avenue's prestige by wealthy neighborhoods to the west. Single-family homes had been turned into multifamily dwellings, and monuments were obscured by trees. To restore the avenue, the commission advocated landscaping and adding seven more statues of Confederate heroes further west on the avenue. No new monuments were erected, though, and the restoration of the neighborhood ultimately depended more on individual renovators and the nearby presence of the new and growing Virginia Commonwealth University.[25]

Educational benefits for veterans and the arrival of new residents, along with the technical needs of new businesses, increased the demand for higher education in the city. Richmond's colleges and universities experienced the same postwar expansion that other schools across the nation experienced. In 1968, Richmond Professional Institute merged with the venerable and vital Medical College of Virginia to form Virginia Commonwealth University, adding particular strengths in the arts, social work, and urban affairs to the longtime medical research presence in the city. Richmond also held Virginia Union University, a historically black college, and a cluster of institutions and facilities forming the Richmond Theological Center; these institutions added diversity and vitality to the central city as well as a center of stability to neighborhoods. With its campus in the handsome West End suburbs, the University of Richmond's long connection with the Southern Baptist Convention and with the city's solid middle class made it an unlikely site for avant garde arts or policy reconsiderations. But that image began to change when the university acquired a large endowment from local pharmaceutical manufacturer E. Claiborne Robins—an endowment that was conditioned on an end to Baptist control over the university. The endowment permitted the University of Richmond to begin a serious physical and program expansion, including a quest for established scholars in a variety of fields.[26]

Richmond Forward, formed in 1964 as a replacement for the Richmond Citizens' Association, began as a white-controlled group concerned with annexation and urban development. As the decade passed, its overriding concern came to be the growth of black political power in the city and the concurrent threat to control by the white civic leaders. The Richmond Crusade for Voters, which had been registering black voters in the city for almost a decade, expanded after the Voting Rights Acts of 1965, a constitutional amendment, and Supreme Court decisions ended the poll tax and forced a state reapportionment that shifted power to city and suburban voters.

The city's business progressivism, under assault by new voters, intensified its annexation efforts and began to focus more on race issues than on the traditional practice of incorporating new neighborhoods and exchanging services for taxes. Richmond looked for room to grow in the suburbs after the 1960 census indicated that the city was losing population to outlying areas. Annexation efforts by the city had almost always been successful, but this time the city encountered serious opposition both from adjacent suburban counties, especially Henrico and Chesterfield, and from the Crusade for Voters, which soon perceived that annexation of the Henrico or Chesterfield suburbs would dilute black voting power in the city.

Their perception was correct. After 1965, and certainly after the 1968 city council election in which three men endorsed by Crusade for Voters won, the goals of the annexation became more fixed on expanding the base of white voters. The plan to annex part of Chesterfield County was the product of private meetings among city and county leaders and involved explicit trade-offs not aired in public. After a long court suit, the city annexed twenty-three square miles of that suburban county and 47,000 of its residents—most of them white.[27] This annexation sparked a series of federal court battles in the next decade.

By the end of the sixties, concerned central Richmond citizens had begun to find each other and to form organizations in support of the public schools. The family of Linwood Holton, who was elected governor in 1969, provided much-needed symbolic support by attending public schools. At the time of the *Brown* decision in 1954, Richmond's segregated public schools were three-fifths white and two-fifths black. Seven years later, in the first year of a token integration, the white percentage had dropped by 15 percent, but this change was

Gov. Linwood Holton walks his daughter Tayloe into John F. Kennedy High School in Richmond on the first day of classes in 1970. The Holtons' choice to send their children to predominantly black city schools during the tempestuous days of the busing controversy in Richmond was a dramatic and symbolic act. Courtesy of the Virginia Historical Society, Richmond

due more to increased black enrollment than to white decline in numbers. Only 2,000 white students had left the school system, while 6,000 black students had entered. By 1969, the last school year before the annexation of the Chesterfield suburbs, the percentage of white pupils had dropped to under a third, which represented a loss of 6,000 white students over the decade of the sixties and a gain of almost 9,000 blacks.[28]

While enjoying the nation's material prosperity and the fruits of technology in the postwar decades, Richmonders had also experienced a challenge to Jim Crow that seemed to overshadow all other events. The physical demolition that leveled old neighborhoods and carved paths for highways was, in part, an effort to shore up traditional political and racial systems as well as the downtown commercial center. When the city government optimistically planned to change postwar Richmond, their vision of highways, suburban annexation, and a revitalized downtown had not included either protracted legal resistance to annexation from groups outside and inside the city, legal challenges to all forms of segregation, or the mass hysteria known as massive resistance. Local efforts to use planned change as a mechanism for maintaining both downtown business and white city government had taken a heavy toll on neighborhood life in the center city.

CHAPTER TWELVE

The Suburban City

In the summer of 1963, a longtime leader in Richmond's preservation efforts evoked images of Yankee profiteers, invasive toll roads, and the dark totalitarian future of George Orwell's *Nineteen Eighty-Four* to express her vision of the effects of urban renewal in Richmond. In a letter to the editor of the *Richmond Times-Dispatch*, Mary Wingfield Scott protested the city's designation of a part of Jackson Ward as a slum and angrily concluded: "Well, Big Brother knows best, so let us sweep away the fine ante-bellum houses, put the people into barracks like Mosby Court, and hope some financial giants from the North will profit by cheap land to erect Berkshires [high-rise apartments] to enjoy the noise along the toll road."[1]

Miss Scott and her fellow preservationists were angered by the city's plans to demolish much of the historic Jackson Ward neighborhood in an effort to acquire federal dollars for urban renewal. The concern for preservation and restoration was a long tradition in Richmond, expressed first in the Association for the Preservation of Virginia Antiquities and enlarged in the 1930s and 1940s through the efforts of Scott and others. The establishment of the Historic Richmond Foundation in 1956 gave a broader base to efforts at preserving Richmond's architecture and neighborhoods. Mary Wingfield Scott's objections to the piecemeal demolition of a black neighborhood were eloquent but ineffective. The city's urban renewal, annexation, and commercial revitalization schemes followed the pattern of many American cities—belatedly and on a smaller scale, but with many of the same consequences.

Richmond's desire to restructure its downtown was part of a national effort to modernize American cities still organized around streetcar patterns. It was also an effort to respond to the shabby or deteriorated central city housing, which was mostly, although not entirely, occupied by blacks. Generations of civic neglect and decades of federal discrimination in housing policy placed dwellings with the fewest city services and amenities closest to the commercial and retail center. Demolition of these neighborhoods seemed in keeping with both the southern Progressive tradition and with federal policy, but resistance from residents, preservationists, and conservatives who wanted no government programs delayed the planners and forced downtown business leaders to form a series of organizations to press for their agendas.[2]

In the 1970s, long, enduring civic disputes and cross-pressures over the physical growth of the city, the composition and fate of its neighborhoods and schools, and the authority of its local government culminated in seismic shifts in Richmond's shape, demography, and politics. The race-based struggles over public schools, suburban annexation, the racial composition of city government, and policies for downtown renewal no longer identified Richmond as a southern city. These scenarios were now nationwide, played out in almost every American city. But in some ways Richmond gave national urban problems a local flavor through a time-honored emphasis on legal battles and a self-conscious sense of the city's place in history.

While the city embarked on experiments with urban renewal, the school system gradually acquired a black majority, and Richmond lost population, dropping back to its 1960 level despite the boost given by the 1970 annexation, while the suburbs expanded. By the early seventies, it was no longer white flight from the city but migration to the region that accounted for suburban growth. Colleges and universities increased enrollment, and both state and city government offices added workers. The particularly Richmond version of the southern accent became a minority dialect. As Richmond spread out, it prepared to meet the southern tip of the Washington suburbs and to become part of the interconnected urban region that ran from Boston to Norfolk and Virginia Beach.

In the continuing legal combat over integration of the Richmond school system, local lawyers who prepared briefs for opposing positions studied case law and the Constitution like medieval Scholastics reasoning out holy writ. The long conflict entered a new era in 1970, when district judge Robert Merhige ordered intracity busing to achieve racial balance in the city's schools. In 1973, the Supreme Court heard a request from the Richmond City Schools that they be permitted to extend their busing to the predominantly white Henrico County suburbs. Justice Lewis Powell, chairman of Richmond's school board in the era just after the *Brown* decision, recused himself from the case, but his fellow justices produced a tie vote, and the Court determined that busing plans could not cross county boundaries. As suburbs continued to spread widely across administrative lines, this court decision meant they would be increasingly independent of the city's school problems.[3]

Annexation of part of the Chesterfield County suburbs, accomplished in 1970 after a decade of litigation, drew a legal challenge initiated by black community activist Curtis Holt, who claimed that the goal of annexation was to dilute the black vote. The addition of the

After federal judge Robert R. Merhige, Jr., ruled that the school districts of Richmond City, Henrico County, and Chesterfield County should be merged through a busing plan, many white Richmonders protested the decision. The plan was eventually overturned on appeal. Photograph of 1970 antibusing protest, from the Valentine, Richmond, Virginia

new suburbs and old farms south of the James River had indeed created 43,000 new white voters and only 4,000 new black voters, reducing Richmond's black voting power from 52 to 42 percent. The federal district court suspended voting in the city while it determined whether annexation was a rational pursuit of Richmond's needs, as the city claimed, or an expediency for racial control. In 1975, the Supreme Court—again without the participation of Justice Powell—upheld the suburban annexation but required that the at-large system of voting be replaced with a ward/district system.

Citywide elections in 1977 under the new ward system created a black majority on the city council, and that majority elected the city's first black mayor, Henry L. Marsh, a lawyer active in civil rights litigation. Marsh opened the city's boards and commissions to people with new perspectives and relied on the majority black vote on the city council. Some Richmond whites feared that the black majority on the city council would now force white Richmond to experience political powerlessness, and this fear seemed confirmed by the firing of a white city manager and the council's racial divisions over the next five years. But there were divisions among the black members, and the new leadership showed no inclination to abandon Project One, the downtown improvement plan adopted by the previous administration. Mayor Marsh's willingness to cooperate with the completion of a hotel–convention center–office center complex spoke for the black leadership's continuity with past commitments and the hope for a biracial political alliance. Such an alliance of middle-class blacks and white business elites had emerged in other cities, from New York to Atlanta.[4]

By the late seventies it was clear that the economic growth in southern cities had a sustainable vigor of its own, which might finally bring them to parity with northeastern cities.

The annexation of 1970, which made a large part of Chesterfield County part of Richmond, brought many new white voters and needed tax dollars into the city. African Americans fought the annexation, which they saw as a way of forestalling black political power. The legacy of race as an issue in annexation has prevented the further expansion of the corporate limits of Richmond and has stifled regional cooperation. Courtesy of Richmond Newspapers, Inc.

The obvious growth in population, industry, and prosperity was variously attributed to the presence of cheap nonunionized labor, expanding markets, a pleasant climate (especially when moderated by air conditioning), abundant natural resources, less expensive land, favorable amenities for living, regional promotional efforts, and the flow of federal funds. But the most important factors were the interstate highway systems, which had begun in the fifties, and the dismantling of segregation, which brought southern cities closer to the rest of the nation and freed them from the burden of maintaining racial separation at the cost of all other goals; the qualities that made southern cities attractive were then more apparent. Because Richmond was a late and limited participant in the demolition aspects of urban renewal, the city boasted an old housing stock, like that of Charleston and Savannah, as well as a solid and diversified business economy.

Richmond is a city of neighborhoods, but some of those neighborhoods fared better than others during the changes of the postwar decades. The neighborhoods of modest postwar brick houses, the more imposing residences of the West End, and the newest tracts and developments across the river in Chesterfield or further out in Henrico County prospered as national branching and regional expansion of business brought new employees to the area. The older city neighborhoods offered visual evidence of the variety of strategies used by the city in its efforts to revitalize the center.

Typical of privately financed restoration and renovation was the Fan District, an architecturally pleasing district with homes built between 1880 and 1920 and with Monument Avenue as its Main Street. This area, the scene of speculative real estate schemes since the early nineteenth century, became first a streetcar suburb and then slightly shabby during the 1930s

Henry Marsh (center) is honored at a testimonial dinner by then–state senator L. Douglas Wilder (speaking) in 1970. Marsh was Richmond's first black mayor, elected by a black majority on city council in 1977. From the Valentine, Richmond, Virginia

and 1940s as old homes were converted to apartments or boardinghouses. But young families moved in during the 1950s, and one street was reportedly nicknamed "Stork Alley" for its contribution to postwar population growth. The establishment of Virginia Commonwealth University in 1968 both anchored and stabilized the Fan District and gave the predominantly townhouse section a mildly bohemian air.

On Church Hill, where council member Richard Adams once laid out lots and offered land for the state capitol, the solidly middle-class structures built on both sides of Broad Street had declined in status and appearance. Private renovation and restoration began in the 1950s in the area near St. John's Church, a site almost as monumental for its own long history as for the day when Patrick Henry spoke there. But on Church Hill on Broad Street's north side—a working-class neighborhood with many antebellum houses—there was little change until the mid-1980s. Then a group of white urban homesteaders asked for a historic district designation in a working-class black neighborhood where residents resented restrictions on exterior changes to their dwellings and feared that higher property taxes would drive them from their homes. In this dilemma, race and class were again profoundly intertwined.[5]

At the beginning of the seventies, Richmond had initiated four separate urban redevelopment projects involving more than one thousand acres of densely populated streets and neighborhoods, at a cost of $100 million. Fulton, a predominantly black working-class neighborhood built over some of the city's earliest material history, was the site of Richmond's one neighborhood-wide urban renewal demolition. Fulton Hill was where Christopher Newport and John Smith are said to have met with Parahunt, son of Powhatan, in May 1607. In the early 1700s, seafarer Robert Rocketts bought extensive property along the James and established a ferry between Rocketts Wharves and the south bank of the James. A few blacks lived in Fulton after the Civil War, and more moved there at the turn of the century, holding factory jobs and

supporting churches. The exodus of white families from Fulton Bottom took more than two generations and was never complete. Annexed to the city in 1867, the section was commercially viable until the mid-twentieth century.[6]

In the 1960s, Fulton was home to low- or moderate-income blacks with varied perspectives on the neighborhood and on their own personal futures. World War II and postwar prosperity had brought new jobs and greater income to many Richmond blacks. Older family heads, typically vigilant against the sins of sloth and self-indulgence, believed that a Jim Crow world allowed them only a tenuous grip on stability. This seemed excessively cautious to their children, whose postwar world included the movement for civil rights, improved access to factory work and, through their participation in the nation's postwar consumption boom, an expanded set of expectations.

The federal urban renewal and community development programs of the sixties and seventies provided an opportunity for new voices and tactics. The authority of black ministers, lawyers, and the Crusade for Voters was intermittently challenged by more confrontational activists, who questioned the old legalistic and procedural tactics. Like many black neighborhoods, Fulton was torn between its admiration for those who succeeded by using mainstream rules and values and those who successfully flouted the rules.

Recalling Fulton in the late 1960s, a lifelong resident said, "Fulton at that time, like people said, was a bad neighborhood, but it was only bad housing. We wouldn't call it a bad neighborhood as far as crime or anything of that nature."[7] Almost half of Fulton residents owned their homes, and the housing authority's original plan to raze the area and convert it into an industrial park, with a few new dwellings set near a city landfill, caused residents to organize and protest their eviction from a community they cared about. In an effort to control development and prevent bulldozing, Fulton residents got assistance from the Richmond Community

The destruction of the Fulton neighborhood was one of the last and most controversial "slum clearances" under urban renewal in Richmond. A neighborhood anchored by the C&O switching yards, the Richmond Cedar Works, Millhiser Bag Factory, and the city docks, it suffered from falling wages, absentee landlords, and neglect. Battered by severe flood damage in the early 1970s, the community was entirely cleared and new housing was proposed. Only a few new units have yet been built, despite the twenty-odd years since Fulton's destruction. The failure to replace razed housing has been a central failure of urban renewal in Richmond. Photograph of new housing in Fulton area, c. 1980s, courtesy of Richmond Newspapers, Inc.

Action Program, a part of the federal antipoverty program, and drew up a plan that emphasized spot clearance and new schools, parks, and traffic design. Residents thought they had gotten guarantees of rehabilitation, but actually the area was consigned to demolition.

A revised plan limited the industrial site and marked the rest for housing, but condemnation proceedings and title searches slowed rebuilding on half-cleared sites. While the city praised citizen involvement, its plan contained no criteria, and targeted no areas, for rehabilitation. Longtime residents coexisted uneasily with the plywood-boarded windows and yellow signs announcing that the property now belonged to the Richmond Redevelopment Housing Authority. Most residents forced to move from the area were never able to return. Fewer Fulton residents went into public housing or dilapidated housing than did residents of other neighborhoods involved in urban renewal, but Fulton lay demolished and empty for over a decade before it was rebuilt with moderate-income housing above the flood plain level.[8]

In the mid-1970s, when federal funds encouraged restoration while, at the same time, gasoline prices doubled, the city turned to neighborhood rehabilitation, which had been proceeding privately since the 1950s. In 1976, a Richmond Housing Action Plan was adopted; this plan's ambitious agenda proposed to preserve the existing housing supply and encourage historic preservation as well as to redevelop substandard areas in order to attract high-income families and nonresident uses. Conservation became the new investment frontier for developers, who had previously focused on suburban growth. These speculative enterprises included conversion of the old city hall to an office complex, Shockoe Slip warehouses to restaurants and shops, and the Main Street train station to a shopping arcade, as well as the restoration of the formerly elegant downtown Jefferson Hotel.[9]

In 1982, a racially balanced coalition of public and private sector individuals, led by Mayor Henry Marsh and attorney T. Justin Moore, Jr., organized Richmond Renaissance. A primary

Completed in 1994, the Richmond floodwall brings to an end the historic flooding that periodically afflicted much of Shockoe Bottom and the riverfront. This accelerated yet another major shift in the central business district, with its service, information, and entertainment core moving toward the waterfront. From the Valentine, Richmond, Virginia

goal of this coalition was to channel cash commitments from the city and from private corporations toward revitalization of the city center and to create jobs for central city residents. The ascendancy of Richmond Renaissance assured that public officials would continue to consult the city's business leaders and that black political leadership would not significantly change the direction of the city's goals for economic development. Despite tensions, this understanding held steady throughout the eighties under Roy West, who had often opposed Marsh and who was elected as the city's second black mayor in 1982.

Richmond Renaissance planned to use the old downtown section of Jackson Ward as the site for both a major convention hotel — Jackson Place — and the Sixth Street Marketplace. The coalition hired James Rouse, the developer of Boston's Quincy Market and Baltimore's Inner Harbor, to draw up specific plans. The Sixth Street Festival Marketplace opened with high local expectations in September 1985; it extended from the Richmond Blues Armory on the north side of Broad Street to the major department stores of Thalhimer's and Miller & Rhoads on the south side of Broad Street, with an enclosed pedestrian bridge constructed over Broad to connect the two sections. The *Richmond Times-Dispatch* noted approvingly: "It is appropriate that the main architectural feature of the [Sixth Street] Marketplace is the Bridge [across Broad Street] . . . between the predominantly white communities to the south and the predominantly black communities to the north. It is perhaps the epochal turn in the road from the past to the future."[10]

In 1986, a Metropolitan Richmond Convention and Visitors Bureau pamphlet welcomed readers to Richmond and described the downtown as divided into four shopping sections connected by an interurban bus. Those sections were: the Sixth Street Marketplace; Main Street Station and, next to it, the old Farmer's Market; the traditional Broad-Grace retail section; and the renovated section on lower Main called Shockoe Slip, converted from warehouses

Broad Street has long been a symbol of racial division in Richmond, separating predominantly black Jackson Ward from the white retail and commercial district to the south. The Sixth Street Marketplace, a project of Richmond Renaissance, was intended to literally and symbolically bridge the divide between the white and black communities and to create a downtown retail hub. Financial problems have plagued the project, as did the closing of retail anchors Miller & Rhoads and Thalhimers. Photograph of opening of Sixth Street Marketplace, 1985, from the Valentine, Richmond, Virginia

to restaurants and specialty shops. These configurations resembled suburban shopping malls brought downtown; dozens of other American cities were attempting the same reordering of space, signaling that the future of American downtowns was deeply invested in sales, service, and tourism. A half dozen years later, though, only the privately developed Shockoe Slip has truly prospered, and the ancient Farmer's Market, surrounded by warehouses turned to condominiums and lunch counters become ambitious restaurants, continues to offer its humble produce—now valued as authentic, if not strictly organic. Main Street Station closed in 1988, and the Sixth Street Marketplace has been attached to life support systems. The enterprise did indeed draw visitors to the city, but success in booking conventions did not extend to the collection of boutiques, food stands, restaurants, and specialty shops at the Sixth Street Marketplace, and those expectations were quickly disappointed.[11]

Contemporaneous with the difficulties of downtown malls was the other downtown eighties investment—a readily apparent building boom. Richmond's skyline rose in imitation of the Dow Jones averages as a series of chrome, glass, and granite skyscrapers inhabited by

Shockoe Slip (left) has led a resurgence of Richmond's historic waterfront as a retail and shopping district. Photograph of Shockoe Slip area, 1980s, courtesy of Richmond Newspapers, Inc.

The Shockoe Bottom area (below) has enjoyed a revival since the building of the Richmond floodwall, and the "First Market" at Seventeenth Street still stands on its original site. Photograph, 1993, courtesy of Richmond Newspapers, Inc.

law firms, insurance companies, banks, and financial services composed a new skyline between Capitol Square and the James River. These buildings, built in an international corporate style, would be as much at home in Houston or Denver as they are in Richmond. Anchored by the construction of a new Federal Reserve Building, other business and financial centers rose in the same area, including Kanawha Plaza, Riverfront Plaza, and the James Center. The quick-return possibilities of financial investments, real estate, and mergers made some headway among more cautious traditions. The eighties growth, often financed by money that was several times removed from the production of goods and services, encouraged investment and construction. It also met occasional stubborn resistance from local family-run corporations accustomed to a smaller scale and a more personal style of management.

Since Willow Lawn opened in 1957, Richmond has seen an explosion of mall development, especially in the western and southern suburbs. Regency Square Mall (left) opened in 1975. From the Valentine, Richmond, Virginia

In the late eighties, the city witnessed the failure of a hostile takeover attempt against a midsized publishing conglomerate that was based in Richmond and represented a central part of the city's history. Media General Inc.—a communications company with varied southern newspaper, magazine, and television holdings, which included Richmond's two newspapers—was owned by the Bryan family, Richmond newspaper publishers for one hundred years. Described in articles as "genteel, aristocratic . . . old money," with "a business tradition based on familial obligation and reverence for history," the Bryans fended off the West Coast–based attempt to buy the company but, a few years later, found it necessary to close down their afternoon paper, the *Richmond News-Leader*.[12]

A full-page advertisement in the *Wall Street Journal* in 1987 asked in large headlines, "What are 14 Fortune 500 Headquarters Doing in Quiet, Conservative Old Richmond?" It was characteristic of Richmond that the answer was, most often: "They were born here." The Ethyl Corporation, James River Corporation, Chesapeake Corporation, Reynolds, E. R. Carpenter, and others were outgrowths of the region's diverse industrial and business enterprises. However, the allure of these corporate giants obscured the fact that most national business growth has in recent years been created by companies that employ fewer than twenty in processing and merchandising. The true economic strength of Richmond may lie in the cautious but assiduous growth of small local companies.[13]

Civic boosters promoted the South's advantages in agriculture, energy, and air and water quality, but a decade-long study by the Southern Growth Policies Board, issued in 1980, recommended controlled growth through banking reform, financial support for education, and expansion of port facilities. Eager to acquire or keep plants and payrolls, Richmond—like the rest of the South—made only minimal efforts to control or regulate growth. A by-product of that approach was an increasing strain on the region's water, air, and soil.

Richmond had always dumped its waste into the James, believing in the river's ability to clean itself, eventually, somewhere downstream. In 1958, the city of Richmond began operating the first primary sewage treatment plant on the river, but the plant was small and ineffective, and the city was regularly cited by state authorities for the overflow of its storm and sewer system. By the sixties, the effect of generations of increasingly toxic dumping in the James River was apparent to fishermen and state regulatory agencies. Fewer shad and herring made the spawning run, and sturgeon had disappeared. The eagles and ospreys that had once nested along the river were gone. The Commission of Game and Inland Fisheries brought in tougher fish, like smallmouth bass, to restock the river.[14]

The State Water Control Board, aided by the federal Clean Water Act and the Environmental Protection Agency, acquired the power to demand treatment of industrial and urban waste. Some progress was made, but compared to the effect of dumping chemicals in the river, the progress was negligible. Since the 1950s, the Allied Chemical Corporation in Hopewell had been manufacturing chlordecone, an organochloride, marketed as Kepone and designed to kill insects on vegetables. Kepone, a long-lasting and water-soluble chemical, is highly toxic to the nervous system. Allied regularly dumped its Kepone waste into the James; but it was not until a subsidiary Allied company with the inspired name of Life Sciences began producing three to six thousand pounds of Kepone daily, operating night and day, that the Kepone levels changed from a long-term problem to an immediate threat, apparent to all by the mid-1970s. Signs of poisoning were apparent in workers' neurological systems and in the river's fishlife. The river was closed to commercial fishing, and while state authorities argued over how much Kepone was permissible, many people simply stopped buying fish from Virginia.

Cleanup of the Kepone—a costly and difficult enterprise—still continues. In the time since, there have been other reminders of the James River's close connection with the citizens of Richmond. In 1981, a bright green algae in the river, encouraged by the sun and by fertilizers from lawns and fields, gave a strange odor to all the water in Richmond. It was essentially harmless but reminded Richmonders that what goes into the river will flavor the city's morning coffee. By the end of the eighties, there was cautious optimism that the problems of sewage and industrial waste had peaked and that a slow reversal of their effects again permitted fishing and perhaps swimming in the James River.[15]

Just occasionally, it was still possible for a breeze to bring the sweet aroma of tobacco to downtown Richmond. Unlike many American cities, Richmond maintained an industrial core near its center into the late twentieth century. Slowly, in the last decades of the twentieth century, the old tobacco plants closed. It was the end of a very long era of tobacco warehousing and processing at those sites. In 1970, Liggett & Myers left the old Allen and Ginter plant in the warehouse district on the site of William Byrd's village, and American Tobacco closed its last plant in the city in 1988. Philip Morris closed two of its three remaining warehouse district sites in 1993.

Richmond also suffered the sale of locally owned Best Products and its slide into receivership; and A. H. Robins Pharmaceuticals paid vast damages to women injured by its birth control product, the Dalkon Shield, before the local family-run company was also sold. These reverses were at least balanced by new data-processing services, telecommunication centers, and retail outlets, such as Circuit City, as well as other service and information businesses. Virginia Commonwealth University, with its medical research and teaching hospital, the Medical College of Virginia, employed increasingly higher percentages of city residents. The Richmond Area Metropolitan Economic Development Council promoted Richmond's low labor costs, its educated workforce, its position as a state capital, the Fifth Federal Reserve District Bank, and the presence of important southern law firms, advertising agencies, and banks. Especially noted as attractions were the city's historic buildings.

As the fast-money frenzy of the 1980s drew to a close, the amount of wealth invested conservatively, together with a large public service employment base, made certain that the city would survive into another century. In the late eighties, economists predicted "steady, lackluster growth" for the metropolitan area, where almost two-thirds of all employment was divided equally between trade, government, and services.[16]

At the start of the century's last decade, the city witnessed another dramatic ritual in Capitol Square. In January 1990, L. Douglas Wilder, whose ex-slave grandparents had moved from

Supreme Court Justice Lewis Powell administers the oath of office to L. Douglas Wilder, Virginia's first black governor, in 1990. Courtesy of Richmond Newspapers, Inc.

rural Goochland County to Richmond in the 1880s, was inaugurated as governor by retired Supreme Court justice Lewis F. Powell, Jr., son of the young man from Southampton County who was dazzled by his arrival in Richmond on New Year's Day 1899. On this cold but sunny day in January, Powell was clearly delighted to administer the oath of office to the first elected black governor in the nation.

Earlier, at nearby St. Paul's Episcopal Church, where Jefferson Davis had worshipped during his years in Richmond, the long preinaugural worship service ended with congregational singing of "The Battle Hymn of the Republic." Two blocks from St. Paul's, on Broad Street, the downtown Miller & Rhoads, one of the city's two venerable department stores, had closed its doors after 105 years, and its windows announced the auction of its merchandise, down to the store fixtures. The city's other major department store, Thalhimer's, closed shortly thereafter. Among the other recent closures was the Home for Confederate Women, which moved its last eight frail residents to a suburban retirement village.[17]

South of the James, the suburbs of Chesterfield County were home to almost 200,000 of the Richmond metropolitan region's estimated 650,000 residents. Over half of the metropolitan area's workers were white-collar, employed in national or regional corporate headquarters, government offices, medical centers and hospitals, colleges and universities, or banks and insurance companies. The high-rise city empties at night except for the renovated Shockoe Slip area and Shockoe Bottom, where upscale specialty shops, idiosyncratic art shops, and restaurants draw tourists and men and women from nearby offices.[18]

The decay of the down-town has been symbolized by the closing of many Richmond landmarks, including the two major retail anchors, Miller & Rhoads (right) and Thalhimers, as well as the Hotel John Marshall (left). Courtesy of Richmond Newspapers, Inc.

In the old residential section near the capitol, the area known recently as Court End but longer as part of Shockoe Hill, Clay and Marshall streets contain several blocks of surviving gentry residences. On one block, the Valentine Museum of the Life and History of Richmond has carefully restored the 1812 city home of Federalist lawyer John Wickham. Nearby is the house that Chief Justice John Marshall built and lived in for most of his life. One block at the end of Clay Street is dominated by buildings that house the Museum of the Confederacy and the recently restored White House of the Confederacy. During the mid-1980s the Valentine began a reinterpretation of the city's history, featuring exhibitions on antebellum black life in Richmond, the Jim Crow experience in Richmond, the history of Jews in the city, women in Richmond's workforce, and other previously unexplored topics. In 1991, the Valentine and Ethyl Corporation, owner of the Tredegar Iron Works on the Kanawha Canal, entered into an agreement for the Valentine to use the site for new museum galleries and historic attractions depicting the life of the city, with an emphasis on the nineteenth century and Richmond's industrial past.[19]

In nearby Hanover County, heirs to John Wickham's plantation, Hickory Hill, negotiated to sell it for a commercial and residential planned community. Speculative preliminary plans for the tract called for homes, office parks, light industry, a golf course, a health center, and restoration of the manor house.[20] The popular planned towns of the suburbs recall Richmond's entrepreneurial origins in William Byrd's 1737 plan. Developers have attempted to create suburban shopping downtown, city planning has been planted in the suburbs, and the two are tied together by ribbons of highway; in effect, the sprawling present-day city recreates the same distances between interconnected clusters that characterized the neighborhoods of seventeenth-century Virginia.

While the urban economic dilemmas of a diminishing tax base and a disappearing middle class have captured the most attention, the nature of the postwar suburbs and even more re-

Richmond's cityscape holds both the old and the new. In the foreground is Valentine Riverside, an outdoor museum on the site of the Tredegar Iron Works. Valentine Riverside opened in May 1994, converting an industrial site to a new industry—tourism. In the background, the towers of Richmond's financial, information, and service industries hold sway. From the Valentine, Richmond, Virginia

cent ones has changed markedly since the early fifties. The suburbs have urbanized and now have their own centers of employment—mostly based on informational and knowledge work, but including some of the small amount of remaining industry. Domestic service had almost disappeared as an employment category by the 1980s, and few aproned housewives remain in suburban homes. Most middle-class American blacks live in the suburbs, where the new wave of Hispanic and Asian immigrants has also settled. Coincident with their suburban construction, shopping centers, banks, department stores, and supermarkets extended their hours to accommodate the "second shift" of working women. With two-income families a national and local standard, the absence of women's labor as civic volunteers and caregivers is evident in the proliferation of fast food restaurants, day care centers, and nursing homes.[21]

At the beginning of the 1980s, women workers were primarily concentrated in lower-paying clerical and service occupations, with professional and factory or craft employment as lesser, but still important, categories. The long and emotionally tangled relationship between black domestic workers and their white women employers, marked by centuries of deference, dissembling, anger, and affection, declined and effectively ended. Black women sought employment more consistent with their training or simply declined day work in households.[22] One hundred years earlier, Richmond's work force had changed as women and children of both races entered the factories and white women found work in new offices and department

Recent disputes over regional cooperation are well illustrated by Henrico County's proposal to build its own water treatment plant—a plan opposed by Richmond City, which now sells water to Henrico. Richmond has felt the competitive pressure from other areas with consolidated governments, such as Charlotte, Nashville, and Jacksonville, which can resolve jurisdiction disputes and consolidate metropolitan government. Photograph of Richmond water treatment plant, courtesy of Richmond Newspapers, Inc.

stores. In the decades after 1970, new workers again found new employment in Richmond. White-collar occupations expanded for black men and women after the 1960s, while the largest group of new workers was married women with children. As the workplace became more integrated by sex and race, it appeared to sort out more sharply by class. Just when blacks and women found barriers to skilled labor lowered through legislation, factory employment diminished.

While the traditional industrial and commercial jobs that long sustained Richmond declined nationally and locally, service sector and professional work increased. As a midsized southern city, Richmond was poised to take advantage of two developments within the national economy: its regionalization and, concurrently, its transformation into a service and administrative economy, dominated by the professions of banking, insurance, law, medicine, and education. Apparent in the new economy is a biracial upper-middle-class workforce of two-income Richmonders in sharp contrast to an increasingly feminized poverty.[23]

In the 1980s the Census Bureau merged the Richmond metropolitan area with that of Petersburg; together their population is expected to reach one million after the turn of the century. The core city lost population in the eighties at a rate faster than it had in the previous two decades. Of the metropolitan counties, Chesterfield County, south of the James River and long connected with the city, grew most rapidly, and Chesterfield and Henrico are each expected to surpass the city in population by the year 2000. There is no indication that cars will be abandoned for public transport. These suburbs, often with their own centers, may exert more influence on the old central city in the twenty-first century than it exerts on them.[24]

The ideal American family, for whom the suburbs were constructed, no longer lives there or anywhere else. The people in those houses reconstruct their own vision of family roles and ethnic or regional identity as their lives change to accommodate new realities. The cost of land, oil, and mortgages, a long-term rise in the divorce rate, and the fall in household size affected the functions as well as the meanings of suburban communities. Suburbia, generally viewed as an intellectual wasteland and an architectural hymn to conformity and mediocrity, has begun to reinvent itself to provide new services to new populations. The suburban connection with the historic central city is less commercial, more tied to administrative and intellectual functions in a new way.[25]

Much of the late-twentieth-century South seemed to move quickly from a rural to a postindustrial economy, from the countryside to the suburbs, and from the solid Democratic South to the Republican party. As a factory town, Richmond's metropolitan experience combined Rustbelt trauma with Sunbelt solace, losing industry to knowledge work and middle-class urbanites to suburbs. The new economy has expanded employment for women and loosened social constraints on them, but service sector work is neither paid well enough nor organized well enough to permit most working women to maintain traditional family structures. This may be nothing new for the generations of factory women and shop girls in the city—especially those who continued to work after marriage—but a much larger percentage of women have now experienced these dual demands. The necessary accommodations and compromises are far from worked out.[26]

The 1980s saw a business revival for many downtowns, including Richmond, but downtown building booms failed to provide jobs for downtown unemployed. The new two-level service economy has boosted workers with knowledge functions, while low-level service workers are paid little and remain in poverty even while employed. Luxury hotels and "trophy" office buildings coexist with crime, homelessness, welfare dependency, lethal drug use and rising murder rates. A 1986 study by the Southern Growth Policies Board described the "sunshine on the sunbelt" as "a narrow beam of light" falling chiefly on the urban South and cited the region's need for educated workers and investment. Just as the New South of the late nineteenth century was urban and industrial and tilted toward the Piedmont, the Sunbelt—whose definition is equally ephemeral—is metropolitan and service-oriented, tilting back toward the cities and suburbs in the Atlantic seaboard states.[27]

Quality-of-life ratings based on the environment, the economy, education, public welfare, and quality of government continued to rank the South and Virginia low, but this was not how locals viewed it. As John Shelton Reed noted, such sociological renderings are "a Yankee way of knowing" and do not speak to the many southerners who overwhelmingly name someone they know as the person they most admire and choose where they are as where they want to live.[28]

Near the end of the twentieth century, Richmond was an old city by American standards and was a mix of families long resident in the region and newcomers. Few cities that served as the capital of a defeated nation have been as thoroughly enshrined and enfolded into national history as Richmond has. But late-twentieth-century Richmond experienced its history as a dilemma. The city feared losing its past to the neon glare, subdivision mazes, and postmodern facades common to American cities but, to some extent, feared keeping it as well. The city wanted tourist dollars but did not want to point to its slave-based past and its role as capital of the Confederacy in a city with a black administration and a majority-black school population. As in the past, Richmond's residents edged toward solutions that acknowledged current realities without abandoning a conservative perspective or a mythic past.

One block down from the Valentine Museum, the Museum of the Confederacy began, in the late 1980s, to offer tours of the newly redecorated and reopened White House of the Confederacy. Despite its immense popularity among tourists, the museum and the Confederate White House, decorated to reflect its interior in 1862, were not on the list of approved museums for Richmond school groups to visit at the time of its reopening. In the summer of 1991, the Museum of the Confederacy opened a major exhibition on slavery in the Old South. The venerable Virginia Historical Society, often a participant in shaping as well as recording Richmond and Virginia history, expanded both its research facilities and its research agenda beginning in the late 1980s.

In 1986, Richmond's school board ordered an end to busing, which, they concluded, was

no longer necessary in a school system that was 87 percent black.[29] In 1989, the descendants of Albert and Lucy Brooks held a Brooks family reunion in Richmond and, wearing reunion T-shirts, took a bus tour of the sites where the slave family had lived and worked in the city.

The Virginia Council on Indians stopped receiving state financial aid in 1991, but the eight tribes, with a total of 15,000 members, were experiencing a revival of interest in their culture, and the Upper Mattaponi of the Powhatan Confederacy announced plans for an Indian village near Richmond, a village designed to be a major tourist attraction.[30] In July 1992, the three toll plazas on Interstate 95 shut down, and for the first time in thirty-four years, motorists no longer had to stop to pay for the highway, which had long since been paid off.[31]

As the oldest part of the city moved toward becoming a place of office towers, government buildings, tourist shops, and restaurants, the city's history continued to be told, casually or didactically, by many voices. Past the old market, near the store where Samuel Smith boxed up Henry Brown, where the Confederates burned tobacco, where floods and freshets left high water marks over decades, where William Byrd II reluctantly permitted a town grid to be imposed, Richmond poet Dave Smith captured one vision of driving a car in pale Sunday morning light:

I ride through Richmond over gray
cobblestones, passing porticoed houses,

. . . .

through Shockoe Bottom
where the state began; slaves, produce markets,
centuries of tobacco. Now boutiques, bars,
condos, all-night joints for lawyers cruising
after coke in Volvos.[32]

There are other visions too. Richmond families, black and white, told stories as they always had—about the war, about the idiosyncrasies of famous Richmonders, about the true parentage of certain mulatto families, about political decisions made by a few men in a small room. The storytelling itself was part of the history. As ever, some parts of the city's history were forgotten or selectively remembered, some mythologized beyond recognition. Parts were in dispute and other parts were being retold with a new emphasis. Like the tumbling of multi-colored stones in a kaleidoscope, any shift in historic interpretation in the city changes the whole prism of understanding.

Notes

CHAPTER ONE

1. Accounts of the voyage upriver are given in George Percy, "Observations Gathered Out of a Discourse of the Plantation of the Southern Colonies in Virginia by the English, 1606," in *The Jamestown Voyages Under the First Charter, 1606–1609*, 2d ser., no. 136, ed. Philip Barbour (London: Published for the Hakluyt Society by Cambridge University Press, 1969), 129–46; Gabriel Archer, "A Relatyon of the Discovery of Our River," 80–98, and "Description of the River and Country," 98–102, in Barbour, *Jamestown Voyages*; and Wirt Armistead Cate, "History of Richmond," 3 vols. (unpublished manuscript held at Valentine Museum, Richmond, c. 1944), 1:8–9. For discussions of the natural history of the Chesapeake and the upper James River, see Virginia Academy of Sciences, *The James River Basin: Past, Present, and Future* (Richmond: Virginia Academy of Sciences, 1950), 154, 191, 350, 358, 374, 388–99, 422, 439–40; Anne Woodlief, *In River Time: The Way of the James* (Chapel Hill: Algonquin Books, 1985); Donald Meinig, *Atlantic America, 1491–1800*, vol. 1 of *The Shaping of America* (New Haven: Yale University Press, 1986), 28–35, 144–48; and Helen Rountree, "The Land and Its Resources," in *The Powhatan Indians of Virginia* (Norman: University of Oklahoma Press, 1989), esp. 24–25, 29.

2. The most detailed research on the lives of the Powhatans is Rountree, *Pocahontas's People* (Norman: University of Oklahoma, 1990) and *The Powhatan Indians*. Jeffrey Hantman, "From Powhatan to Quirank: Reconstructing Monacan Culture and History in the Context of Jamestown" (unpublished paper in author's possession, 1989) explores a nearby group. See

also James Axtell, "The Rise and Fall of the Powhatan Empire," in *After Columbus: Essays in the Ethnohistory of Colonial North America* (New York: Oxford University Press, 1988): 182–221.

3. Richard Hakluyt, *A Discourse on Western Planting*, in *Collections of the Maine Historical Society*, 2d ser., vol. 2, ed. Charles Deane (Cambridge: John Wilson and Son, 1877), 60–61; see also pp. 157–58, 36–37. See also Nicholas Canny, "The Ideology of English Colonization from Ireland to America," *William and Mary Quarterly*, 3d ser., 30 (1973): 575–98; Meinig, *Shaping of America*, 28–30, 39. For the circumstances of early migrants to Virginia, see Eric Wolf, *Europe and the People without History* (Berkeley and Los Angeles: University of California Press, 1982); Edmund Morgan, *American Slavery, American Freedom: The Ordeal of Colonial Virginia* (New York: W. W. Norton, 1975); and James Horn, "Servant Emigration to the Chesapeake in the Seventeenth Century," in *The Chesapeake in the Seventeenth Century: Essays on Anglo-American Society*, ed. Thad Tate and David Ammerman (Chapel Hill: University of North Carolina Press for the Institute of Early American History and Culture, 1979): 51–95.

4. Percy, "Observations Gathered Out of a Discourse," 140–41.

5. Archer, "A Relatyon of the Discovery of Our River," 86, 89.

6. J. Frederick Fausz, "An 'Abundance of Blood Shed on Both Sides': England's First Indian War, 1609–1614," *Virginia Magazine of History and Biography* 98 (January 1990): 3–57, esp. 4, and "The Invasion of Virginia: Indians, Colonialism, and the Conquest of Cant: A Review Essay on Anglo-Indian Relations in the Chesapeake," *Virginia Magazine of History and*

Biography 95 (April 1987): 145.

7. See the Bibliographic Essay for sources on interpretations of Pocahontas over time.

8. "A Coppie of the Subscription for Maydes," quoted in David R. Ransome, "Wives for Virginia, 1621," *William and Mary Quarterly*, 3d ser., 48, no. 1 (January 1991): 3–18; the quote appears on p. 7. See also Morgan, *American Slavery, American Freedom*, 44–47; Cate, "History of Richmond," 1:14; Julia Cherry Spruill, *Women's Life and Work in the Southern Colonies* (1938; reprint, New York: W. W. Norton, 1972), 7–9.

9. Susan Kingsbury, *Records of the Virginia Company*, in Wesley Frank Craven, *White, Red and Black: The Seventeenth-Century Virginian* (Charlottesville: University Press of Virginia), 55; J. Leitch Wright, Jr., *The Only Land They Knew: The Tragic Story of the American Indians in the Old South* (New York: Free Press, 1981), 77–81.

10. Meinig, *Atlantic America*, 144–46; Darrett and Anita Rutman, *A Place in Time: Middlesex County, Virginia, 1650–1750* (New York: W. W. Norton, 1984), 44–48.

11. Craven, *White, Red and Black*, 54–57; Rountree, *Pocahontas's People*, 84–88.

12. W. W. Hening, *Statutes at Large*, in Cate, "History of Richmond," 1:16–17; Wright, *The Only Land They Knew*, 22, 87; Peter Wood, "Recounting the Past," *Southern Exposure* 16, no. 2 (Summer 1988): 30–37; Warren Billings, ed., *The Old Dominion in the Seventeenth Century: A Documentary History of Virginia, 1606–1689* (Chapel Hill: University of North Carolina Press for the Institute of Early American History and Culture), 243.

13. Christopher Hill, *Reformation to Industrial Revolution: The Making of Modern English Society, 1530–1780* (New York: Pantheon

Books, 1967), 123–28, 185–87; Wolf, *Europe and the People without History*, 158–63, 195–96; Carole Shammas, "English Commercial Development and American Colonization, 1560–1620," in *The Westward Enterprise: English Activities in Ireland, the Atlantic, and America, 1480–1650*, ed. K. R. Andrew, N. P. Canny, and P. E. H. Hair (Liverpool: Liverpool University Press, 1978), 151–74.

14. Jane Carson, *Bacon's Rebellion: 1676 to 1976* (Jamestown: The Jamestown Foundation, 1976), 4–5; Wilcomb Washburn, *The Governor and the Rebel: A History of Bacon's Rebellion in Virginia* (Chapel Hill: University of North Carolina Press, 1957), 29, 186n.

15. John Berry and Francis Moryson, *A True Narrative*, quoted in Howard Mumford Jones, *The Literature of Virginia in the Seventeenth Century*, 2d ed. (Charlottesville: University Press of Virginia, 1968), 118. See also Washburn, *The Governor and the Rebel*, 35.

16. Spruill, *Women's Life and Work*, 233–36.

17. See reference to Aphra Behn's *The Widow Ranter, or the History of Bacon in Virginia*, in Carole Shammas, "English-Born Creole Elites in Turn-of-the-Century Virginia," in Tate and Ammerman, *The Chesapeake in the Seventeenth Century*, 275–77. Byrd was granted Bacon's seized land on 15 March 1676. See Louis H. Manarin and Clifford Dowdey, *The History of Henrico County* (Charlottesville: University Press of Virginia, 1984), 53–54.

18. Interpretations of Bacon's Rebellion are discussed in the Bibliographic Essay. See also Rountree, *Powhatan Indians of Virginia*, 96–99.

19. Rountree, *Pocahontas's People*, 109–10, places these cabins at the north end of the modern Mayo's Bridge, a low-lying area of railroad track at the base of overarching patterns of expressways, thoroughfares, and highways.

20. Sir William Berkeley in Hening, *Statutes at Large*, quoted in Billings, *Old Dominion*, 118. See also Robert Beverley, *The History and Present State of Virginia*, quoted in Billings, *Old Dominion*, 235.

21. Meinig, *Atlantic America*, 149; Stephen Innes, ed., *Work and Labor in Early America* (Chapel Hill: University of North Carolina Press for the Institute of Early American History and Culture, 1988), 6–7; Jack P. Greene, *Pursuits of Happiness: The Social Development of Early Modern British Colonies and the Formation of American Culture* (Chapel Hill: University of North Carolina Press, 1988), 12–18.

CHAPTER TWO

1. Donald W. Meinig, *Atlantic America, 1491–1800*, vol. 1 of *The Shaping of America* (New Haven: Yale University Press, 1986), 153–55.

2. Jeffrey L. Hantman, "Between Powhatan and Quirank: Reconstructing Monacan Culture and History in the Context of Jamestown" (unpublished paper in author's possession, 1989); Wirt Armistead Cate, "History of Richmond," 3 vols. (unpublished manuscript held at Valentine Museum, Richmond, c. 1943), 1:20; Louis H. Manarin and Clifford Dowdey, *The History of Henrico County* (Charlottesville: University Press of Virginia, 1984), 41, 72–74.

3. Margaret Kern, *The Trail of the Three-Notched Road* (Richmond: William Byrd Press, 1928), 13–15; Drew J. Carneal, "A History of the Fan District" (unpublished manuscript in author's possession, n.d.), 1–3; J. Leitch Wright, Jr., *The Only Land They Knew: The Tragic Story of the American Indians in the Old South* (New York: Free Press, 1981), 96; Manarin and Dowdey, *Henrico County*, 46.

4. Darrett and Anita Rutman, *A Place in Time: Middlesex County, Virginia, 1650–1750* (New York: W. W. Norton, 1984), 7, 120, 126, 188, 239; Cate, "History of Richmond," 1:30–31; Wright, *The Only Land They Knew*, 135, 148.

5. Virginia Academy of Sciences, *The James River Basin: Past, Present, and Future* (Richmond: Virginia Academy of Sciences, 1950), 360–64; Jack Temple Kirby, "Virginia's Environmental History," *Virginia Magazine of History and Biography* 99, no. 4 (October 1991): 454–57; Manarin and Dowdey, *Henrico County*, 57.

6. Meinig, *Atlantic America*, 155–57; Richard B. Sheridan, "The Domestic Economy," in *Colonial British America: Essays in the New History of the Early Modern Era*, ed. Jack P. Greene and J. R. Pole (Baltimore: Johns Hopkins University Press, 1984), 45.

7. Dell Upton, "New Views of the Virginia Landscape," *Virginia Magazine of History and Biography* 96, no. 4 (October 1988): 421–24; Cary Carson et al., "Impermanent Architecture in the Southern American Colonies," *Winterthur Portfolio* 16 (Summer/Autumn 1981): 135–36, 138, 141, 158, 163–64.

8. "Narrative of John F. D. Smythe, 1769–1775," in *Travels in Virginia in Revolutionary Times*, ed. Andrew J. Morrison (Lynchburg, Va.: J. P. Bell Company, 1922), 13. See also Paul Clemens, "The Commercial Character of the Early American South: The Case of the Chesapeake" (paper presented to the Southern Historical Association, Norfolk, Va., November 1988), 5–7; Manarin and Dowdey, *Henrico County*, 57; Gary B. Nash, "Social Development," in Greene and Pole, *Colonial British America*, 242–43; and Lorena S. Walsh, "Urban Amenities and Rural Sufficiency: Living Standards and Consumer Behavior in the Colonial Chesapeake, 1643–1777," *Journal of Economic History* 43 (March 1983): 109–17.

9. See Jack P. Greene, *Pursuits of Happiness: The Social Development of Early Modern British Colonies and the Formation of American Culture* (Chapel Hill: University of North Carolina Press, 1988), for a portrayal of the Chesapeake as the model for American cultural development.

10. T. H. Breen and Stephen Innes, *'Myne Own Ground': Race and Freedom on Virginia's Eastern Shore, 1640–1676* (New York: Oxford University Press, 1980), 119n; Lois Green Carr and Lorena S. Walsh, "The Planter's Wife: The Experience of White Women in Seventeenth-Century Maryland," *William and Mary Quarterly*, 3d ser., 34, no. 4 (October 1977): 542–43; Edmund Morgan, *American Slavery, American Freedom: The Ordeal of Colonial Virginia* (New York: W. W. Norton, 1975), 304–5.

11. Philip Curtin, *The Atlantic Slave Trade: A Census* (Madison: University of Wisconsin Press, 1969), 157; Morgan, *American Slavery, American Freedom*, 308–9, 312–13, 320, 325, 327–37, 363–87.

12. Lois Green Carr and Lorena Walsh, "Economic Diversification and Labor Organization in the Chesapeake, 1650–1820," 148–49, 176–77, and Philip Morgan, "Task and Gang Labor Systems," 190–91, 200–201, in *Work and Labor in Early America*, ed. Stephen Innes (Chapel Hill: University of North Carolina Press for the Institute of Early American History and

Culture, 1988); Rutman and Rutman, *A Place in Time*, 238–45; Alden Vaughn, "The Origins Debate: Slavery and Racism in Seventeenth-Century Virginia," *Virginia Magazine of History and Biography* 97, no. 3 (July 1989): 311–54.

13. Henrico County Deed Book, 1677–1692, quoted in *The Old Dominion in the Seventeenth Century: A Documentary History of Virginia, 1606–1689*, ed. Warren Billings (Chapel Hill: University of North Carolina Press for the Institute of Early American History and Culture, 1975), 161–63.

14. W. W. Hening, *Statutes at Large*, in Philip Schwarz, *Twice Condemned: Slaves and the Criminal Laws of Virginia* (Baton Rouge: Louisiana State University Press, 1988), 16–17; Rutman and Rutman, *A Place in Time*, esp. 204–7; Carr and Walsh, "Economic Diversification," 144–49, 157–63.

15. Simon Shama, *The Embarrassment of Riches: An Interpretation of Dutch Culture in the Golden Age* (New York: Knopf, 1987), 195, speaks provocatively, if briefly, of the clay pipe as "peace pipe" and as icon in Dutch portraiture; see also John Noble Wilford, "Old Pipes Offer New View of Black Life in Colonies," *New York Times*, 12 July 1988. See John Michael Vlach, "Afro-American Domestic Artifacts in Eighteenth-Century Virginia," *Material Culture* 19, no. 1 (1987): 3–23, and Theresa Singleton, "The Archeology of Slave Life," in *Before Freedom Came: African American Life in the Antebellum South* (Richmond: University Press of Virginia for the Museum of the Confederacy, 1991), 158.

16. Julia Cherry Spruill, *Women's Life and Work in the Southern Colonies* (1938; reprint, New York: W. W. Norton, 1972), 186–87.

17. Carville Earle and Ronald Hoffman, "The Urban South: The First Two Centuries," in *The City in Southern History: The Growth of Urban Civilization in the South*, ed. Blaine A. Brownell and David R. Goldfield (Port Washington, N.Y.: Kennikat Press, 1977), 23, 26–27; David R. Goldfield and Blaine A. Brownell, *Urban America: A History*, 2d ed. (Boston: Houghton Mifflin, 1990), 21–25.

18. Meinig, *Atlantic America*, 157; M. E. Bristow, "Money and Banking," in *Richmond, Capital of Virginia: Approaches to Its History*, ed. H. J. Eckenrode (Richmond: Whittet and Shepperson, 1938); Jacob

Price, "The Rise of Glasgow in the Chesapeake Tobacco Trade," *William and Mary Quarterly*, 3d ser., 11 (April 1954): 179–99, and "Buchanan and Simpson, 1759–1763: A Different Kind of Glasgow Firm Trading with the Chesapeake," *William and Mary Quarterly*, 3d ser., 40 (January 1983): 3–41; Joseph A. Ernst and H. Roy Merrens, "'Camden's Turrets Pierce the Skies!': The Urban Process in the Southern Colonies," *William and Mary Quarterly*, 3d ser., 30 (October 1973): 549–55, 573, 574.

19. William Byrd, "A Journey to the Land of Eden," quoted in Cate, "History of Richmond," 1:3.

20. John W. Reps, *Tidewater Towns: City Planning in Virginia and Maryland* (Charlottesville: University Press of Virginia for the Colonial Williamsburg Foundation, 1972), 267, 213.

21. See *Richmond's Historic Waterfront: Rockett's Landing to Tredegar, 1607–1865* (Richmond: Historic Richmond Foundation, 1988); Mechal Sobel, *The World They Made Together: Black and White Values in Eighteenth-Century Virginia* (Princeton: Princeton University Press, 1987), 100; Lois Green Carr and Lorena S. Walsh, "Changing Lifestyles and Consumer Behavior in the Colonial Chesapeake" (paper presented at the United States Capitol Historical Society, Washington, D.C., 1989), 3; Billings, *Old Dominion*, 161–63.

22. Cate, "History of Richmond," 1:38–41, 1:48; Carneal, "History of the Fan District," 1.

23. Klaus Wust, *The Virginia Germans* (Charlottesville: University Press of Virginia, 1969), 24. See also *Virginia Gazette*, 9 June 1738, and Henrico County Order Book, in Edward V. Valentine, "Richmond on the James: Historical Notes and Personal Recollections," 5 vols. (unpublished typescript held at Valentine Museum, Richmond, n.d.), 1:n.p.

24. Hening, *Statutes at Large*, in Cate, "History of Richmond," 1:55–56, 1:52–54. See also Samuel Mordecai, *Virginia, Especially Richmond, in By-Gone Days*, 2d ed. (Richmond: West and Johnston, 1860), 32–33; Rhys Isaac, *The Transformation of Virginia, 1740–1790* (Chapel Hill: University of North Carolina Press for the Institute of Early American History and Culture, 1982), 94–104.

25. Carr and Walsh, "Changing Life-

styles," 29–30; John Stilgoe, *The Common Landscape of America: 1580–1845* (New Haven: Yale University Press, 1982), 258–59.

26. Marion Tinling, ed., *The Correspondence of the Three William Byrds of Westover, Virginia, 1684–1776*, 2 vols. (Charlottesville: University Press of Virginia, 1977), 2:623–26; quote appears on p. 626. See also Cate, "History of Richmond," 1:57–59; Spruill, *Women's Life and Work*, 179–80; Linda Kerber, *Women of the Republic: Intellect and Ideology in Revolutionary America* (Chapel Hill: University of North Carolina Press for the Institute of Early American History and Culture, 1980), 9, 119–21; Suzanne Lebsock, *"A Share of Honour": Virginia Women, 1600–1945*, 2d ed. (Richmond: Virginia State Library, 1987), 43–44.

27. *Pennsylvania Gazette*, 20 August 1767, 4. Copy in Virginius Dabney papers, Alderman Library, University of Virginia; original held at Virginia Historical Society.

28. *Virginia Gazette*, 20 August 1767, quoted in Cate, "History of Richmond," 1:61, 1:57–59, 1:62–63; Carneal, "History of the Fan District," 4, 5; Reps, *Tidewater Towns*, 269.

CHAPTER THREE

1. "Narrative of John F. D. Smyth, 1769–1775," in *Travels in Virginia in Revolutionary Times*, ed. Andrew J. Morrison (Lynchburg, Va.: J. P. Bell Company, 1922), 12–13.

2. *Virginia Gazette*, 30 May and 6 June 1771, in Wirt Armistead Cate, "History of Richmond," 3 vols. (unpublished manuscript held at Valentine Museum, Richmond, c. 1944), 1:64–66; *Richmond Compiler*, 20 July 1842, in Edward V. Valentine, "Richmond on the James: Historical Notes and Personal Recollections," 5 vols. (unpublished typescript held at the Valentine Museum, Richmond, n.d.), 1:n.p.

3. T. H. Breen, *Tobacco Culture: The Mentality of the Great Tidewater Planters on the Eve of Revolution* (Princeton: Princeton University Press, 1985), 123; Jack P. Greene, *Pursuits of Happiness: The Social Development of Early Modern British Colonies and the Formation of American Culture* (Chapel Hill: University of North Carolina Press, 1988), 90–93.

4. Breen, *Tobacco Culture*, 129, 131–32; Samuel Mordecai, *Richmond in By-Gone Days*, 2d ed. (Richmond: West and Johnston, 1860), 35–37.

5. Harry M. Ward and Harold E. Greer, Jr., *Richmond during the Revolution, 1775–1783* (Charlottesville: University Press of Virginia for the Richmond Independence Bicentennial Commission, 1977), 123, and Allan Kulikoff, *Tobacco and Slaves: The Development of Southern Cultures in the Chesapeake, 1680–1800* (Chapel Hill: University of North Carolina Press for the Institute of Early American History and Culture, 1986), 124, note that the Upper James River had become the center of the Virginia slave trade in the decades before the American Revolution.

6. Breen, *Tobacco Culture*, 125–27, 129, 131–32, 142; Mordecai, *Richmond in By-Gone Days*, 35–37. See also a related economic analysis by Jacob M. Price, *Capital and Credit in British Overseas Trade: The View from the Chesapeake, 1700–1776* (Cambridge: Harvard University Press, 1980).

7. Ward and Greer, *Richmond during the Revolution*, 24–29.

8. Valentine, "Richmond on the James," 1:n.p.; Drew J. Carneal, "A History of the Fan District" (unpublished manuscript in author's possession, n.d.), 8.

9. Ward and Greer, *Richmond during the Revolution*, 74–88; Sylvia Frey, "Between Slavery and Freedom: Virginia Blacks in the American Revolution," *Journal of Southern History* 49, no. 3 (August 1983): 396–97.

10. Carneal, "History of the Fan District," 9; Ward and Greer, *Richmond during the Revolution*, 82–93; Luther P. Jackson, "Virginia Negro Soldiers and Seamen in the American Revolution," *Journal of Negro History* 27, no. 3 (July 1942): 253, 259.

11. Donald Meinig, *Atlantic America, 1492–1800*, vol. 1 of *The Shaping of America* (New Haven: Yale University Press, 1986), 156; David R. Goldfield and Blaine A. Brownell, *Urban America: A History*, 2d ed. (Boston: Houghton Mifflin, 1990), 23; John W. Reps, *Tidewater Towns: City Planning in Colonial Virginia and Maryland* (Charlottesville: University Press of Virginia for the Colonial Williamsburg Foundation, 1972), 269, 271.

12. "Letter of Eliza J. Ambler to Mrs. Dudley," in Ward and Greer, *Richmond during the Revolution*, 41. See also Mary Mann Page Newton, *Colonial Virginia: A Paper Read Before the Historical Congress at Chicago, July 13, 1893* (Richmond: West, Johnston, 1893).

13. "A List of the Inhabitants and Property in the City of Richmond, 1782," *City of Richmond Common Hall Records* no. 1, in *Heads of Families at the First Census of the United States Taken in the Year 1790. Records of the State Enumerations: 1782–1785* (Baltimore: Genealogical Publishing Company, 1966), 111–19; Raymond Pinchbeck, *The Virginia Negro Craftsman and Artisan* (Richmond: William Byrd Press, 1926), 39–40.

14. Henrico and Chesterfield petition to General Assembly, 14 November 1789, in Valentine, "Richmond on the James," 1:15–16.

15. Jay Worrall, "The Friendly Virginians: A History of America's First Quakers" (unpublished manuscript in author's possession, 1992), 340, 377, 344.

16. Rhys Isaac, *The Transformation of Virginia, 1740–1790* (Chapel Hill: University of North Carolina Press for the Institute of Early American History and Culture, 1982), 143–47, 163–67, 282–95; Mechal Sobel, *Trabelin' On: The Slave Journey to an Afro-Baptist Faith* (Westport, Conn.: Greenwood Press, 1979), 3–5, 5–17, 19–20, 48–49; Donald Mathews, *Religion in the Old South* (Chicago: University of Chicago Press, 1977), xiv, xv, 14, 16; Blanche Sydnor White, *History of the First Baptist Church, Richmond, Virginia, 1790–1955* (Richmond: Whittet and Shepperson, 1956), 1.

17. Julia Cherry Spruill, *Women's Life and Work in the Southern Colonies* (1938; reprint, New York: W. W. Norton, 1972), 247–49.

18. Worrall, "Friendly Virginians," 343, 393.

19. Louis H. Manarin and Clifford Dowdey, *The History of Henrico County* (Charlottesville: University Press of Virginia, 1984), 152–54; Virginius Dabney, *Richmond: The Story of a City*, 2d ed. (Charlottesville: University Press of Virginia, 1990), 32, 40.

20. Robert Saunders, "Modernization and the Free Peoples of Richmond: The 1780s and the 1850s" (unpublished paper in author's possession, c. 1985), 25.

21. John S. Adams, ed., *An Autobiographical Sketch by John Marshall*, in *John Marshall*, ed. Stanley Kutler (Englewood Cliffs, N.J.: Prentice Hall, 1972), 18.

22. "History of the Memorial Home for Girls, Formerly Female Humane Society 1805–1938," pamphlet in Virginia Women's History Project files, Archives Division, Virginia State Library, Richmond; Myron Berman, *Richmond's Jewry: Shabbat in Shockoe, 1769–1976* (Charlottesville: University Press of Virginia for Jewish Community Federation of Richmond), 85.

23. On the consumer revolution, see Neil McKendrick, John Brewer, and J. H. Plumb, *The Birth of a Consumer Society: The Commercialization of Eighteenth-Century England* (London: Indiana University Press, 1982); Mary Newton Stanard, *Richmond News Leader*, 29 December 1924, in Valentine Museum vertical file.

24. Thomas Jefferson to James Madison, 20 September 1785, quoted in Reps, *Tidewater Towns*, 273. See also Mary Wingfield Scott, *Old Richmond Neighborhoods* (Richmond: Valentine Museum, 1950), 64; Dell Upton, "New Views of the Virginia Landscape," *Virginia Magazine of History and Biography* 96, no. 4 (October 1988): 451–57; Mark R. Wenger, "Thomas Jefferson and the Virginia State Capitol," *Virginia Magazine of History and Biography* 101, no. 1 (January 1993): 82, 85, 88–92; Edward C. Carter II, John C. Van Horne, and Charles E. Brownell, eds., *Latrobe's View of America, 1795–1820: Selections from the Watercolors and Sketches* (New Haven: Yale University Press, 1985), 66–69, 72–75, 104–5.

25. See Linda Kerber, *Women of the Republic: Intellect and Ideology in Revolutionary America* (Chapel Hill: University of North Carolina Press for the Institute of Early American History and Culture, 1980).

26. *Heads of Families at the First Census of the United States*, 116.

27. Philip J. Schwarz, "Gabriel's Challenge: Slaves and Crime in Late Eighteenth-Century Virginia," *Virginia Magazine of History and Biography* 90, no. 3 (July 1982): 283–306; Douglas Egerton, "Gabriel's Conspiracy and the Election of 1800," *Journal of Southern History* 56, no. 2 (May 1990): 191–214; Douglas Egerton, letter to author, 6 January 1993.

28. Testimony of Ben Woolfolk (first quote) and of of Prosser's Ben (second quote) at trial of Prosser's Gabriel, Calendar of Virginia State Papers, Negro Insurrection, Executive Papers, James Monroe, September 1800, Box 114, Virginia State Library, Richmond.

29. Philip Schwarz, *Twice Condemned: Slaves and the Criminal Laws of Virginia* (Baton Rouge: Louisiana State University Press, 1988), 242, 263–64, 267, 271; Egerton, "Gabriel's Conspiracy."

CHAPTER FOUR

1. Edward V. Valentine, manuscript notes and sketches, n.d., Valentine Museum, Richmond.

2. Virginius Dabney, *Richmond: The Story of a City* (New York: Doubleday, 1976), 78, 84–85; Samuel Mordecai, *Virginia, Especially Richmond, in By-Gone Days*, 2d ed. (Richmond: West and Johnston, 1860), 55–65; John P. Little, *History of Richmond* (1851; reprint, Richmond: Dietz Press, 1933), 103–4.

3. Mordecai, *Richmond in By-Gone Days*, 335; John Mayo daybook (1800–1802), manuscript, Valentine Museum, Richmond; Gregg Kimball, "Afro-Virginians and the Vernacular Building Tradition in Richmond City, 1790–1860," *Perspectives in Vernacular Architecture* (St. Louis: University of Missouri Press, forthcoming), 1–5.

4. Robert M. Saunders, "Crime and Punishment in Early National America: Richmond, Virginia, 1784–1820," *Virginia Magazine of History and Biography* 86 (1978): 33–34; Ira Berlin, *Slaves without Master: The Free Negro in the Antebellum South* (New York: Vintage Books, 1974), 75–85, 182–84.

5. Charles Copland journal and memoir (1823), unpublished manuscript, Virginia State Library and Archive, Richmond. See also Mary Wingfield Scott, *Old Richmond Neighborhoods* (Richmond: Valentine Museum, 1950), xv, 229.

6. Little, *History of Richmond*, 108–17; *Virginia Argus*, 27 February, 27 March, and 31 March 1807, Virginia State Library and Archive, Richmond.

7. William Wirt to John Allan, 1802, Wirt Family Papers (1802–1825), Southern Historical Collection, University of North Carolina, Chapel Hill.

8. Gordon S. Wood, *The Radicalism of the American Revolution* (New York: Knopf, 1992), 322–25.

9. *Virginia Argus*, 31 March 1807, 3; *Virginia Argus*, 7 April 1807, n.p.

10. William R. Taylor, *Cavalier and Yankee* (1957; New York: Harper Torchbooks, 1969), 68–80.

11. Philip Barrett, *Gilbert Hunt, the City Blacksmith* (Richmond: James Woodhouse and Company, 1859), 29–31. See also Wirt Armistead Cate, "History of Richmond," 3 vols. (unpublished manuscript held at Valentine Museum, Richmond, c. 1943), 3:775; Little, *History of Richmond*, 119–26; Agnes Bondurant, *Poe's Richmond* (1942; reprint, Richmond: Poe Associates, 1978), 130–31; W. Asbury Christian, *Richmond: Her Past and Present* (Richmond: L. H. Jenkins, 1912), 78–79.

12. "History of the Memorial Home for Girls, Formerly Female Humane Society 1805–1938," pamphlet held in Virginia Women's History Project files, Archives Division, Virginia State Library, Richmond, 11–13; Daniel Walker Howe, "The Evangelical Movement and Political Culture in the North during the Second Party System," *Journal of American History* 77, no. 4 (March 1991): 1216–39; Patricia Click, *The Spirit of the Times: Amusements in Nineteenth-Century Baltimore, Norfolk, and Richmond* (Charlottesville: University Press of Virginia, 1989), 77–80. For a locally published admonition to young ladies, see Virginia Cary, *Letters on Female Character* (Richmond: Ariel Works, 1830).

13. [George Mayo Carrington], *To the Public* (Richmond, 1835).

14. Dabney, *Richmond*, 74–75; Little, *History of Richmond*, 118.

15. Quoted in Robert Heilbroner, *The Economic Transformation of America* (New York: Harcourt, Brace, Jovanovich, 1977), 25.

16. David R. Goldfield and Blaine A. Brownell, *Urban America: A History*, 2d ed. (Boston: Houghton Mifflin, 1990), 127–30.

17. "Report of the Committee on Roads and Internal Navigation," 23 December 1815, Virginia *Journal of the House of Delegates* (1815–1816), in *Virginia since 1789: A Select Bibliography and Collection of Primary Sources*, comp. Daniel Jordan (unpublished manuscript in author's possession, 1974), 12–15; William Shelton, *The Means of Improving Richmond and the State of Virginia, Consisting of Various Essays Written on this Interesting Subject, by Different Personns* (Richmond: Shepherd and Pollard, 1817), 25.

18. *Richmond Daily Compiler*, 2 February 1814; Bondurant, *Poe's Richmond*, 43.

19. J. H. Harrison, Jr., "Oligarchs and Democrats—The Richmond Junto," *Vir-*

ginia Magazine of History and Biography 78, no. 2 (April 1970): 194–97; F. Thornton Miller, "The Richmond Junto: Secret All-Powerful Club or—Myth," *Virginia Magazine of History and Biography* 99, no. 1 (January 1991): 63–80; Bondurant, *Poe's Richmond*, 31.

20. "Mechanic" letter quoted in Shelton, *The Means of Improving Richmond*, 25; David R. Roediger, *The Wages of Whiteness: Race and the Making of the American Working Class* (London: Verso, 1991), 50–51.

21. Benjamin Brand to R. R. Gurley, 3 January 1832, reel 12, no. 5981, American Colonization Society Papers, Library of Congress, Washington, D.C.; J. B. Taylor, *Biography of Elder Lott Cary* (Baltimore: Armstrong and Berry, 1837), 15–16, 28–31. See also Barrett, *Gilbert Hunt*, 12–16; Marie Tyler-McGraw, "Richmond Free Blacks and African Colonization," *Journal of American Studies* 21 (1987): 210, 212–17.

22. Dabney, *Richmond*, 104.

23. Cate, "History of Richmond," 3:995.

24. Margaret Meagher, *History of Education in Richmond* (Richmond: Richmond City School Board, 1939), 61; Jane Austen, *Emma* (1816; reprint, New York: New American Library/Penguin, 1969), 52.

25. *Richmond Daily Compiler*, 31 December 1817, in Virginia Women's History Project files, Archives Division, Virginia State Library, Richmond. See also Suzanne Lebsock, *"A Share of Honour": Virginia Women, 1600–1945*, 2d ed. (Richmond: Virginia State Library, 1987), 60–62, and *The Free Women of Petersburg* (New York: W. W. Norton, 1984), 173–76, 204–5.

26. *Richmond Enquirer* (29 October 1824) quoted in Edgar Ewing Brandon, *Lafayette, Guest of the Nation*, 3 vols. (Oxford, Ohio: Oxford Historical Society, 1957), 2:99.

27. Brandon, *Lafayette*, 2:96–103.

28. Lois Banner, *American Beauty* (New York: Knopf, 1983), 250–51; Karen Halttunen, *Confidence Men and Painted Women: A Study of Middle-Class Culture in America, 1830–1870* (New Haven: Yale University Press, 1982), 74–75.

29. *Richmond Enquirer*, 29 October 1824, quoted in Brandon, *Lafayette, Guest of the Nation*, 3:93.

30. Alison Goodyear Freehling, *Drift Toward Dissolution: The Virginia Slavery Debate of 1831–1832* (Baton Rouge: Louisiana

State University Press, 1982), 44, 47, 51, 58, 71, 77–81. See also Dickson Bruce, *The Rhetoric of Conservatism: The Virginia Convention of 1829–1830 and the Conservative Tradition of the South* (San Marino, Calif.: Huntington Library, 1982).

CHAPTER FIVE

1. "Reveille for Bondsmen," Richmond *Daily Dispatch*, 18 August 1853, quoted in Claudia Dale Goldin, *Urban Slavery in the American South, 1820–1860: A Quantitative History* (Chicago: University of Chicago Press, 1976), xvi; Edward V. Valentine, manuscript notes, Valentine Museum, Richmond.

2. William Still, *The Underground Railroad* (1969; reprint, New York: Arno Press, 1972), 48, 81–86; Henry Brown as told to George Stearns, *Narrative of the Life of Henry Box Brown* (Boston: Brown and Stearns, 1849), 58–62; Patricia Hickin, "Antislavery in Virginia, 1831–1861" (Ph.D. diss., University of Virginia, 1968), 77–78, 85–90; Edward V. Valentine, manuscript notes, Valentine Museum, Richmond.

3. Inventory of Amanda Cousins, Richmond Hustings Court Will Book 20, pp. 267–69, 1 July 1860, Manuscript Division, Virginia State Library and Archive, Richmond; Suzanne Lebsock, "Free Black Women and the Question of Matriarchy," in *Sex and Class in Women's History*, ed. Judith L. Newton, Mary P. Ryan, and Judith R. Walkowitz (London: Routledge and Kegan Paul, 1983), 156.

4. Rodney Green, "Urban Industry, Black Resistance, and Racial Restriction in the Antebellum South: A Model and a Case Study in Urban America" (Ph.D. diss., American University, 1980), 291; Randall Miller, "Immigrants in the Old South," *Immigrant History Newsletter* 10 (November 1978): 9; Richard C. Wade, *Slavery in the Cities: The South, 1820–1860* (New York: Oxford University Press, 1964), 327.

5. Richmond Police Daybook, 1834–43, manuscript copy in Valentine Museum, Richmond.

6. Runaway advertisement and paper scraps in "Description of Slaves Belonging to Miss McCall's Estate, Tappahannock County," Leesburg Papers 8557a, Box 19, Alderman Library, University of Virginia, Charlottesville.

7. Ibid.

8. Alison Goodyear Freehling, *Drift toward Dissolution: The Virginia Slavery Debate of 1831–32* (Baton Rouge: Louisiana State University Press, 1982), 166, 126, 130.

9. Freehling, *Drift toward Dissolution*, 122–69, 170–74, 189.

10. Edgar Poe to John Allan, in *The Black Experience: An Anthology of American Literature for the 1970s*, ed. Francis E. Kearns (New York: Viking Press, 1970), 10–11, 14.

11. *Southern Literary Messenger* 2 (April 1836): 339, quoted in David K. Jackson, *Poe and the* Southern Literary Messenger (1934; reprint, New York: Haskell House, 1970), 77–78. See also Agnes Bondurant, *Poe's Richmond* (1942; reprint, Richmond: Poe Associates, 1978), 5n.

12. Jay B. Hubbell, *The South in American Literature* (Durham: Duke University Press, 1954), 21, 23, 431; Richard Beale Davis, *Intellectual Life in Jefferson's Virginia* (Chapel Hill: University of North Carolina Press, 1964), 312–13; William J. Van DeBurg, *Slavery and Race in American Popular Culture* (Madison: University of Wisconsin Press, 1984), 15–16; Kearns, *The Black Experience*, 66–67.

13. Samuel Mordecai, *Virginia, Especially Richmond, in By-Gone Days*, 2d ed. (Richmond: West and Johnston, 1860), 354–55.

14. Mrs. Burton Harrison [Constance Cary Harrison], *Flower de Hundred, The Story of a Virginia Plantation* (New York: Cassell, 1890), 54; John O. Beaty, *John Esten Cooke, Virginian* (New York: Columbia University Press, 1922), 15, 19, 30, 31; Bondurant, *Poe's Richmond*, 106; Clement Eaton, *The Freedom-of-Thought Struggle in the Old South* (New York: Harper and Row, 1964), 268; Hubbell, *South in American Literature*, 13–14, 29.

15. Kathleen Bruce, *Virginia Iron Manufacture in the Slave Era* (New York: Century, 1931), 323; Green, "Urban Industry," 313–28, 213–20, 228–29.

16. Robert Heilbroner, *The Economic Transformation of America* (New York: Harcourt, Brace, Jovanovich, 1977), 34; W. F. Dunaway, *History of the James River and Kanawha Company* (1922; reprint, New York: AMS Press, 1969), 116, 129.

17. William J. Ernst, *Urban Leaders and Social Change: The Urbanization Process in Richmond, 1840–1880* (Ph.D. diss., University of Virginia, 1978), 35–38.

18. Miss Mendel, *Notes of Travel and Life* (New York, 1854), quoted in Patricia Click, "Leisure in the Upper South in the Nineteenth Century: A Study of Trends in Baltimore, Norfolk, and Richmond" (Ph.D. diss., University of Virginia, 1980), 10; Mordecai, *Richmond in By-Gone Days*, 246.

19. David Goldfield, *Urban Growth in the Age of Sectionalism* (Baton Rouge: Louisiana State University Press, 1977), 4–48; Michael Chesson, *Richmond after the War: 1865–1890* (Richmond: Virginia State Library and Archive, 1981), 8; Charles B. Dew, *Ironmaker to the Confederacy: Joseph Anderson and the Tredegar Iron Works* (New York: Yale University Press, 1966), 22, 32–39.

20. Goldfield, *Urban Growth*, 60, 130–37, 144.

21. Linden B. Waller, "Notes on Richmond Residences and Families" (unpublished manuscript held at Valentine Museum, Richmond, 1906), 18–19.

22. Myron Berman, *Richmond's Jewry: Shabbat in Shockoe, 1769–1976* (Charlottesville: University Press of Virginia for the Jewish Confederation of Richmond, 1976), 237–38. Ira Berlin and Herbert Gutman, "Natives and Immigrants, Free Men and Slaves: Urban Working Men in the Antebellum South," *American Historical Review* 88, no. 5 (December 1983): 1175–1200.

23. *Richmond Times*, quoted in Mary Wingfield Scott, *Old Richmond Neighborhoods* (Richmond: Valentine Museum, 1950), 210; see also pp. 20, 208–11, 283, 287–89, 292. See also Frederick Law Olmsted, *The Slave States*, rev./enl., ed. Harvey Wish (New York: Capricorn Books, 1959), 45; Green, "Urban Industry," 295n; Gregg Kimball, "Black Housing in Antebellum Richmond" (draft essay, Valentine Museum, 1989), 1–12.

24. Patricia Click, *The Spirit of the Times: Amusements in Nineteenth-Century Baltimore, Norfolk, and Richmond* (Charlottesville: University Press of Virginia, 1989), 77–81; Lucian Minor, "The Temperance Reformation in Virginia," *Southern Literary Messenger* 16 (1850): 427, 430.

25. Klaus Wust, *The Virginia Germans* (Charlottesville: University Press of Virginia, 1969), 205; Marie Tyler-McGraw and Gregg D. Kimball, *In Bondage and Freedom: Antebellum Black Life in Richmond, Virginia* (Richmond: Valentine Museum, 1988), 35–41.

26. Mary Jo Bratton, ed., "Fields's Observations: The Slave Narrative of a Nineteenth-Century Virginian," *Virginia Magazine of History and Biography* (January 1980): 82.

27. Goldin, *Urban Slavery*, 21, 36; Green, "Urban Industry," 258; Gregg Kimball, "African-Virginians and the Vernacular Building Tradition in Richmond City," in *Perspectives in Vernacular Architecture 4* (St. Louis: University of Missouri Press, forthcoming), 5.

28. Richmond/Henrico Society for the Prevention of the Abducting and Absconding of Slave Property, New-York Historical Society, photocopies in manuscript division of Alderman Library, University of Virginia, Charlottesville.

29. David Goldfield, "The Triumph of Politics over Society, Virginia 1851–1861" (Ph.D. diss., University of Maryland, 1970), 17–22; David Goldfield and Blaine Brownell, *Urban America: A History*, 2d ed. (Boston: Houghton Mifflin, 1990), 105, 111.

30. Dew, *Ironmaker to the Confederacy*, 2–13, 16, 22–24.

31. *Richmond Enquirer*, 12 June 1847, quoted in Dew, *Ironmaker to the Confederacy*, 26.

32. John T. O'Brien, "Freedom's Ferment: The Reconstruction Experiment in Virginia" (unpublished manuscript in author's possession, 1988), 123; *Richmond Enquirer*, 27 August 1857, quoted in Goldin, *Urban Slavery*, 31. See also Dew, *Ironmaker to the Confederacy*, 28–32.

33. Dew, *Ironmaker to the Confederacy*, 31–34.

34. The difficulty in assessing how many slaves were sold south from Richmond or Virginia in the late antebellum era is suggested by Chesson, *Richmond after the War*, 134, 214, 20n, 10, 215, and Barbara Jeanne Fields, *Slavery and Freedom on the Middle Ground* (New Haven: Yale University Press, 1985), 17, 214.

35. Chesson, *Richmond after the War*, 8–9; Harrison Ethridge, "The Jordan Hatcher Affair of 1852: Cold Justice and Warm Compassion," *Virginia Magazine of History and Biography* 84, no. 4 (October 1976): 446–63.

36. Click, *Spirit of the Times*, 75. See listings in William Montague, *The Richmond City Directory and Business Advertiser for 1852* (Baltimore: J. W. Woods, 1852), and M. Ellyson, *The Richmond Directory and Business Advertiser for 1856* (Richmond: H. K. Ellyson, 1856).

37. John O'Brien, "Factory, Church, and Community: Blacks in Antebellum Richmond," *Journal of Southern History* 44, no. 4 (November 1978): 515–18; Click, *Spirit of the Times*, 76–77.

38. Chesson, *Richmond after the War*, 10, 214–15; John S. Wise, *The End of an Era* (New York: Farrar Straus, 1899), 78–88; Goldfield, *Urban Growth*, 120–21; Virginius Dabney, *Virginia, The New Dominion* (New York: Doubleday, 1971), 47, 228–29, 240–43; Edward V. Valentine, manuscript notes, "Traders (Negro)," Valentine Museum, Richmond; Templeman and Goodwin Account Book 1849–50 (Richmond), Southern History Collection, Wilson Library, University of North Carolina, Chapel Hill.

39. Elizabeth Varon, "The Ladies Are Whigs," *Virginia Cavalcade* 42, no. 2 (Autumn 1992): 72–83; Anne F. Scott, *Natural Allies: Women's Associations in American History* (Urbana: University of Illinois Press, 1991), 2–4, 13, 19; Suzanne Lebsock, *The Free Women of Petersburg: Status and Culture in a Southern Town, 1784–1860* (New York: W. W. Norton, 1985), 196–201.

40. O'Brien, "Freedom's Ferment," 27.

41. John O'Brien, "From Bondage to Citizenship: The Richmond Black Community, 1865–1867" (Ph.D. diss., University of Rochester, 1974), 14–15, 20–25; Green, "Urban Industry," 286–87; Herman Schuricht, *History of the German Element in Virginia*, 2 vols. (Baltimore, 1898; reprint, Baltimore: Genealogical Publishing Company, 1977), 2:33–39.

42. "'An Ordinance Concerning Negroes': The Richmond Black Code (1859)," in "A Richmond Reader," ed. Daniel Jordan (unpublished manuscript in author's possession), 1974.

CHAPTER SIX

1. For more information on Wise and the People's Convention, see Daniel Crofts, *Reluctant Confederates: Upper South Unionists in the Secession Crisis* (Chapel Hill: University of North Carolina Press, 1989), and Craig Saunders, *A Good Southerner: The Life of Henry A. Wise of Virginia* (Chapel Hill: University of North Carolina Press, 1985). See also John B. Jones, *A Rebel War Clerk's Diary*, ed. Howard Swiggert, 2 vols. (Philadelphia: John B. Lippincott, 1866), 1:16–17; Henry T. Shanks, *The Secession Movement in Virginia, 1847–1861* (Richmond: Garrett and Massie, 1934), 122, 202–4; Emory M. Thomas, *The Confederate State of Richmond: A Biography of the Capital* (Austin: University of Texas Press, 1971), 8–11; and J. Cutler Andrews, *The South Reports the Civil War* (1970; reprint, Pittsburgh: University of Pittsburgh Press, 1985), 20–22, 26n.

2. Michael Holt, *The Political Crisis of the 1850s* (New York: John Wiley and Sons, 1978), 38, 226–28, 238–39, 207, 215; David Potter (completed and edited by Donald E. Fehrenbacher), *The Impending Crisis of the Union* (New York: Harper and Row, 1976), 438–39, 443; "Report of the Joint Committee of the General Assembly of Virginia on the Harper's Ferry Outrage," 26 January 1860, quoted in James M. McPherson, "The War of Southern Aggression," *New York Review of Books*, 19 January 1989, 16.

3. *Richmond Daily Examiner*, 3 December 1860, quoted in McPherson, "War of Southern Aggression," 16.

4. Letcher quoted in Beverly B. Munford, *Virginia's Attitude toward Slavery and Secession* (Richmond: L. H. Jenkins, 1909), 248–49. See also Potter, *Impending Crisis*, 477, 500–501, 529, and Virginius Dabney, *Virginia, The New Dominion* (Garden City, N.Y.: Doubleday, 1971), 159.

5. Thomas, *Confederate State of Richmond*, 8.

6. Thomas, *Confederate State of Richmond*, 4–6, 34; Crofts, *Reluctant Confederates*, 320–22. The most frequently used accounts of the day's turbulent events are from the diaries of John B. Jones and Sallie Brock Putnam and from the *Richmond Daily Dispatch* and the *Richmond Enquirer* for 15 April 1861. For a more skeptical view by an ordinary Richmonder, see Ernest Walthall, *Hidden Things Brought to Light* (Richmond: privately printed, 1908), 17–19.

7. Michael Chesson, *Richmond after the War, 1865–1890* (Richmond: Virginia State Library, 1981), 4, 8–12; Thomas, *Confederate State of Richmond*, 20–24, 23n.

8. *The Stranger's Guide and Official Directory of the City of Richmond* (Richmond: G. P. Evans, 1863).

9. Robert Waitt, Jr., *Confederate Military Hospitals in Richmond* (Richmond: Rich-

mond Civil War Centennial Commission, 1964), 6–7, 14, 29.

10. Waitt, *Confederate Military Hospitals*, 20, 32–33.

11. Sarah Agnes Rice Pryor quoted in Richard Wheeler, *Sword over Richmond: An Eyewitness Account of McClellan's Peninsula Campaign* (New York: Harper and Row, 1986), 325–26. See also Phoebe Yates Pember, *A Southern Woman's Story: Life in Confederate Richmond*, ed. Bell Irvin Wiley (Jackson, Tenn.: McCowat-Mercer Press, 1959), 5–7, 28–29, 153–57, and James H. Brewer, *The Confederate Negro: Virginia's Craftsmen and Military Laborers, 1861–65* (Durham: Duke University Press, 1969), xii, 95–118.

12. *Sixteenth Annual Report of Richmond and Danville Railroad* (Richmond, 1863), in Angus James Johnson II, *Virginia Railroads in the Civil War* (Chapel Hill: University of North Carolina Press, 1961), 218–22; Thomas, *Confederate State of Richmond*, 60–61.

13. Johnson, *Virginia Railroads*, 7; Edward R. Crews, "The Industrial Bulwark of the Confederacy," *Invention and Technology* (Winter 1992): 9–17.

14. Quotations from William Stiner, "My experiences . . . during and after the late war," manuscript collection, New-York Historical Society, New York City. See also Emory Thomas, *The Confederacy as a Revolutionary Experience* (Englewood Cliffs, N.J.: Prentice-Hall, 1971), 88, and Crews, "Industrial Bulwark," 12–14.

15. Wheeler, *Sword over Richmond*, 325–26; Thomas, *Confederate State of Richmond*, 156; Mary H. Mitchell, *Hollywood Cemetery: The History of a Southern Shrine* (Richmond: Virginia State Library, 1985), 52–53.

16. E. V. Valentine Papers, Box 7, Theater Folder 1, Valentine Museum, Richmond.

17. Thomas, *Confederate State of Richmond*, 81–84, 106, 157, 172; Louis H. Manarin, ed., *Richmond at War: The Minutes of the City Council, 1861–65* (Chapel Hill: University of North Carolina Press for the Richmond Civil War Centennial Commission, 1966), 127–28, 374–75.

18. Van Lew papers, folder 4, Manuscript and Rare Books Department, Swem Library, College of William and Mary, Williamsburg, Va., and Manuscripts Division, Virginia State Library, Richmond;

Thomas McNiven, "Recollection of Thomas McNiven and his Activities in Richmond during the Civil War," Personal Papers Collection, Virginia State Library and Archive, Richmond.

19. Susan Barber, "The Quiet Battles of the Homefront War: Civil War Bread Riots and the Development of a Confederate Welfare System" (M.A. thesis, University of Maryland, 1986), 58.

20. Constance Cary Harrison, *Recollections Grave and Gay* (New York: Charles Scribner's Sons, 1911), 82. See also Johnson, *Virginia Railroads*, 56–57, and Thomas, *Confederate State of Richmond*, 93–94.

21. Harrison, *Recollections*, 83–84.

22. Peter Randolph, *From Slave Cabin to the Pulpit* (Boston: James H. Earle, 1893), 81; Thomas, *Confederate State of Richmond*, 19–22; Manarin, *Richmond at War*, 627–34.

23. Barber, "Quiet Battles," 21, 28–35; Thomas, *Confederate State of Richmond*, 117–18; Brewer, *Confederate Negro*, 6–7; Michael Chesson, "Harlots or Heroines?: Another Look at the Richmond Bread Riot," *Virginia Magazine of History and Biography* 92, no. 2 (April 1984): 131–75 (see especially pp. 139–46).

24. Barber, "Quiet Battles," 21–26, and Chesson, "Harlots or Heroines?," 131–75. Both Barber and Chesson present thoughtful analysis of the bread riot, with slightly different emphases. Barber notes the conditions under which such riots appear in other cities, while Chesson examined the court record to determine the backgrounds and the sentences of those arrested.

25. Barber, "Quiet Battles," 103.

26. Sallie Brock Putnam, *In Richmond during the War: Four Years of Personal Observation* (New York: G. W. Carleton, 1867), 250–54; Varina Davis, "Women in War Time," unidentified newspaper clipping (1893), vertical file, Valentine Museum, Richmond. See also Georgia Dickinson Wardlaw, "Women of the South Overcame Hardships," *Richmond Times-Dispatch*, 3 September 1962.

27. Crews, "Industrial Bulwark," 16.

28. Walthall, *Hidden Things*, 34; Brewer, *Confederate Negro*, xi–xii, 6–8.

29. *Norfolk Virginian-Pilot*, 30 November 1969, in Virginius Dabney papers, Alderman Library, University of Virginia, Charlottesville.

30. Emma Mordecai Diary, Southern Historical Collection, Wilson Library, University of North Carolina, Chapel Hill; C. Vann Woodward, ed., *Mary Chesnut's Civil War* (New Haven: Yale University Press, 1981); Ladies' Gunboat Society papers, Museum of the Confederacy, Richmond.

31. Katharine M. Jones, *Ladies of Richmond, Confederate Capital* (Indianapolis: Bobbs-Merrill, 1962), 276–77.

32. Putnam, *In Richmond during the War*, 174. See also Mary Elizabeth Massey, *Bonnet Brigades* (New York: Knopf, 1966), 138–39, and Leah Fortson, "The Working-Class Women of Confederate Richmond" (paper presented for a seminar, Columbia University, December 1987), 5–12.

33. John B. Jones, *Rebel War Clerk's Diary*, 1:99–100; *Southern Punch*, occasional newspaper issues held at Valentine Museum, Richmond.

34. Thomas, *Confederate State of Richmond*, 157–60, 167–70, 182, 185.

35. Two explicit references to this evolution in Richmond's meaning are in Thomas, *Confederate State of Richmond*, 177–78, and Douglas Southall Freeman, "The Confederate Tradition of Richmond," *Civil War History* 3, no. 4 (December 1957): 369–73, reprinted from the *Richmond Magazine* Confederate reunion souvenir issue (1932). Freeman noted that "Richmond was a name in 1860; the War Between the States made her a symbol" (p. 369).

CHAPTER SEVEN

1. Michael Chesson, *Richmond after the War, 1865–90* (Richmond: Virginia State Library, 1981), 57–59; Rembert W. Patrick, *The Fall of Richmond* (Baton Rouge: Louisiana State University Press, 1960), 42–45, 61; Charles L. Perdue, Jr., Thomas E. Barden, and Robert K. Phillips, *Weevils in the Wheat: Interviews with Virginia Ex-Slaves* (Bloomington: University of Indiana Press, 1980), 145–46.

2. Patrick, *Fall of Richmond*, 67, 68–70, 70–73; Chesson, *Richmond after the War*, 59.

3. Lincoln quote in Shelby Foote, *Civil War*, quoted in James M. McPherson, *Battle Cry of Freedom: The Civil War Era*, vol. 6 of *Oxford History of the United States*, ed. C. Vann Woodward (New York: Oxford University Press, 1988), 846–47.

4. Patrick, *Fall of Richmond*, 127–34; Eric Foner, *Reconstruction: America's Unfinished Revolution, 1863–1877* (New York: Harper and Row, 1988), 73; John T. O'Brien, "Reconstruction in Richmond: White Restoration and Black Protest, April–June 1865," *Virginia Magazine of History and Biography* 89 (July 1981): 259–81; quote appears on 261–62. Accounts differ on the time and agenda of Lincoln's visit. See John B. Jones, *A Rebel War Clerk's Diary*, ed. Howard Swiggert, 2 vols. (Philadelphia: John B. Lippincott, 1866), 2:466–73, for a less jubilant version.

5. O'Brien, "Reconstruction in Richmond," 266–69; Foner, *Reconstruction*, 154, 209–11; Chesson, *Richmond after the War*, 59–60, 66–67; William Joel Ernst, "Urban Leaders and Social Change: The Urbanization Process in Richmond, Virginia, 1840–1880" (Ph.D. diss., University of Virginia, 1978), 212–14.

6. J. T. Trowbridge, *The South: A Tour of its Battlefields and Ruined Cities* (Hartford, Conn.: L. Stebbins, 1866), 178–79. See also Chesson, *Richmond after the War*, 68–71, 88, 91.

7. Maria S. Peck to Daniel G. Marrow, 9 May 1865, in *Refugees in Richmond: Civil War Letters of a Virginia Family*, ed. Henry C. Blackiston (Princeton: privately printed by Princeton University Press, 1989), 60–61.

8. *New York Tribune*, 17 June 1865, cited in Charlotte K. Brooks et al., *A Brooks Family Chronicle: The Life and Times of an African-American Family* (Washington, D.C.: Brooks Associates, 1989), 61–62, 183–86. See also Peter Randolph, *From Slave Cabin to the Pulpit* (Boston: James H. Earle, 1893), 81, 61; O'Brien, "Reconstruction in Richmond," 266, 272, 274–80; A. A. Taylor, "The Negro in the Reconstruction of Virginia (Part 1)," *Journal of Negro History* 11, no. 2 (April 1926): 243–415 (quote appears on 282–83); and Chesson, *Richmond after the War*, 57, 72–74.

9. Chesson, *Richmond after the War*, 74–75; Peter Rachleff, *Black Labor in the South: Richmond, Virginia, 1865–1890* (Philadelphia: Temple University Press, 1984), 14–15, 35–37; Foner, *Reconstruction*, 155; O'Brien, "Reconstruction in Richmond," 259–61.

10. Elizabeth Van Lew papers, folder 4, Manuscript and Rare Books Department, Swem Library, College of William and Mary, Williamsburg, Va.; Rachleff, *Black Labor*, 39; Taylor, "Negro in Reconstruction (Part 1)," 304–6.

11. *Richmond Enquirer and Examiner*, 17 March 1869, in Virginia Women's History Project Files, Archives Division, Virginia State Library, Richmond; capitals in original. See also Suzanne Lebsock, *The Free Women of Petersburg: Status and Culture in a Southern Town, 1784–1860* (New York: W. W. Norton, 1984), 239–44; *Richmond Evening Journal* (n.d., circa 1900) in Elizabeth Van Lew papers, New York Public Library, on Miscellaneous Reel 14 at the Virginia State Library, Richmond; Susan Barber, "'The Quiet Battles of the Home Front War': Civil War Bread Riots and the Development of a Confederate Welfare System" (M.A. thesis, University of Maryland, 1986), 74–75; and Chesson, *Richmond after the War*, 75–76.

12. John B. Jones, *Rebel War Clerk's Diary*, 2:470; Rachleff, *Black Labor*, 30.

13. Brooks et al., *Brooks Family Chronicle*, 165–66, 8, 94–99. See also Rachleff, *Black Labor*, 30, 32–33, and Jacqueline Jones, *Labor of Love, Labor of Sorrow: Black Women, Work, and the Family from Slavery to the Present* (New York: Basic Books, 1985), 46.

14. Patrick, *Fall of Richmond*, 127–34; Foner, *Reconstruction*, 73; Lawrence W. Levine, *Black Culture and Black Consciousness: Afro-American Folk Thought from Slavery to Freedom* (New York: Oxford University Press, 1977), 32–33, 137–38; Randolph, *From Slave Cabin*, 59.

15. "A Patriotic Barber," "Negroes: Richmond" clipping file, Valentine Museum, Richmond; Taylor, "Negro in Reconstruction (Part 1)," 246–47; Brooks et al., *Brooks Family Chronicle*, 164–66.

16. McPherson, *Battle Cry of Freedom*, 818–19.

17. James W. Hunnicutt, *The Conspiracy Unveiled: The South Sacrificed and the Horrors of Secession* (Philadelphia: John B. Lippincott, 1863), 241–62; S. J. Quinn, *History of Fredericksburg, Virginia* (Richmond: The Hermitage Press, Inc., 1908), 77; Ernst, "Urban Leaders," 210–14; Howard Rabinowitz, "Continuity and Change: Southern Urban Development, 1860–1900," in *The City in Southern History: The Growth of Urban Civilization in the South*, ed. Blaine Brownell and David Goldfield (Port Washington, N.Y.: Kennikat Press, 1977), 92–122; Chesson, *Richmond after the War*, 105, 109–10; A. A. Taylor, "The Negro in the Reconstruction of Virginia (Part 2)," *Journal of Negro History* 11, no. 3 (July 1926): 425–537 (see especially p. 459).

18. Chesson, *Richmond after the War*, 107–8; Rachleff, *Black Labor*, 39; Orlando Brown to General Schofield, 20 May 1867, and Paul Hambrick to Orlando Brown, 25 May 1867, Freedmen's Bureau Records, National Archives, in Freedom History Project, University of Maryland, College Park.

19. See Rabinowitz, "Continuity and Change"; John W. Cell, *The Highest Stage of White Supremacy: The Origins of Segregation in South Africa and the American South* (Cambridge: Cambridge University Press, 1982); Taylor, "Negro in Reconstruction (Part 1)," 294–96, and "Negro in Reconstruction (Part 2)," 465; Ernst, "Urban Leaders," 226–31; Rachleff, *Black Labor*, 40, 42–43; and Chesson, *Richmond after the War*, 102–3.

20. Ernst, "Urban Leaders," 231; Taylor, "Negro in Reconstruction (Part 2)," 382–83, 389, 390, 396, 480–82.

21. Randolph, *From Slave Cabin*, 96.

22. Foner, *Reconstruction*, 282, 304–5, 310–24, 327–28; Rachleff, *Black Labor*, 44–49, 242–43; Taylor, "Negro in Reconstruction (Part 1)," 296; Chesson, *Richmond after the War*, 106–7, 110.

23. Alexander H. H. Stuart, "A Narrative of the Leading Incidents to Secure the Restoration of Virginia to the Union" (Richmond: William Ellis Jones, 1889), 9–25; Rachleff, *Black Labor*, 49–50.

24. Chesson, *Richmond after the War*, 96, 105, 112–14; Ernst, "Urban Leaders," 207; Rabinowitz, "Continuity and Change," 98.

25. Chesson, *Richmond after the War*, 68, 71, 75–78; Ernst, "Urban Leaders," 283–92; Rachleff, *Black Labor*, 38–40.

26. *The Southern Opinion*, 14 September 1867, issue held at Valentine Museum, Richmond. See also Foner, *Reconstruction*, 213, 391; Charles Dew, *Ironmaker to the Confederacy: Joseph R. Anderson and the Tredegar Iron Works* (New Haven: Yale University Press, 1966), 305–11, 318; and Chesson, *Richmond after the War*, 150–54.

27. Sally Flocks, "'In the Hands of Others': The Development of Dependence of Richmond's Manufacturers on Northern Financiers" (paper presented at

annual meeting of the Southern Historical Association, Norfolk, Va., November 1988); Chesson, *Richmond after the War*, 68–70. Flocks believes dependence on northern capital undermined Richmond's industrial recovery, while Chesson holds that lack of a true capitalist mentality defeated the postbellum city.

28. Chesson, *Richmond after the War*, 68, 65–66; Ernst, "Urban Leaders," 211; Paul Dulaney, *The Architecture of Historic Richmond*, 2d ed. (Charlottesville: University Press of Virginia, 1976), 17.

29. Clyde A. Haulman, "Changes in Wealth-Holding in Richmond, Virginia, 1860–1870," *Journal of Urban History* 13, no. 1 (November 1986): 54–71; Rachleff, *Black Labor*, 310; James K. Sanford, ed., *Richmond: Her Triumphs, Tragedies, and Growth* (Richmond: Metropolitan Richmond Chamber of Commerce, 1975), 10–12.

30. Foner, *Reconstruction*, 535; Dew, *Ironmaker to the Confederacy*, 318; Rachleff, *Black Labor*, 70–71.

CHAPTER EIGHT

1. Gaines M. Foster, *Ghosts of the Confederacy: Defeat, The Lost Cause, and the Emergence of the New South* (New York: Oxford University Press, 1987), 37, 45, 59; Charles Reagan Wilson, *Baptized in Blood: The Religion of the Lost Cause* (Athens: University of Georgia Press, 1980), 18–24.

2. Paul M. Gaston, *The New South Creed: A Study in Southern Myth-Making* (Baton Rouge: Louisiana State University Press, 1970), is the classic study. The Richmond experience supports the analysis of Don Doyle, *New Men, New Cities, New South: Atlanta, Nashville, Charleston, Mobile, 1860–1910* (Chapel Hill: University of North Carolina Press, 1990), 315.

3. Gavin Wright, *Old South, New South: Revolutions in the Southern Economy since the Civil War* (New York: Basic Books, 1986), 156–57, 162–75; Maury Klein and Harvey A. Kantor, *Prisoners of Progress: American Industrial Cities, 1850–1920* (New York: Macmillan, 1976), 22–24. See Michael Chesson, *Richmond after the War, 1865–1890* (Richmond: Virginia State Library, 1981), chapter 7; Edward L. Ayers, *The Promise of the New South* (New York: Oxford University Press, 1992), 55–56; Jack Temple Kirby, "Virginia's Environmental History: A Prospectus,"

Virginia Magazine of History and Biography 99, no. 4 (October 91): 461–62; and Doyle, *New Men, New Cities, New South*, 13–14. Ayers and Chesson see leadership issues in the fate of southern cities. See Ayers, *Promise of the New South*, 59, on Birmingham, and Chesson, *Richmond after the War*, 210, on Richmond.

4. Christopher Silver, *Twentieth-Century Richmond* (Knoxville: University of Tennessee Press, 1984), 27–28, 31; Chesson, *Richmond after the War*, 123–27.

5. Foster, *Ghosts of the Confederacy*, 53–61; Wilson, *Baptized in Blood*, 119–27.

6. Foster, *Ghosts of the Confederacy*, 38, 40–41; Mary H. Mitchell, *Hollywood Cemetery: The History of a Southern Shrine* (Richmond: Virginia State Library, 1985), 64–73.

7. Virginius Dabney, *Richmond: The Story of a City*, rev. ed. (Charlottesville: University Press of Virginia, 1990), 242–43; Foster, *Ghosts of the Confederacy*, 98–100; Wilson, *Baptized in Blood*, 136.

8. Peter Rachleff, *Black Labor in the South: Richmond, Virginia, 1865–1890* (Philadelphia: Temple University Press, 1984), 55–57.

9. Chesson, *Richmond after the War*, 163–64, 198–99; Wright, *Old South, New South*, 156–58, 164–66; Nannie Mae Tilley, *The Bright Tobacco Industry, 1860–1929* (Chapel Hill: University of North Carolina Press, 1948), 570–72; Dabney, *Richmond*, 224–25.

10. Andrew Morrison, comp., *Richmond, Virginia, and the New South* (Richmond: William Ellis Jones [printed for George W. Engelhardt and Company, Chicago and Richmond], 1888), 100–106, 187; W. D. Chesterman, *Guide to Richmond and the Battlefields* (Richmond: James Goode, 1894), 143.

11. Chesson, *Richmond after the War*, 190; Gregg Kimball, "The Working People of Richmond," *Labor's Heritage* 3, no. 2 (April 1991): 56–58; Leon Fink, *Workingmen's Democracy: The Knights of Labor and American Politics* (Urbana: University of Illinois Press, 1983), 150–52; Rachleff, *Black Labor*, 110–11.

12. Rachleff, *Black Labor*, 114–15, 117, 129–23, 163, 171–78; Fink, *Workingmen's Democracy*, 154–55, 14, 163–65.

13. William Joel Ernst, "Urban Leaders and Social Change: The Urbanization Process in Richmond, Virginia, 1840–1880" (Ph.D. diss., University of Virginia,

1978), 214; Gregg Kimball, "The Working People of Richmond" (draft catalog essay, Valentine Museum, 1990), 11–13; Morrison, *Richmond, Virginia, and the New South*, 94, 137; Fink, *Workingmen's Democracy*, 150, 153–58.

14. Ann Field Alexander, "Black Protest in the New South: John Mitchell, Jr. (1863–1929) and the Richmond *Planet*" (Ph.D. diss., Duke University, 1973), 257–66; Kimball, "Working People of Richmond," 11–13; Chesson, *Richmond after the War*, 186.

15. C. Vann Woodward, *Origins of the New South, 1877–1913* (Baton Rouge: Louisiana State University Press, 1951), 61; Jack Temple Kirby, *Darkness at the Dawning: Race and Reform in the Progressive South* (Philadelphia: Lippincott, 1972), 15; Chesson, *Richmond after the War*, 187.

16. Typescript reminiscences of John F. O'Grady, 1960, Valentine Museum, Richmond (courtesy of Gregg Kimball, archivist).

17. Chesson, *Richmond after the War*, 229f.; Rachleff, *Black Labor*, 40; Robert C. Scribner and W. Edwin Hemphill, "Richmond's Electric Streetcar System: First Successful Pioneer in a Municipal Transit Revolution," *Virginia Cavalcade* (Autumn 1958): 21–31.

18. Morrison, *Richmond, Virginia, and the New South*, 1. See also David R. Goldfield and Blaine A. Brownell, *Urban America: A History*, 2d ed. (Boston: Houghton, Mifflin, 1990), 263.

19. Board of Health report quoted in Ernst, "Urban Leaders," 93.

20. Robert Cutchins, *Memories of Old Richmond, 1881–1944* (Verona, Va.: McClure Printing Co., 1943), 17, 19, 28, 30; quote appears on p. 17. See also Robert Beverly Munford, Jr., *Richmond Homes and Memories* (Richmond: Garrett and Massie, 1936), 218.

21. Ellen Glasgow, *The Woman Within* (New York: Harcourt Brace, 1954), 19–22, 215; quote appears on p. 215. See also Ernst, "Urban Leaders," 387–93.

22. *Richmond Dispatch* quoted in Howard Rabinowitz, "Continuity and Change: Southern Urban Development, 1860–1900," in *The City in Southern History: The Growth of Urban Civilization in the South*, ed. Blaine Brownell and David Goldfield (Port Washington, N.Y.: Kennikat Press, 1977), 113.

23. Goldfield and Brownell, *Urban*

America, 259–66; Silver, *Twentieth-Century Richmond*, 20, 37–40; John R. Stilgoe, *Borderlands: Origins of the American Suburb, 1820–1939* (New Haven: Yale University Press, 1988), 16.

24. Suzanne Lebsock, *"A Share of Honour": Virginia Women, 1600–1945*, 2d ed. (Richmond: Virginia State Library, 1987), 109–14; Kathleen Berkeley, "'Colored Ladies Also Contributed': Black Women's Activities from Benevolence to Social Welfare, 1866–1896," in *The Web of Southern Social Relations: Women, Family, and Education*, ed. Walter J. Fraser, Jr., R. Frank Saunders, Jr., and Jon L. Wakelyn (Athens: University of Georgia Press, 1985), 182–83, 186, 196.

25. Anne Goodwyn Jones, *Tomorrow Is Another Day: The Woman Writer in the South, 1859–1936* (Baton Rouge: Louisiana State University Press, 1981), 225–31, 265–66.

26. *Richmond Dispatch*, 19 June 1886, quoted in Jay Killian Bowman Williams, *Changed Views and Unforeseen Prosperity* (Richmond: privately published, 1969), 30, 33, 36–37.

27. *Richmond Planet* quoted in Williams, *Changed Views*, 60–61, 53–57. See also Dabney, *Richmond*, 241–43.

28. Quotations from *Richmond Dispatch*, 30 June 1896, 19–21. See also Foster, *Ghosts of the Confederacy*, 133, 139, 142, 167.

29. Wilson, *Baptized in Blood*, 136–37; James M. Lindgren, "'For the Sake of Our Future': The Association for the Preservation of Virginia Antiquities and the Regeneration of Traditionalism," *Virginia Magazine of History and Biography* 97, no. 1 (January 1989): 47–74; Williams, *Changed Views*, 58; Dabney, *Richmond*, 244, 245.

30. Cutchins, *Memories of Old Richmond*, 25; Dabney, *Richmond*, 245; Goldfield, *Urban Growth*, 277–79.

31. Gregg D. Kimball, "Life and Labor in an Industrial City, 1865–1920," *Labor's Heritage* 3, no. 2 (April 1991): 44–65, 56; Robert L. Scribner, "Fitzhugh Lee: Ex-Confederate in Blue," *Virginia Cavalcade* 49 (Spring 1956): 16–21.

32. Silver, *Twentieth-Century Richmond*, 46–47.

33. Kimball, "Life and Labor," 55–59; Silver, *Twentieth-Century Richmond*, 53–60. Kimball's work has documented higher levels of union membership and more labor actions after the 1890s than was

known to or acknowledged by historians.

34. Alexander, "Black Protest in the New South," 327–28.

35. Rachleff, *Black Labor*, 55; Ernst, "Urban Leaders," 65, 356–60, 300–303.

CHAPTER NINE

1. Louis F. Powell, *Recollections and Observations* (Richmond: privately printed, 1958), 24.

2. Powell, *Recollections*, 30; Blaine Brownell, "The Urban South Comes of Age, 1900–1940," in *The City in Southern History: The Growth of Urban Civilization in the South*, ed. Blaine Brownell and David Goldfield (Port Washington, N.Y.: Kennikat Press, 1977), 123–58 (see especially 124–25).

3. Richmond Chamber of Commerce, "City of Richmond, of Historic Fame, of Great Commercial Prestige" (Richmond, 1905), 2–4; Gregg Kimball, "Life and Labor in an Industrial City, 1865–1920," *Labor's Heritage* 3, no. 2 (April 1991): 42–65 (see especially 56–60).

4. See Kathy Peiss, *Cheap Amusements: Working Women and Leisure in Turn-of-the-Century New York* (Philadelphia: Temple University Press, 1986), for a view of working women's lives that has application to Richmond.

5. Ellen Glasgow, *The Woman Within* (New York: Harcourt Brace, 1954), 217–18.

6. Wythe Holt, Jr., "The Virginia Constitutional Convention of 1901–1902: A Reform Movement Which Lacked Substance" (Ph.D. diss., University of Virginia, 1979), 2–3; Charles Reagan Wilson, *Baptized in Blood: The Religion of the Lost Cause, 1865–1920* (Athens: University of Georgia Press, 1980); Angie Parrott, "'Love Makes Memory Eternal': The Daughters of the Confederacy in Richmond, Virginia, 1897–1920," in *The Edge of the South: Life in Nineteenth-Century Virginia*, ed. Edward L. Ayers and John C. Willis (Charlottesville: University Press of Virginia, 1991), 219–38.

7. Robert A. Cutchins, *Memories of Old Richmond, 1881–1944* (Verona, Va.: McClure Printing Company, 1973), 17–19, 28, 30; YWCA Records, Virginia Commonwealth University Library and Archives, Richmond; Christopher Silver, *Twentieth-Century Richmond: Planning, Politics, and Race* (Knoxville: University of Tennessee Press, 1984), 29–31, 113–14; Virginius Dabney, *Virginia,*

the New Dominion (Garden City, N.Y.: Doubleday, 1971), 286.

8. Brownell, "Urban South," 138–41; Raymond Gavins, *The Perils and Prospects of Southern Black Leadership: Gordon Blaine Hancock, 1884–1970* (Durham: Duke University Press, 1977), 259–60; Silver, *Twentieth-Century Richmond*, 32–34.

9. Dewey W. Grantham, *Southern Progressivism: The Reconciliation of Progress and Tradition* (Knoxville: University of Tennessee Press, 1983), 202; Parrott, "'Love Makes Memory Eternal'"; Suzanne Lebsock, *"A Share of Honour": Virginia Women, 1600–1945*, 2d ed. (Richmond: Virginia State Library, 1987).

10. *Southern Workman* (January 1922), quoted in Betsy Brinson, "Helping Others to Help Themselves: Social Advocacy and Wage-Earning Women in Richmond, Virginia, 1910–1932" (Ph.D. diss., Union Graduate School, 1984), 22–23; boarding-house information in Women and Labor Survey (1911), box 11, file 25, YWCA Papers, Virginia Commonwealth University Library and Archives, Richmond.

11. Jack Temple Kirby, *Darkness at the Dawning: Race and Reform in the Progressive South* (Philadelphia: Lippincott, 1972), 3–4, 49; Grantham, *Southern Progressivism*, xv–xxii; William Link, *The Paradox of Southern Progressivism, 1880–1930* (Chapel Hill: University of North Carolina Press, 1992), 95–96, 203–4.

12. Howard Rabinowitz, "Continuity and Change: Southern Urban Development, 1860–1900," in Brownell and Goldfield, *City in Southern History*, 107–10; Leon Fink, *Workingmen's Democracy: The Knights of Labor and American Politics* (Urbana: University of Illinois Press, 1983), 150; Elsa Barkley Brown, "Womanist Consciousness: Maggie Lena Walker and the Independent Order of St. Luke," *Signs* 14 (Spring 1989): 610–53.

13. James D. Watkinson, "William Washington Browne and the True Reformers of Richmond, Virginia," *Virginia Magazine of History and Biography* 97, no. 3 (July 1989): 375–98; Gavins, *Gordon Blaine Hancock*, 43–45; Andrew Buni, *The Negro in Virginia Politics, 1902–1965* (Charlottesville: University Press of Virginia, 1967), 39–40.

14. Ann Field Alexander, "Black Protest in the New South: John Mitchell, Jr., and the Richmond *Planet*" (Ph.D. diss., Duke

University, 1972), 169, 283–85.

15. William Wells Brown, *My Southern Home* (1880; reprint, New York: Negro Universities Press, 1969), 204; William E. Hatcher, *John Jasper, the Unmatched Negro Philosopher and Preacher* (New York: F. H. Revell Company, 1908), 31, 88, 47–57, 89–93, 121–49.

16. Andrew Montague to Henry St. George Tucker, 22 November 1901, in Wythe Holt, "Virginia's Constitutional Convention of 1901–1902," 153, 1–3, 24.

17. Alexander, "Black Protest in the New South," 271–80.

18. Brownell, "Urban South," 142, 150–58; Silver, *Twentieth-Century Richmond*, 4, 9–10.

19. Silver, *Twentieth-Century Richmond*, 21; Allan Moger, *Virginia: Bourbonism to Byrd, 1870–1925* (Charlottesville: University Press of Virginia, 1968), 130–31; Grantham, *Southern Progressivism*, xv–xx.

20. Silver, *Twentieth-Century Richmond*, 42–56.

21. Brownell, "Urban South," 151.

22. Barton Heights Realty and Finance Corporation, advertisement in *Richmond Virginian*, 9 June 1912; M. Omohundro, "Oak Park: Queen of Suburbs," pamphlet advertisement (1911), 5, 14.

23. Silver, *Twentieth-Century Richmond*, 86, 89–90; Dabney, *Virginia*, 279.

24. "History of WCTU," Virginia Women's History Project file, Archives Division, Virginia State Library, Richmond. See also Anne Scott, cited in Anne Goodwyn Jones, *Tomorrow Is Another Day: The Woman Writer in the South, 1859–1936* (Baton Rouge: Louisiana State University Press, 1981), 33; Brinson, "Helping Others," 25–26.

25. Robert A. Hohner, "The Prohibitionists: Who Were They?," *South Atlantic Quarterly* 68 (Autumn 1969): 499–500.

26. Grantham, *Southern Progressivism*, 363, 160–72; Hohner, "Prohibitionists," 502–4.

27. James M. Lindgren, "'For the Sake of Our Future': The Association for the Preservation of Virginia Antiquities and the Regeneration of Traditionalism," *Virginia Magazine of History and Biography* 97, no. 1 (January 1989): 65, 68, 69, 73–74, and "'Virginia Needs Living Heroes': Historic Preservation in the Progressive Era," *Public Historian* 13, no. 1 (Winter 1991): 10, 11, 15–16, 19–20, 23.

28. Silver, *Twentieth-Century Richmond*; Lebsock, *"Share of Honour,"* 114–16; Louis Harlan, *Separate and Unequal* (Chapel Hill: University of North Carolina Press, 1958), 168.

29. Quoted in Sarah McCulloh Lemmon, "Munford, Mary Cooke Branch," in *Notable American Women*, 4 vols., ed. Edward T. James et al. (Cambridge: Belknap Press of Harvard University Press), 2:600–601.

30. Lebsock, *"Share of Honour,"* 114.

31. Gavins, *Gordon Blaine Hancock*, 266–67.

32. Quotes (including *Richmond Planet*, 14 July 1900) from Alexander, "Black Protest in the New South," 169. See also Anne Firor Scott, "Most Invisible of All: Black Women's Voluntary Associations," *Journal of Southern History* 56, no. 1 (February 1990): 3–22 (see especially 9–12, 20–22); Barkley Brown, "Womanist Consciousness," 614–15, 620–21, 622, 625–26.

33. Anne Goodwyn Jones, *Tomorrow Is Another Day*, 186, 184, 225.

34. Glasgow, *Woman Within*, 185–87.

35. Robert Merritt, "Adele Clark Cast a Long Shadow," *Richmond Times-Dispatch*, 12 June 1983, J-4.

36. *Virginia Suffrage News*, December 1914, in Brinson, "Helping Others," 25, 27.

37. *The Woman Patriot*, 30 August 1919, quoted in Elna Green, "The Ideology of Southern Antisuffragism: White Supremacy vs. White Monopoly" (paper presented to the Southern Association of Women Historians, Chapel Hill, N.C., June 1991), 3.

38. Suzanne Lebsock, "Woman Suffrage and White Supremacy: A Virginia Case Study" (paper presented to the Southern Association of Women Historians, Norfolk, Va., 10 November 1988).

39. Link, *Paradox of Southern Progressivism*, 300; "World War Gripped Richmond as Spanish One Never Did," *Richmond Times-Dispatch*, 8 September 1937; James Sanford, *Richmond: Her Triumphs, Tragedies, and Growth* (Richmond: Metropolitan Richmond Chamber of Commerce, 1975), 112–13.

40. Joseph C. Robert, *Gottwald Family History: The First Century of the Gottwalds and Freyvogles in Richmond, Virginia, 1822–1922* (Richmond: privately printed, 1984), 78–79.

41. "Report of War Activities, 1917–1918," published by Richmond Public Schools, 1918, held in Virginia State Library and Archive, Richmond.

42. Maurine Greenwald, *Women, War, and Work: The Impact of World War I on Women Workers in the United States* (Westport, Conn.: Greenwood Press, 1980), xx, xxiv, 13, 45; Colleen Callahan, "Dressed for Work: Women's Clothing on the Job, 1900–1990," *Labor's Heritage* 4, no. 1 (Spring 1992): 33–34.

43. Dabney, *Virginia*, 468–69.

44. Lebsock, *"Share of Honour,"* 12.

45. Alexander, "Black Protest in the New South," 332–34, 339–40; Watkinson, "William Washington Browne," 396–98.

46. Julius R. Raper, *Ellen Glasgow's Reasonable Doubts: A Collection of Her Writings* (Baton Rouge: Louisiana State University Press, 1987), 54 (n. 1), 55 (n. 3), 58 (n. 6), 61 (n. 8); James Latimer, "Gubernatorial Election of 1921 Was 'Odd' One," *Richmond Times-Dispatch*, 27 September 1981, G-1; Gavins, *Gordon Blaine Hancock*, 259, 271.

CHAPTER TEN

1. Tazewell Carrington, telephone interview with author, 19 March 1992.

2. Christopher Silver, *Twentieth-Century Richmond: Planning, Politics, and Race* (Knoxville: University of Tennessee Press, 1984), 130–31; Blaine Brownell, *The Urban Ethos in the South, 1920–1930* (Baton Rouge: Louisiana State University Press, 1975), 188.

3. Silver, *Twentieth-Century Richmond*, 86–93, 101, 106–9.

4. Orie Latham Hatcher, *Rural Girls in the City for Work* (Richmond: Garrett and Massie, 1930), 58–59; Southern Women's Educational Alliance, cited in Betsy Brinson, "Helping Others to Help Themselves: Social Advocacy and Wage-Earning Women in Richmond, Virginia, 1910–1936" (Ph.D. diss., Union Graduate School, 1984), 56–57. See June Purcell Guild, "Black Richmond," *Survey Graphic* (June 1934): 276–78, and Charles L. Knight, *Negro Housing in Certain Virginia Cities* (Richmond: William Byrd Press for the University of Virginia, Phelps Stokes Fellowship Papers, 1927), among the city studies done between 1914 and 1930.

5. Virginius Dabney, *Richmond: The Story of a City*, rev. ed. (Charlottesville: University Press of Virginia, 1990), 297, 311; Paul Dulaney, *The Architecture of Historic Rich-*

mond (Charlottesville: University Press of Virginia, 1968), 163.

6. Silver, *Twentieth-Century Richmond*, 109; David R. Goldfield and Blaine A. Brownell, *Urban America: A History*, 2d ed. (Boston: Houghton Mifflin, 1990), 292–96; Dabney, *Richmond*, 304; James Lindgren, "'For the Sake of Our Future': The Association for the Preservation of Virginia Antiquities and the Regeneration of Traditionalism," *Virginia Magazine of History and Biography* 97, no. 1 (January 1989): 65–69.

7. *Richmond News Leader*, December 1925, 27 August 1927, 15 August 1928.

8. Goldfield and Brownell, *Urban America*, 289–91; Phyllis Palmer, *Domesticity and Dirt: Housewives and Domestic Servants in the United States, 1920–1945* (Philadelphia: Temple University Press, 1989), 167n.

9. *Section: Windsor Farms* and *Houses: Agecroft* (promotional brochure), vertical file, Valentine Museum, Richmond; William B. O'Neal and Christopher Weeks, *The Work of William Lawrence Bottomley in Richmond* (Charlottesville: University Press of Virginia, 1985); Dabney, *Richmond*, 310–11.

10. Daniel Singal, *The War Within: From Victorian to Modernist Thought in the South, 1919–1945* (Chapel Hill: University of North Carolina Press, 1982), 35–36, 83, 87–91, 108–9, 111.

11. Singal, *War Within*, 83–87; James Branch Cabell, *Let Me Lie* (New York: Farrar, Straus, 1947), 203–4, 213–26; Dabney, *Richmond*, 300–301.

12. Virginius Dabney, *Across the Years: Memories of a Virginian* (Garden City, N.Y.: Doubleday, 1978), 116–20; John T. Kneebone, *Southern Liberal Journalists and the Issue of Race* (Chapel Hill: University of North Carolina Press, 1985), xvii, 4.

13. Kneebone, *Southern Liberal Journalists*, xiii–xiv, 24–25, 105, 148, 202–3; Walter Russell Bowie, *Sunrise in the South: The Life of Mary-Cooke Branch Munford* (Richmond: William Byrd Press, 1942), 157.

14. Richard Sherman, "'The Last Stand': The Fight for Racial Integrity in Virginia in the 1920s," *Journal of Southern History* 54, no. 1 (February 1988): 71–73.

15. Sherman, "'Last Stand,'" 73, 77, 82–87; Helen Rountree, *Pocahontas's People: The Powhatan Indians of Virginia through Four Centuries* (Norman: University of Oklahoma Press, 1990), 219–21.

16. Dabney, *Richmond*, 303–4; Samuel Shepherd, "Churches at Work: Richmond, Virginia, White Protestant Leaders and Social Change in a Southern City, 1900–1929" (Ph.D. diss., University of Wisconsin, 1980), 67–86.

17. George Brown Tindall, *The Emergence of the New South, 1913–1945* (Baton Rouge: Louisiana State University Press, 1967), 184–218; Bill Malone, *Southern Music, American Music* (Lexington: University Press of Kentucky, 1979), 62–64; Kip Lornell, *Virginia Blues, Country, and Gospel Records, 1902–1943: An Annotated Discography* (Lexington: University Press of Kentucky, 1989), 134–35, 155–57; Annabell Morris Buchanan quoted in Suzanne Lebsock, *"A Share of Honour": Virginia Women, 1600–1945*, 2d ed. (Richmond: Virginia State Library, 1987), 126–27.

18. "WRVA: Serving You for Fifty Golden Years" (Richmond: WRVA, 1974), a4–a6; Freeman obituary, *Richmond Times-Dispatch*, 14 June 1953, 1.

19. Virginius Dabney, *Virginia Commonwealth University: A Sesquicentennial History* (Charlottesville: University Press of Virginia, 1987), xviii, 132, 171; Sarah McCulloh Lemmon, "Hatcher, Orie Latham," in *Notable American Women*, 4 vols., ed. Edward T. James et al. (Cambridge: Belknap Press of Harvard University Press), 2:152–53.

20. M. Pierce Rucker, "Rebel Obstetrician: An Autobiography and Biographical Sketches" (unpublished typescript in possession of Rucker/Powell families, Richmond, 1950), 35–37, 64; Guild, *Negro in Richmond*, ix.

21. Lucy Randolph Mason, *To Win These Rights: A Personal Story of the CIO in the South* (New York: Harper and Bros., 1952), 1–2, 5, 8; Naomi Cohn obituary, *Richmond Times-Dispatch*, 21 October 1982, in Virginia Women's History Project Files, Archives Division, Virginia State Library, Richmond.

22. V. O. Key, *Southern Politics in State and Nation* (New York: Knopf, 1949), 19–33.

23. Virginius Dabney, *Virginia, the New Dominion* (Garden City, N.Y.: Doubleday, 1971), 488.

24. Pete Daniel, *Breaking the Land: The Transformation of Cotton, Tobacco, and Rice Cultures since 1880* (Urbana: University of Illinois Press, 1985); Ronald L. Heinemann,

Depression and New Deal in Virginia: The Enduring Dominion (Charlottesville: University Press of Virginia, 1983), 8–10, 12, 16–18, 26–28.

25. Heinemann, *Depression and New Deal*, 18; Dabney, *Richmond*, 313–15.

26. Introduction to James C. Cobb and Michael V. Namorato, eds., *The New Deal and the South: Essays* (Jackson: University Press of Mississippi, 1984), 7.

27. Heinemann, *Depression and New Deal*, 5–12, 28, 30–31, 39–41, 156; Dabney, *Virginia*, 408–9.

28. *Richmond News Leader*, 30 July 1930, 18 March 1933, 10 October 1933. See *Richmond Times-Dispatch*, 4 October 1933, for a report on the referendum.

29. *Richmond Times-Dispatch*, 19 April 1937, 1.

30. Heinemann, *Depression and New Deal*, 60–67; Dabney, *Richmond*, 313; *Richmond News Leader*, 9 October 1936, 1; Goldfield and Brownell, *Urban America*, 328.

31. Heinemann, *Depression and New Deal*, 76; Dabney, *Richmond*, 315.

32. Heinemann, *Depression and New Deal*, ix, x, 58, 85, 156, 157, 36–39, 83, 143.

33. Alice Jackson Stuart, interview with author (Richmond), 24 February 1992 and 18 March 1992.

34. Alan Brinkley, "The New Deal in Southern Politics," in Cobb and Namorato, *New Deal and the South*, 101; Heinemann, *Depression and New Deal*, 168–69.

35. For a discussion of the lack of change in Virginia, see Numan V. Bartley, "New Deal as a Turning Point in Southern History," in Cobb and Namorato, *New Deal in the South*, 145; Brinkley, "The New Deal and Southern Politics," 98; Key, *Southern Politics*, 29, 32, 33.

36. Goldfield and Brownell, *Urban America*, 328–32.

37. Daniel, *Breaking the Land*, xii, 214; Garland Pollard, "So Long, Tobacco Queen," *Style Weekly*, 14 March 1990, 34.

38. Francis Earle Lutz, *Richmond in World War II* (Richmond: Dietz, 1951), 8–12, 15–16.

39. Ibid., 22, 18.

40. Lutz, *Richmond in World War II*; Silver, *Twentieth-Century Richmond*.

41. Lutz, *Richmond in World War II*, 67, 109–11.

42. Ibid., 65–68; YWCA Annual Reports (1942), p. 1, Industrial Department, box 1, Virginia Commonwealth University

Library and Archives, Richmond; Goldfield and Brownell, *Urban America*, 336–41.

43. YWCA Annual Reports (1942), Industrial Department, box 1; YWCA Annual Reports (1945), Industrial Department, box 1.

44. Lutz, *Richmond in World War II*, 39, 41. For the relation between fashion, work, and war in Richmond, see especially Colleen Callahan, "Dressed for Work: Women's Clothing on the Job, 1900–1990," *Labor's Heritage* 4, no. 1 (Spring 1992): 31–36, 38–42.

45. *Richmond News Leader*, 21 July 1943, 3; "Second Street," essay and video for an exhibition held February–August 1990, Valentine Museum, Richmond.

46. Lutz, *Richmond in World War II*, 59–64.

47. Ibid., 18; *Richmond News Leader*, 7 February 1942, 10; 5 May 1942, 1; 12 May 1942, 10; 16 October 1942, 1, 10; 2 December 1942, 1; 19 February 1943, 1; 8 March 1943, 1; 24 March 1943, 12; 16 March 1943, 10; 21 April 1943, 10; *Richmond Times-Dispatch*, 21 March 1943, 1.

48. Lutz, *Richmond in World War II*, 34, 40.

49. Introduction to Margaret R. Higonnet, ed., *Behind the Lines: Gender and the Two World Wars* (New Haven: Yale University Press, 1987), 7, 8; Sheila Tobias and Lisa Anderson, "What Really Happened to Rosie the Riveter?," in Linda Kerber and Jane De Hart Mathews, *Women's America: Refocusing the Past* (New York: Oxford University Press), 354–73.

CHAPTER ELEVEN

1. *Richmond Times-Dispatch*, 5 December 1945, 7; 9 December 1945, 12-D; and 11 December 1945. *Richmond News Leader*, 24 December 1945, 1; Francis Earle Lutz, *Richmond in World War II* (Richmond: Dietz Press, 1950), 426.

2. Francis M. Foster, "Remembering the Ward," *Style Weekly*, 2 February 1988, 32.

3. Garland Pollard, "So Long, Tobacco Queen," *Style Weekly*, 14 March 1990, 32–35; J. Harvie Wilkinson, III, *Harry Byrd and the Changing Face of Virginia Politics, 1945–1966* (Charlottesville: University Press of Virginia, 1968), 177; James Sanford, ed., *A Century of Commerce* (Richmond: Richmond Chamber of Commerce, 1967), 185–88, 206.

4. Sanford, *Century of Commerce*, 204, 206; Edward F. Haas, "The Southern Metropolis, 1940–1976," in *The City in Southern History: The Growth of Urban Civilization in the South*, ed. Blaine A. Brownell and David R. Goldfield (Port Washington, N.Y.: Kennikat Press, 1977), 160–61, 173–76; David R. Goldfield, *Promised Land: The South since 1945* (Arlington Heights, Ill.: Harlan Davidson, 1987), 33–34, 206; Virginius Dabney, *Richmond: The Story of a City*, rev. ed. (Charlottesville: University Press of Virginia, 1990), 334; Christopher Silver, *Twentieth-Century Richmond: Planning, Politics, and Race* (Knoxville: University of Tennessee Press, 1984), 225–28.

5. Suzanne Lebsock, *"A Share of Honor": Virginia Women, 1600–1945*, 2d ed. (Richmond: Virginia State Library, 1987), 130, 133–34; Loren Baritz, *The Good Life: The Meaning of Success for the American Middle Class* (New York: Knopf, 1989), 191–95; Haas, "Southern Metropolis," 160; Goldfield, *Promised Land*, 22–27; Pete Daniel, *Breaking the Land: The Transformation of Cotton, Tobacco, and Rice Cultures since 1880* (Urbana: University of Illinois Press, 1985), 256–57, 265–67.

6. Harland Bartholomew and Associates, *Richmond, Virginia: A Master Plan* (Richmond: City Planning Commission, 1946), 84–90, 46–47, 58–59, 74, 155; Kenneth Jackson, *Crabgrass Frontier: The Suburbanization of the United States* (New York: Oxford University Press, 1985), 214; Silver, *Twentieth-Century Richmond*, 160–61, 164, 167–68, 174, 176–78.

7. David R. Goldfield and Blaine A. Brownell, *Urban America: A History*, 2d ed. (Boston: Houghton Mifflin, 1990), 330, 343–48, 350; John Moeser and Rutledge Dennis, *The Politics of Annexation: Oligarchic Power in a Southern City* (Cambridge, Mass.: Schenkman, 1982), 29–30; Jackson, *Crabgrass Frontier*, 190–91, 203–10, especially 213–15; Robert A. Pratt, "School Desegregation in Richmond, Virginia, 1954–1984: A Study of Race and Class in a Southern City" (Ph.D. diss., University of Virginia, 1987), 160–61.

8. Wilkinson, *Harry Byrd*, 179; Oliver Hill, "Tribute to Lewis Powell," *Harvard Law Review* 101 (December 1987): 415; Dabney, *Richmond*, 334–35; Silver, *Twentieth-Century Richmond*, 178.

9. James Latimer, "Virginia Politics in the 1950s" (typewritten manuscript in author's possession, Richmond), 64–65, and "Longest Day Brought New Dawn for Virginia Politics," *Richmond Times-Dispatch*, 4 March 1990, F-9; V. O. Key, *Southern Politics in State and Nation* (New York: Knopf, 1949), 19; Wilkinson, *Harry Byrd*, 179; Goldfield, *Promised Land*, 35–39; thanks to Ann Hobson Freeman for clarity in phrasing.

10. Richard Kluger, *Simple Justice: The History of* Brown v. Board of Education *and Black America's Struggle for Equality* (New York: Knopf, 1976), 128–31, 480–506; Ann Hobson Freeman, *The Style of a Law Firm: Eight Gentlemen From Virginia* (Chapel Hill: Algonquin Books, 1989), 259–60 (nn. 42–52), 138–41; Peter Wallenstein, "'I Went to Law School to Fight Segregation': Oliver W. Hill vs. Jim Crow in Virginia" (paper presented at annual meeting of Southern Historical Association, Atlanta, Ga., November 1992), 4, 11, 18.

11. Robert Johnson, *Richmond Afro-American*, 22 May 1954, quoted in Pratt, "School Desegregation," 10–11.

12. Pratt, "School Desegregation," 10–11, 13n; Latimer, "Virginia Politics," 51–52; Wilkinson, *Harry Byrd*, 113–54, 237–40.

13. Kilpatrick quoted in Steven A. Smith, *Myth, Media, and the Southern Mind* (Fayetteville: University of Arkansas Press, 1985), 39.

14. Dabney, *Richmond*, 345, 350; John T. Kneebone, *Southern Liberal Journalists and the Issue of Race, 1920–1944* (Chapel Hill: University of North Carolina Press, 1985), 220–22; Smith, *Myth, Media, and the Southern Mind*, 39–40; Goldfield, *Promised Land*, 10–11, 52–54; Raymond Gavins, *The Perils and Prospects of Southern Black Leadership: Gordon Blaine Hancock, 1884–1970* (Durham: Duke University Press, 1977), 139–41, 161–62, 169; Wilkinson, *Harry Byrd*, 129.

15. Kilpatrick quoted in Wilkinson, *Harry Byrd*, 127.

16. Lindsay Almond, from *Southern School News*, October 1957, quoted in Pratt, "School Desegregation," 26; Pratt, "School Desegregation," 16–21, 28–29; Benjamin Muse, *Virginia's Massive Resistance* (Bloomington: Indiana University Press, 1961), 92–94, 111–18; Wilkinson, *Harry Byrd*, 138.

17. Pratt, "School Desegregation," 35–37, 40, 42, 50, 52–55, 63, 81, 94, 95; *Richmond*

Times-Dispatch, 11 January 1972; Wilkinson, *Harry Byrd*, 143, 166; Dabney, *Richmond*, 336–37.

18. Dabney, *Richmond*, 336; Richmond newspaper photograph files, Valentine Museum, undated; Clayborne Carson, *In Struggle: SNCC and the Black Awakening of the 1960s* (Cambridge: Harvard University Press, 1981), 10–11.

19. Barry Pearson, "Bowling Green John Cephas and Harmonica Phil Wiggins: D.C. Country Blues," *Living Blues* 63 (January–February 1985): 14–20; Bill Malone, *Southern Music, American Music* (Lexington: University Press of Kentucky, 1979), 142–45; YWCA survey of member attitudes (1946), Richmond YWCA archives, Virginia Commonwealth University, Richmond. See also Charles Keil, *Urban Blues* (Chicago: University of Chicago Press, 1966).

20. John Tansey quote from interview with Chris Fullerton, 23 February 1990; transcript in Chris Fullerton's possession. *Nashville Tennessean*, 15 June 1979, and Country Music Foundation clipping file, courtesy of Chris Fullerton.

21. Tom Mitchell, telephone interview by Karen Holt Luetjen, 28 February 1990, transcript in Valentine Museum, Richmond.

22. Dabney, *Richmond*, 313, 346, 349, 354. J. Ronald Oakley, *God's Country: America in the Fifties* (New York: Dembner, 1986), 9.

23. Silver, *Twentieth-Century Richmond*, 212–13, 256, 258, 173, 184, 186–88, 192–93, 196–97, 219.

24. Silver, *Twentieth-Century Richmond*, 272, 278–80; Wilkinson, *Harry Byrd*, 180; *Richmond News Leader*, 24 December 1954.

25. Richmond City Planning Commission, *Design for Monument Avenue* (Richmond: City Planning Commission, 1965), 4.

26. Haas, "Southern Metropolis," 178–79; Dabney, *Richmond*, 340, 342–43.

27. Silver, *Twentieth-Century Richmond*, 278–80; Peter Wallenstein, "Federal Courts and Southern Politics in the 1960s: The Reapportionment Revolution in Virginia in Historical Perspective," *Virginia Social Science Journal* 26 (1991): 1–10 (see especially 1, 5, 6).

28. Pratt, "School Desegregation," 220.

CHAPTER TWELVE

1. Mary Wingfield Scott, letter to *Richmond Times-Dispatch*, 12 June 1963.

2. Christopher Silver, *Twentieth-Century Richmond: Planning, Politics, and Race* (Knoxville: University of Tennessee Press, 1984), 142, 259–80; Kenneth Jackson, *Crabgrass Frontier: The Suburbanization of the United States* (New York: Oxford University Press, 1985), 213–17.

3. Edward F. Haas, "The Southern Metropolis, 1940–1976," in *The City in Southern History: The Growth of Urban Civilization in the South*, ed. Blaine A. Brownell and David R. Goldfield (Port Washington, N.Y.: Kennikat Press, 1977), 177; Robert A. Pratt, "School Desegregation in Richmond, Virginia, 1954–1984: A Study of Race and Class in a Southern City" (Ph.D. diss., University of Virginia, 1987), 161–62, 162 (n. 18), 181–82; James L. Doherty, *Race and Education in Richmond* (Richmond: privately printed, 1972), 5–13.

4. David Goldfield, *Black, White and Southern: Race Relations and Southern Culture, 1940 to the Present* (Baton Rouge: Louisiana State University Press, 1990), 186; John Moeser and Rutledge Dennis, *The Politics of Annexation: Oligarchic Power in a Southern City* (Cambridge, Mass.: Schenkman, 1982), 145–72, 181–83; Robert Goldblum, "Henry Marsh's Unfinished Business," *Style Weekly* (October 1988), 33–37; Silver, *Twentieth-Century Richmond*, 206, 316.

5. See Drew Carneal, "A History of the Fan District" (unpublished manuscript in author's possession, n.d.); and John F. Harris, "Battle over Historic Status Turns Racial in Richmond," *Washington Post*, 22 October 1990.

6. See *Richmond's Historic Waterfront: Rocket's Landing to Tredegar, 1607–1865* (Richmond: Historic Richmond Foundation, 1989); Scott C. Davis, *The World of Patience Gromes: Making and Unmaking a Black Community* (Lexington: University of Kentucky Press, 1989), 9–11.

7. A. J. Fleming quoted in *Richmond News Leader*, 20 July 1983.

8. Silver, *Twentieth-Century Richmond*, 289–310; Davis, *World of Patience Gromes*, 3–6, 65–68, 71–72, 90; *Richmond News Leader*, 20 July 1983.

9. Silver, *Twentieth-Century Richmond*, 313–14.

10. *Richmond Times-Dispatch* (n.d.) quoted in Edwin Slipek, Jr., "The Suburbanization of Downtown," *Style Weekly* (29 October 1991). See also Jeanne Cummings, "Renaissance Chairman Plans to Step Down," *Richmond News Leader*, 1 November 1985; Silver, *Twentieth-Century Richmond*, 316, 319; John Teaford, *The Rough Road to Renaissance: Urban Revitalization in America, 1940–85* (Baltimore: Johns Hopkins University Press, 1990), 272–75.

11. David Hilzenrath, "Festival Marketplaces Have Few Developers Cheering," *Washington Post*, 1 October 1988.

12. Ostler and Wiles, "A Publishing Empire under Attack," *Style Weekly* (1988), 33–35, 37; Mollie Gore, "*News Leader* Will Be Merged with *Times-Dispatch* June 1," *Richmond Times-Dispatch*, 5 September 1991.

13. *Wall Street Journal*, 19 November 1987, 9; James C. Cobb, *The Selling of the South: The Southern Crusade for Industrial Development* (Baton Rouge: Louisiana State University Press, 1982), 261; John M. Berry, "James River Flows On, Quietly," *Washington Post*, 10 October 1988.

14. Data cited in Charles P. Roland, "Sun Belt Prosperity and Urban Growth," in *Interpreting Southern History*, ed. John B. Boles and Evelyn Thomas Nolen (Baton Rouge: Louisiana State University Press, 1987), 440–41; Ann Woodlief, *In River Time: The Way of the James* (Chapel Hill: Algonquin Books, 1985), 156–62, 182–84.

15. Woodlief, *River Time*, 185–92. For examples of the ongoing tug-of-war between state agencies and the city, see *Richmond News Leader*, 29 September 1970, 17 November 1970, and 21 March 1989.

16. Cindy Elmore, "A 'Sleepy Southern Town' Wakes Up," *Washington Post*, 4 July 1988; Alan M. Gayle and Christine Chmura, "The Richmond-Petersburg MSA Economy" (Crestar Investment Bank, Richmond, 1990).

17. *Richmond Times-Dispatch*, 14 January 1990; *Washington Post*, 14 January 1990; *Richmond Times-Dispatch*, 18 March 1990; *Washington Post*, 14 April 1989; *Washington Post*, 1 October 1988.

18. *Washington Post*, 1 October 1988; *Atlanta Constitution*, 2 February 1988; *Washington Post*, 4 July 1988.

19. Valerie Hubbard, "22.5 Million Dollar Riverside Museum Planned by the Valentine, Ethyl," *Richmond Times-Dispatch*,

23 January 1991, A1, 7.

20. *Richmond Times-Dispatch*, 31 August 1988.

21. Michael Elliott, "America: The Old Country," *The Economist*, 26 October 1991, 3–26; William Schneider, "The Suburban Century Begins," *Atlantic Monthly* (June 1992): 33–58; Susan Strasser, *Never Done: A History of American Housework* (New York: Pantheon Books, 1982), 301–2; Suzanne Lebsock, *"A Share of Honour": Virginia Women, 1600–1945*, 2d ed. (Richmond: Virginia State Library, 1987), 131, 134–35.

22. Judith Rollins, *Between Women Domestics and Their Employers* (Philadelphia: Temple University Press, 1985), 173–78; Susan Tucker, *Telling Memories among Southern Women: Domestic Workers and Their Employers in the Segregated South* (Baton Rouge: Louisiana State University Press, 1988).

23. "Beyond the Glass Ceiling: Business Women in the '90s," *Richmond News Leader*, 26 June 1989, B1–B23; "Working Women," *Southern Exposure* 9 (Winter 1981): 1–129; Andrew Hacker, "Women at Work," *New York Review of Books*, 14 August 1986, 26–32; Julia Martin and Donna Tolson, "Family Composition in Virginia Female-Headed Families, 1970–1980" (Charlottesville: University of Virginia Institute of Government, 1983).

24. Andrew Holliday, *An Economic Profile of the Richmond-Petersburg MSA* (Charlottesville: University of Virginia Center for Public Service, 1990), 000; Robert Black, "The Future of the Capital Area: What It May Be, What It Should Be" (Virginia Intergovernmental Institute, 0000).

25. David R. Goldfield, "Neighborhood Preservation and Community Values in Historical Perspective," in *Neighborhood and Community Environments*, vol. 9 of *Human Behavior and Environment: Advances in Theory and Research*, ed. Irwin Altman and Abraham Wandersman (forthcoming), 5, 45; Jackson, *Crabgrass Frontier*, 298–303.

26. Lebsock, *"A Share of Honor,"* 134–36; Julia Kirk Blackwelder, "Race, Ethnicity, and Women's Lives in the Urban South," in *Shades of the Sunbelt: Essays on Ethnicity, Race, and the Urban South*, ed. Randall Miller and George E. Pozzetta (New York: Greenwood, 1988), 75–91 (see especially 75–77, 88–89).

27. Quoted in *The Economist*, 2 May 1992, 28. See also Joel Garreau, "Where the Voters Are," *Washington Post*, 2 August 1992; *The Economist*, 2 May 1992, 31; *The Economist*, 9 May 1992, 21, 24.

28. Cobb, *Selling of the South*, 264–65; John Shelton Reed, *One South: An Ethnic Approach to Regional Culture* (Baton Rouge: Louisiana State University Press, 1982).

29. Robert Pratt, "School Desegregation," iv.

30. *Richmond Times-Dispatch*, 9 April and 25 July 1991.

31. Donald P. Baker, "At Midnight, Virginia's I-95 Tolls Reach the End of the Road," *Washington Post*, 30 June 1992.

32. Dave Smith, "To Isle of Wight," in *Cuba Night* (New York: William Morrow, 1990), 17–18.

Bibliographic Essay

This selective bibliographic essay features those sources that have been most useful to me and to the Valentine Museum in interpreting the history of Richmond. Some sources listed here appear frequently in the notes, but this essay is also an opportunity to acknowledge uncited works that shaped thinking in large and important ways. Certain useful works that appear in the notes are not cited further here. The scholarship of many monographs and journal articles has been supplemented by primary research, much of which has been done by the Valentine Museum staff and interns in relation to museum exhibitions. Selectively, newspapers, public records, institutional archives, letter collections, and archaeological findings have been perused and census data tabulated. The essay is somewhat chronological, but many themes are discussed in their entirety when they first appear.

Native Americans, English Adventurers, African Captives, and Settlement at the Falls

The archaeological and anthropological attention paid in the last twenty years to the Indian tribes of the eastern part of North America has extended the human history of the James River and Chesapeake Bay back by centuries. It has also given balance to the seventeenth-century encounter between the English and the Powhatan Indians; both groups are now more clearly seen in terms of what their values caused them to expect from the other. J. Leitch Wright, in *The Only Land They Knew: The Tragic Story of the American Indians in the Old South* (New York: Free Press, 1981), and James Axtell, in *The Invasion Within: The Contest of Cultures in Colonial North America* (New York: Oxford University Press, 1985), have described the Indians' populations and temporal and geographical range on the southern land. Bernard Sheehan, in *Savagism and Civility: Indians and Englishmen in Colonial Virginia* (Cambridge: Cambridge University Press, 1980), and Gary Nash, in *Red, White, and Black: The Peoples of Early America* (1974; 2d ed., Englewood Cliffs, N.J.: Prentice Hall, 1982), explored the English image of the Virginia Indians and added to the visual study by Hugh Honour, *The New Golden Land: European Images of America from the Discoveries to the Present Time* (New York: Pantheon, 1975). Winthrop Jordan's still-monumental *White Over Black: American Attitudes toward the Negro, 1550–1812* (Chapel Hill: University of North Carolina Press, 1968) provided a similar context for European attitudes toward Africans.

For the area at the falls of the James River, ongoing research by archaeologists such as Daniel Mouer, Mark Wittkofski, and Theodore Reinhart III make current assumptions tentative. In Mouer's *Archaeology in Henrico, 1980–*, and Wittkofski and Reinhart's *Paleoindian Research in Virginia* (Special Publication No. 19 of the Archeological Society of Virginia, Richmond, 1989), a clear picture is emerging of a people whose governmental seat and trade center was at the falls. The research of Helen C. Rountree is indispensable for an understanding of Virginia Indians near the falls. Her published work includes *Pocahontas's People: The Powhatan Indians of Virginia through Four Centuries* (Norman: University of Oklahoma Press, 1990) and *The Powhatan Indians of Virginia: Their Traditional Culture* (Norman: University of Oklahoma Press, 1989). Jeffrey Hantman ("Between Powhatan and Quirank: Reconstructing Monacan Culture and History in the Context of Jamestown," unpublished essay, 1989) has studied the Monacan tribes just above the falls, and Frederick Fausz has convincingly reinterpreted the relations between the Indians and the English in the first years of contact, in "The Invasion of Virginia: Indians, Colonialism, and the Conquest of Cant: A Review Essay on Anglo-Indian Relations in the Chesapeake," *Virginia Magazine of History and Biography* 95, no. 2 (April 1987): 1333–56, and "'An Abundance of Blood Shed on Both Sides': England's First Indian War, 1609–1624," *Virginia Magazine of History and Biography* 98, no. 1 (January 1990): 3–57. Early descriptions of Virginia and its inhabitants, useful for a contemporary perspective, include Robert Beverley's *The History and Present State of Virginia*, edited with an introduction by Louis B. Wright (Chapel Hill: University of North Carolina Press, 1947); Thomas Jefferson's *Notes on Virginia*, edited with an introduction by William Peden (Chapel Hill: University of North Carolina Press, 1958); and William Byrd's *Natural History of Virginia, or the Newly Discovered Eden*, edited by Richard Beatty and William Molloy (Richmond: Dietz Press, 1940).

The sense of a changing and dynamic English world and the fear of chaos is brought to life in Carl Bridenbaugh's *Vexed and Troubled Englishmen, 1590–1642* (New York: Oxford University Press, 1968), and two books by Christopher Hill: *Reformation to Industrial Revolution: The Making of Modern English Society, 1530–1780* (New York: Pantheon Books, 1967) and *The World Turned Upside Down: Radical Ideas during the English Revolution* (New York: Viking Press, 1972). The ambitions of gentlemen adventurers are described in Anthony Esler's

The Aspiring Mind of the Elizabethan Younger Generation (Durham, N.C.: Duke University Press, 1966). Bacon's Rebellion of 1676 gave evidence of later forms of English ambition and involved English, Africans, and Indians near the falls; several works have examined this subject, including Jane Carson, *Bacon's Rebellion: 1676 to 1976* (Jamestown, Va.: The Jamestown Foundation, 1976); Wilcomb Washburn, *The Governor and the Rebel: A History of Bacon's Rebellion in Virginia* (Chapel Hill: University of North Carolina Press, 1957); Stephen Saunders Webb, *1676: The End of American Independence* (New York: Knopf, 1984); and T. J. Wertenbaker, *Bacon's Rebellion, 1676*, rev. ed. (Charlottesville: University Press of Virginia, 1957). Wertenbaker ennobled Bacon as "torchbearer of the Revolution" in his effort to find the origins of the American Revolution in the rebellion, and Washburn's 1957 study redressed the balance in favor of Governor Berkeley. Edmund Morgan's *American Slavery, American Freedom: The Ordeal of Colonial Virginia* (New York: W. W. Norton, 1975) remains the most persuasive attempt to sort out the mix of peoples that created both slavery and a rhetoric of freedom in Virginia, and his comments on Bacon's Rebellion and the Virginia frontier are perceptive. Wilcomb Washburn's assessment of Bacon's motives stands up well when considered in conjunction with Rountree's and Fausz's more recent accounts of the history of Anglo-Powhatan relations. Another work, both useful and readable, is W. Stitt Robinson, *The Southern Colonial Frontier, 1607–1763* (Albuquerque: University of New Mexico Press, 1979).

For the English experience of the New World, there is no substitute for reading the vivid accounts of the dramatis personae, beginning with the two Richard Hakluyts, who provide a pragmatic rationale for colonization and are the first of an army of promoters for Virginia. See Richard Hakluyt, "Particular Discourse of the Western Planting," in E. G. R. Taylor, ed., *The Original Writings and Correspondence of the two Richard Hakluyts*, Hakluyt Society Publications, 2d ser. (London, 1935). Accounts of Virginia by John Smith, Ralph Hamor, John Rolfe, Gabriel Archer, and William Strachey have been republished many times since their first appearances in

London. The first American collection was Peter Force, coll., *Tracts and Other Papers Relating Principally to the Origin, Settlement and Progress of the Colonies in North America*, 4 vols. (Washington, 1836–46). More recently, Philip Barbour edited *The Complete Works of Captain John Smith*, 3 vols. (Chapel Hill: University of North Carolina Press for the Institute of Early American History and Culture, 1986). John Stilgoe's *The Common Landscape of America: 1580–1845* (New Haven: Yale University Press, 1982) and D. W. Meinig's *The Shaping of America: A Geographical Perspective on 500 Years of History*, vol. 1: *Atlantic America, 1492–1800* (New Haven: Yale University Press, 1988) offer broad studies that place Virginia and the site of Richmond in a continental geographic and historical context. The names and histories of early English women settlers in Virginia are also beginning to emerge. See David Ransome's "Wives for Virginia, 1621," *William and Mary Quarterly*, 3d ser., 48, no. 1 (January 1991), 3–18, including the debate in his footnotes over data used to assess social and geographic origins.

Native Americans grew in symbolic importance as they declined in numbers and power. Pocahontas has been a literary inspiration for Americans and Europeans for more than three centuries, and generations of black and white Richmonders have claimed her as an Indian foremother. Jay Hubbell's "The Smith-Pocahontas Story in Literature," *Virginia Magazine of History and Biography* 65 (July 1957): 275–300, traces this usage. See also Philip Barbour, *Pocahontas and Her World: A Chronicle of America's First Settlement* (Boston: Houghton Mifflin, 1970); E. McClung Fleming, "The American Image as Indian Princess, 1765–1783," *Winterthur Portfolio* 2 (1965): 65–81, and "From Indian Princess to Greek Goddess: The American Image," *Winterthur Portfolio* 3 (1967): 37–66; G. W. P. Custis, *Pocahontas: Or, The Settlers of Virginia* (Philadelphia: C. Alexander, 1830); and Rayna Green, "The Pocahontas Perplex: The Image of Indian Women in American Culture," *Massachusetts Review* 16 (Autumn 1975): 698–714.

Four intriguing articles that describe the changing relations between three races in Virginia are featured in *Virginia Magazine of History and Biography* 95, no. 2 (April

1987), a special issue. See also Peter Wallenstein, "Indian Foremothers: Race, Sex, Slavery, and Freedom in Early National Virginia" (paper presented at the meeting of the Society of Historians of the Early American Republic, Gettysburg, Pa., July 1992), and James H. Johnston, "Documentary Evidence of the Relations of Negroes and Indians," *Journal of Negro History* 14, no. 1 (January 1929): 29–30.

Colonial Virginia: Planters, Slaves, Towns, and Trade

Chesapeake studies, especially the works of cultural and social history written since 1970, vastly enlarge an understanding of life at and near the falls of the James River before the American Revolution. Studies by Cary Carson, Dell Upton, Lois Green Carr, Lorena Walsh, Philip D. Morgan and others, individually and in various collaborations, have appeared regularly in *Winterthur Portfolio*, *William and Mary Quarterly*, *Virginia Magazine of History and Biography*, and such essay collections as Thad Tate and David Ammerman, eds., *The Chesapeake in the Seventeenth Century: Essays on Anglo-American Society* (Chapel Hill: University of North Carolina Press, 1979); Stephen Innes, ed., *Work and Labor in Early America* (Chapel Hill: University of North Carolina Press, 1988); Jack P. Greene and J. R. Pole, eds., *Colonial British America: Essays in the New History of the Early Modern Era* (Baltimore: Johns Hopkins University Press, 1984); and Lois Green Carr, Philip Morgan, and Jean B. Russo, eds., *Colonial Chesapeake Society* (Chapel Hill: University of North Carolina Press, 1988). Much of their research concerns the immigration ratios, domestic consumption, and marriage patterns of male and female whites in the Chesapeake area, and the evolution of their gender expectations. Darret and Anita Rutman's *A Place in Time: Middlesex County, Virginia, 1650–1750* (New York: W. W. Norton, 1984) is exemplary in its depiction of a dispersed but fully connected and kinship-centered rural community in seventeenth-century Virginia; it provides a model that can be applied to Henrico.

Town development in Virginia was erratically encouraged by British colonial policy but was more often the product of natural and convenient sites for trade and land speculation by a proprietor. Town planning and its relation to speculative and commercial aspirations in Virginia is well documented in John Reps, *Tidewater Towns: City Planning in Colonial Virginia and Maryland* (Williamsburg: Colonial Williamsburg Foundation, 1972); Joseph A. Ernst and H. Roy Merrens, "'Camden's Turrets Pierce the Sky!': The Urban Process in the Southern Colonies during the Eighteenth Century," *William and Mary Quarterly*, 3d ser., 30 (October 1973): 549–74; Carville Earle and Ronald Hoffman, "The Urban South: The First Two Centuries," in Blaine Brownell and David R. Goldfield, *The City in Southern History: The Growth of Urban Civilization in the South* (Port Washington, N.Y.: Kennikat Press, 1977). Brownell and Goldfield note that southern towns often developed for the convenience of the countryside and that this distinction from northern cities continued over time.

In his *An Historical Geography of Urban System Development: Tidewater Virginia in the Eighteenth Century* (York University Geographical Monographs, no. 13, 1983), James O'Mara argues that Virginia planters desired towns, perhaps more than the British crown did; but William Byrd, proprietor at the falls of the James, did not desire to give up his trade monopoly. Colonial policy, however, prevailed over private profit. Jacob Price, in *Capital and Credit in British Overseas Trade: The View from the Chesapeake, 1700–1766* (Cambridge: Harvard University Press, 1980), has traced the tobacco trade and the Scottish firms who had agents and stores up the rivers from the Chesapeake. Lois Green Carr and Lorena Walsh's "Changing Lifestyles and Consumer Behavior in the Colonial Chesapeake" (unpublished paper presented to the United States Capitol Historical Society, Washington, D.C., 1989), is an excellent study on changes in stores, merchants, and consumer goods in the late seventeenth and early eighteenth centuries; it demonstrates how similar the lives of the early planters were to the lives of people who owned very little land. Patterns changed in the eighteenth century as merchandise grew more available and planters acquired more consumer goods that set them apart from their neighbors.

Improving conditions in England and increased opportunities north of the Chesapeake reduced the number of indentured servants in Virginia in the late 1600s, and the Royal African Company stepped up its slave importations. Winthrop Jordan's argument that slavery and concepts of racial inferiority reinforced each other as the need for black labor grew remains persuasive for the area of the Chesapeake frontier that became Richmond. When the Royal African company lost its slave trade monopoly in 1698, other companies raced to bring Africans to the Chesapeake. The debate over the evolution of Chesapeake slavery is reviewed in Alden Vaughn, "The Origins Debate: Slavery and Racism in Seventeenth-Century Virginia," *Virginia Magazine of History and Biography* 97 (July 1989): 311–54, but without resolution. Edmund Morgan's analysis of the conditions that brought about Virginia slavery still seems to be the best source; see Morgan, *American Slavery, American Freedom: The Ordeal of Colonial Virginia* (New York: W. W. Norton, 1975). On the construction of race as an important ideology in Virginia, see two articles by Barbara J. Fields: "Ideology and Race in American History," in *Region, Race, and Reconstruction: Essays in Honor of C. Vann Woodward*, J. Morgan Kousser and James McPherson, eds. (New York: Oxford University Press, 1982), and "Slavery, Race, and Ideology in the United States of America," *New Left Review* 181 (May–June 1990): 95–118.

As Ira Berlin noted in "Time, Space and the Evolution of Afro-American Society on British Mainland North America," *American Historical Review* 85 (1980): 44–78, Chesapeake slavery was the first to develop and differed from slavery to the north and to the south. Tobacco, Virginia's first staple crop, did not use a labor force in the same way that rice, cotton, or sugar would. In the vast and variegated international slave trade of the sixteenth through nineteenth centuries, North America received only 5 percent of the slaves transported from Africa, but by the mid-nineteenth century, primarily through natural increase, this continent had a majority of the slaves. See Philip Curtin, *The Atlantic Slave Trade: A Census* (Madison: University of Wisconsin Press, 1969), and James A. Rawley, *The Transatlantic Slave Trade: A History* (New York: W. W. Norton, 1981).

We know little about the lives of ex-indentured servants and families with small holdings in the colonial Chesapeake. What we do know comes from the work of Carr and Walsh, the Rutmans, and pioneer researchers like Julia Cherry Spruill, *Women's Life and Work in the Southern Colonies* (1938; reprint ed., New York: W. W. Norton, 1972). Ordinary people, indignant or fearful, boisterous or subdued, come to us in their own words in the court documents of the colonial period—for example, those collected in Warren Billings, ed., *The Old Dominion in the Seventeenth Century: A Documentary History of Virginia, 1606–1689* (Chapel Hill: University of North Carolina Press for the Institute of Early American History and Culture, 1975). The massive importation of Africans into Virginia in the mid-eighteenth century brought the social and economic change described in Allan Kulikoff's *Tobacco and Slaves: The Development of Southern Culture in the Chesapeake, 1680–1800* (Chapel Hill: University of North Carolina Press for the Institute of Early American History and Culture, 1986). Kulikoff also speculates on the origins of the African American family in "The Origins of Afro-American Society in Tidewater Maryland and Virginia, 1700–1790," *William and Mary Quarterly*, 3d ser., 35 (April 1978): 226–59. In his *The Negro in Eighteenth-Century Williamsburg* (Williamsburg: Colonial Williamsburg Foundation, 1965), Thad Tate presents aspects of urban colonial Virginia black life as Richmond was about to grow from Williamsburg transplants.

Planter society became distinct and distinctly visible in the 1720s and 1730s, when successful landholders built imposing residences and began to elaborate a culture and society in which they meant to aggrandize their wealth by displaying it. Here the ethnographic studies of Rhys Isaac, T. H. Breen, and others are very important in determining the significance of dress, gesture, leisure activity, architectural style, ritual, and display in colonial Virginia. In *The Transformation of Virginia, 1740–1790* (Chapel Hill: University of North Carolina Press, 1982), Isaac describes a Virginia gentry that first elaborated a hierarchy and then saw it weakened by Baptist evangelicalism and patriotic republicanism. Isaac also describes the system of signs on the landscape and establishes the dual visions and merged visions of African Virginians and Anglo-Virginians which are central to understanding Richmond's culture for the next two centuries. Breen's *Tobacco Culture: The Mentality of the Great Tidewater Planters on the Eve of the Revolution* (Princeton: Princeton University Press, 1985) focuses on tobacco planters and the manner in which the indebtedness and borrowing characteristic of tobacco culture was expressed in planter politics and society. The legal status of their wives and other colonial women gets an initial exploration in Suzanne Lebsock, *"'A Share of Honour'": Virginia Women, 1600–1945* (Richmond: Virginia State Library, 1987), chapter 2.

Landscape and the Built Environment

Architecture in colonial Virginia is examined in Cary Carson et al., "Impermanent Architecture in the Southern American Colonies," *Winterthur Portfolio* 16 (Summer/ Autumn 1981): 135–96. This article provides a careful view of the Chesapeake frontier landscape and describes as characteristic both an impermanent architecture and a "Virginia house" that, together, best met the needs of early settlement. John M. Vlach, in "Afro-American Domestic Artifacts in Eighteenth-Century Virginia," *Material Culture* 19 (Spring 1987): 3–23, and Mechal Sobel, in *The World They Made Together: Black and White Values in Eighteenth-Century Virginia* (Princeton: Princeton University Press, 1987), document their conviction that Africans in eighteenth-century Virginia contributed to the style and standards for housing, music, religious belief, food preparation, and other aspects of Virginia culture. In his *Pursuits of Happiness: The Social Development of Early Modern British Colonies and the Formation of American Culture* (Chapel Hill: University of North Carolina Press, 1988), Jack P. Greene proposed that the Chesapeake represented the real origins of American society, while New England was something of an aberration. Greene's thesis strengthens the case for the nation as an African and European culture. Richmond provides evidence that aspects of culture, material and other, were transmitted in both directions, while political and economic power remained predominantly in white hands.

Richmond's homes, neighborhoods, and architecture can be explored in a variety of sources. The best primary sources for domestic furnishings are found in the wills and probate inventories of county records, although these sources may neglect humble but significant items. The policies of the Mutual Assurance Society, held at the Valentine Museum in Richmond, and the files and publications of the Virginia Historic Landmarks Commission contain information on many specific early residences. Henry Glassie's *Pattern in the Material Folk Culture of the Eastern United States* (Philadelphia: University of Pennsylvania Press, 1969) and *Folk Housing in Middle Virginia: A Structural Analysis of Historic Artifacts* (Knoxville: University of Tennessee Press, 1975) trace the migration of folk architecture and other material forms in the countryside surrounding Richmond. Dell Upton's "New Views of the Virginia Landscape," *Virginia Magazine of History and Biography* 96 (Oct 1988): 403–70, is a useful overview of suburbanization and combines landscape, architecture, and domestic interiors in Virginia. His assessment of the consumer revolution of the eighteenth century is particularly pertinent for Richmond and its rapid growth after the Revolution.

Mary Wingfield Scott was simultaneously pioneering and elegiac as she documented and photographed hundreds of Richmond houses from the 1930s through the 1950s in *Houses of Old Richmond* (New York: Bonanza Books, 1941) and *Old Richmond Neighborhoods* (Richmond: Whittet and Shepperson, 1950). Her ability to see merit in modest structures and her well-founded fears for their survival combined to give Richmond an outstanding history of its houses and neighborhoods, supplemented with public record research on each building. Other contributions to a pictorial history of Richmond and regional architecture include Paul Dulaney's *The Architecture of Historic Richmond* (Charlottesville: University Press of Virginia, 1968) and Robert P. Winthrop's *Architecture in Downtown Richmond* (Richmond: Junior Board of the Historic Richmond Foundation, 1982). Good general sources include David Lowenthal's "Age and Artifact: Dilemmas of Interpretation," in D. W.

Meinig, ed., *The Interpretation of Ordinary Landscape* (New York: Oxford University Press, 1979), 103–28, and Lowenthal's "Past Time, Present Place: Landscape and Memory," *Geography Review* 65 (January 1975), 1–36, for understanding the role of commemorative public space over time. On the work of particular architects in Richmond, see Sarah Shields Driggs, "Otis Manson and Neoclassicism in Central Virginia" (M.A. thesis, University of Virginia, 1988); William B. O'Neal and Christopher Weeks, *The Work of William Lawrence Bottomley in Richmond* (Charlottesville: University Press of Virginia, 1985); Edward Carter, John C. Van Horne, and Charles E. Brownell, eds., *Latrobe's View of America, 1795–1820: Selections from the Watercolors and Sketches* (New Haven: Yale University Press, 1983); and Edward Zimmer and Pamela Scott, "Alexander Parris, Benjamin Henry Latrobe, and the John Wickham House in Richmond, Virginia," *Journal of the Society of Architectural Historians* 41 (1982): 202–11.

One can find early evidence of Richmond land speculation and the development of suburban living in Samuel Mordecai's *Virginia, especially Richmond, in By-Gone Days*, 2d ed. (Richmond: West and Johnson, 1860), which describes the real estate boom and bust of 1816–20. In "A History of the Fan District" (unpubl. ms. in author's possession), Drew Carneal discusses the land promotion and development schemes of some early city fathers who owned land west of the capitol. A similar history of Church Hill, to the east, awaits its chronicler, although Mary Wingfield Scott's research of the neighborhoods provides a good start. John Stilgoe's *Borderlands: Origins of the American Suburb, 1820–1939* (New Haven: Yale University Press, 1988) traces the American dream of the suburban middle landscape right back to the time of Mordecai's account and demonstrates that Richmond followed national trends in suburban development and architectural style. Abundant examples of late-nineteenth- and twentieth-century promotional brochures extolling the sunlight and air of Richmond's suburban subdivisions exist in the Virginia State Library. They are remarkable for their similarity of values, whether addressed to elite white families or to middle-class black families.

The Revolutionary Era and a New Capital

The work of Allan Kulikoff and T. H. Breen explores the effect of the Revolution on Chesapeake gentry and slaves; see Kulikoff, *Tobacco and Slaves: The Development of Southern Culture in the Chesapeake, 1680–1800* (Chapel Hill: University of North Carolina Press for the Institute of Early American History and Culture, 1986), and Breen, *Tobacco Culture: The Mentality of the Great Tidewater Planters on the Eve of the Revolution* (Princeton: Princeton University Press, 1985). In addition to Edmund Morgan's study of the ideology of slavery and freedom in Virginia (*American Slavery, American Freedom: The Ordeal of Colonial Virginia* [New York: W. W. Norton, 1975]), useful studies of this convoluted topic include Robert McColley, *Slavery and Jeffersonian Virginia*, 2d ed. (Urbana: University of Illinois Press, 1973), and John Chester Miller, *The Wolf by the Ears: Thomas Jefferson and Slavery* (New York: Free Press, 1977). In *Richmond during the Revolution* (Charlottesville: University Press of Virginia, 1977), Harry M. Ward and Harold E. Greer, Jr., supply anecdotes of Richmond's experience in the Revolutionary era.

Richmond after the Revolution was a growing city that embraced both republicanism and capitalism. Joyce Appleby's view of capitalism as an intellectual adjunct to republicanism, put forth in *Capitalism and a New Social Order: The Republican Vision of the 1790s* (New York: New York University Press, 1984), fits the small, ambitious city. Thomas Doerflinger, in *A Vigorous Spirit of Enterprise* (Chapel Hill: University of North Carolina Press, 1986), described the entrepreneurial spirit of American cities in the early republic and suggested that Virginians erred in not gaining control of the tobacco trade from the exiting British. But it is not clear that merchants in Richmond or other Virginia towns could have successfully competed with the more developed trade systems of the major port cities—New York, Philadelphia, and Baltimore.

The republican doctrines so ardently espoused from the 1770s until the 1820s were the basis for the conspiracy of the Richmond slave Gabriel in 1800. This attempted slave revolt has now begun to receive the close study it deserves, in Philip Schwarz, *Twice Condemned: Slaves and the Criminal Laws of Virginia* (Baton Rouge: Louisiana State University Press, 1988), and Douglas Egerton, *Gabriel's Rebellion: The Virginia Slave Conspiracies of 1800 and 1802* (Chapel Hill: University of North Carolina Press, 1993). Studies that trace Virginia politics in this era include Richard Beeman, *The Old Dominion and the New Nation, 1788–1801* (Lexington: University Press of Kentucky, 1972), and Drew McCoy, *The Elusive Republic: Political Economy in Jeffersonian Virginia* (Chapel Hill: University of North Carolina Press, 1980).

Thomas Haskell's "Capitalism and the Origins of the Humanitarian Sensibility," *American Historical Review* 90, nos. 2 and 3 (April–June 1985): 339–61, 547–66, links the spread of humanitarianism with the values of early capitalism; this connection may explain the number of schools and benevolent societies that appeared in Richmond in the 1790s, many of them founded by or for women. Suzanne Lebsock's important work *The Free Women of Petersburg: Status and Culture in a Southern Town, 1784–1860* (New York: W. W. Norton, 1983) notes the increase in separate estates for women as well as the increase in female benevolence through the antebellum period. She finds that in Petersburg, by the 1850s men had taken over the societies begun by women; there is little evidence of this change in Richmond, however. The proliferation and diversity of schools, listed in Margaret Meagher's *History of Education in Richmond* (Richmond: Works Progress Administration, 1939), suited the capital of a new state; schools were also appropriate as a concern of mothers in a republic. For more commentary on "republican mothers," see Linda Kerber, *Women of the Republic: Intellect and Ideology in Revolutionary America* (Chapel Hill: University of North Carolina Press, 1980), and Mary Beth Norton, *Liberty's Daughters: The Revolutionary Experience of American Women, 1750–1800* (Boston: Little, Brown, 1980). For a general discussion of antebellum education, see Joseph Kett, *Rites of Passage: Adolescence in America, 1790 to the Present* (New York: Basic Books, 1977).

Four unpublished works proved to be very useful sources of information about eighteenth- and nineteenth-century Richmond. The manuscript history of Richmond to 1860 by Wirt Armistead Cate (typescript, Valentine Museum collections, circa 1943) was useful for its detailed listings of theaters, schools, and the physical structures of early Richmond. Drew Carneal ("A History of the Fan District," unpubl. ms. in author's possession) has done much the same for the Fan District in a manuscript especially valuable for its imaginative use of public documents. The five-volume typescript "Richmond on the James," circa 1925–27, by Edward Valentine (Valentine Museum collections) provides corroborating detail on a variety of subjects, and his effort to map neighborhoods of the 1790s, dwelling by dwelling, enables one to "tour" the early city with confidence. Jay Worrall's three-volume history of the Quakers in Virginia ("Friendly Virginians," 1991, typescript in author's possession) contains much information about that group's activities and members in Richmond in the early republic.

Richmond in the Early Republic

Richmond's planter-connected politicians, merchants, and lawyers developed a distinctive culture. Bertram Wyatt-Brown, in *Southern Honor: Ethics and Behavior in the Old South* (New York: Oxford University Press, 1982); Edward L. Ayers, in *Vengeance and Justice: Crime and Punishment in the Nineteenth-Century American South* (New York: Oxford University Press, 1984); and A. G. Roeber, in *Faithful Magistrates and Republican Lawyers: Creators of Virginia Legal Culture, 1680–1810* (Chapel Hill: University of North Carolina Press, 1981), have explored aspects of this conjunction of legal and social culture, its connection with republicanism, and its symbols. Richmond lawyer William Wirt's rhetoric and his writing (*The Letters of the British Spy, The Old Bachelor, A Life of Patrick Henry*), which extolled a lost and perhaps imaginary Virginia planter society, is the most eloquent example of this style. This culture reflected the presence of a civic elite of lawyers and wealthy merchants connected by kinship and business with the state's planters. These connections are examined in two studies of pivotal political moments in 1829 and 1831: Alison Goodyear Freehling's *Drift toward Dissolution: The*

Virginia Slavery Debate of 1831–1832 (Baton Rouge: Louisiana State University Press, 1982), and Dickson Bruce's *The Rhetoric of Conservatism: The Virginia Conventions of 1829–1830 and the Conservative Tradition of the South* (San Marino, Calif.: Huntington Library, 1982). Letters, newspapers, and patent applications suggest that planter dominance in politics and society did not preclude entrepreneurial ambition. In addition, as the city grew, a web of slave and free black connections spread out within it; evidence of this growing web can be found in church and benevolent society records, police daybooks, runaway ads, employee lists, and probate records.

Patricia Click's University of Virginia dissertation ("Leisure in the Upper South in the Nineteenth Century: A Study of Trends in Baltimore, Norfolk, and Richmond" [1980]) and her book, *The Spirit of the Times: Amusements in Nineteenth-Century Baltimore, Norfolk, and Richmond* (Charlottesville: University Press of Virginia, 1989), describe gentry and popular amusements and note the effect of both evangelicalism and loss of exclusivity on horse racing, dancing, theaters, and other forms of entertainment. The rise of the evangelical woman, as described by Donald Mathews in *Religion in the Old South* (Chicago: University of Chicago Press, 1977), was apparent in Richmond at this period, and these women appeared to be more numerous, influential, and self-aware than the "republican mothers" of an earlier generation. Books of moral direction and household management published in Richmond and letters between Richmond family members—for example, the Wickham family letters held at the Virginia Historical Society—point to a new emphasis on the domestic circle and the mother's role, as suggested by Jan Lewis's *The Pursuit of Happiness: Family and Values in Jefferson's Virginia* (New York: Cambridge University Press, 1983) and the first section of Karen Halttunen's *Confidence Men and Painted Women: A Study of Middle-Class Culture in America, 1830–1870* (New Haven: Yale University Press, 1982). Although Jean Friedman, in *The Enclosed Garden: Women and Community in the Evangelical South, 1830–1900* (Chapel Hill: University of North Carolina Press, 1985), concludes that a male-dominated evan-

gelicalism constricted women, Richmond evidence suggests that it gave women—and blacks—social space and an opportunity for a little discreet independence. In *Poe's Richmond* (reprint ed., Richmond: Poe Associates, 1978), Agnes Bondurant admirably brings forward the popular culture and commercial base of the city from the 1820s through the 1840s.

Richmond as an Antebellum Industrial City

Perhaps the key question for the antebellum period is this: what difference did urban slave and free black labor make in Richmond's industrial expansion and class formation? In its pragmatic business orientation, its evangelical enthusiasm, and the formation of its middle class, it appears much like the New York described by Mary Ryan in *Cradle of the Middle Class: The Family in Oneida County, New York, 1790–1865* (Cambridge: Cambridge University Press, 1981), and by Paul Johnson in *A Shopkeeper's Millenium: Society and Revivals in Rochester, New York, 1815–1837* (New York: Hill and Wang, 1978). However, the formation of Richmond's urban free black and slave families is not yet factored in adequately, although Marie Tyler-McGraw and Gregg Kimball's *In Bondage and Freedom: Antebellum Black Life in Richmond, Virginia* (Richmond: The Valentine Museum, 1988) makes a beginning. Nor is the impact of women on the formation of those values considered "middle-class" sufficiently understood. Two books that supplement the class hypothesis that Stuart Blumin puts forth in *The Emergence of the Middle Class: Social Experience in the American City, 1760–1900* (Cambridge: Cambridge University Press, 1989) are Anne Firor Scott, *Natural Allies: Women's Associations in American History* (Urbana: University of Illinois Press, 1991), and Mary P. Ryan, *Women in Public: Between Banners and Ballots 1825–1880* (Baltimore: Johns Hopkins University Press, 1990).

The number of hired slaves, the nature of their work, the skill levels of immigrant labor, and the rate at which labor, free and slave, left the city are a few of the many questions that surround the late-antebellum period, when Richmond industrialized rapidly and attracted sig-

nificant immigration. In his *Slavery in the Cities: The South, 1820–1860* (New York: Oxford University Press, 1964), Richard C. Wade suggested that hired slaves were being pulled from the cities in the late-antebellum era because urban slavery was destabilizing to the system. Claudia Goldin, author of *Urban Slavery in the American South, 1820–1860: A Quantitative History* (Chicago: University of Chicago Press, 1976), believed that late-antebellum urban slaves were being pushed to the cotton fields. In *Slavery and Freedom on the Middle Ground: Maryland during the Nineteenth Century* (New Haven: Yale University Press, 1985), Barbara Fields argued that slavery could not provide the basis for urban or industrial development. Baltimore is her example of a city where slavery declined and growth was rapid, but Baltimore also had superior natural advantages for trade. Richmond was more dependent on tobacco factories, in which hired slave labor appeared to have been a rational choice. Hired slaves were cost-effective for Richmond and aided rather than impeded Richmond's industrial growth. The extent to which local skilled slave labor was sold out of the city is also unknown. The fact that Richmond was a major slave market does not mean that most or many of the slaves were local. Slaves sold to the South from Richmond came from Virginia and even North Carolina plantations, and the sales were handled by local agents.

Important studies of free blacks, immigrant labor, and industrial slavery, mostly in Richmond, include Ira Berlin, *Slaves Without Masters: The Free Negro in the Antebellum South* (New York: Pantheon, 1974); John T. O'Brien, "Factory, Church, and Community: Blacks in Antebellum Richmond," *Journal of Southern History* 44 (November 1978): 509–36; and Rodney D. Green, "Industrial Transition in the Land of Chattel Slavery: Richmond 1820–1860" (Ph.D. diss., American University, 1980). Industrial slavery is covered in Robert Starobin, *Industrial Slavery in the Old South* (New York: Oxford University Press, 1970); Ronald L. Lewis, *Coal, Iron, and Slaves: Industrial Slavery in Maryland and Virginia, 1715–1865* (Westport, Conn.: Greenwood Press, 1979); and Charles B. Dew, *Ironmaker to the Confederacy: Joseph R. Anderson and the Tredegar Iron Works* (New Haven: Yale

University Press, 1966). The earlier work of Kathleen Bruce, *Virginia Iron Manufacture in the Slave Era* (New York: Century, 1931), remains useful as well.

It is true that Richmond attracted a high percentage of skilled immigrants who came purposefully to the city for specific jobs; see Ira Berlin with Herbert Gutman, "Natives and Immigrants, Free Men and Slaves: Urban Workingmen in the Antebellum South," *American Historical Review* 88 (December 1983): 1175–1200, and three articles by Randall Miller: "Immigrants in the Old South," *Immigrant History Newsletter* 10 (November 1978): 8–12; "The Fabric of Control: Slavery in Antebellum Southern Textile Mills," *Business History Review* 55 (1981): 471–90; and "The Enemy Within: Some Effects of Foreign Immigrants on Antebellum Southern Cities," *Southern Studies* 24 (Spring 1985): 30–53. However, the percentages presented by Berlin and Gutman seem extremely high. Gregg Kimball of the Valentine Museum has made a start at reevaluating skilled and unskilled categories in Richmond. See Gregg D. Kimball, "African-Virginians and the Vernacular Building Tradition in Richmond City, 1790–1860," in *Perspectives in American Vernacular Architecture* (St. Louis: University of Missouri Press, forthcoming); "Race and Class in a Southern City: Richmond, 1865–1920" (unpublished paper presented to the Organization of American Historians, Louisville, Ky., April 1991); and "The Working People of Richmond: Life and Labor in an Industrial City, 1865–1920," *Labor's Heritage* 3, no. 2 (April 1991): 66–77.

The work of John Blassingame, Eugene Genovese, Herbert Gutman, Ira Berlin, and Lawrence Levine is useful for understanding the nature of the slave communities in Richmond during the decades before the Civil War. Blassingame, in *The Slave Community: Plantation Life in the Antebellum South* (New York: Oxford University Press, 1972), and Genovese, in *Roll, Jordan, Roll: The World the Slaves Made* (New York: Vintage Books, 1974), evoke a slave world where kinship ties and religious belief mitigate against the loss of self in a white-dominated society. The plantation model on which these studies are based is useful for Richmond because most hired slaves grew up in the surround-ing countryside before being hired out. Levine's *Black Culture and Black Consciousness: Afro-American Folk Thought from Slavery to Freedom* (New York: Oxford University Press, 1977) crosses from the antebellum to the postbellum eras, and that span is particularly useful for assessing Richmond, where African Americans maintained cultural continuity despite Emancipation. The Brooks family of Richmond is an excellent example of the pre–Civil War move from slavery to freedom, as illustrated in *A Brooks Family Chronicle*, by Walter and Charlotte Brooks (Washington, D.C.: typescript, 1989).

Richmond trailed behind as the South moved toward secession; the prospect of secession was painful for civic leaders and most residents. David Goldfield's *Urban Growth in the Age of Sectionalism: Virginia, 1847–1861* (Baton Rouge: Louisiana State University Press, 1977) sketches the economy and politics of late-antebellum Richmond. The city was an exception to the southern urban pattern, which centered on agricultural processing; it aspired to further industrial expansion within a national economy. Daniel W. Crofts's *Reluctant Confederates: Upper South Unionists in the Secession Crisis* (Chapel Hill: University of North Carolina Press, 1989) explores the dilemmas faced by Unionists in the Virginia secession convention and, in particular, draws out the implications of behind-the-scenes maneuvering by fire-eaters.

Civil War and Reconstruction

Historians have frequently noted that secession and the Civil War finally did what the South feared the federal union would do: first interfered with slavery and then ended it. The vast bibliography of the Civil War has treated Richmond as the center of Confederate political and military strategy and has usually focused on the activities of high-ranking officers and officials and their diary-keeping wives. But the city was also a place under constant siege—a place of refugees, shortages, illegal trade, spies, martial law, industrial expansion, technological experimentation, hospitals, and the extensive employment of black and female labor. James McPherson's *Battle Cry of Freedom: The Civil War Era* (New York: Oxford University Press, 1988) provides a useful background for a consideration of Richmond's Civil War experience and reaffirms that slavery was the central divisive issue. Another recent overview—*Why the South Lost the Civil War*, by Richard E. Beringer et al. (Athens: University of Georgia Press, 1986), reviews the reasons for the Confederacy's loss and concludes that it was an insufficient sense of nationalism, rather than insufficient industrial capacity, men, and supplies. Richmond's Confederate nationalism, scarcely in evidence before secession, quickly became and remained highly visible, although it was arguably more a reaction to war than an embrace of secessionist doctrine. Emory Thomas, in *The Confederacy as a Revolutionary Experience* (Englewood Cliffs, N.J.: Prentice Hall, 1971), looked at how wartime exigencies reshaped fundamental institutions and assumptions in the South and certainly in Richmond.

For a specific focus on Richmond, see Emory Thomas, *The Confederate State of Richmond: A Biography of the Capital* (Austin: University of Texas Press, 1971); Louis H. Manarin, ed., *Richmond at War: The Minutes of the City Council, 1861–1865* (Chapel Hill: University of North Carolina Press, 1966); and Katharine Jones, *Ladies of Richmond: Confederate Capital* (Indianapolis: Bobbs-Merrill, 1962), which provides first-person accounts. Richmond newspapers were never more important than during the Civil War, which they reported, criticized, and influenced. A good account with Richmond at the center is J. Cutler Andrews, *The South Reports the Civil War* (Pittsburgh: University of Pittsburgh Press, 1985). Richmond's railroads and iron foundries were vital to the Confederacy; these two concerns are covered in Angus Johnston's *Virginia Railroads in the Civil War* (Chapel Hill: University of North Carolina Press, 1961) and Charles B. Dew's *Ironmaker to the Confederacy: Joseph R. Anderson and the Tredegar Iron Works* (New Haven: Yale University Press, 1966). The city council's efforts to proceed with local matters, manfully if occasionally dimly, while the Confederacy and the state government usurped city space and prerogatives, is revealed in *Richmond At War: The Minutes of the City Council, 1861–1865*, edited by Louis Manarin (Chapel

Hill: University of North Carolina Press for the Richmond Civil War Centennial Committee, 1966).

The first real attention historians paid to southern women was to document their activities during the Civil War. In Richmond, as elsewhere, the diaries and memoirs written by women in that painful period aided researchers in that documenting process. Most frequently cited are the diary of Mary Chesnut, *Mary Chesnut's Civil War*, edited by C. Vann Woodward (New Haven: Yale University Press, 1981); the memoir of hospital matron Phoebe Yates Pember, *A Southern Woman's Story: Life in Confederate Richmond*, edited by Bell Wiley (Jackson, Tenn.: McCowat-Mercer Press, 1959); and Sally Putnam's *In Richmond during the War: Four Years of Personal Observation* (New York: G. W. Carleton, 1867). While women's heroism and sacrifice in the Confederate capital has long been celebrated, historians are now beginning to disaggregate women's experience to gauge the extent of class tensions, disaffection with the war, and disruption of southern institutions. Drew Gilpin Faust, in "Altars of Sacrifice: Confederate Women and the Narratives of War," *Journal of American History* 76, no. 4 (March 1990): 1200–1228, has provided an analysis of the ideological goals of Confederate public discourse and suggested that the failure of the Confederacy occurred when women deserted the cause and abandoned the altars of sacrifice. Two analyses of the Bread Riot—Michael Chesson's "Harlots or Heroines?: A New Look at the Richmond Bread Riot," *Virginia Magazine of History and Biography* 92 (April 1984): 131–75, and Susan Barber's "'The Quiet Battles of the Home Front War': Civil War Bread Riots and the Development of a Confederate Welfare System" (M.A. thesis, University of Maryland, 1988)—consider its organization and participants and, in so doing, expose a new side of Confederate Richmond. Tracey Weiss considers the changes in the lives of Richmond's black women during the 1860s in two papers: "What Price Freedom?: Emancipation and African American Property Holding in Richmond, Virginia" (paper presented to the Social Science History Association, Minneapolis, Minn., October 1990) and "The Transition to Free Labor Reconsidered: Households,

Domesticity, and Property in the Emancipation Experiences of African American Women in Richmond" (paper presented to the Southern Association of Women Historians, Chapel Hill, N.C., June 1991).

In *A Rebel War Clerk's Diary*, 2 vols. (Philadelphia: John B. Lippencott, 1867), J. B. Jones recounts the hardships of his family but comes truly alive when describing the bureaucratic infighting, the vendettas and invective, of his Confederate department. In other Confederate endeavors, Richmond slaves as well as free blacks were conscripted or hired for every sort of labor, as described by James H. Brewer in *The Confederate Negro: Virginia's Craftsmen and Military Laborers, 1861–1865* (Durham, N.C.: Duke University Press, 1969), despite the wishes of their masters.

Although Eric Foner has little to say about Richmond, his *Reconstruction: America's Unfinished Revolution* (New York: Harper and Row, 1988) is essential background reading for this era. The historiographic questions about the Reconstruction era in Richmond concern the role and status of the freedmen, the nature of the economic recovery effort, and the creation of an acceptable public rationale for the Civil War. Michael Chesson's well-researched and thoughtfully organized *Richmond after the War, 1865–1890* (Richmond: Virginia State Library, 1981) examines this period, and the author argues, against his own powerful evidence, that after 1885 Richmond businessmen chose not to compete vigorously in industry and commerce.

Two important studies—Peter Rachleff's *Black Labor in the South: Richmond, Virginia, 1865–1890* (Philadelphia: Temple University Press, 1984), and John O'Brien's "From Bondage to Citizenship: The Richmond Black Community, 1865–1867" (Ph.D. diss., University of Rochester, 1975)—focus on the black response to emancipation and demonstrate high levels of black expectation and organization. Those high hopes must be measured against the evidence presented in Howard N. Rabinowitz's *Race Relations in the Urban South, 1865–1890* (New York: Oxford University Press, 1978) and John W. Cell's *The Highest Stage of White Supremacy: The Origins of Segregation in South Africa and the American South* (Cambridge: Cam-

bridge University Press, 1982). The works by Rabinowitz and Cell indicate that antebellum urban ordinances restricting slaves and free blacks were models for the legal development of postbellum segregation. At the same time, Richmond's long and uneven movement toward Jim Crow also supports C. Vann Woodward's *Origins of the New South* (Baton Rouge: Louisiana State University Press, 1951) and *The Strange Career of Jim Crow*, 3rd ed. (New York: Oxford University Press, 1974), which pointed out that there was a generation of uncertainty before the triumph of legal segregation.

Scholars frequently debate the sources and assumptions for black family formation after the Civil War. See Jacqueline Jones, *Labor of Love, Labor of Sorrow: Black Women, Slavery, and the Family from Slavery to the Present* (New York: Basic Books, 1985), and Deborah Gray White, *"Ar'n't I a Woman?": Black Women, Work, and the Family from Slavery to the Present* (New York: W. W. Norton, 1985). Richmond evidence suggests that black women left the labor force after the Civil War if they had male support. The city's black churches—sources of benevolence, political debate, and middle-class status—encouraged a patriarchal family structure, and most postbellum black leadership stemmed from such a family structure. Conversely, the paid labor of black women both burdened them and gave them a certain autonomy. Kinship networks and factory "families" supported the women who depended on wage labor. These women were the ones who organized into Knights of Labor assemblies, and later generations remained receptive to collective action.

The Lost Cause and the New South in Richmond

Parallel to the rebuilding of the city's industry was a restructuring of its image. Charles Reagan Wilson's *Baptized in Blood: The Religion of the Lost Cause* (Athens: University of Georgia Press, 1980) and Gaines M. Foster's *Ghosts of the Confederacy: Defeat, the Lost Cause, and the Emergence of the New South* (New York: Oxford University Press, 1987) describe the growth of the Lost Cause as either a "civil religion" or a "revitalization movement," with particular emphasis on Richmond; and Paul Gaston has described, in *The New South Creed: A Study in Southern Mythmaking* (New York: Knopf, 1970), the creation of a New South business boosterism based primarily on mythmaking. As Gaston notes, the New South and Lost Cause ideologies could coexist harmoniously, and they certainly did in Richmond. This harmony found a physical expression in Monument Avenue, which enshrined Confederate generals while it promoted suburban development. Drew Carneal's "History of the Fan District" (unpubl. ms. in author's possession) and Jay K. B. Williams's *Changed Views and Unforeseen Prosperity: Richmond of 1890 Gets a Monument to Lee* (Richmond: privately printed, 1969) offer good perspectives on this development.

In an age of industrial labor organizing and strike activity, Richmond labor had the difficult task of organizing a work force that included men and women of every ethnicity. The fateful Knights of Labor convention in Richmond in 1886 marked the high point of these efforts. Gregg Kimball has written perceptively about labor in Richmond and has emphasized this era in his article "The Working People of Richmond: Life and Labor in an Industrial City, 1865–1920," *Labor's Heritage* 3, no. 2 (April 1991): 66–77. Extremely useful for analysis of the southern economy since the Civil War are Gavin Wright, *Old South, New South: Revolutions in the Southern Economy since the Civil War* (New York: Basic Books, 1986), and Don Doyle, *New Men, New Cities, New South: Atlanta, Nashville, Charleston, Mobile* (Chapel Hill: University of North Carolina Press, 1990).

Change in the personnel and goals of Richmond's city government from the 1840s to the 1880s is ably examined by William Ernst in "Urban Leaders and Social Change" (Ph.D. diss., University of Virginia, 1978), while the development of a distinct black community voice is described by Ann Field Alexander in "Black Protest in the New South: John Mitchell, Jr., 1863–1929, and the Richmond *Planet*" (Ph.D. diss., Duke University, 1973). While Wendell Dabney's *Maggie L. Walker and the I.O. of St. Luke: The Woman and her Work* (Cincinnati: Dabney Publishers, 1927) describes some of her enterprises, Maggie L. Walker—Richmond's premier

example of mingled philanthropic and entrepreneurial vision—lacks an adequate biography. Elsa Barkley Brown has made a start with her article "Womanist Consciousness: Maggie Lena Walker and the Independent Order of St. Luke," *Signs* 14 (1989): 610–33. Michael Chesson has discussed "Richmond's Black City Councilmen, 1871–1896" in Howard Rabinowitz, ed., *Southern Black Leaders of the Reconstruction Era* (Urbana: University of Illinois Press, 1982), 191–222.

The post–Civil War public school system, new gasworks and water treatment facilities, electric streetcar system, parks, and suburb planning are best treated as part of national trends to modernize and beautify cities. David Goldfield and Blaine Brownell's *Urban America: A History*, 2d ed. (Boston: Houghton Mifflin, 1990) and Christopher Silver's *Twentieth-Century Richmond: Planning, Politics, and Race* (Knoxville: University of Tennessee Press, 1984) put these events in context, while local memoirs—like Charles Wallace's *Boy Gangs of Richmond in the Dear Old Days* (Richmond: Dietz Press, 1938) and John Wise's *The End of an Era* (Boston: Houghton Mifflin, 1899)—describe city childhoods through children's street games and gangs.

The proliferation of organizations in Richmond took various forms. Two articles by James M. Lindgren, "'For the Sake of Our Futures': The Association for the Preservation of Virginia Antiquities and the Regeneration of Traditionalism," *Virginia Magazine of History and Biography* 97, no. 1 (January 1989): 47–74, and "'Virginia Needs Living Heroes': Historic Preservation in the Progressive Era," *The Public Historian* 13, no. 1 (Winter 1991): 9–24, portray preservation as a revitalization movement similar to Gaines Foster's Confederate societies. Angie Parrot's essay "'Love Makes Memory Eternal': The United Daughters of the Confederacy in Richmond, Virginia, 1897–1920," in Edward L. Ayers and John C. Willis, eds., *The Edge of the South: Life in Nineteenth-Century Virginia* (Charlottesville: University Press of Virginia, 1991), 219–38, sees the Daughters as powerful arbiters of education and culture in Richmond. The Virginia Women's History Project, based at the Virginia State Library, holds a diverse collection of records for women's

organizational activities in Richmond at the end of the nineteenth century, confirming much activity and some overlapping personnel. This topic is explored in Betsy Brinson's "'Helping Others to Help Themselves': Social Advocacy and Wage-Earning Women in Richmond, Virginia, 1910–1932" (Ph.D. diss., Union for Experimenting Colleges and Universities, 1984). The records of the Women's Christian Temperance Union and the Young Women's Christian Association, held at Virginia Commonwealth University, may also provide light on this issue.

The Early Twentieth Century

Scholars of the South continue to revisit the era when Jim Crow took firm hold, and they do so for good reason. For many, the generation before legal segregation still holds instructive information on how the issue of race affected class and gender relations and the reformation of southern economies before those relations were limited by segregation laws. The thematic threads usually followed to link the late nineteenth century with the early twentieth are the Progressive movement, the rise and pervasiveness of Jim Crow, and the development of New South industry and labor relations. Aspects of C. Vann Woodward's enduring *Origins of the New South, 1877–1913* (Baton Rouge: Louisiana State University Press, 1951) and George Tindall's *The Emergence of the New South, 1913–1945* (Baton Rouge: Louisiana State University Press, 1967), which together cover the period, echo in Richmond's post-Reconstruction industrial and racial experience. In the last decade, the Progressive movement in the South has been reexamined in William A. Link, *The Paradox of Southern Progressivism, 1880–1930* (Chapel Hill: University of North Carolina Press, 1992). Dewey Grantham's *Southern Progressivism: The Reconciliation of Progress and Tradition* (Knoxville: University of Tennessee Press, 1983) provides the best-known analysis of the reform impetus in the South, while Edward Ayers's *The Promise of the New South: Life after Reconstruction* (New York: Oxford University Press, 1992) provides a panoramic examination of the energetic transformation of all sections and classes of the varied South.

In Richmond, Progressivism divided into several branches, each with roots in earlier eras. For the city's white male leadership, Progressivism's scientific efficiency seemed to promise more services at less cost—an aspect of their city planning that Christopher Silver has traced well in his *Twentieth-Century Richmond: Planning, Politics, and Race* (Knoxville: University of Tennessee Press, 1984). In regard to the era's antialcohol bent, Virginius Dabney's *Dry Messiah: The Life of Bishop Cannon* (New York: Knopf, 1949; reprint ed. Westport, Conn.: Greenwood Press, 1970) approaches Prohibition as a political issue and treats its Protestant proponents as H. L Mencken or Sinclair Lewis would have. Women's suffrage was both opposed and supported by women of every status and ethnicity; each tangled motive awaits further unraveling. The papers of Adele Clark, at Virginia Commonwealth University, and of Lila Meade Valentine and Mary-Cooke Branch Munford, at the Virginia State Library, may reveal more of this history and of the social justice and education concerns of these and other Progressive women.

The early twentieth century saw a genuine literary boom in Richmond. Anne Goodwyn Jones' *Tomorrow Is Another Day: Southern Women Writers, 1859–1939* (Baton Rouge: Louisiana State University Press, 1981) includes thoughtful essays on Ellen Glasgow and Mary Johnston. The novels of Glasgow and Johnston grew in complexity and subtlety, and as Johnston moved to rural Virginia, James Branch Cabell began to publish. The best account of their work in relation to its time is Daniel Joseph Singal's *The War Within: From Victorian to Modernist Thought in the South, 1919–1945* (Chapel Hill: University of North Carolina Press, 1982). The white youth of the city who published little magazines such as *Black Swan* and *The Reviewer* in the 1920s modeled themselves after the Baltimore iconoclast H. L. Mencken. The debunking style of the period also produced books like Emily Clark's *Stuffed Peacocks* (New York, 1927), a barely disguised attack on legendary locals. John Kneebone, in *Southern Liberal Journalists and the Issue of Race, 1920–1944* (Chapel Hill: University of North Carolina Press, 1985), has written with perception about the liberal southern editors who appeared in the 1920s and 1930s at southern urban newspapers, including Virginius Dabney of the Richmond *Times Dispatch.*

Modern Times and After

The percentages of male and female, black and white migrants to Richmond in the early twentieth century are not precisely known, but historians have documented an increasing number of new jobs for women and suggest that more African American female domestic workers entered the city after 1900. Evidence for who came and how long they stayed remains anecdotal, but it is certain that, by the 1920s, child labor had decreased, while factories continued to offer black and white women very separate spheres of labor.

The rapid advance of mass entertainment after World War I, the backlash of nativism, the youth culture of the 1920s and their desire to be modern, and the advent of Prohibition and then the Great Depression were all national events in which Richmond participated with a local emphasis. Race issues deeply affected Richmond's version of national trends in the expansion of suburbs and popular culture, the professionalization of social work, and the wage scales for labor. Just as the social reform concerns of middle-class whites and blacks reached toward organizational merger rather than parallel efforts, biological racism reached its peak in the Anglo-Saxon clubs and the new Ku Klux Klan. The adaptive strategies of black social activists in Richmond from the 1920s through the 1940s are suggested in Raymond Gavins, *The Perils and Prospects of Southern Black Leadership: Gordon Blaine Hancock, 1884–1970* (Durham: Duke University Press, 1970), but this is an era in need of more scholarly attention.

Advertising and consumption, a new emphasis on leisure, and the automobile affected all groups. Early local radio programming is described in Bill Malone's *Southern Music, American Music* (Lexington: University Press of Kentucky, 1979) and Kip Lornell's *Virginia's Blues, Country, and Gospel Records, 1902–1943: An Annotated Bibliography* (Lexington: University Press of Kentucky, 1989). The effect of the new national popular culture on women's lives and self-perception is described by Lois Banner in *American Beauty* (Chicago: University of Chicago Press, 1983) and by William Chafe in *The American Woman: Her Changing Social, Economic, and Political Roles, 1920–1970* (New York: Oxford University Press, 1974).

The very visibility of change in women's lives and roles between 1920 and 1945—from twenties flapper to anxious mother of the Great Depression to Rosie the Riveter—obscures the extent to which women's lives remained constant through these decades even as their roles were reinterpreted to meet changing economic conditions. Nancy Cott, in *The Grounding of Modern Feminism* (New Haven, Yale University Press, 1987), suggests that women lost their symbolic identity as a collective subordinate group and fragmented once they obtained the vote. But those Richmond women who had been active in suffrage continued to be active in the new League of Women Voters and old benevolent societies, and women were increasingly visible in business. In *To Work and to Wed: Female Employment, Feminism, and the Great Depression* (Westport, Conn.: Greenwood Press, 1980), Lois Scharf notes that in the twenties educated women said they wanted to work in order to use their training, but during the depression they argued that their income was needed. Delores Janiewski's *Sisterhood Denied: Race, Gender, and Class in a New South Community* (Philadelphia: Temple University Press, 1985) confirms and extends the differences between the work culture of black and white women in the textile and tobacco factories and adds, for the 1930s, the indifference of craft labor unions to the concerns of working women.

The New Deal often accommodated Richmond's political machines and traditions. Industrial labor unions contested the dominant craft unions. The NAACP challenged segregation in higher education. On Richmond's politics in the 1920s and 1930s, see Virginius Dabney, *Virginia, The New Dominion* (New York: Doubleday, 1971). Dabney is at the height of his powers describing Virginia and Richmond in this period. The best approach to federal policy and the Depression South is the collection of essays edited by James C.

Cobb and Michael V. Namaroto, *The New Deal in the South* (Jackson: University of Mississippi Press, 1984). More analysis of federal programs and their effects appears in Robert L. Heineman's *Depression and New Deal in Virginia: The Enduring Dominion* (Charlottesville: University Press of Virginia, 1983). Many writers have chronicled Virginia's Byrd machine, which deeply influenced Richmond politics. See, for example, Harvie Wilkinson, *Harry Byrd and the Changing Face of Virginia Politics* (Charlottesville: University Press of Virginia, 1968).

The Douglas Southall Freeman index of newspaper articles about Richmond in the 1920s and 1930s, taken from the Richmond *News-Leader* (which he edited) and available on microfilm at several repositories, is an excellent source for this period in the city's history. Richmond's concerns, as expressed in those articles, are much the same as those described in Blaine Brownell's *The Urban Ethos in the South, 1920–1930* (Baton Rouge: Louisiana State University Press, 1985). Francis Earl Lutz's *Richmond in World War II* (Richmond: Dietz Press, 1951) is based on newspaper accounts and essentially carries the Freeman index through another decade.

Changing Times

The literature for the post–World War II civil rights movement is extensive, and Richmond has received its share of attention. For analysis of massive resistance, see Numan V. Bartley, *The Rise of Massive Resistance: Race and Politics in the South during the 1950s* (Baton Rouge: Louisiana State University Press, 1969); Benjamin Muse, *Virginia's Massive Resistance* (Bloomington: Indiana University Press, 1961); Robbins L. Gates, *The Making of Massive Resistance: Virginia's Politics of Public School Desegregation, 1954–1956* (Chapel Hill: University of North Carolina Press, 1964); and James Ely, Jr., *The Crisis of Conservative Virginia: The Byrd Organization and the Politics of Massive Resistance* (Knoxville: University of Tennessee Press, 1971). Richard Kluger's *Simple Justice: The History of* Brown v. Board of Education *and Black America's Struggle for Equality* (New York: Knopf, 1976) tells the national legal story, which is important for understanding Richmond. Robert Pratt's

dissertation, "School Desegregation in Richmond, Virginia, 1954–1984: A Study of Race and Class in a Southern City" (University of Virginia, 1987), asserts that Richmond substituted "passive resistance" for "massive resistance" and thus gave white city residents time to move to the suburbs before schools were integrated. It is, however, important to note that the move out of the city began after World War II, when federal policies for veterans, for highways, and for cities made the suburbs both attractive and accessible for white families with moderate incomes, which confining black families with moderate incomes to intown neighborhoods.

Technology and transformation came late to both farmers and workers within the tobacco culture supporting Richmond. See two works by Pete Daniel: *Breaking the Land: The Transformation of Cotton, Tobacco, and Rice Cultures since 1880* (Urbana: University of Illinois Press, 1985), and *Standing at the Crossroads: Southern Life in the Twentieth Century* (New York: Hill and Wang, 1986). The urban histories by David Goldfield and Blaine Brownell—especially Brownell and Goldfield, eds., *The City in Southern History: The Growth of Urban Civilization in the South* (Port Washington, N.Y.: Kennikat Press, 1977), and Goldfield and Brownell, *Urban America: A History*, 2d ed. (Boston: Houghton Mifflin, 1990)—offer invaluable comparative information for American cities over time and provide a constant monitoring of urban trends, with a special emphasis on the South. Especially for the period after World War II, Goldfield has carefully analyzed issues of region, race, urbanization, and industrial transformation; see his *Cotton Fields and Skyscrapers: Southern City and Region, 1607–1980* (Baton Rouge: Louisiana State University Press, 1982) and *Black, White, and Southern* (Baton Rouge: Louisiana State University Press, 1989). Any approach to Richmond's place in the urban south since 1945 must begin with Goldfield and Brownell and continue with Christopher Silver's *Twentieth-Century Richmond: Planning, Politics, and Race* (Knoxville: University of Tennessee Press, 1984), which delineates the racial control aspects of Richmond's annexation and urban renewal policies in that period. John V. Moeser and Rutledge M. Dennis, in *The Politics of Annexation: Oligarchic Power in a*

Southern City (Cambridge, Mass.: Shenkman Publishing, 1982), take the story of annexation from the 1950s through the 1970s. The political stakes make a dramatic story of what might have been a simple civics lesson.

Ann Woodlief (*In River Time: The Way of the James* [Chapel Hill, N.C.: Algonquin Books, 1985]) has written eloquently of the James River and its history. She surveys the damage done by toxic waste, especially since World War II, and notes how reluctant officials have been to deal with it. Local resident James L. Doherty has written an account of 1970—a painful year in Richmond's public school system—and recorded the exhausting debate over busing for racial balance; see Doherty, *Race and Education in Richmond* (privately published, Richmond, 1972).

Recent studies of American culture from the 1950s through the 1970s debate how healthy or repressive it was. Some of the most useful studies include Elaine Tyler May, *Homeward Bound: American Families in the Cold War Era* (New York: Basic Books, 1988); Rickie Solinger, *Wake Up Little Susie: Single Pregnancy and Race before* Roe v. Wade (New York and London: Routledge, 1992); Stephanie Koontz, *The Way We Never Were: American Families and the Nostalgia Trap* (New York: Basic Books, 1992); and Ruth Schwartz Cowan, *More Work for Mother: The Ironies of Household Technology from the Open Hearth to the Microwave* (New York: Basic Books, 1983).

John Shelton Reed combines good humor with sociology to ask variations on the question, "Is the South still southern?" In books such as *One South: An Ethnic Approach to Regional Culture* (Baton Rouge: Louisiana State University Press, 1982), his tentative answer is yes. Still, James Cobb's work on southern efforts since the 1930s to attract or develop industry does not give much hope to those who wish to see the South avoid the industrializing errors of the North. See James C. Cobb, *The Selling of the South: The Southern Crusade for Industrial Development, 1935–1980* (Baton Rouge: Louisiana State University Press, 1982) and *Industrialization and Southern Society* (Lexington: University Press of Kentucky, 1984).

Interviews with Richmond citizens conducted by the Valentine Museum staff provide commentary on events of the recent past. Economic and urban analysts from Virginia Commonwealth University and Crestar Bank have contributed information on the city's recent business history and projections for the future. Both David Goldfield, in *Cotton Fields and Skyscrapers: Southern City and Region, 1607–1980* (Baton Rouge: Louisiana State University Press, 1982) and *Black, White, and Southern* (Baton Rouge: Louisiana State University Press, 1989), and Jon C. Teaford, in *The Rough Road to Renaissance* (Baltimore: Johns Hopkins University Press, 1990), have examined the uncertain future of "festival marketplaces" and similar late-twentieth-century urban headaches.

The dramatic ironies and tensions of Richmond's political and demographic shifts within the generation after 1965 obscured other changes in daily life, which included the entry of more women into the work force, the decline of skilled labor, and a more integrated white-collar work force. Basic changes in what is considered civil behavior; in family, work, and consumption patterns; and in the use of public space have occurred quickly and provoked both cheers and jeremiads. One work that is particularly useful for understanding Richmond and the broad issues surrounding the meaning of family in postindustrial America is Jane Sherron De Hart and Donald Mathews's *Sex, Gender, and the Politics of ERA: A State and the the Nation* (New York: Oxford University Press, 1990). Their analysis of Upper South politics, gender issues, and the effort to impose cultural norms suggests that the century will end as it began—in tension between attempts to expand public services to new constituencies and attempts to reform those services through revitalized traditions.

Index

Page numbers in italic type
refer to illustrations.

A. H. Robins Pharmaceuticals, 310
Academy of Arts and Sciences, 72
Academy Theater, 249
Adams, Richard, 69, 302
African Americans. *See* Blacks
African colonization, 94–95
Agriculture, 139; Indian, 13, 16, 35;
    slavery and, 94, 117; mechanization
    of, 280
Air conditioning, 279
Airports, 248
Algonquian Indians, 11
Allan, Frances Valentine, 108
Allan, John, 96, 108
Allegre, Jane, 72
Allen, Otway, 207–8
Allen and Ginter tobacco company,
    190
Allied Chemical Corporation, 309
Almond, Lindsay, 287
Amalgamated Iron and Steel, 193
Ambler, Eliza, 65
Ambler, Jacquelin, 65
Ambler, Mary Willis, 70
Ambler, Rebecca, 65
American colonies, 10, 14, 56, 59
American Colonization Society, 94–95
American Federation of Labor (AFL),
    214, 265
American Indians, 6; James River set-
    tlements, 1, 2, 9, 11, *12*, 13; encoun-
    ters with English settlers, 4, 9,
    11–13, 14, 16; agriculture, 13, 16, 35;
    women, 13–14; wars with English,
    18, 21, 22, 23, 27; English subjection
    of, 23, 24, 26, 29–30, 32; enslave-
    ment of, 30, 32, 33; tobacco use,
    41–42. *See also* names of individual
    tribes
American Locomotive Company, 238

American Missionary Association, 175
American (Know-Nothing) Party, 129
American Revolution, 56, 108, 109; in
    Richmond, 62–63, 64; blacks and,
    63–64, 67, 76
American Telephone & Telegraph
    Company (AT&T), 292
American Tobacco Companies, 265,
    271, 277, 310
Amicable Club, 70
Anderson, Archer, 209
Anderson, Henry, 243
Anderson, Joseph Reid, 120–21, 144–
    45, 153, 172
Anglo-Powhatan Wars, 18, 22
Anglo-Saxon Clubs of America, 255,
    256
Annexations, 51, 227, 228, *map* 229; of
    1793, 78; of 1867, 173, 174, 185; of
    1892, 208; of 1906–14, 222; Man-
    chester, 222; of 1942, 271; Henrico
    County, 271, 296; Chesterfield
    County, 271, 296, 299–300, 301; of
    1970, 296, 299–300, 301
Antiliquor movement, 231–32, 238. *See
    also* Temperance movement
Anti-Saloon League, 231
Appomattox River, 32, 44
Architecture, 56, 72, 205–6, 248, 249,
    251, 306–7
Armistead, James. *See* Lafayette, James
    Armistead
Armistead, William, 64
Armory Battalion, 156
Army of Northern Virginia, 162
Arnold, Benedict, 62
Arrohattec village, 18
Art Club of Richmond, 236
Association for the Preservation of
    Virginia Antiquities (APVA), 206,
    232, 248, 298
Association of the Army of Northern
    Virginia, 188

Atlanta, Ga., 185
Austen, Jane, 110
Automobiles, *230*; and suburbanization,
    244, 247, 249, 277; and city planning,
    248; Great Depression and, 261;
    World War II and, 274

Bacon, Nathaniel, 26, 27–29
Bacon's Rebellion, 27–29, 53
Bagby, George W., 134
Bahen, James, 199
Baliles, Gerald, 317
Baltimore, Md., 123
Baltimore Evening Sun, 253
Bank of the United States, 90
Bank of Virginia, 90
Banks, 90, 180, 181–82, 222, 240, 242
Baptist Church, 68
Baptists, 58, 176; evangelicalism, 4, 68
Barbershops, 118
Barrett, Kate Waller, 206
Bartholomew Plan (1946), 281–82,
    283, 284, 292
Barton, James, 205
Barton Heights, 205
Basie, Count, 276
Battle Abbey, 249, 292
Battlefield Park, 266
Baughman Brothers print shop, 196
Beaurepaire, Quesnay de, 72
Beckley, John, 67
Bell, John, 133
Belle Isle prison camp, 142, 143
Belvidere house, *47*, 50, 51
Berkeley, William, 26, 27–29, 30
Bermuda Hundred, 1, 38, 40
Best Products, 310
Beth Shalome Hebrew Congregation,
    69
Beverly, Robert, 42
Bills of exchange, 57
Birmingham, Ala., 185
Birth of a Nation (film), 234

Blacks, 2, 4, 5; women, 3, 107, 168, 223, 234–35, 238, 265, 313; plantation labor, 25; in Revolutionary War, 63–64; artisans, 65, 78–79, 105, 117, 182, 193, 200–201, 225; churches, 68, 112, 116, 176; local restrictions on, 80, 108, 117, 131, 166; and African colonization, 94–95; population in Richmond, 99, 136, 222, 271; white fear of employment competition from, 105, 112; assistance to runaway slaves, 107, 118; neighborhoods and housing, 114, 173–74, 222, 247, 269–70, 282–83, 294–95, 298; middle class, 116, 170, 224–25, 226, 313; tobacco factory workers, 117, 182, 194, 223, 265; business ownership, 118, 225, 226, 240, 276–77; in Civil War, 137, 139, 149, 152–53, 159; punishment by whipping, 149, 166; in Union-occupied Richmond, 166–67; militia units, 167; voting rights granted to, 173, 296; and Republican Party, 174, 177, 199, 200, 225, 243; and Jackson Ward politics, 174, 196–97, 199, 227; struggles for integration, 174, 213, 214, 268–69, 275, 288; education of, 175, 225–26, 233, 287–88; citizenship rights, 176; police officers, 177; Reconstruction and, 178; organization of labor unions, 182, 189, 193, 195, 196, 214; city council members, 197, 227, 300; Democratic Party and, 199, 225, 227; streetcar boycott of 1904, 214–15; incomes, 222; Progressive movement and, 224, 226, 240; self-help movement, 225, 226, 234; disfranchisement of, 226, 227; political campaigns, 243; and racial cooperation movement, 255; New Deal and, 268, 269, 272; in World War II, 272, 273, 275; urban renewal and, 294–95; public school population, 296–97, 299, 316–17; and suburban annexation, 299–300; white-collar employment, 314. *See also* Segregation; Slaves

Black Swan, 251
Bonsack, James A., 190
Bonsack cigarette machine, 190
Booth, Edwin, 84
Booth, John Wilkes, 84, 146
Booth, Junius Brutus, *84,* 146
Bottomley, William Lawrence, 251
Botts, John Minor, 147
Bourbon Democrats, 199
Bowser, Mary, 147
Bowser, Rosa Dixon, 206
Bowser, Wilson, 147
Bradshaw, Booker T., 283
Brady, Mathew, 141
Bread Riot (1863), 151, 157
Breckinridge, John C., 133
Bridgwood, John C., 60
Briggs, London, 79–80
Bright, Fulmer, 245, 263
Broad Street, 247, *267, 279,* 302, 305, 306
Broad Street Railroad Station, 248
Brockenbrough, John, 90
Brockenbrough, William, 90
Brooks, Albert, 154, 170–71, 317
Brooks, David Burr, 154
Brooks, Lucy, 154, 170, 317
Brooks, Margaret Ann, *124*
Brown, Henry ("Box"), 103–4
Brown, John, 129, 130, 133
Brown, Orlando, 166
Browne, William Washington, 225, 240
Brown's Island, 79
Brown's Island Ordnance Laboratory, 150
Brown v. Board of Education of Topeka, Kansas (1954), 284, 285, 286–87, 296

Bryan, Isobel Stewart, 212
Bryan, Joseph, 210–12; and family, as owners of communications company, 308
Buchanan, Annabel, 257
Buchanan's Spring, 78
Building Aid Society, 182
Bureau of Refugees, Freedmen, and Abandoned Lands. *See* Freedmen's Bureau
Burr, Aaron, 81, 82
Burr, David, 154
Busing, 299, 300, 316–17
Butler, Benjamin F., 167
Byrd, Elizabeth Hill Carter, 47, 50–51
Byrd, Harry F.: political machine of, 260–61, 269, 284; and New Deal, 263, 267, 269; and school desegregation, 285
Byrd, Susan, 42
Byrd, Ursula, 42
Byrd, William, I, 3, 6, 42, 200; land holdings, 26, 27, 29, 45; Indian trade, 26, 32, 33; in Bacon's Rebellion, 27, 29; slave trade, 33, 40
Byrd, William, II, 42, 43; founding of Richmond, 43, 44, 48, 312; Westover home, 45, *47;* death of, 50
Byrd, William, III: Belvidere home, *47,* 50, 51; sale of lands by lottery, 51, 52, 60; suicide of, 51–53
Byrd Airport, 248, 271
Byrd Park, 203, 294
Byrd Theater, 276

C. F. Sauer and Company, 189–90
Cabell, James Branch, 219, 253, *254*
Calhoun, John C., 93, 286
Calloway, Cab, 277
Cannon, Bishop James, Jr., 231, 232, 256, 270–71
Capitalism, 1, 267
Capitol Square, 99, 101, 131, 146, 150,

151, 160, 166, 168, 174, 221, 307, 310

Capitol Theater, 249

"Carpetbaggers," 173

Carrington, Eliza Ambler, 70

Carrington, Magdelena, 86

Carrington and Michaux tobacco company, 265

Carter, Robert, 67

Cary, Lott, 95, 96

Cary Street Center, 281

Cemeteries, 146, 187

Census Bureau, 314

Censuses: of 1669, 30; of 1800, 78; of 1820, 93; of 1860, 123; of 1870, 172, 174; of 1960, 296

Central National Bank, 247

Central Trades and Labor Council, 237

Chahoon, George, 177, 178

Charles, Fort, 23

Charles I (king of England), 20

Cheek, Leslie, Jr., 292

Chemical industry, 189

Chesapeake and Ohio Railroad, 181

Chesapeake Corporation, 308

Chesapeake region, 35, 36, 37, 38, 57, 89

Chesnut, Mary Boykin, 154, 155

Chesterfield (Rocky Ridge), 54, 62

Chesterfield County, 301, 311, 314; annexations of, 271, 296, 299–300

Chiesman, Lydia, 29

Childbirth, 258

Child labor, 223, 260

Children, 72–74

Chimborazo Hospital, 139, 140–41

Chimborazo Park, 203

Christian and White's Grocery, 203

Christianity, 38, 68

Churches, 68–69, 116

Church Hill, 69, 113, 203, 302; railroad tunnel collapse, 257

Church of England, 58

Church societies, 116

Cigarette production, 261, 270, 277; advertising, 190, 192; mechanization of, 190–93. See also Tobacco

Cigar making, 194

Circuit City Stores, Inc., 310

Citizens' Service Exchange of Richmond, 266–67

City Battalion, 150

City beautification movement, 207

Civilian Conservation Corps (CCC), 266

Civil rights movement, 284, 288

Civil War, 4; Lost Cause iconography, 5, 6, 184–85, 187, 188, 209–10, 215–17, 221, 253; effects on Richmond, 5, 136–38, 139–40, 164–65, 172; blacks in, 137, 139, 149, 152–53, 159; women in, 137, 141, 151, 154–56, 167; blockade of Virginia, 138, 152; prison camps, 142–43, 156; southern industry in, 144–45, 153; martial law in Richmond, 146, 147; espionage, 147–48; siege of Richmond, 148; conscription, 149, 157; Richmond-area battlefields, map 150; fall of Richmond, 157–58, 159–62; surrender of Confederate armies, 162–64

Clark, Adele, 236, 243

Clark, Emily Tapscott, 253–54

Class structure, 6, 113–14, 125, 217. See also Middle class; Working class

Clay, Henry, 93, 127–28, 131

Clay, Laura, 236

Clay Street, 312

Clean Water Act (1972), 309

Cleveland, Grover, 200

Clinton, Sir Henry, 62

Clowes, E. H., 209

Coal mining, 62, 111, 120, 122

Cocke, Thomas, 38, 45

Coercive Acts (1774), 59

Coffee trade, 123

Cohn, Naomi, 260

Coleman, Mrs. Clayton Glanville, 236

Colonial Dames, 219

Colored National Labor Union, 189, 193

Commission of Game and Inland Fisheries, 309

Commission on Interracial Cooperation (CIC), 254–55

Committees of Correspondence, 59

Committee to Defend America by Aiding the Allies, 270–71

Common Hall, 69, 90, 93

Commonwealth Club, 219, 264, 271

Confederacy: memorialization of in Richmond, 4, 5, 169, 183, 184–85, 186–87, 208–9, 210, 211; Lost Cause iconography, 5, 6, 184–85, 187, 188, 209–10, 215–17, 221, 253; Richmond as capital of, 5, 136–40, 147; hospitals, 140–41; employment of women, 141, 155–56; prison camps, 142–43; industrial production, 144–45, 153; elections, 146; espionage against, 147–48; fortification of Richmond, 148; conscription, 149; taxation, 149; impressment of black labor, 149, 153; impressment of food, 150; defense of Richmond, 157–58; evacuation of Richmond, 159, 160, 162; surrender of, 162–64; veterans, 184, 209, 211, 249

Confederate armies, 159, 162–64

Confederate Congress, 138, 139, 149, 150

Confederate Memorial Association, 292

Confederate Memorial Institute, 210, 249

Confederate Memorial Literary Society, 210, 212

Confederate Soldiers' Home, 211

Congress of Industrial Organizations (CIO), 265, 269
Conscription, 149, 270
Conservative Party, 177, 178, 199
Constitutional Union Party, 133
Continental Congress, 59
Cook, Fields, 116, 189
Cooke, John Esten, 110
Copland, Charles, 80
Cornwallis, Charles, first marquis, 63
Cotton production, 117, 181
Counties, 22, 260–61
Country Club of Virginia, 251
Country Magazine, 56
Court End, 312
Cousins, Amanda, 104
Cox, Earnest, 255
Cox, Joseph, 176
Crane, William, 95
Crowe, Eyre, 118, 124
Crump, Rev. L. C., 265
Culpepper, Frances, 26
Curles Plantation, 26
Cutchins, Robert, 207

Dabney, Virginius, 254, 256, 275, 286, *287*
Dahlgren, Ulric, 156
Dale, Sir Thomas, 18
Daniel, John M., 134, 135
Darwin, Charles R., 256–57
Daughters of the American Revolution, 206
Davis, Daniel Webster, 225, 234
Davis, Jefferson, 142, 156; arrival in Richmond, 136; Richmond residence of, 138, 155; inauguration as president, 146; and Bread Riot, 151, 152; federal charges against, 171; Hollywood Cemetery monument, *221*
Davis, Varina, 152, 155
Deepwater Terminal, 270, 271

Democratic Party: lack of support in Richmond, 127; National Convention of 1860, 133; and black voters, 199, 225, 227; in Virginia, 199, 260–61, 269; and enactment of Prohibition, 231–32; and school desegregation, 285
Democratic-Republican Party, 70
Department stores, 203, 247, 276, 289
Douglas, Stephen A., 133
Downtown Expressway, 294
Drewry's Bluff fortifications, 148
Drummond, Sarah, 29
Dueling, 50, 212
Duke, James B., 190
Du Pont Company, 248, 261, 271, 272

E. R. Carpenter Company, Inc., 308
Early, Jubal A., 187, 189
Economic conditions: recession of 1819, 93; southern economic independence, 117–18, 119; recession of 1837, 120; depression of 1873, 178, 181–82, 183; depression of 1893, 227; Great Depression, 261–63, 266
Edgeworth Tobacco Station, 257
Education: of Indians, 21; of women, 72, 96–97; private schools, 96; of blacks, 175, 225–26, 233, 287–88; desegregation of universities, 268–69. *See also* Public schools
Ege, Elizabeth, *68*, 72
Ege, Jacob, 48, *68*
Ege, Samuel, Jr., 74
Ege family house, 248
Elections: city council, 129, 227, 296, 300; of 1860, presidential, 133; of 1870, mayoral, 178; of 1921, state, 243; of 1928, presidential, 256
Elizabeth I (queen of England), 9
Ellie (Cooke), 110
Ellington, Duke, 277
Ellyson, Henry, 177, 178

Emancipation Day, 210
Emancipation law, Virginia. *See* Manumission Act
Emancipation Proclamation (1863), 174
Embargo Act (1807), 88
Enabling Act (1870), 177
England: trade in America, 9–10, 14, 25, 42–44, 56–57, 88; wars with Netherlands, 25; union with Scotland, 44; colonial rebellion against, 56, 59, 62–63; wars with France, 57–58; taxation of colonies, 58–59, 67; American boycotts against, 59, 88; War of 1812, 86, 89
English law, 21, 38, 56
English settlers: James River settlements, 3, 4, 9, 16–18, 22–23; James River exploration, 4, 9, 10; encounters with Indians, 4, 9, 11–13, 14, 16; migration to Virginia, *24*; wars with Indians, 18, 21, 22, 23, 27; land grants to, 21, 26–27; subjection of Indians, 23, 24, 26, 29–30, 32; wars with Dutch, 25; mortality rates, 30; agriculture, 35
Enlightenment, 56, 68, 70, 72
Environmental Protection Agency, 309
Episcopal congregation, 85
Espionage, Civil War, 147–48
Ethyl Corporation, 308, 312
Evangelicalism, 84, 86, 116; Baptist, 4, 68
Evans, Lewis, 265
Evins, William, 167
Ezrat Orchim, 70

Falling Gardens, 77
Family Service Society, 263
Fan District, 205–6, 301–2
Farmers, 261. *See also* Planters
Farmer's Bank, 90

Farmer's Market, 305, 306

Farrar, Judge, 209

Federal Emergency Relief Act (1933), 266, 268

Federal Housing Administration (FHA), 282–83

Federalist Party, 70, 82, 93

Federal Reserve Act (1913), 240

Federal Reserve Building, 307

Federal Reserve Commission, 222

Federal Reserve District Bank, 240, 310

Female Academy, 97

Female Charitable Association, 86

Female Humane Society, 70, 86

Fire companies, 127

Fire department, 180

First African Baptist Church, 116

Fisher, Flavius, 109

Fishing, 13, 309, 310

Flexner Report (1913), 258

Flood of 1771, 54–56, 57

Flour mills, 112, 123, 136, 180, 182, 185

Flowerdew Hundred, 41

Forest Hill Park, 203

Foster, John, 105

Foushee, William, 67, 69

France, 57–58, 89

Freedmen's Bureau, 165–66, 175

Freedmen's Savings Bank, 182

Freedmen's Schools, 225

Freeman, Douglas Southall, 248, 257, 270

French and Indian War, 58

Friedman-Marks Clothing, 271

Frye, Joshua, 49

Fulton Hill, 302, 303

Fulton neighborhood, 114, 247, 302–4

Fur trade, 25, 33

Gabriel's Conspiracy, 2, 3, 74–76, 80

Gallego flour mill, 123, 182, 189

Galt, Gabriel, 72

Gamble Hill, 203

Gamble's Hill Park, 203

Gasoline tax, 248

Gasworks, 180

Gentrification, 303

German Americans: immigration, 48, 112, 113, 115, 117; neighborhoods, 114, 196–97; militias, 125; Civil War and, 156; in politics, 173; World War I and, 238

German Sick Assistance Association, 116

GI Bill, 281

Gilliat, Sy, 79–80, 102

Ginter, Lewis, 205

Ginter Park, 203, 205

Girardin, Louis, 83

Gladman, Sally, 94

Glasgow, Cary, 236

Glasgow, Ellen, 219–20, 254; literary career, 207, 235, 253; in politics, 236, 243

Glass, Carter, 240, 263

Gottwald, Dewey, 238

Grain production, 35, 36

Grand Arch, 184

Grand United Order of True Reformers, 225

Great Depression, 261–63, 266

Grendon, Sarah, 29

Hagar (Johnston), 235

Hakluyt, Richard, 14

Halleck, Henry W., 164, 166

Hampton Institute, 255

Hancock, Gordon Blaine, 247, 260, 286

Hanover County, 58, 312

Harland Bartholomew and Associates, 281

Harpers Ferry raid, 129–30, 133

Harper's Weekly, 144, 152

Harris, Jordan, 105

Harrison, Constance Cary, 110, 148, 155

Harrison, William Henry, 127

Harvie-Wickham house, 66

Hatcher, Jordan, 125

Hatcher, Orie Latham, 258

Haxall-Crenshaw flour mill, 182, 189, 227

Hay, George, 80

Haymarket Gardens, 77

Heath, James Ewell, 109

Hebrew Cemetery, 146

Henrico County, 45, 301; founding and settlement of, 22–23, 25, 32; Indian conflict in, 29–30; in American Revolution, 59; annexations in, 271, 296; busing controversy, 299; population, 314; water treatment plant, 314

Henrico County Courthouse, 69

Henrico County Jail, 69

Henrico garrison, 18, 21

Henry, Patrick, 4, 59, 60, 76

Hermitage house, 79

Hibbs, Henry, 258

Hibernian Guard, 125

Hickory Hill plantation, 312

Highway construction, 279, 282, 293, 294, 301

Hill, Oliver, 283–84, 285

Hippodrome Theatre, 250, 277

Historic preservation, 206, 232, 298, 304

Historic Richmond Foundation, 298

Hobson, Frederick, 105

Hollywood Cemetery, 145, 146, 169, 187, 188, 221

Hollywood Memorial Association, 187, 188

Holmes, Rev. J. H., 168

Holt, Curtis, 299

Holton, Linwood, 296, 297

Holton, Tayloe, *297*
Home for Confederate Women, 311
Hoover, Herbert C., 256
Hopewell, 238
Hospitals, 140–41, 258
Hotel John Marshall, 312
Houdon, Jean-Antoine, 73
Housing, *281*, 301, 304; plantation, 35, 45, *47*, 56–57; suburban, 205; residential segregation, 222, 282, 298; inner-city deterioration, 247, 282, 294–95, 298; public, 294
Housing Acts (1949, 1954), 292
Houston, Nora, 236, 243
Hunnicutt, James W., 173, 174, 176
Hunt, Gilbert, 84, 95, 104, *118*
Hutchings, Martha, 74
Hylton, Daniel, 51

Immigration, 48, 112, 127, 129, 156
Imperial Quartette, 209
Indentured servitude, 10, 29, 37, 38, 109
Independent Order of Saint Luke, 234
Industrial History of the Negro Race (Jackson and Davis), 225
Industrialization, 5, 105, 120, 189, 263–64, 269. *See also* Manufacturing
Instructional Visiting Nurses Association (IVNA), 233
Interstate 95, 317
Irish Americans: immigration, 112, 113, 117; neighborhoods, 114, 196–97; militias, 125
Irish National League, 197
Iron industry, 62, 110, 120, 122–23, 144–45, 185, 271
Iroquois Indians, 11, 23

Jackson, Alice, 268–69
Jackson, Andrew, 93, 127
Jackson, Giles B., 225, 228–29
Jackson, James, 269

Jackson, Thomas J. ("Stonewall"), 184, 221, 249
Jackson Place, 305
Jackson's Gardens, 77
Jackson Ward: annexation of, 174; blacks and politics in, 174, 196–97, 199, 227; political abolition of, 227; housing deterioration in, 247, 294; highway construction in, 282, 293, 294; urban renewal in, 294, 298, 305
James I (king of England), 9, 14
James Center, 307
James River, 1, 2, 51; Indian settlements on, 1, 2, 9, 11, *12*, 13; English settlement on, 3, 4, 9, 16–18, 22–23; English exploration of, 4, 9, 10; fishing, 13, 77, 310; Dutch invasions of, 25; tobacco production and trade on, 35, 44, 57; Richmond–Rocky Ridge ferry, 48; flood of 1771, 54–56, 57; speculators' claims to, 65–67; port construction, 180, 181, 270, 271, 308; pollution of, 309–10
James River and Kanawha Canal, *106*, 110–11, 120, 181
James River and Kanawha Company, 110
James River Company, 89
James River Corporation, 308
Jamestown, 3, 22; settlement of, 9, 10, 18, 21; Bacon's siege of, 27–29; historic preservation in, 232
Jamestown Ter-Centennial (1907), 225
Jasper, Rev. John, 168, 226
Jefferson, Peter, 49
Jefferson, Thomas: as governor of Virginia, 62, 63, 68; and relocation of capital to Richmond, 64; agricultural republican ideal, 70, 89; design of capitol building, 72, 73; and trial of Burr, 82; as president, 88; and Missouri Compromise, 93

Jefferson Hotel, 304
Jefferson Park, 203
Jefferson Ward, 173, 178
Jim Crow laws. *See* Segregation
Jockey Club, 99
Johnson, Andrew, 165, 166, 171, 172
Johnson, Marmaduke, 135
Johnson, William, 103
Johnston, Mary, 235, 236
Jones, J. B., 138
Jones, Rev. William, 187

Kanawha Plaza, 307
Kepone, 309
Kilpatrick, James Jackson, 285, 286, 287
Kline Car Corporation, 230
Kneller, Sir Godfrey, 43
Knights of Labor, 193–96, 200, 214, 234
Know-Nothing Party, 129
Ku Klux Klan, 234, 254, 256

Labor strikes: streetcar workers, 1, 213–14, 217; against slave labor, 112, 121–22; Knights of Labor, 193–96; tobacco workers, 265
Labor unions, 189, 193, 214, 237, 265, 269
Ladies Gunboat Society, 154
Ladies' Hebrew Benevolent Society, 222
Ladies' Lee Monument Association, 188–89, 207–8
Lafayette, James Armistead, 64, 67, 99, 109, 226
Lafayette, Marquis de, 62–63, 95–96, *97*, 99, 101
Lakeside Park, 203
Lambert, David, 69
Land: colonial grants, 21, 26–27; Indian cessions, 23
Landon, Alfred M., 268

Larus & Brothers Tobacco Company, 257, 265, 271, 277, 291

Latrobe, Benjamin Henry, 47, 71, 72, 73, 78, 79

Law and Order League, 196

Lawyers, 80–81

League of Women Voters, 240

Lee, Fitzhugh, 189, 196, 208, 212, 213

Lee, Richard M., 137

Lee, Robert E., 153, 209, 212, 221; defense of Richmond, 157–58; surrender of, 162; death of, 188

Lee, Camp, 238, 270

Lee Camp of United Confederate Veterans, 219

Lee (Robert E.) Monument, 200, 208–9, 211

Leigh, Benjamin Watkins, 101

Letcher, John, 134, 135, 136, 151

Letters of the British Spy (Wirt), 81

Libby, Luther, 142

Libby Hill, 203

Libby Prison, 142, 143, 144, 156

Liberia, 95

Libraries, 247–48

Liggett & Myers (Liggett Group, Inc.), 265, 277, 310

Lincoln, Abraham, 161; and secession, 2, 132, 135; elected president, 133; and fall of Richmond, 160–62; assassination of, 162

Lincoln Mounted Guard, 174

Lindsay, Lewis, 176

Lipscomb, Martin Meredith, 128, 136

Literature, 108–9, 235, 253

Little Hickories, 244

Loew's Theater, 250

London, Daniel, 118–19

Lost Cause, 5, 184–85, 187, 188, 209–10, 215–17, 221, 253

L'Ouverture, Toussaint, 76

Lucas, Mary, 65

McCaw, James, 84, 141

McFarland, William H., 135

McKinley, William, 212–13

MacLeod, William, 106

Madison, James, 101

Maggie Walker High School, 266

Mahone, William, 199, 200

Main Street Station, 305, 306

Malvern Hill plantation, 38

Manakintown, 32

Manassas, first battle of, 140, 142

Manchester, Va., 1, 58, 63, 140, 159, 165, 193, 203; annexation of, 222

Manufacturing, 89, 93, 145, 189, 190, 193, 219. See also Industrialization

Manumission Act (1782), 65, 67, 80

Marriage, 168

Marsh, Henry L., 288, 300, 302, 304, 305

Marshall, John, 83, 99, 114; home of, 3, 70, 232, 248, 312; legal career, 69–70, 80; in trial of Burr, 81, 82; and voting rights, 101–2; burial place, 187

Marshall, Thurgood, 268–69

Marshall, William, 69

Marshall Ward, 173

Martin, John B., 64

Mason, Lucy Randolph, 223, 260

Masonic Hall, 72

Masonic Order, 70

"Massive resistance," 5, 285–86, 287, 297

Maternal Welfare Committee, 260

Maury, Matthew Fontaine, 249

May Campaign, 233

Mayo, George, 84

Mayo, John, 79–80

Mayo, Joseph (of Powhatan Seat), 42, 45

Mayo, Joseph (mayor of Richmond), 136, 149, 151, 158, 159, 166

Mayo, Louisa, 84

Mayo, William, 42, 44–45, 46

Mayo's Bridge, 159, 165

Meade, William, 84

Mechanic's Institute, 139

Mechanics Savings Bank of Richmond, 242

Mechanics' Trade Union, 189

Media General, Inc., 308

Medical College of Virginia, 140, 258, 266, 293–94, 295, 310

Medical Society of Virginia, 260

Meherrin Indians, 11

Memminger, Christopher, 148, 156

Mencken, H. L., 253, 254

Mercer, Charles Fenton, 94

Merchants, 32, 57, 58, 152, 182

Merhige, Robert R., Jr., 299, 300

Merrimac, USS, 145

Methodists, 68, 69, 176

Metropolitan Richmond Convention and Visitors Bureau, 305

Middle class, 6, 220; blacks, 116, 170, 224–25, 226, 313; use of streetcars, 205; in Progressive movement, 223–24; and suburbanization, 249, 312–13

Militias, 125, 167

Miller, Polk, 209, 258

Miller, Tony, 209

Miller & Rhoads department store, 203, 247, 276, 288, 306, 311, 312

Missouri Compromise, 93, 94

Mitchell, John, 199, 209, 214, 216, 225, 242, 243

Mitchell, Robert, 69

Mobile, Ala., 172

Monacan Indians, 11, 16, 32

Monitor, USS, 145, 148

Monroe, James, 74, 88, 101, 129, 187

Montgomery Guard, 125

Monumental Church, 85

Monument Avenue, 208, 249, 295

Moore, Samuel Preston, 140

Moore, T. Justin, Jr., 304
Mordecai, Emma, 154
Mordecai, Samuel, 58, 109–10, 113
Morissey, James, 176
Mortality rates, 30; maternal, 258–60
Mosque Theater, 270, 273, 276
Mother's Aid, 264
Movie theaters, 249, 250
Mulatto Jack (slave), 41
Munford, Beverly, 233
Munford, Mary Cooke Branch, 233, 255
Museum of the Confederacy, 312, 316
Museums, 210
Music, 257, 288–90

National Association for the Advancement of Colored People (NAACP), 268–69, 275, 284–85
National Industrial Recovery Act (1933), 266, 268
Nationalism, 93
National Unemployed Council, 263
Native Americans. See American Indians
Natural resources, 180
Navigation Acts (1650–96), 25
Navy Hill neighborhood, 114
Negro Fairs, 234
Negro Welfare Survey Committee, 247
Neighborhoods, 6, 114, 247, 292–93, 295, 301
Netherlands, 25
New Deal, 245, 263–68, 269–70, 283
New England, 88, 90
New Market, 203
New Orleans, La., 3, 172
Newport, Christopher, 9, 10, 16, 302
New South, 212, 213, 218; Lost Cause and, 184–85, 210, 217; Sunbelt South and, 263–64, 315–16
Newspapers, 308; and slavery, 134; and secession, 134, 135; and Civil War,

147; German-language, 197; provocation of duels, 212; and public schools, 233; and New Deal, 267–68; and civil rights movement, 286
New York Tribune, 166
Nixon, Richard M., 283
Norfolk, 3, 185, 287
Northside Land Company, 205
Nottoway Indians, 11
Nurses, 206, 233, 258
Nurses' Settlement House, 233

Oak Park, 228–29
Oakwood Cemetery, 146
Occaneechee Indians, 27
Old Dominion Barn Dance, 290
Old Dominion Iron and Nail Works, 196
Old Market, 203
Old South Quartette, 259
Old Stone House, 232, 248
Opechancanough (Powhatan chief), 22, 23
Ord, O. C., 164, 166
Ordinance Concerning Negroes (1859), 131
Oregon Hill neighborhood, 114, 294
Osterbind, Anton, 215
Osterbind, Carter Clarke, 215
Osterbind, Henry Carter, 215
Overton, Samuel, 79

Pamunkey Indians, 11, 16, 23, 27, 30
Panic of 1873, 181, 182
Paper industry, 190, 271
Parahunt, 11, 16, 302
Parks, 203–4
Parrish, J. Scott, 260
Parrish, Mrs. J. Scott, 260
Patrick, Marsena, 164, 166
Patriotic societies, 206
Paul, R. A., 199
"Pawnee Sunday," 135–36

Payne, John Barton, 292
"Peace Convention" (1861), 134
Pember, Phoebe Yates, 141–42
Peninsular Campaign, 148, 154, 157
Pennsylvania Gazette, 51
"People's Convention" (1861), 132, 135
Petersburg, 3, 44, 117, 185, 314
Philip Morris Companies, Inc., 265, 277, 310
Piedmont region, 1, 13, 125, 185
Pierpont, Francis, 165, 166
Plantations, 5, 21; slave labor on, 25, 58, 94; tobacco, 32, 35, 57; houses, 35, 45, 47, 56–57
Planters: and slavery, 4, 38, 58; as merchants, 25, 32, 33; land grants to, 21, 26–27; in Bacon's Rebellion, 27, 29; attacks on Indians, 30; as elite class, 30–31; credit and indebtedness, 37, 56, 57, 58; government relief for flood of 1771, 54, 56; and location of state capital, 64
Pleasants, Robert, 67, 68
Plecker, W. A., 255
Plessy v. Ferguson (1896), 284
"Plug-Uglies," 146
Pocahontas, 4, 18, 19, 255–56
Poe, Edgar Allan, 96, 108–9
"Poe Shrine," 248
Police, 150, 177–78, 180
Poll tax, 227, 243, 296
Porter, David, 162
"Post Office Gang," 199
Poverty, 314, 315
Powderly, Terence V., 193, 196
Powell, John, 255, 256
Powell, John Wesley, 257
Powell, Lewis F., Jr., 283, 287, 299, 300, 311
Powell, Louis, 218
Powhatan. See Wahunsonacock
Powhatan Confederacy, 27, 317

Powhatan Indians: James River settle-
ments, 3, 9, 11, *12, 15*, 30, 32;
encounter of English settlers, 4, 9,
11, 16; agriculture, 13, 35; wars with
English, 18, 21, 22, 23
Powhatan Seat house, 45
Presbyterians, 58, 85
Presley, Elvis, 290
Prince Edward County, 285
Printing and publishing industry, 271
Prison camps, 142–43
Progressive Literary Association,
206
Progressive movement, 239–40; and
racial segregation, 223–24, 226, 227,
231; and political reforms, 226, 228,
245, 283; and historic preservation,
232; and racial cooperation, 254;
and urban renewal, 298
Prohibition, 254; state referendum of
1914, 231–32; passage of Eighteenth
Amendment, 238, 239, 240, 247;
repeal of, 264
Project One, 300
Property tax, 178
Prosser, Thomas, Jr., 74
Protestant Episcopal Church, 68
Protestantism, 56, 68, 84, 87
Providence Baptist Church, 95
Pryor, Sarah Rice, 142
Public Guard, 80, 150, 151
Public health, 260
Public housing projects, 294
Public schools, 178; segregated, 175,
227, 233; desegregation of, 284–85,
286–87, 296–97; white resistance to
desegregation, 285–86, 287–88,
297; busing for integration, 299,
300, 316–17
Public Works Administration (PWA),
266, 268
Pupil Placement Board, 287, 288

Quakers, 67, 68, 69
Queen Anne style, 205

Race relations, 227, 254
Racial cooperation, 255
Racial Integrity Act (1924), 255
Racism, 234
Radio, 257, 288–89, 290–91
Railroads, 111–12, 136, 180; Civil War
and, 144, 165; state sale of, 181; seg-
regation on, 227; Church Hill tunnel
collapse, 257
Randolph, Edmund, 72
Randolph, George Wythe, 135, 145–46
Randolph, John, 101
Randolph, Mary, 88
Randolph, Peter, 170, 176
Randolph, Peyton, 51
Randolph neighborhood, 294
Rationing, World War II, 273–74
Readjuster Party, 199–200
Reconstruction, 164, 171–72, 176, 178,
182, 220
Reconstruction Act (1867), 174
Red Cross, 263, 273
Redlining, 269–70, 282–83
Reed, John Shelton, 316
Regency Square Mall, *308*
Reid, William Ferguson, 288
Religion, 68–69, 170
Religious fundamentalism, 254,
256–57
Republicanism, 4, 56, 76, 122, 128
Republican Party, 129, 200, 315; in
1860 election, 133; in Reconstruc-
tion, 173, 176, 178; blacks and, 174,
177, 199, 200, 225, 243
Reservoir Park, 203
Reviewer, 254
Reynolds' Female Seminary, 96
Reynolds Metal Company, 272, 308
Rice, John Holt, 84
Richard Evelyn Byrd Field, 248, 271

Richmond, 1–7; role of James River
in, 1, 2, 4, 9, 181; role of slavery in,
1, 3–4, 5, 90, 94, 112–13; role of
women in, 2–3, 5, 86, 167–68, 232–
33; physical landscape, 3, 53, 77, *106,
313*; segregation in, 5, 174–75, 200–
201, 222, 276–77, 282; class structure, 6, 113–14, 125; neighborhoods, 6, 114, 247, 292–93, 295, 301;
founding of, 43, 44–45, *map* 46, 48;
population, 48, 51, 60, 78, 104–5,
136, 185, 271, 279, 280, 296, 299,
314; immigration to, 48, 112, 117,
127, 129, 156; street layout, 49;
James River flood of 1771, 54–56,
57; American Revolution and, 56,
62–63, 64; architecture, 56, 72,
205–6, 248, 249, 251, 306–7; slave
rebellions and, 74, 76, 80, 107–8;
theater fire of 1811, 83–84, *85*; in
War of 1812, 88, 89; black population, 99, 136, 222, 271; railroads in,
111–12, 136, 144, 180, 181; water
supplies, 112, 150, 180, 202, 309–10;
militia units, 125, 167; port facilities,
180, 181, 270, 271, 308; rural migration to, 185–86, 218; parks construction, 203–4; suburbanization,
205–6, 207, 217, 222, 228, 249–51,
279, 299, 312–13; historic preservation, 206, 232, 298, 304; youth
gangs, 244; twentieth-century modernization, 244, 245, 258; effects of
automobiles on, 244, 248, 249, 277;
housing deterioration, 247, 282,
294–95, 298; highway construction,
282, 293, 294; floodwall, *305*; sewage
treatment plant, 309; metropolitan-
area consolidation, 314
—annexations, 51, 227, 228, *map* 229;
of 1793, 78; of 1867, 173, 174, 185;
of 1892, 208; of 1906–14, 222; Manchester, 222; of 1942, 271; Henrico

County, 271, 296; Chesterfield
County, 271, 296, 299–300, 301; of
1970, 296, 299–300, 301
—and Civil War: as center of Confederate memorialization, 4, 5, 169, 183,
184–85, 186–87, 208–9, 210, 211;
effects of war on, 5, 136–38, 139–
40, 164–65, 172; as Confederate
capital, 5, 136–40, 147; and secession, 133, 134–36; martial law in,
146, 147; espionage, 147–48; Union
siege of (1862), 148; battlefields, *map*
150; Bread Riot (1863), 151, 157;
Confederate defense of, 157–58;
Confederate evacuation of, 159, *160*,
162; evacuation fire, 159–60, 162,
164–65, 172; Union occupation of,
160, 163, 165–67; Reconstruction
and, 172, 177, 178
—economy: role of trade in, 3, 5,
32–33, 53, 65; role of tobacco production in, 3, 36–37, 58, 123–25,
136, 180, 219, 270, 271, 277, 278;
industrialization, 5, 105, 120, 189–
90, 263–64, 269; iron industry, 62,
110, 120, 122–23, 144–45, 185, 271;
manufacturing in, 89, 93, 145, 189,
190, 193, 219; recession of 1819, 93;
major industries, 122–23, 136, 185,
271; Civil War and aftermath, 139,
180–81; depression of 1873, 178,
181–82, 183; real estate development, 227; World War I production,
238–39; tourism in, 248–49, 313,
316; Great Depression in, 261–63,
264; World War II production, 271–
72, 273, 277; post–World War II
boom, 279–81; boom of 1980s, 307,
310, 315; corporations and, 308;
poverty, 314, 315; service sector,
314, 315
—government: county seat moved to,
49; Virginia capital moved to, 64–

65; construction of public buildings,
70, *71*, 72, *73*; restrictive ordinances
on slaves and free blacks, 80, 117,
131, 149; Board of Public Works, 90;
Whig control of, 127; and Civil War
espionage, 147–48; police department, 150, 177–78, 180; Common
Council, 175, 189; modernization of
infrastructure, 178–80, 264, 266;
Board of Health, 202; Committee
on Streets, 202; Board of Aldermen,
227; concerns with wasteful spending, 227–28; Administrative Board,
228; city charter, 228, 245, 283; zoning law, 229–31, 282; Public Works
Department, Bureau of Design,
245–47; city planning, 245–47, 248,
281, 292; Bartholomew Plan, 281–
82, 283, 284, 292; city manager system, 283–84; urban renewal, 292–
93, 294–95, 298, 299, 301, 302; City
Planning Commission, 295; Community Action Program, 303–4;
Housing Action Plan, 304; Redevelopment Housing Authority, 304.
See also Richmond City Council
—politics: Federalist Party dominance,
70, 93; Democratic Party in, 127;
Whig Party dominance, 127, 128–
29; voting rights, 128, 226, 227;
Republican Party in, 129, 173, 176;
blacks in, 173–74, 196–97, 243, 288,
300; mayoral conflict of 1870, 177–
78; "Whiskey Ring" and "Post
Office Gang," 199; Readjuster Party
in, 199–200; labor reform in, 200;
Progressive movement in, 223–24,
226, 228, 239–40, 245; voting fraud,
226; suppression of black votes,
226, 227; enactment of Prohibition,
231–32, 238, 247; women's suffrage
movement, 235–38; New Deal in,
245, 264, 265–68, 269; racial coop-

eration movement, 254–55; repeal
of Prohibition, 264; resistance to
desegregation, 285–86, 287–88,
297; annexation controversies, 296,
299–300
Richmond, Fredericksburg, and
Potomac Railroad, 111
Richmond Academy of Music, 209
Richmond and Danville Railroad, 144
Richmond and West Point Terminal
Railway, 212
Richmond Area Metropolitan Economic Development Council, 310
Richmond Army Air Base, 271
Richmond Blues, 125
Richmond Cedar Works, 189
Richmond Chemical Works, 189
Richmond Citizens' Association, 283,
288, 295
Richmond City Council: restrictions
on slaves, 80, 131; and canal construction, 111; and voting rights
expansion, 128; elections to, 129,
227, 296, 300; in Civil War, 138,
149–50, 157, 165; in Reconstruction,
165, 177; establishment of police
and fire departments, 180; black
members of, 197, 227, 300; and electrification of streetcars, 201; suppression of black votes, 227; and
financing of city services, 227–28;
and racial zoning, 229; and suburban annexation, 296
Richmond City Railway Company, 201
Richmond civic center (Richmond
Centre), 293–94
Richmond Club, 219
Richmond Coliseum, *294*
Richmond College, 251
Richmond Constitutional Whig, 107
Richmond Cotton Manufactory, 89–90
Richmond Council of Social Agencies,
247

Richmond Crusade for Voters, 288, 296, 303

Richmond Daily Examiner, 133–34, 135

Richmond Dispatch, 205

Richmond Education Association, 233

Richmond Engineering Company, 272

Richmond Enquirer, 101, 127, 130, 170

Richmond Enquirer and Examiner, 167–68

Richmond Equal Suffrage League, 236, 237

Richmond Exchange for Women's Work, 222

Richmond Forward, 295, 296

Richmond Greys, 125, *130*

Richmond in By-Gone Days (Mordecai), 109

Richmond Junto, 90

Richmond Light Infantry Blues, 79, 125, 130

Richmond Locomotive Works, 212

Richmond Magazine, 246

Richmond Mother's Club, 206, 222–23

Richmond Motor Company, *246*

Richmond New Nation, 173

Richmond News Leader, 268, 273, 285, 286, 308

Richmond Normal and High School, 225

Richmond Passenger and Power Company, 201, 213

Richmond-Petersburg Turnpike, 293–94

Richmond Planet, 199, 209, 210, 214, 235, 268

Richmond Professional Institute, 295

Richmond Renaissance, 304–5

Richmond School Board, 287–88, 316–17

Richmond School of Social Work and Public Health, 258

Richmond Stove Works, *186*

Richmond Symphony, 291

Richmond Theological Center, 295

Richmond Times, 212

Richmond Times-Dispatch, 233, 255–56, 268, 271, 286, 298, 305

Richmond Traction Company, 201

Richmond Union Foundry, *91*

Richmond Union Passenger Railway Company, 201

Richmond Virginian, 231

Richmond Whig, 132, 171

Richmond Women's Christian Temperance Union (WCTU), 231, 232

Richmond Women's Club, 222

Ritchie, Thomas, 90, 127

Riverfront Plaza, 307

Roane, Spencer, 90

Roanoke, 287

Robb, Charles S., *317*

Robins, E. Claiborne, 295

Robinson, Bill ("Bojangles"), 276

Robinson, Spottswood, III, 284

Rocketts, Robert, 302

Rocketts Landing, 57, 77, *78*

Rocky Ridge, 48

Rolfe, John, 4, 18

Roman Catholic Church, 197

Roman Catholics, 69, 256

Roosevelt, Franklin D., 244–45, 263, 267, 269, 275

Ross, David, 79

Rouse, James, 305

Royal African Company, 25

Sabbath Glee Club, 291

St. Catherine's School, 251

St. Charles Hotel, 140

St. Christopher's School, 251

St. John's Church, 59, *60*, 68, 69, 302

Saint Luke Emporium, 234

Saint Luke Herald, 234

Saint Luke Penny Savings Bank, 234, 236

St. Paul's Episcopal Church, 86, 311

Saloons, 113, 114–15, *198*, 199, 221, 247

Salvation Army, 263

Sanger, William, 258, 260

"Scalawags," 173

Scattergood, Thomas, 69

Schubrick, USS, 212–13

Scotland, union with England, 44

Scott, Ben, 177, 199

Scott, Mary Wingfield, 298

Scott, Sir Walter, 110

Seabrook, John, 93

Seabrook's Tobacco Warehouse, *119*, 140

Seay, Reuben, 105

Secession, 2, 130, 132, 133, 134–35

Second African Baptist Church, 174

Second Street, 277

Segregation: acts of legislation, 5, 200, 214, 215, 220–21, 227, 255; public accommodations, 100, 200–201, 276–77, 288; streetcars, 174–75, 214, 215; public schools, 175, 227, 233; workplace, 193, 196; residential, 222, 282, 298; Progressivism and, 223–24, 226, 227, 231; railroad cars, 227; racial zoning codes, 227, 229–31; racial cooperation movement and, 255; desegregation of universities, 268–69; NAACP and, 268–69, 275, 284–85; military services, 273; public school desegregation, 284–85, 286–87, 296–97; white resistance to desegregation, 285–86, 287–88, 297; public school busing, 299, 300, 316–17

Service economy, 314, 315

Seventeenth Street Bottom, 247

Seven Years' War, 58

Sewage treatment plant, 309

Sheltering Arms Hospital, 222

Sheppard, William, 155

Shiloh Baptist Association of Virginia, 176

Shipbuilding industry, 212, 214

Shockoe, 54

Shockoe Bottom, 305, *307*, 311

Shockoe Cemetery, 146, 187

Shockoe Creek, 54, 77, 202

Shockoe Creek neighborhood, 114

Shockoe Hill, 6, 60, 69, 70, 72, 77, 113–14

Shockoe Slip, 304, 305–6, *307*, 311

Shockoe Valley, 247

Shopping malls, 277–79, 281, 308

Simcoe, John Graves, 62

Simcoe's Rangers, 62

Sinatra, Frank, 276

Sisters of Temperance, 116

Sixth Street Festival Marketplace, 305, 306

Skyscrapers, 306–7

Slave code (1705), 38

Slavery: role in Richmond's development, 1, 3–4, 5, 90, 94, 112–13; Virginia statutes on, 38, 41; white opponents of, 67, 68, 107; Revolutionary rhetoric of liberty and, 67, 76, 93, 95; as national conflict, 93, 94, 128–29; and African colonization movement, 94–95; southern defense of, 109–10, 134; demise of, 172

Slaves: slave rebellions, 3, 74–76, 107–8; plantation, 25, 58, 94; population in Virginia, 30; Indians held as, 30, 32, 33; African sources of, 38, *39*; Virginia statutes on, 38, 41, 67, 80; conversion to Christianity, 38, 68; women, 38, 107; tobacco use, 42; in Revolutionary War, 62, 63–64; emancipation by owners, 65, 67, 80; artisans, 78; hired out by owners, 80, 94, 104, 105, 117, 152–53; local ordinances on, 80, 117, 131, 149; run-

aways, 103, 105–7, 117, 153; urban, 104, 108, 117, 131; rural, 105, 107; relations with owners, 109–10; white fear of employment competition from, 112, 121–22, 125, 127; employed in tobacco factories, 117; employed at Tredegar Works, 121, 122, 125; in Civil War, 137, 152–53; punishment by whipping, 149; prices for, 154; legal emancipation of, 168, 170, 172, 174, 210. *See also* Blacks

Slave trade, 1, 25, 39, 40, 58, 123, 127

Smith, Alfred E., 256

Smith, Dave, 317

Smith, John, 4, 9, 17, 18, 302

Smith, Lomax, 170

Smith, Samuel, 103, 104

Smith, William ("Extra Billy"), 157

Social organizations, 219

Social Service Bureau, 263

Society for the Prevention of the Abducting and Absconding of Slave Property, 117

Sons of Temperance, 115–16

South Carolina, secession of, 133

Southern Baptist Convention, 295

"Southern chivalry," 109, 110

Southern Education Board, 233

Southern Growth Policies Board, 308, 315

Southern Historical Society, 183, 187

Southern Illustrated News, 156, *157*

Southern Literary Messenger, 108, 118, 156

Southern Negro Youth Congress, 265

Southern Planter, 118

Southern Punch, 156, *157*

Southern Rights Association, 118–19

Spanish-American War, 212, 213, 214

Spanish settlers, 11, 25

Speculators, 65–67, 156

Sprague, Frank, 201

Stamp Act (1765), 59

Stanard, Mrs. Robert, 159

Stanley, Thomas B., 285

Stanton, Edwin M., 166–67

States' rights, 129, 133, 187, 286

Statute for Religious Freedom (1786), 68

Steel production, 196

Stegge, Thomas, 26

Stephens, Alexander H., 136, 138

Streetcars, 178; segregation of, 174–75, 214, 215; and suburbanization, 200, 203, 205, 217; electrification of, 201; labor strike of 1903, 213–14, 217; black boycott of 1904, 214–15; demise of, 277, *279*

Street paving, 248

Stuart, Alexander H. H., 177

Stuffed Peacocks (Clark), 253–54

Suburbs, 207, 312–13, 315; streetcars and, 200, 203, 205, 217; architecture, 205–6, 249; and residential segregation, 222; city government and, 227, 247; annexation of, 228, 299–300; automobiles and, 244, 247, 249, 277; shopping malls, 279; population growth in, 282, 299

Sully, R. M., 84

Sumter, Fort, 132, 135

"Sunbelt South," 263–64, 315–16

Surgeon General's report on smoking (1964), 278

Taxation, 264, 269, 312; colonial, 58–59, 67; Confederate, 149; property tax, 178; for public schools, 227; poll tax, 227, 243, 296; gasoline tax, 248

Tazewell, Littleton Waller, 101

Teage, Colin, 95

Television, 292

Temperance movement, 115–16, 198, 231. *See also* Antiliquor movement

Temple Beth Shalome, 70

Terry, Alfred H., 166
Textile industry, 261
Thalhimer, William, 114
Thalhimer's department store, 203, 247, 276, 288, 306, 311, 312
Theater, 82–83, 100
Thornton, William, 288
Tidewater region, 1, 21, 36, 101
"Tidewater Renaissance," 253
Tobacco: trade in, 3, 18, 25, 32, 35, 44, 55, 56, 57, 58; role in Richmond economy, 3, 36–37, 58, 123–25, 136, 180, 219, 270, 271, 277, 278; and settlement in Virginia, 18–21; Charles I's proclamation against, 20; plantations, 32, 35, 57; inspection and grading warehouses, 33, 44; farming practices, 35; prices, 36, 37, 261; clay pipes, 41–42; losses due to flood of 1771, 54, 56; slave cultivation of, 58; taxation of, 58; processing factories, 110, 123, 125, 136; black factory workers, 117, 182, 194, 223, 265; women factory workers, 117, 190–93, 194, 223, 265, 277; depression of 1873 and, 181–82; cigarette advertising, 190, *192*; mechanization of cigarette making, 190–93, 194; labor organization, 193, 265; employment rates, 219; Great Depression and, 261; World War II and, 270; mechanization of farming, 280; plant closings, 310
Tobacco Festival, 278
Tobacco Manufacturing Society, 182
Tobacco Worker's International Union (TWIU), 214, 265
Tompkins, Sally L., 142, *149*, 209
Tourism, 248–49, 313, 316
To Win These Rights (Mason), 260
Trade, 118–19; James River and, 1, 3, 13, 32; slave trade, 1, 25, 39, 40, 58, 123, 127; and growth of Richmond,

3, 5, 32–33, 53, 65; tobacco trade, 3, 18, 25, 32, 35, 44, *55*, 56, 57, 58; with England, 9–10, 14, 25, 42–44, 56–57, 88; English-Dutch trade wars, 25; fur trade, 25, 33; with Indians, 32, 33; grain trade, 35; European wars and, 57–58, 86–89; coffee trade, 123; railroads and, 180
Traveler's Aid, 263
Treaty of 1646, 23
Tredegar Iron Works, 110, 114, 120–21, 123, 312; slave labor at, 121–22, 125; in Civil War, 136, 139, 144–45, 172; in Reconstruction, 180–81; bankruptcy of, 182; in World War I, 238; in World War II, 271
Trigg shipyard, 212–13, *214*
True Reformers Mercantile and Industrial Association, 240
Tschiffele, Samuel, 48–49
Tsenacommacah confederation, 11, 13
Tuckahoe fort, 21
Tucker, Samuel, 284, 288
Turner, Nat, 3, 107–8
Tyler, John, 101, 187

Underground Railroad, 103
Underwood, John, 176
Unemployment rates, 261, 264
Union army, 148, 159–60, 165, 166
Union Burial Ground Society, 116
Union Hill neighborhood, 114
United Cannery Workers, 265
United Confederate Veterans, 209, 249
United Daughters of the Confederacy, 5, 206, 219, 222
United States Congress: European trade embargo, 88; Missouri Compromise, 93; and Reconstruction, 171–72, 174, 176; and New Deal, 263–64, 265, 267; repeal of Prohibition, 264
United States Constitution: Virginia

ratification of, 70; Fourteenth Amendment, 176; Eighteenth Amendment, 240; Nineteenth Amendment, 240; Twenty-First Amendment, 264
United States Customs House, 139
United States Navy, 214, 271
United States Supreme Court: and racial zoning, 229–31; and child labor, 260; and New Deal, 268; and school desegregation, 284, 285, 299; and poll taxes, 296; and Chesterfield County annexation, 300
Universities, 295; desegregation of, 268–69
University of Richmond, 251, 295
Upper Mattaponi Indians, 317
Urban renewal, 292–95, 298–99, 301, 302–3

Valentine, Benjamin, 233
Valentine, Lila Meade, 233, *234*, 236
Valentine, Mann S., 190, 191, 210
Valentine Meat Juice Company, 186, 190, 191
Valentine, the Museum of the Life and History of Richmond, 312
Valentine Riverside, *313*
Van Buren, Martin, 127
Van Lew, Elizabeth, 147, *149*, 167
Variety, 290
Varina, Va., 32, 33
Veterans, 184, 209, 211, 249, 275
Veterans Administration (VA), 283
Virginia, *map* 49, 316; English settlement of, 9, 10–11, 14, 21–22, 30–31, 37; Indian populations, 11, 13, *map* 17, 23, *map* 24; trade with England, 14, 18, 56; role of tobacco production in, 18–21, 36, 56, 58; land grants, 21, 26–27; organization of counties, 22; Indian land cessions to, 23; slave trade in, 25, 38; popula-

tion, 30; slave statutes, 38, 41, 67, 80; in American Revolution, 56, 59; relocation of state capital to Richmond, 64–65; ratification of U.S. Constitution, 70; national importance of, 93–94, 136; constitution of 1776, 101; constitutional convention of 1829, 101–2; voting rights, 101–2, 227, 240, 260; controversy over slavery in, 107, 109; agriculture, 117, 139; constitutional convention of 1850, 128; secession convention of 1861, 132–33, 135, 136; federal blockade of, 138, 152; constitution of 1850, 139; Reconstruction in, 172–73; constitutional convention of 1867, 175, 176; constitution of 1867, 176, 177; state debt, 181, 199; Democratic Party in, 199, 260–61, 269; segregation laws, 214, 215, 255; constitution of 1902, 227, 232, 233; enactment of Prohibition, 240; State Banking Commission, 242; Byrd political machine, 260–61, 269, 284; Department of Public Welfare, 263; fiscal conservatism, 264, 266, 284; resistance to school integration, 269, 286, 287; Commission on the Status of Women, 280; Water Control Board, 309

Virginia (Glasgow), 235

Virginia, CSS, 145

Virginia Abolition Society, 68, 80

Virginia *Argus*, 82

Virginia Association Opposed to Woman Suffrage, 237

Virginia Commonwealth University, 295, 302, 310

Virginia Company, 2, 10, 14–18, 21–22, 30

Virginia Council on Indians, 317

Virginia Equal Suffrage League, 237, 240

Virginia Gazette, 54

Virginia General Assembly, 42, 60, 65, 284; census of 1669, 30; planter delegates to, 33; establishment of Richmond, 48, 49; flood relief to planters, 54, 56; relocation of capital to Richmond, 64; and construction of capitol building, 69; repeal of Manumission Act, 80; and voting rights, 101; slavery debate in, 107; investment in canal construction, 110; and secession, 134; in Civil War, 138, 139, 149, 153, 157; and Reconstruction, 176; and Richmond city government, 177; and Civil War debt, 181; segregation laws, 215, 227; ratification of Prohibition, 240; and school desegregation, 269, 286

Virginia Historical Society, 212, 292, 316

Virginia House, 251

Virginia House of Burgesses, 44, 59

Virginia League for Women Suffrage, 236

Virginia Manufactory of Arms, *121*, 138, 144

Virginia Museum of Fine Arts, 291–92

Virginia Passenger and Power Company, 214

Virginia Rifles, 125

Virginia Society of Friends, 67

Virginia State Capitol, *73*; construction of, *71*, *72*; in Civil War, 139; collapse of 1870, 178, *179*

Virginia State Fair, *120*

Virginia State Library, *268*

Virginia State Penitentiary, *72*, *73*

Virginia Suffrage News, 237

Virginia Union University, 295

Von Groning, Daniel, 154

Voter participation, 260

Voting fraud, 226

Voting rights: property qualifications, 101–2, 128; granted to blacks, 173, 296; disfranchisement of blacks, 226, 227; poll tax, 227, 243, 296; women's, 235, 236–38, 239, 240

Voting Rights Act (1965), 296

Waddell, William, 71

Wagner Act (1935), 265

Wahunsonacock (Powhatan chief), 11–13, 22

Walker, Fannie, 155

Walker, Gilbert, 177

Walker, Maggie Lena, 234, 235, 243

Waller, Linden, 114

Wall Street Journal, 308

Walthall, Ernest, 153

WANT radio, 291

War of 1812, 86, 89, 90

Warehouse Acts (1713, 1730), 33, 44

Warwick, Abram, 123

Washington, Bushrod, 80

Washington, George, 51, 62, *73*

Washingtonians temperance group, 115

Water pollution, 202, 309–10

Waterworks, 112, 150, 180

Watkins, Katherine, 41

Watkins, Henry, 41

Weddell, Alexander, 251

Weitzel, Godfrey, 159, 164

West, Francis, 18

West, Roy, 305

West End neighborhood, 251, 277–79, 280, 301

Westham, 48, 54

Westham Foundry, 62

Westmoreland Club, 219, 220

Westover house, 45, *47*

Whig Party, 127, 128–29, 133

Whipping, public, 149, 166

"Whiskey Ring," 199

White, John, 19

White, Thomas Willis, 109

"White flight," 283, 299
White House, Confederate, 138, *164*, 210, 312, 316
White supremacy, 255, 256, 286
Wickham, John, 79, 80, 81–82, *83*, 114, 187, 312
Wickham, Williams C., 132–33
Wilder, L. Douglas, *302*, 310–11, 317
Wilderness Campaign, 157
Williams, T. C., Jr., 251
Williamsburg, 53, 64, 232, 249
Williamson, Elizabeth Galt, *68*
Williamson, Thomas, *68*
Willow Lawn shopping mall, 277–79, 308
Wilton house, 251
Winder, John H., 146, 147, 150
Winder Hospital, 139, 140
Windsor Farms, 251, *252*, 271
Wirt, William, 80, 81, 82
Wise, Henry, 129–30, 132, 135, 173
Wise, John S., 199
WMBG radio, 291
Women, 2–3, 167–68; English settlers, 2, 21–22; in reform and moral organizations, 3, 5, 86, 222–23, 233, 235–36; blacks, 3, 107, 168, 223, 234–35, 238, 265, 313; Indians, 13–14; indentured servants, 37, 38; legal status of, 38, 51; slaves, 38, 107; public punishment of, 49–50; religion and, 68, 70–71; education of, 72, 96–97; tobacco factory workers, 117, 190–93, 194, 223, 265, 277; clothing and fashions, *126*, 241, 272–73; political participation, 128, 243, 260; in Civil War, 137, 141, 151, 154–56, 167; in Bread Riot, 151, 152; marriages, 168, 280; racial segregation and, 175; and Confederate memorialization, 188–89; in labor movement, 195, 265; employment conditions, 219, 221–22, 223, 280, 313–14, 315; and historic preservation, 232; voting rights, 235, 236–38, 239, 240; in World War I, 239, 241; in World War II, 271–72, 274; poverty among, 314
Women's Christian Temperance Union (WCTU), 231, 232

Wood, Abraham, 32
Wood products industry, 189
Woolfolk, Ben, 74
Working class, 193, 256, 257
Workman, John, 290
Workman, Sunshine Sue, 290
World's Columbian Exposition (1893), 202
World War I, 238–39
World War II, 270–75, 277
Wright's Park, 228
WRTD radio, 291
WRVA radio, 257, 290, 291
WRVA-TV, 292
Wynne, Thomas, 148
Wythe, George, 80

York River Railroad, 157
Young Men's Christian Association (YMCA), 151
Young Women's Christian Association (YWCA), 206, 222–23, 224, 233, 260
Youth gangs, 244

Zoning, 227, 229–31, 282